Drills & Exercises for Pool & Pocket Billiards

How to Become an Expert Pocket Billiards Player

Allan P. Sand
PBIA Certified Instructor

ISBN 978-1-62505-000-7
Print 8.5x11

ISBN 978-1-62505-533-0
eBook format

First edition

Copyright © 2012 Allan P. Sand

All rights reserved under International and Pan-American Copyright Conventions.

Published by Billiard Gods Productions.

Santa Clara, CA 95051

U.S.A.

For the latest information about books and videos, go to: http://www.billiardgods.com

Acknowledgements

Wei Chao created the software that was used to create these graphics.

Table of Contents

Introduction	1
CB Speed/Spin Matrix	3
Your Comfort & Chaos Zones	4
General Observations	4
Know Your Limitations	5
Pocketing Skill Development	**6**
Straight-in Shots	6
Straight-in to Pocket	6
Shallow Angles	8
Shallow Angles to Pocket	9
Progressive Shooting Angles	11
OB to Side Pocket	11
OB to 1D Pocket (on rail)	12
OB to 1 D Pocket (1/2 D from rail)	14
OB 1 D to Pocket (1 D from rail)	15
OB 2 D to Pocket (on rail)	17
OB 2 D to Pocket (1/2 D from rail)	18
OB 2 D to Pocket (1 D from rail)	19
OB 2 D to Pocket (1-1/2 D from rail)	20
OB 2 D to Pocket (2 D from rail)	21
OB 4 D to Corners	22
Precision Shooting	**23**
Standardized CB Speeds	23
Soft 1, 2, 3 Speeds	23
Medium 1, 2, 3 Speeds	24
Hard 1 Speed	24
Wrist Stroke Mastery	25
Nudging Practice Procedure	25
Nudging	26
Back & Forth Nips	26
Come Back Home	27
OB to the Rail & Back	28
Stun the CB	30
Follow It	32
1/2 D	32
1 D	33
2 D	35
3 D	36
4 D	38
Progressive	38
Follow To the Death	39
Draw to the Death	43
Draw to Me	46
1/2 Diamond CB Draw	46
1 Diamond CB Draw	47
1-1/2 Diamond CB Draw	48

  2 Diamond CB Draw..49
  3 Diamond CB Draw..50
  4 Diamond CB Draw..51
  Progressive Draw..52
  Repetitive Draw..55

CB Management...**57**
 Control Path of the Cue Ball (Easy)..57
 Control Path of the Cue Ball (Intermediate)..59
 Control Path of the Cue Ball (Advanced)...60
CB Location Positioning 62

Positioning Skill Development..**64**
Triangle Exercises..64
 Simple Triangles..64
 Intermediate Triangles...67
 Advanced Triangles..68
 Cluster Clearing Triangles 70
Turn the Corner 71
 3 Ball Groups...71
 5 Ball Groups...72
 Advanced Groups...73
Short Stacks..74
Down the Line..75
Side Pocket – Single Groups 77
Side Pocket – Double Groups 79
Double 3 Ball Groups #1..81
Double 3 Ball Groups #2..83
Double 3 Ball Groups #3..85
Around the Table...87
 Single Ball Setups..87
 Double Ball Setups...88
Inside Out 91
 Circle 91
 Box 93
"V" Setups...94
Long Line Setups...96

Banking..**98**
Cross Corner Banks 98
 On Rail Banks..98
 Near Rail Banks...100
 1 D Away Banks 101
 2 D Away Banks 103
Cross Side Banks...104
 On Rail Banks..104
 Near Rail Banks...107
 2 D Away Banks 109
Long Table Banks..110
 On Rail Long Banks...110
 Near Rail Long Banks..112

  2 D Away Long Banks 112
  4 D Away Long Banks 113
  6 D Away Long Banks 114
Combinations & Caroms 115
Dead-on Combo & Carom Examples 115
  Easy Combos 115
  Easy Caroms 116
Combination Exercises 116
  Easy Combinations 116
  Easy Side Combinations 118
  Intermediate Combos...119
  Advanced Combos 120
  Zig-zag Combos 121
  Three Ball Combos 123
  Impossible 4 Ball Combos 124
Caroms 125
  About the Tangent Line 125
  Tangent Line Caroms 126
  Through the Ball Caroms 127
Safeties 129
Distance Safeties..129
Bad Angle 131
On Cushion 133
Hidden Ball Safety 134
CB Control 135
OB Control 137
Kicking 139
Simple Off-Cushion Kicks 139
Cross Side Kicks 140
Long Table Kicks 142
Games to Practice Your Skills 145
Bowliards 145
Bank Pool 146
Equal Offense 147
Chicago (carom-scratch) 148
Chase, a game to learn kicking skills 149
Blank Table Layouts 150

Other books by the author ...

- Why Pool Hustlers Win
- Table Map Library
- Safety Toolbox
- Cue Ball Control Cheat Sheets
- Advanced Cue Ball Control Self-Testing Program
- Drills & Exercises for Pool & Pocket Billiards
- The Art of War versus The Art of Pool
- 3 Cushion Billiards Championship Shots (a series)
- Carom Billiards: Some Riddles & Puzzles
- Carom Billiards: MORE Riddles & Puzzles
- The Psychology of Losing – Tricks, Traps & Sharks
- The Art of Team Coaching
- The Art of Personal Competition
- The Art of Politics & Campaigning
- The Art of Marketing & Promotion
- Kitchen God's Guide for Single Guys

This book is dedicated to my parents, Edmund and Bernadette Sand. They supported and encouraged my interest in pocket billiards.

Introduction

Probably the worst experience to live through when holding a cue stick in your hands is practicing. As much as you love the game, there is something about setting up a shot and shooting it over and over (and over) until you just can't force yourself to continue. You start banging balls around the table with no real focus on accomplishing any kind of improvement.

So, this book could be a waste of time, or it could be an opportunity to take your game from the bar-banger level to the ability to creditably compete in tournaments.

These drills and exercises are based on the concept of progressive advancement. Start with an easy setup, prove that you can make that 4 out of 5 times, and then make it slightly more difficult. Keep on pushing the limits as far as the table edges allow.

Put this book on your eBook reader, smart phone, tablet, or laptop. Bring this to the table along with your paper reinforcement rings (donuts) and you are ready to improve yourself.

This is not a book to be run through a couple of times and then set aside to gather dust in some long unvisited folder on your computing device. Open your online calendar (Google, Yahoo, etc.) and put in reminders every few months to shoot this, that, these, or those pages. In between these scheduled self-testing periods, work with the other Billiard Gods books.

Study this material in two steps. In the comfort of your favorite easy-chair or recliner, review each table layout and thoughtfully consider the ball positions. Could you do the shot at slow, medium and fast CB speeds? Use the "notes" feature of your reader to add assumptions, possibilities, and considerations.

To continue developing yourself as an Intelligent Shooter – you have to get past the "fooling around" stage of your playing career and get serious about becoming a competitive player.

The purpose of the book is to provide a single-source that provides drills to improve almost any skill. Yes, drills are boring. For most people, about all they can handle is 10-15 minutes before they start looking for any excuse to stop practicing. This single source of table layouts and setups can chase away boredom for at least another 20-30 minutes.

The secret to effective practicing is to actually concentrate on improving one thing at a time. Generally, you want to practice a missed shot that cost you a game or match. You can set up and shoot that shot 30, 40, even 50 times before your intense learning desire burns out. But the boredom gremlin eventually manages to get your attention.

This book has hundreds of exercises (and when counting variations – a near infinite variety). When your interest on one exercise fades, select another drill, and so on. Start off a practice session with some ball pocketing exercises. Switch over to some drills that concentrate on making the CB dance to your tune. Then, set up some of the self-pacing practice games at the end of the book to self-demonstrate your improved playing skills.

It is very important that you understand that there are many ways for you to stroke the CB. Keeping it fairly basic, there are 39 different CB speed and spin (CB speed/spin) shot variations. If you want to get real good at pocket billiards, you must make a dedicated effort to "own" these shots. This means that making an object ball (OB) that is 1 diamond requires that you know these 39 basic shots.

Don't let this seeming complexity discourage your learning process. Start with this learning curve using a straight-in shot with the OB 1 diamond from the side pocket, and the CB 1 diamond from the OB in a straight lin. Run the shots with these basics:

- Stun at slow, medium, and fast speeds. Observe the results.
- 12:00/half tip at slow, medium, and fast speeds. Observe the results.
- 12:00/full tip at slow, medium, and fast speeds. Observe the results.
- 6:00/half tip at slow, medium, and fast speeds. Observe the results.
- 6:00/full tip at slow, medium, and fast speeds. Observe the results.

And these are five of the 39 shots. If this is all you decide to use for all the exercises in this book, you will still become a very tough player. The next page contains the entire CB speed/spin definitions.

When you are ready to learn some of the side spin shots, work with both the right and left side at the same practice session. You will need to make some aiming adjustments, but that is easily learned by observing the results of each shot and making appropriate changes.

You must also identify your Comfort/Chaos Zones. When the shot gets too difficult to easily pocket, that is where your Chaos Zone begins. For every drill (and CB speed/spin), mark where this is. Later, as your skills improve, you can compare your last Chaos Zone position and identify which skills have improved.

CB Speed/Spin Matrix

The following table is the matrix of shots to be applied to every shot for every drill and exercise. Some of the slow draw & draw/side spin shots cannot be done because the table cloth wears away at the spin. However, every possibility is shown in this table.

Every shot setup has the following 39 shots that must be practiced and mastered before you can totally "own" that shot. For practical reasons, there are only 30 trustworthy shots that you can truly depend on.

Slow CB speed	Stun	12:00 (1/2 tip)	6:00* (1/2 tip)	10:30 (1/2 tip)	1:30 (1/2 tip)	7:30** (1/2 tip)	4:30** (1/2 tip)
		12:00 (1 tip)	6:00* (1 tip)	10:30 (1 tip)	1:30 (1 tip)	7:30** (1 tip)	4:30** (1 tip)
Medium CB speed	Stun	12:00 (1/2 tip)	6:00 (1/2 tip)	10:30 (1/2 tip)	1:30 (1/2 tip)	7:30** (1/2 tip)	4:30** (1/2 tip)
		12:00 (1 tip)	6:00 (1 tip)	10:30 (1 tip)	1:30 (1 tip)	7:30** (1 tip)	4:30** (1 tip)
Fast CB speed	Stun	12:00 (1/2 tip)	6:00 (1/2 tip)	10:30 (1/2 tip)	1:30 (1/2 tip)	7:30 (1/2 tip)	4:30 (1/2 tip)
		12:00 (1 tip)	6:00 (1 tip)	10:30 (1 tip)	1:30 (1 tip)	7:30 (1 tip)	4:30 (1 tip)

Notes: * Slow speed at 6:00 (reverse spin) is only useful with the CB close to the OB. Otherwise the cloth will wear off the spin and the CB will begin rolling forward.
** At slow & medium speeds, 7:30 and 4:30 speeds are unpredictable. Not recommended

As you gain more experience, you will develop an intuitive skill in determining the correct speed and spin for the CB. This develops from observing the results of hundreds of attempts.

As you master the CB positioning skills, you will stroke the CB at precise speeds with precise CB spins.

Your Comfort & Chaos Zones

When pocketing balls, you (and every other player in the world) have shots that are within comfort zones and chaos zones. When a shot can be made 8 out of 10 times (80%), it is in your comfort zone. When your chances of pocketing the ball are around 3 or 4 times in 10 tries (30-40%) or less, it is within your chaos zone. At 50-60%, it is on the edges of what you can do.

When getting position for another shot, you must move the CB into the comfort zone for that ball. Generally, the least amount of CB travel the better. The more you have to force the CB to move, the easier it is to finish with the CB in your chaos zones.

When you consider an offensive shot, these are the two percentages used to calculate whether to proceed offensively, play a more cautious two-way, or shoot a safety. For example, if you can pocket the ball 8 out of 10 times, but only get shape 3 out of 10 times – that shot falls into your chaos zone. (It also indicates an area that needs practice time.)

When you need to play defense, you want your opponent to have one of these tactical playing situations:

- A shot in his chaos zone – the deeper the better.

- A shot (or two) within his comfort zone, but with a positioning problem in his chaos zone.

General Observations

Closely watch how he handles these shots:

- Long distance shots with various angles from straight-in to sharp cuts.

- Medium distance shots and cuts of various angles.

- Cue and object balls very close together.

- Cross-side, cross-corner, and long-table banks.

- CB draw, follow, speed and spin control.

With this knowledge, you can carefully craft selected safety tactics that are to his greatest disadvantage. This ensures much greater table control. And that is what improves your chances to win the game.

Know Your Limitations

It is very important to know exactly where your shooting and positioning comfort zones are and where the edges are. This requires a level of personal truthfulness that many find painful to admit.

Without this reality-check, you could select offensive shots that you "feel" are within your comfort zone, but actually have a much greater chance of failure. If you constantly select these kinds of shots, you are going to hurt yourself by allowing billiard god luck (chaos) to enter your game. This can be a blind spot in your calculations. The more honest you are with yourself, the better your chances of winning against almost any opponent.

Self-honesty ensures you can make smarter playing and shooting decisions more often. Your choices can be rational and the results match your expectations. This self-knowledge can also be used to configure your practice sessions.

Pocketing Skill Development

This section concentrates on getting the OB into the pocket. There is no concern about where the CB ends up. This is a good time to practice the many CB speed/spin variations. Play at least five shots before changing from one variation to another.

Straight-in Shots

Expertise with these shots requires the skill to pocket the OB using 26 of the 39 CB speed/spin variations.

1. Put CB close to OB, pocket the OB.
2. Re-spot OB and move CB back 1/2 D.
3. Upon a miss, move CB 1/2 D closer to OB.

Proof of competence: Repeat 3 times without miss.

Straight-in to Pocket

1 D

Object: Pocket the OB with CB anywhere on the shaded line.

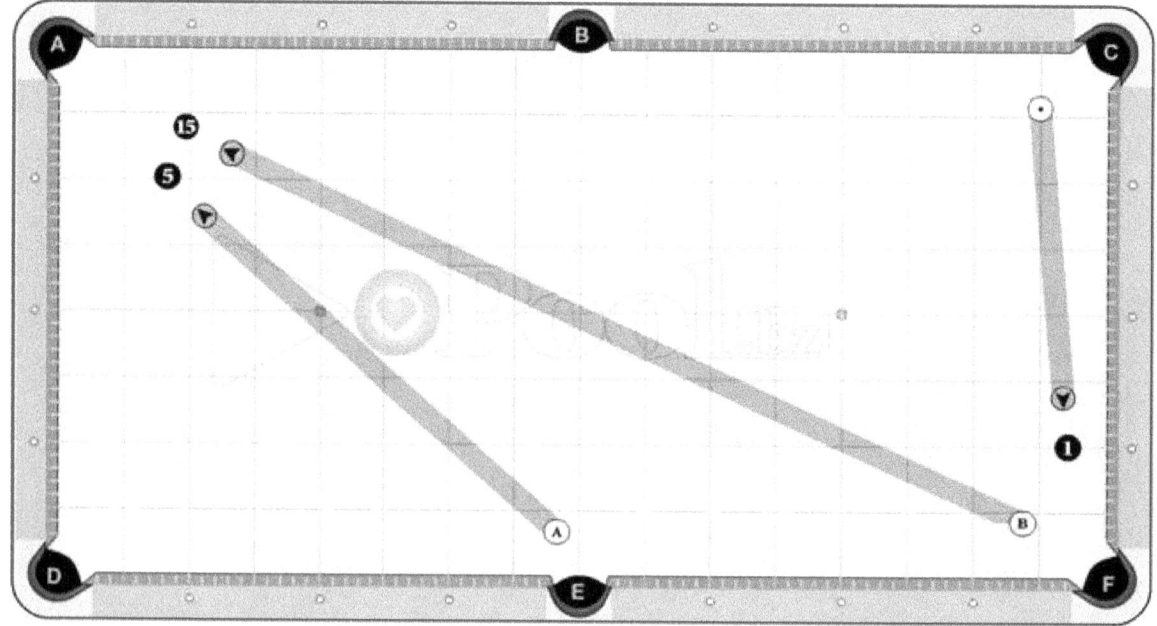

1-1/2 D

Object: Pocket the OB with CB anywhere on the shaded line.

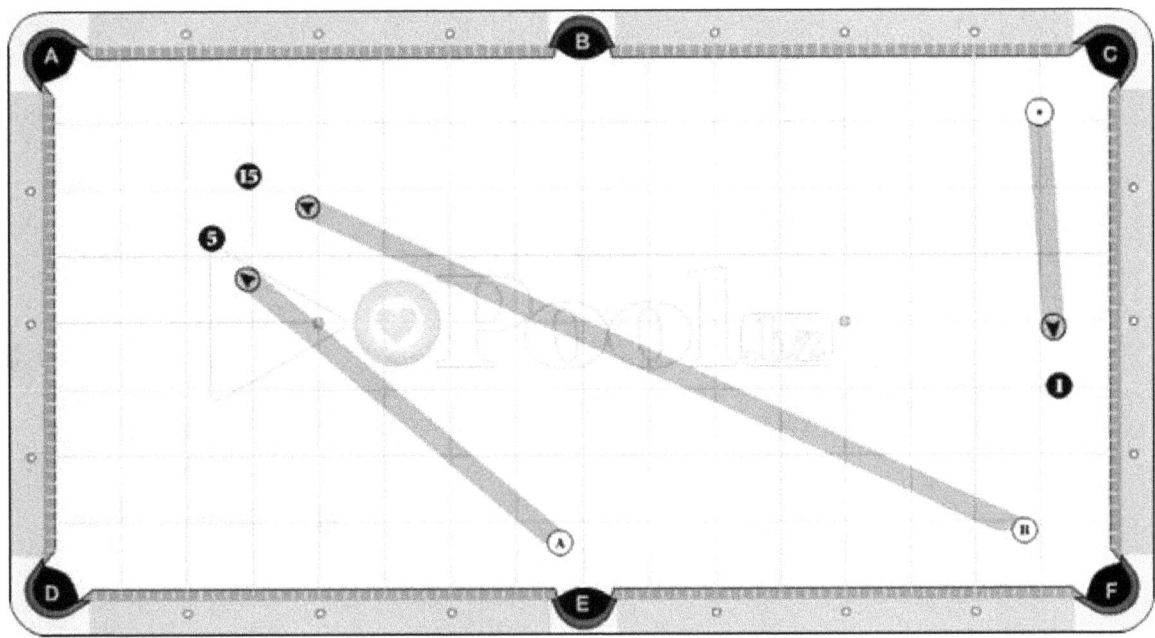

2 D

Object: Pocket the OB with CB anywhere on the shaded line.

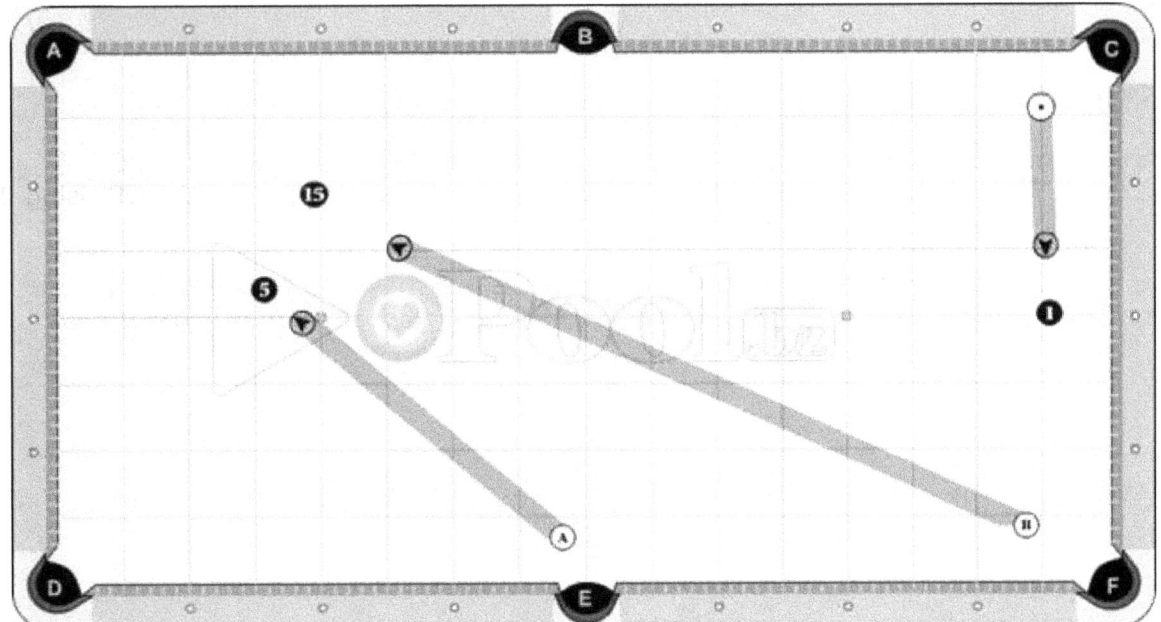

3, 4, 5, 6 D to Pocket

Object: Pocket the OB with CB anywhere on the shaded line.

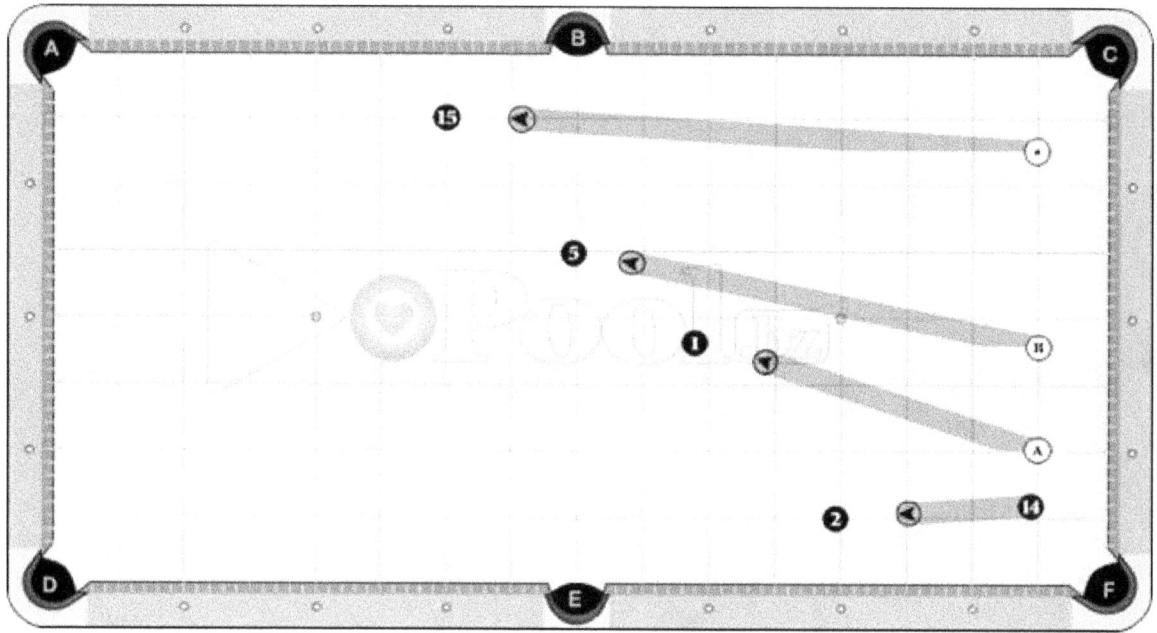

Shallow Angles

Instructions: To begin for the first time, use the stun and medium speed (see *CB Speed/Spin Matrix*). Expertise with these shots requires the skill to pocket the OB using 26 of the 39 CB speed/spin variations.

Drill: Put CB close to OB, pocket the OB. Re-spot OB and move CB back 1/2 D. Upon a miss, move CB 1/2 D closer to OB. *Proof of competence: Repeat 3 times without miss.*

Shallow Angles to Pocket

1 D

Object: Pocket the OB into the side pocket with CB anywhere on the shaded line.

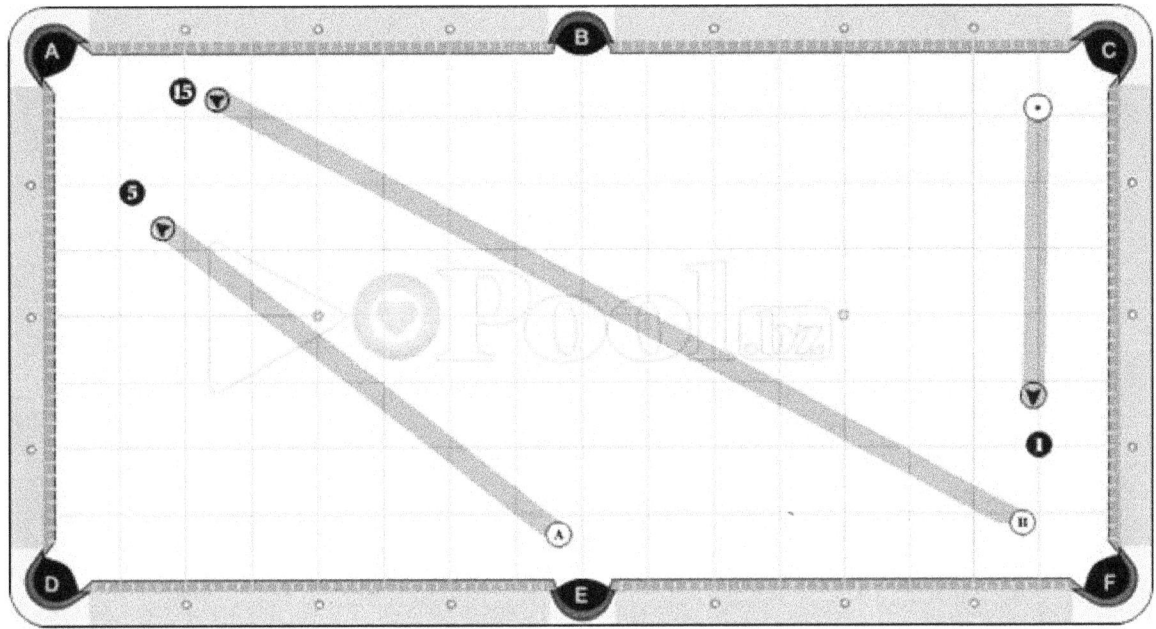

1-1/2 D

Object: Pocket the OB into the nearest pocket with CB anywhere on the shaded line.

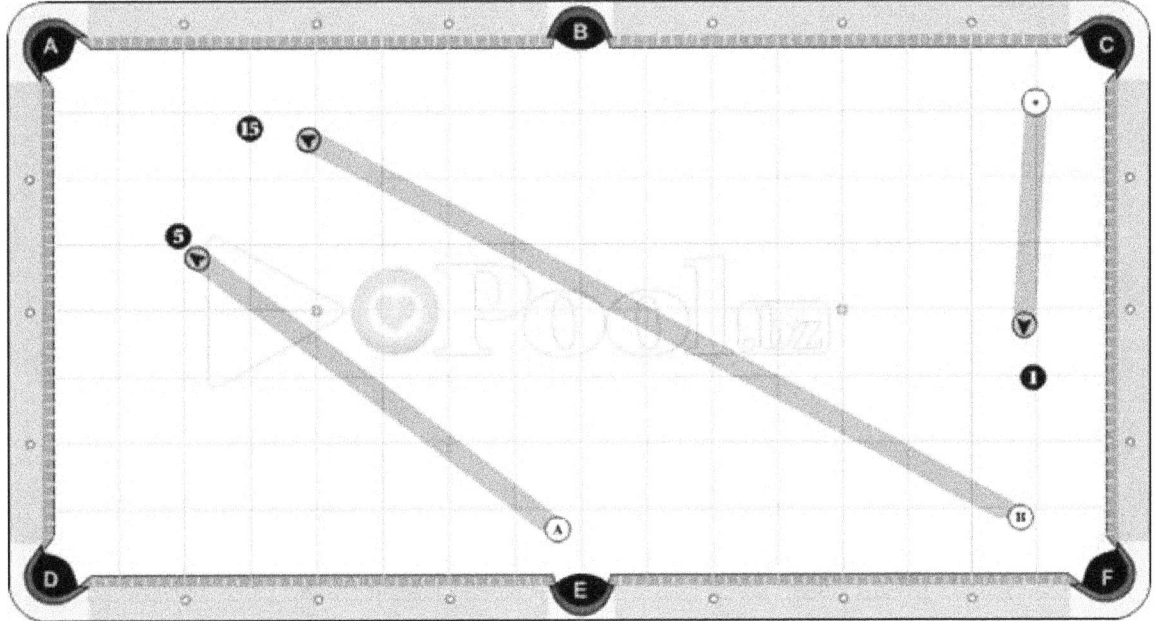

2 D

Object: Pocket the OB into the nearest pocket with CB anywhere on the shaded line.

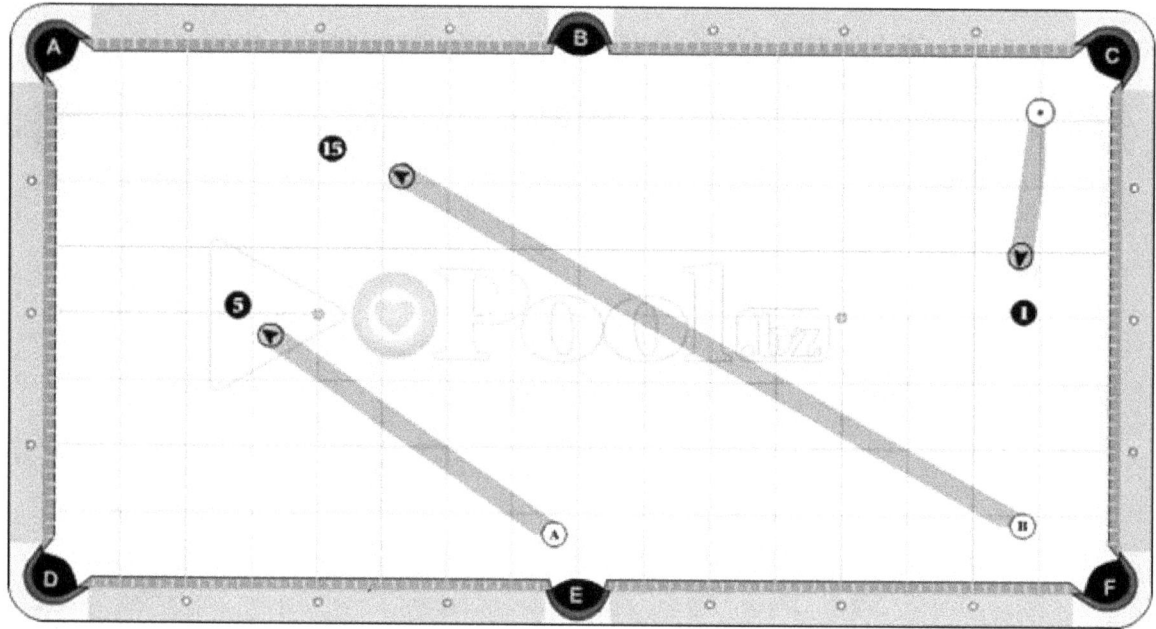

3, 4, 5, 6 D

Object: Pocket the OB into the nearest pocket with CB anywhere on the shaded line.

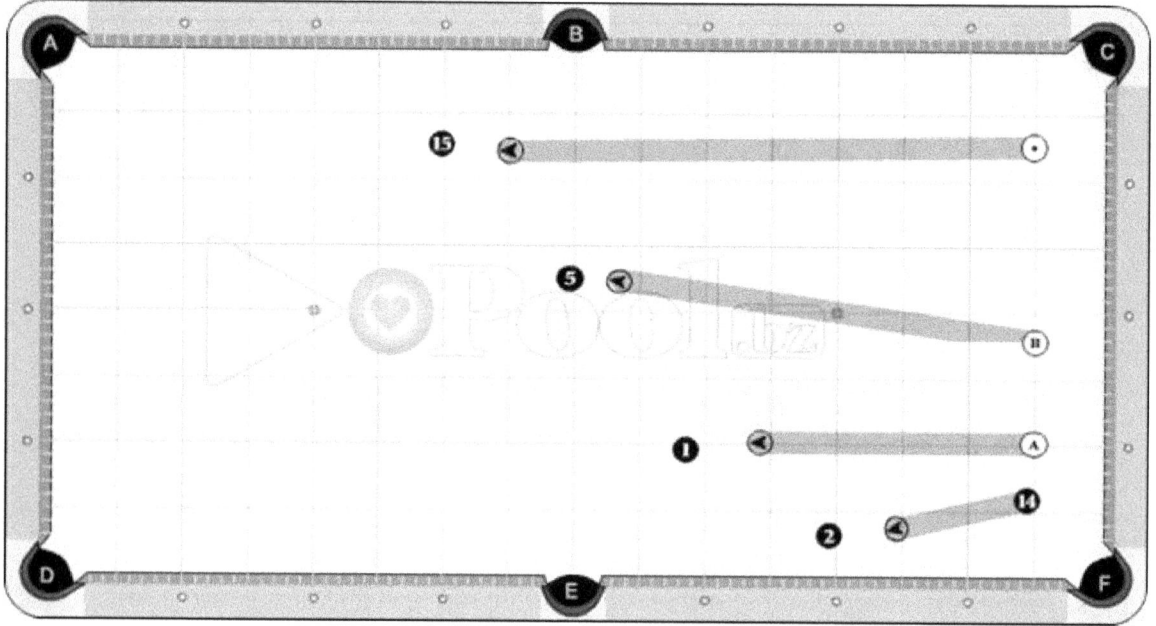

Progressive Shooting Angles

Instructions: To begin for the first time, use the Stun and medium speed (see *CB Speed/Spin Matrix*). Expertise with these shots requires the skill to pocket the OB using 26 of the 39 CB speed/spin variations.

1. Begin the drill with the "stun" position from the *CB Speed/Spin Matrix*. When you identify your Comfort/Chaos Zones for "stun", repeat the process for the other CB speeds and spins.
2. Place the CB on the center spot and shoot at the OB that is 1/2 diamond from the side pocket.
3. Upon pocketing the OB, move the CB 1/2 diamond to the left along the center line.
4. Repeat until a miss, and then backup 1 Diamond and advance from that position.
5. After hitting the beginning of your Chaos Zone on the left side, repeat the steps on the right side.
6. When done, write a note about the Comfort Zone for this left and right edges of your Comfort Zone for the 1/2 diamond.
7. Repeat the process on the OB that is 1 diamond from the side pocket.

Apply each of the 39 CB shots listed in these shots

OB to Side Pocket

Set 1

Object: Pocket the OB into the nearest pocket with CB anywhere on the shaded line.

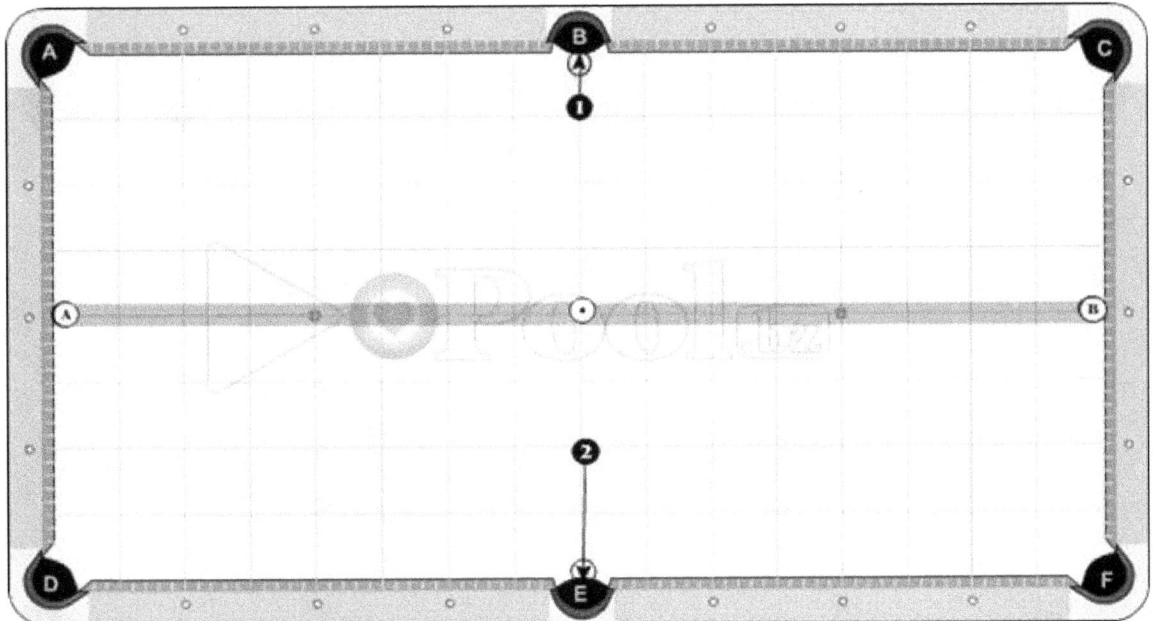

Set 2

Object: Pocket the OB into the side pocket with CB anywhere on the shaded line.

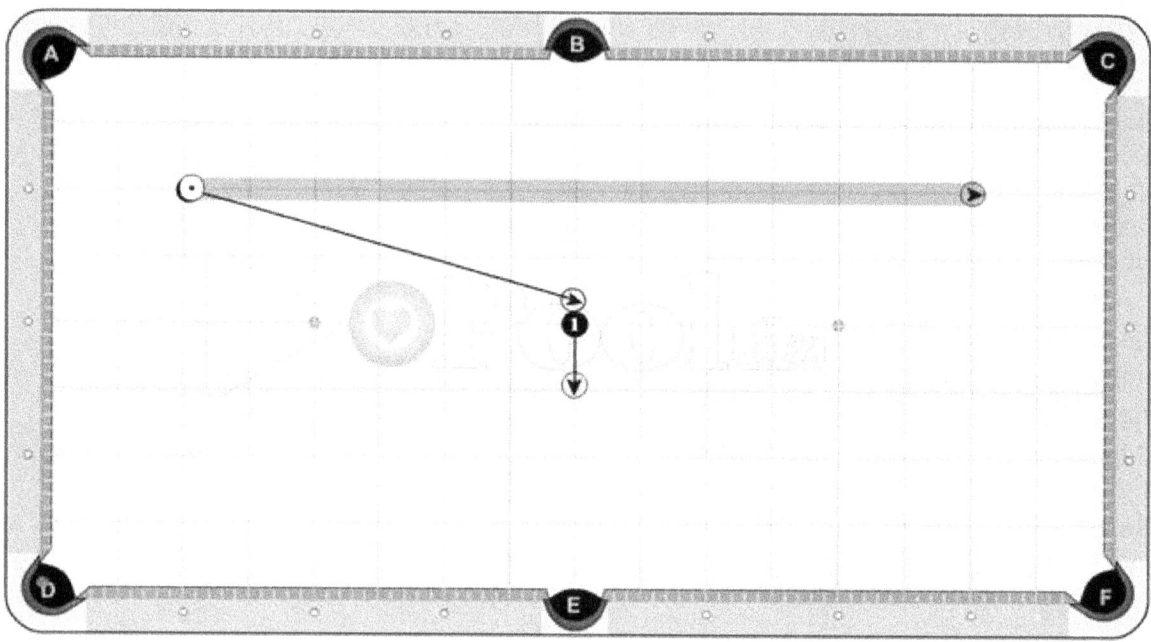

OB to 1D Pocket (on rail)

Object: Pocket the OB into the nearest pocket with CB anywhere on the shaded lines.

Set 1

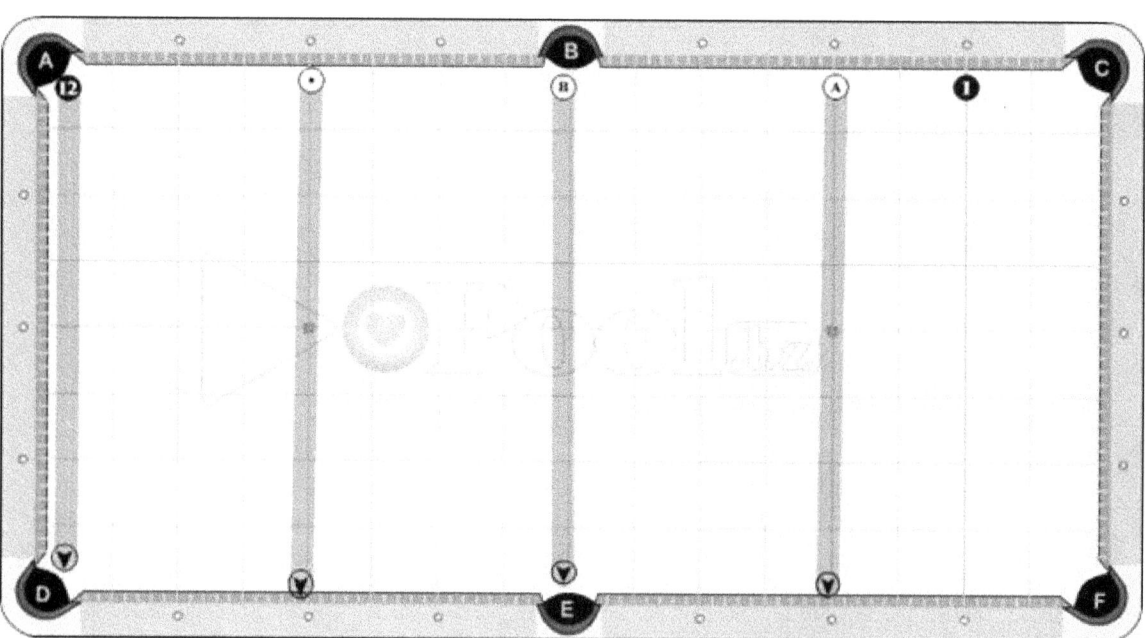

Set 2

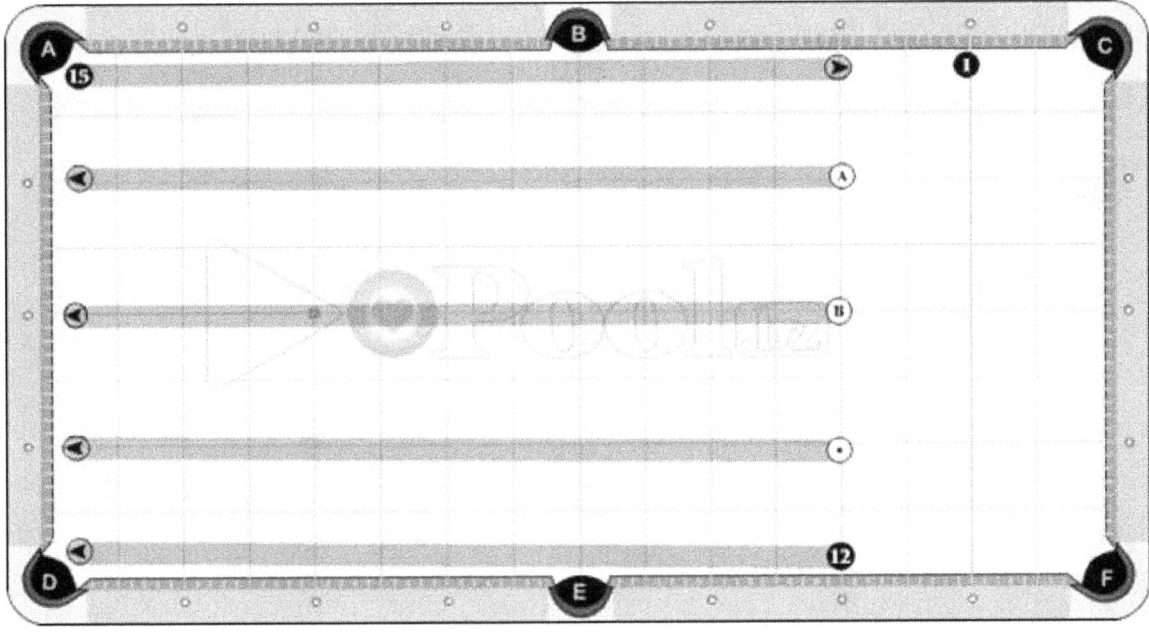

Set 3

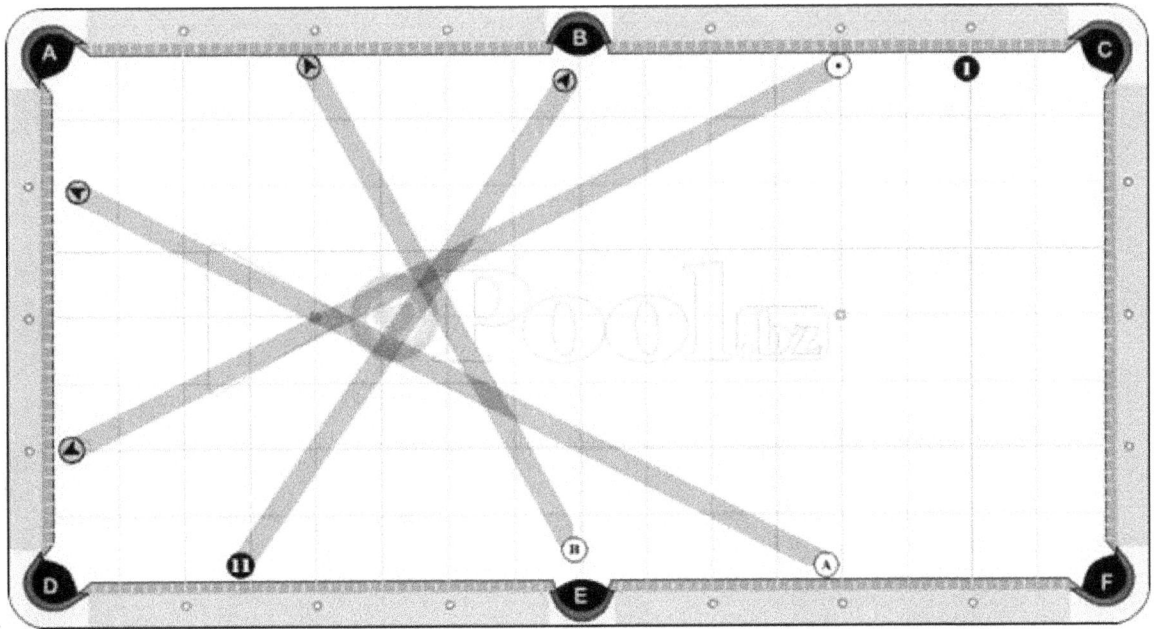

OB to 1 D Pocket (1/2 D from rail)

Object: Pocket the OB into the nearest pocket with CB anywhere on the shaded lines.

Set 1

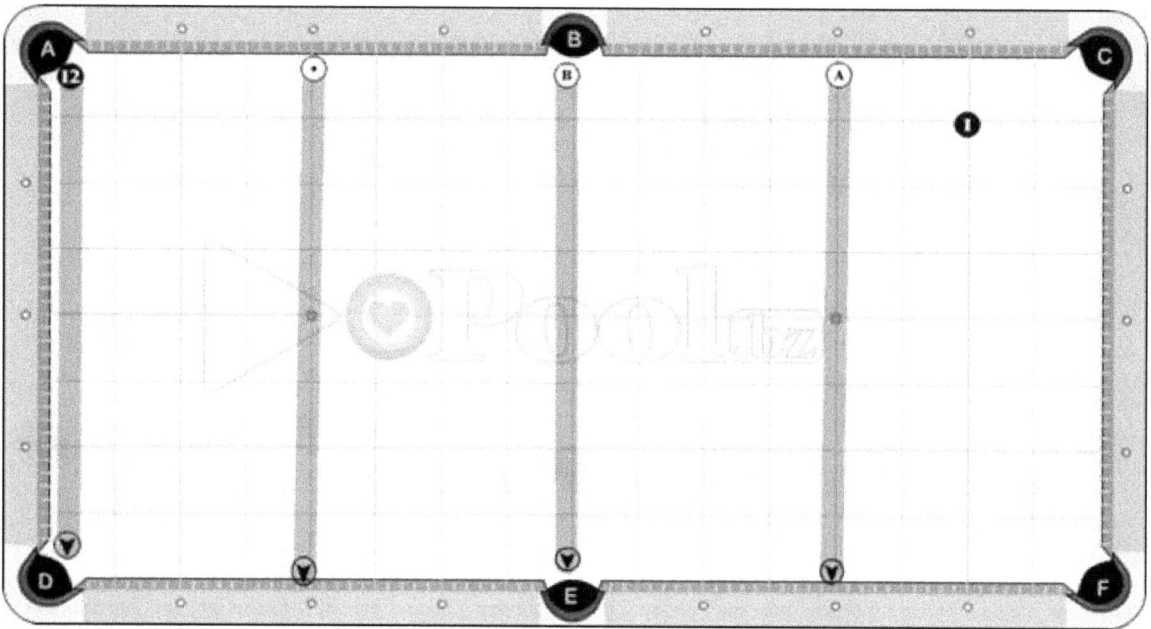

Set 2

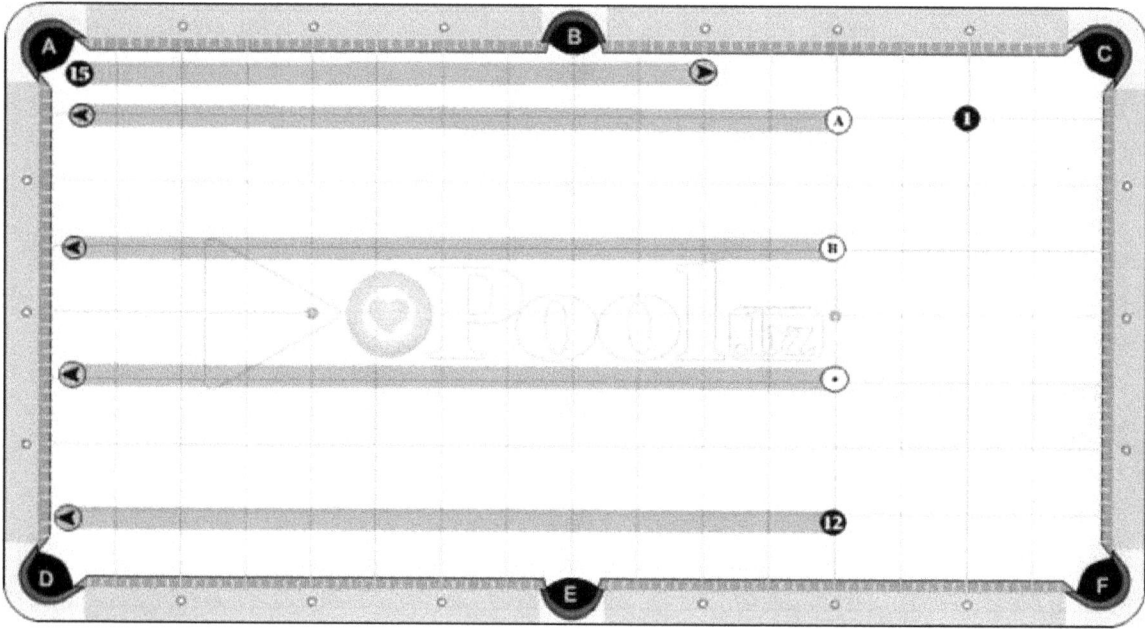

Set 3

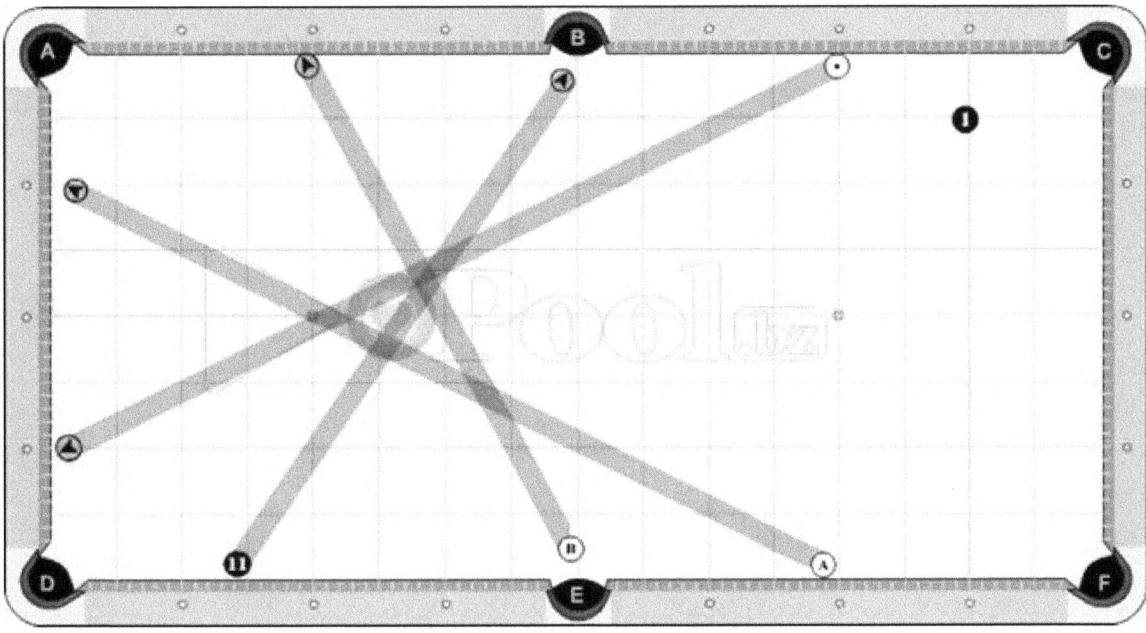

OB 1 D to Pocket (1 D from rail)

Object: Pocket the OB into the nearest pocket with CB anywhere on the shaded lines.

Set 1

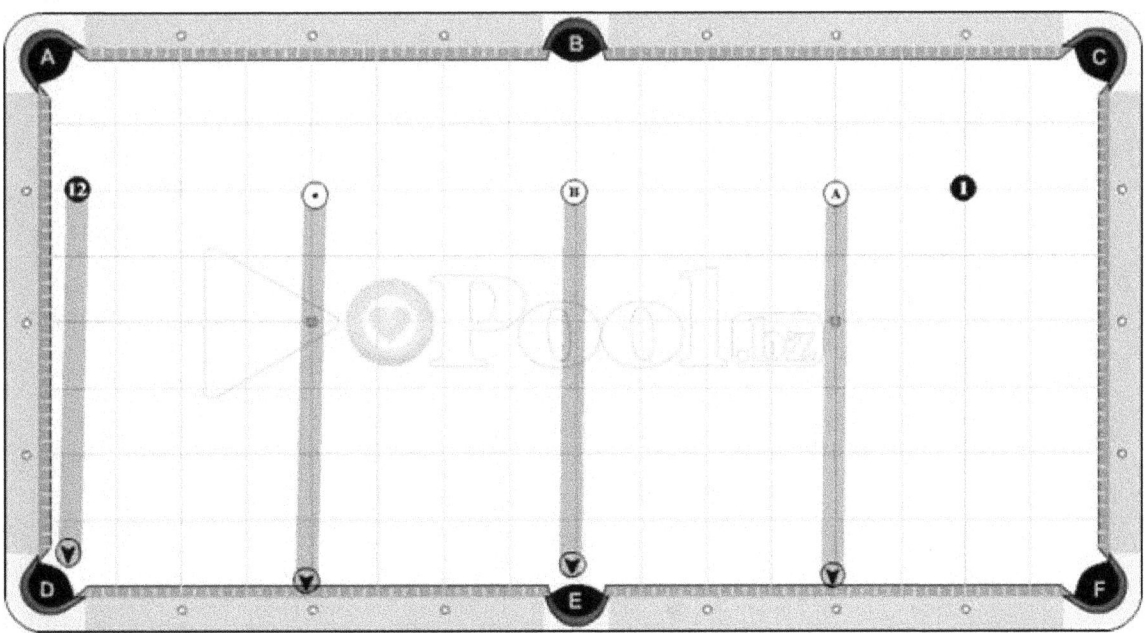

Set 2

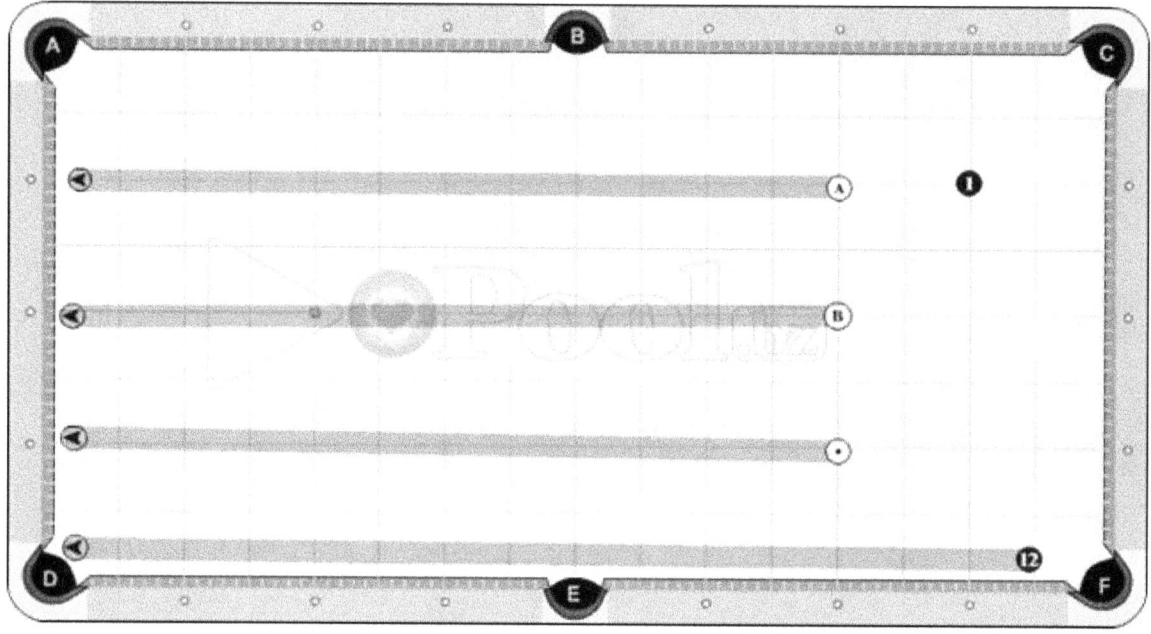

Set 3

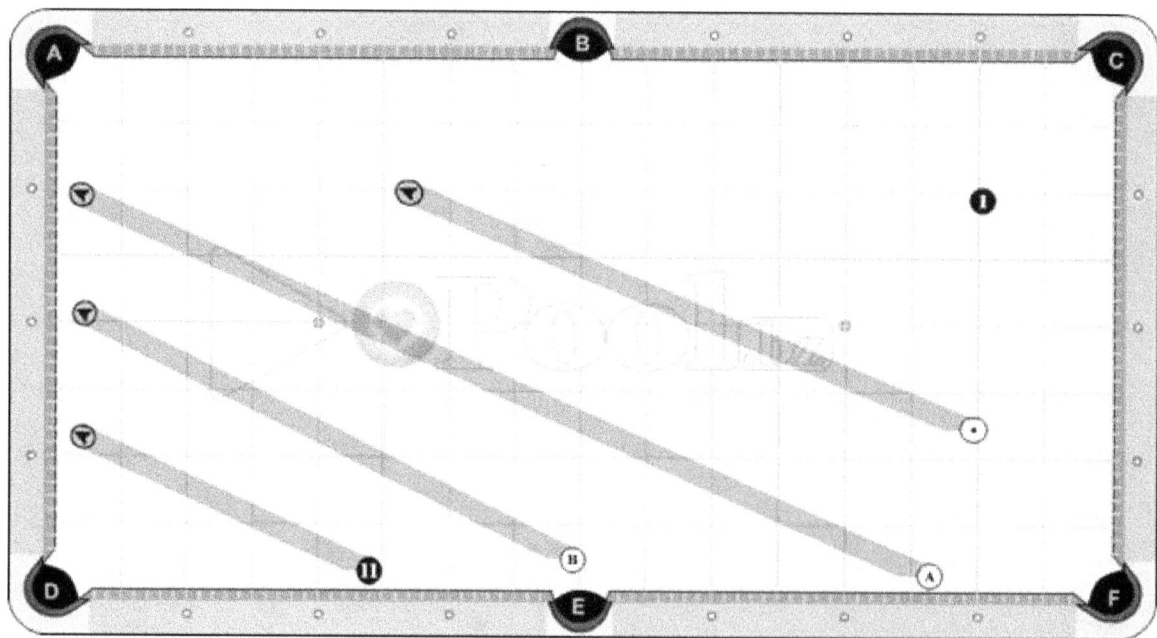

OB 2 D to Pocket (on rail)

Object: Pocket the OB into the nearest pocket with CB anywhere on the shaded lines.

Set 1

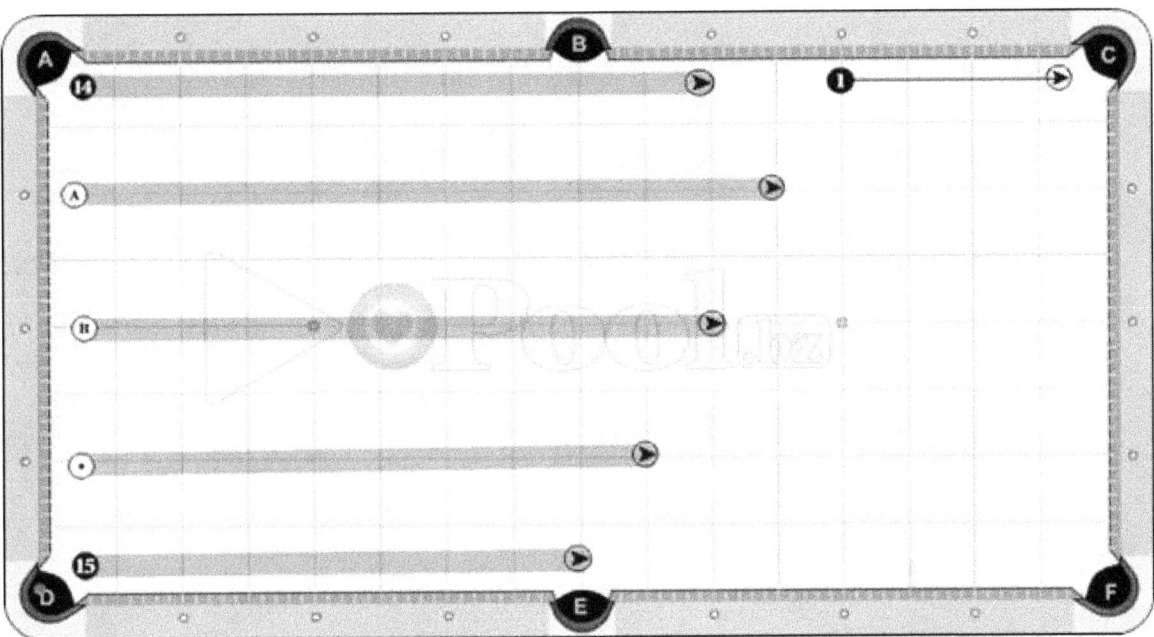

Set 2

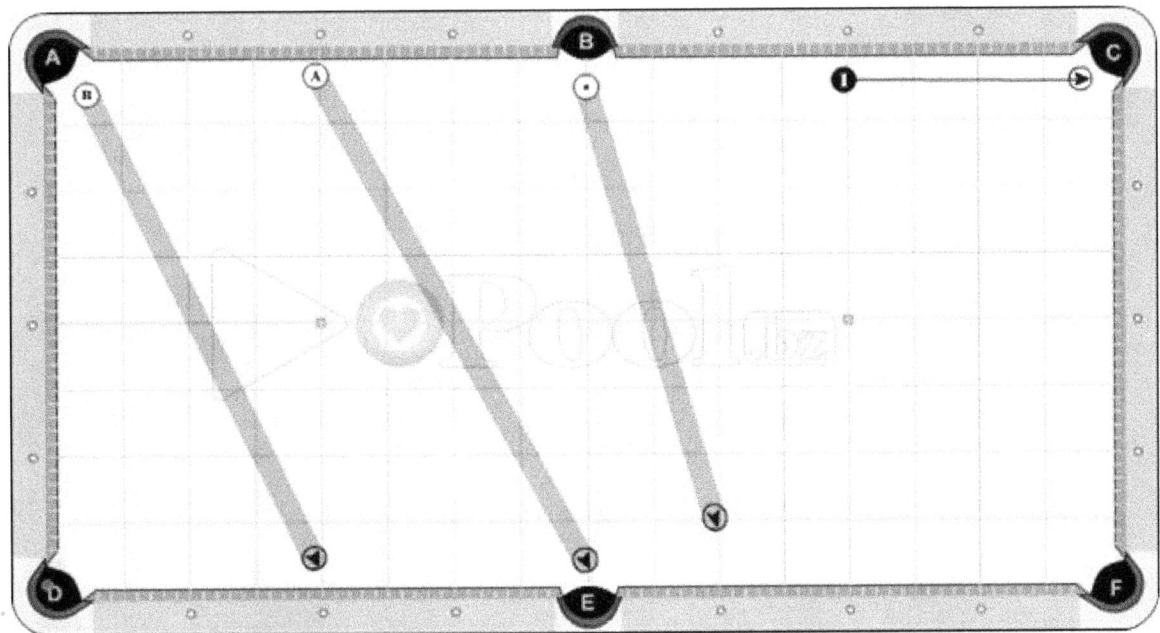

OB 2 D to Pocket (1/2 D from rail)

Object: Pocket the OB into the nearest pocket with CB anywhere on the shaded lines.

Set 1

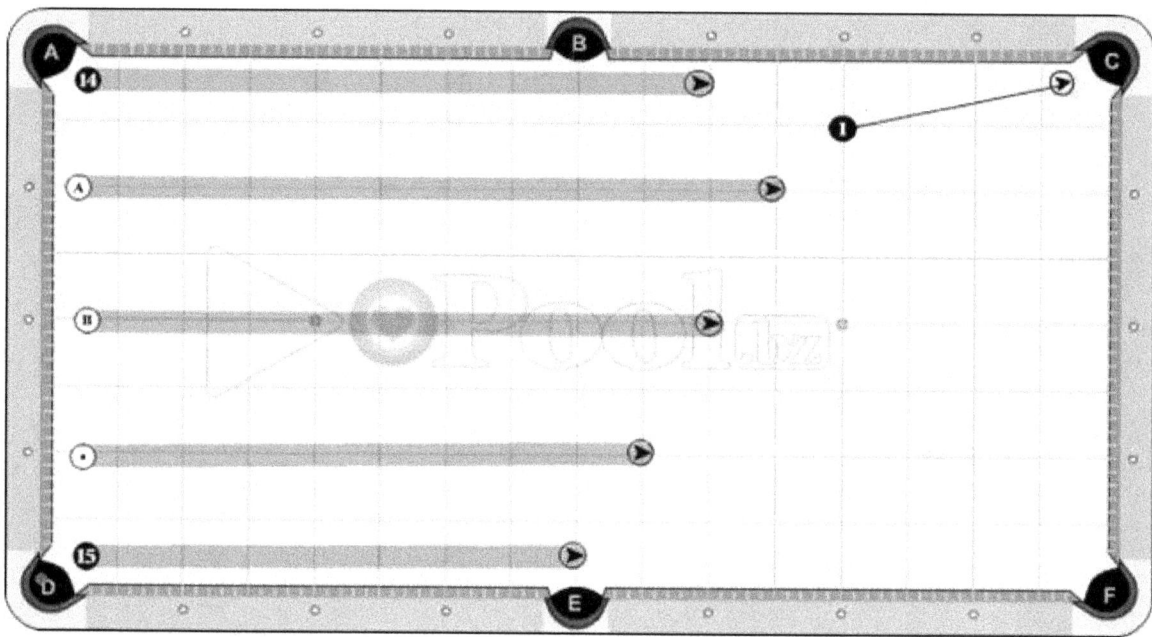

Set 2

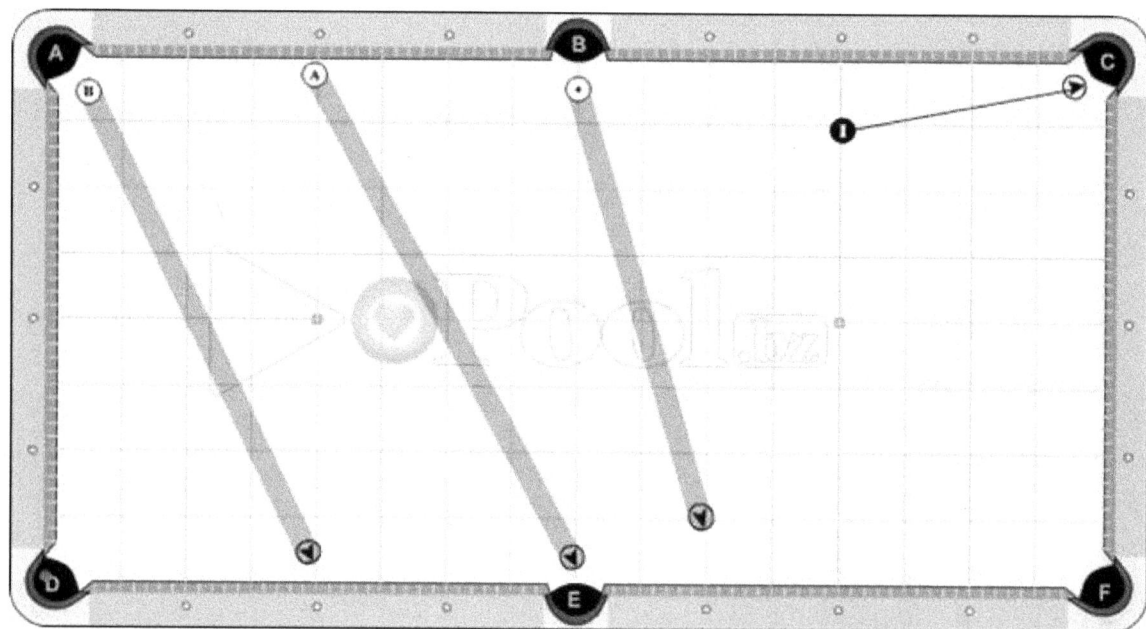

OB 2 D to Pocket (1 D from rail)

Object: Pocket the OB into the nearest pocket with CB anywhere on the shaded lines.

Set 1

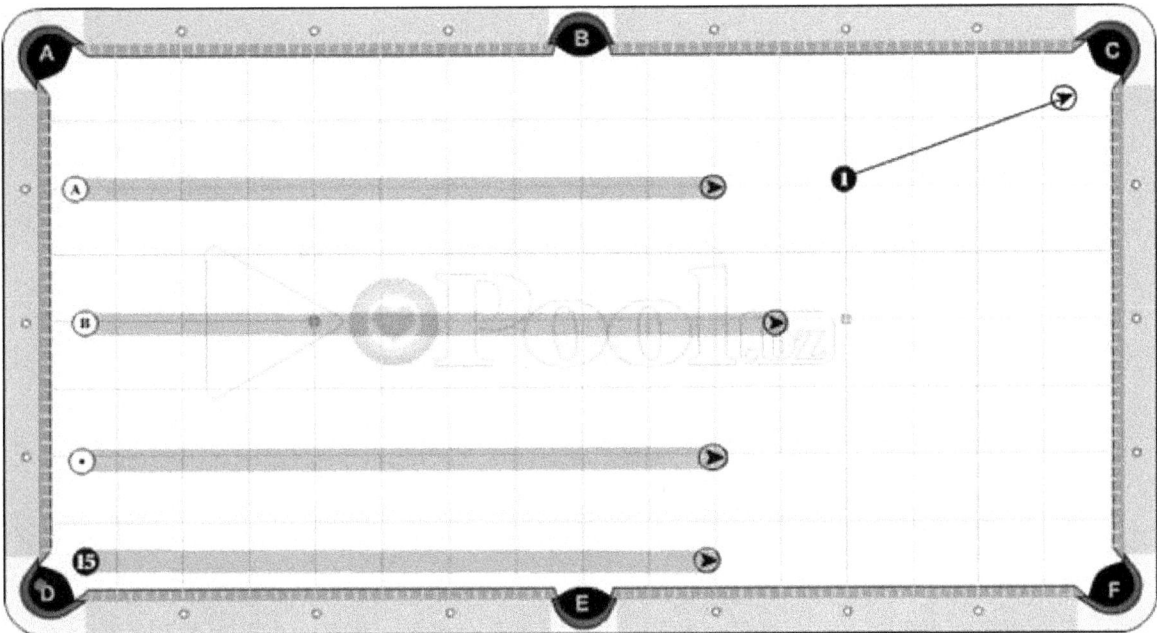

Set 2

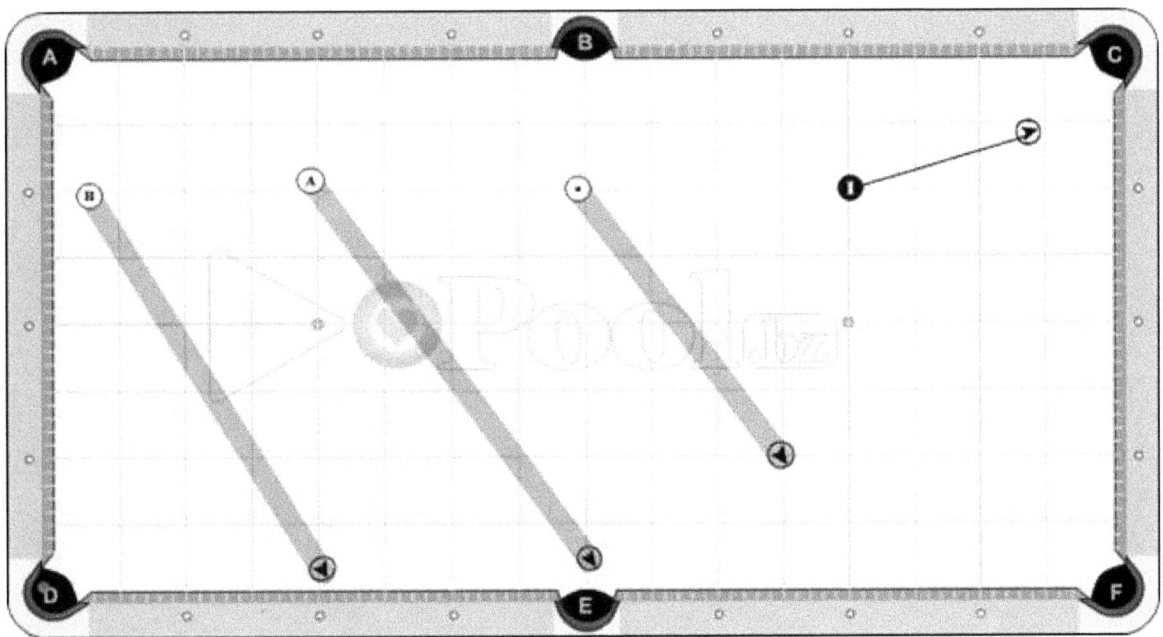

OB 2 D to Pocket (1-1/2 D from rail)

Object: Pocket the OB into the nearest pocket with CB anywhere on the shaded lines.

Set 1

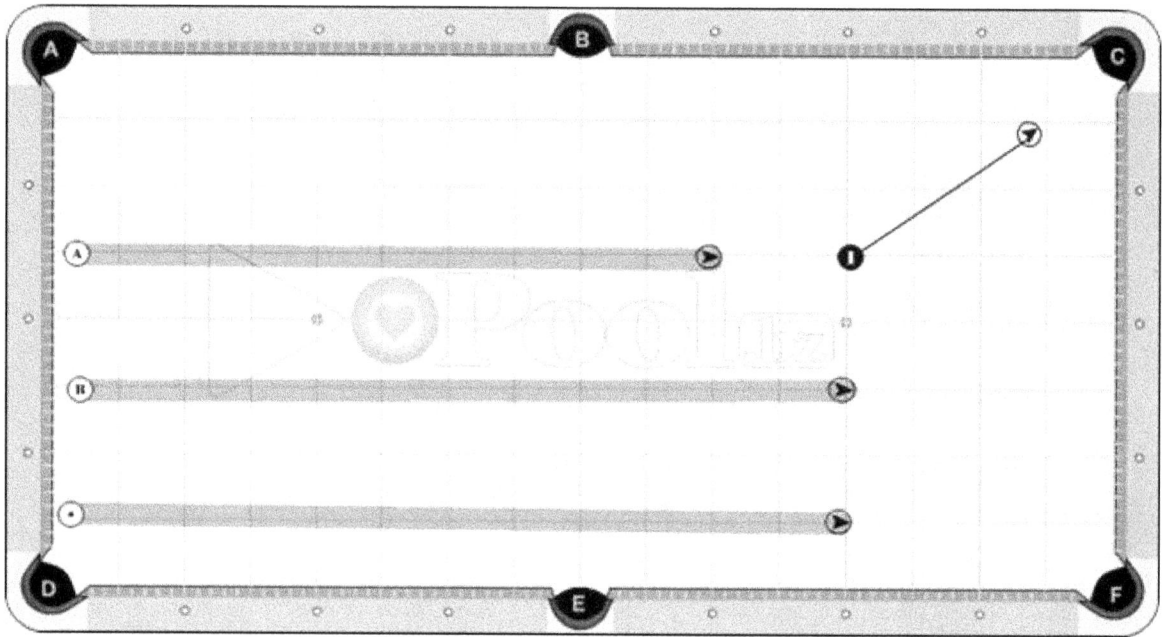

Set 2

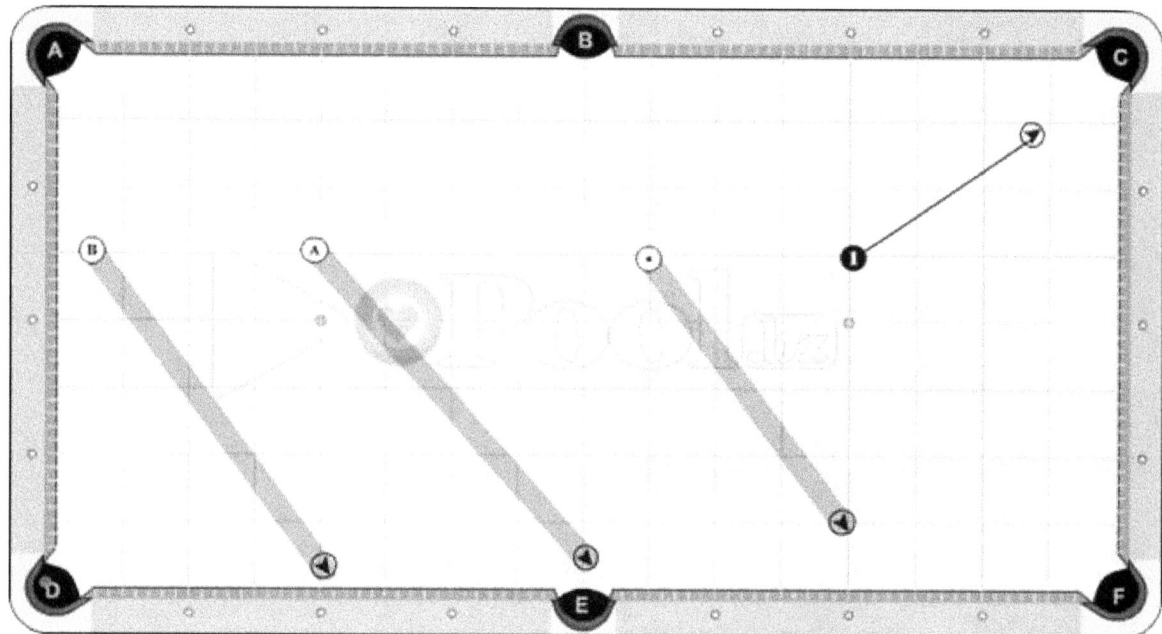

OB 2 D to Pocket (2 D from rail)

Object: Pocket the OB into the nearest pocket with CB anywhere on the shaded lines.

Set 1

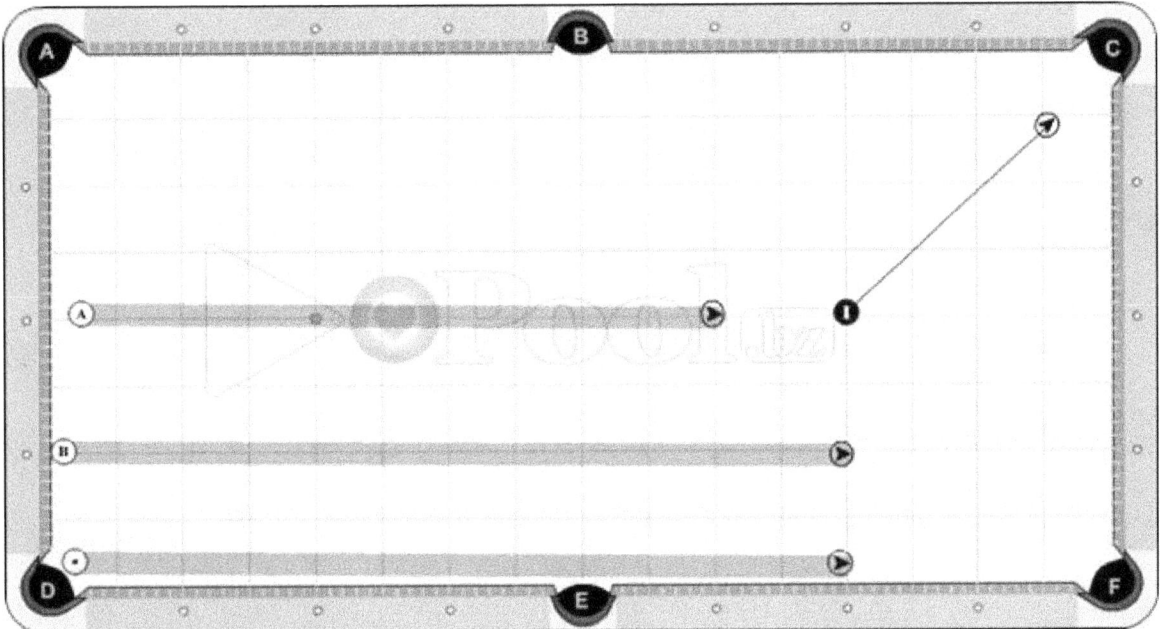

Set 2

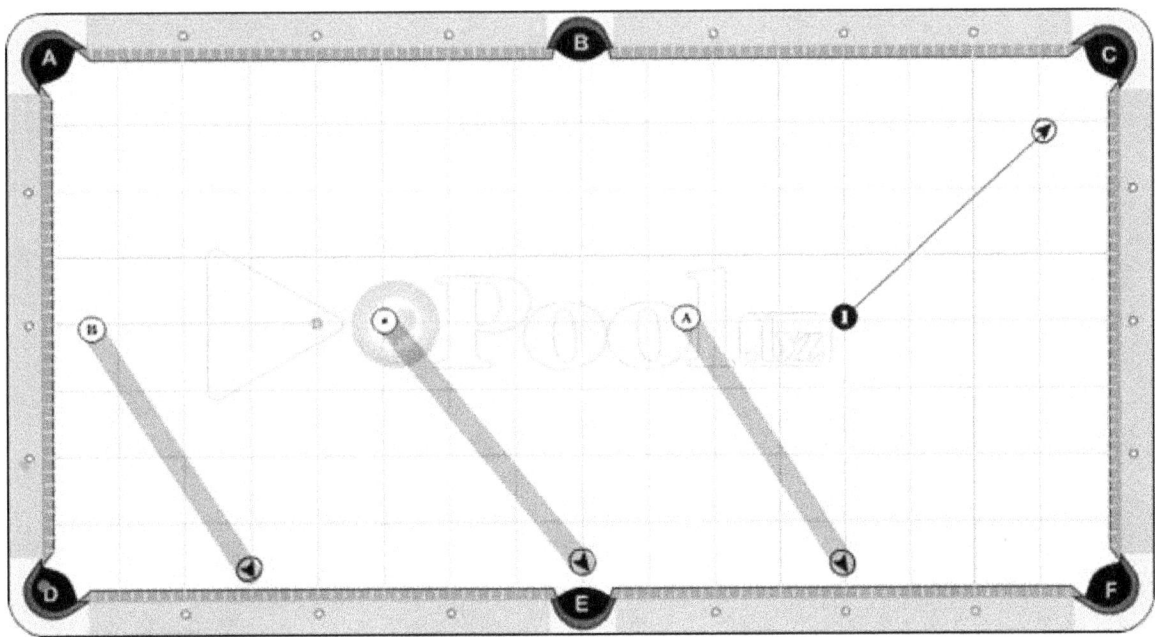

OB 4 D to Corners

Options: OB on center spot and CB on any position in shaded lines. Pocket into any corner.

Set 1

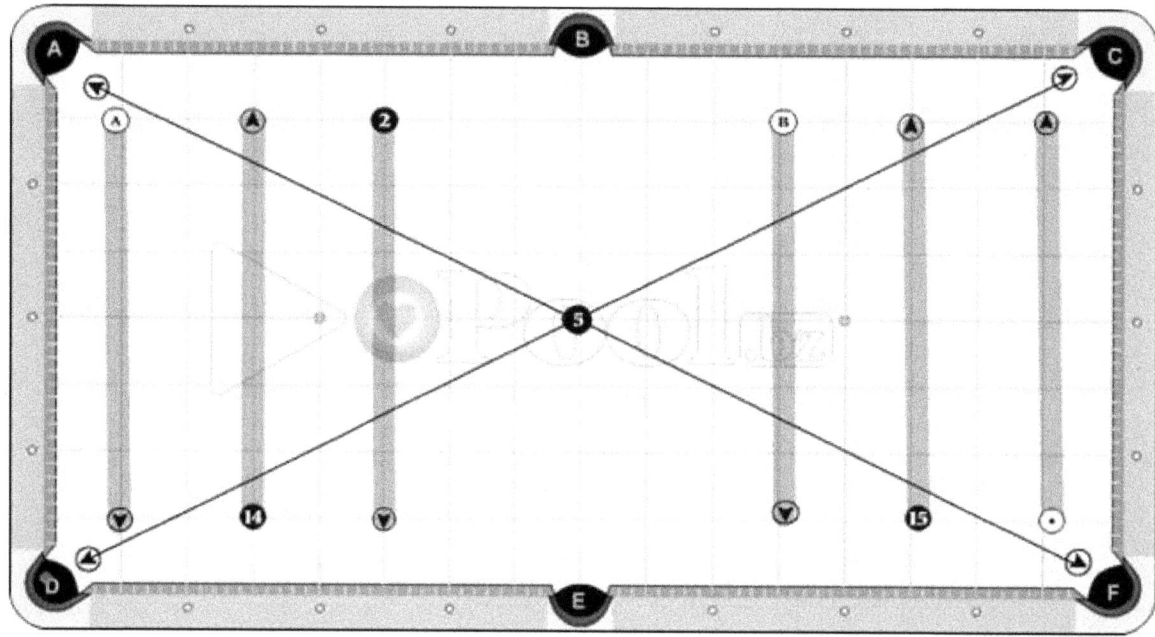

Set 2

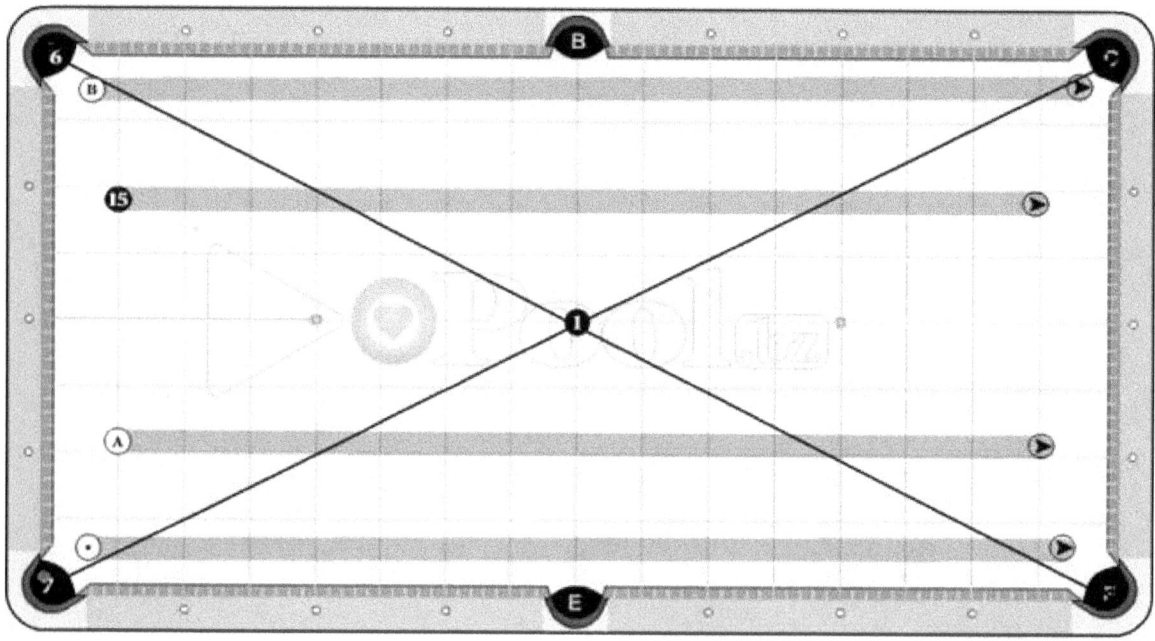

Precision Shooting

These subjects and exercises help you master the necessary skills to accomplish exactly what you intend, when you intend.

Standardized CB Speeds

It is impossible to consistently play position until you have figured out how hard or soft to hit the CB. Speed control is one of the deep secrets to playing with intelligence. Putting a pre-selected and precise amount of energy into the CB is necessary for defensive and offensive shots. With it you can perform miracles. Without it you will not achieve the personal greatness to which you aspire.

This is a physical skill that takes some serious practice to master and own. At first, it might seem a little tricky, but it does not take long before you get a handle on controlling the speed of the CB. Owning this skill has immediate benefits.

The speed settings provided here are somewhat subjective. Work to achieve the rolls shown in the table layout. Line up a row of several balls so that you can go down the line shooting one after the other. Do not quit until you can get these results 9 out of 10 times. As your ability to control improves, you can automatically select speeds by "feel" just by knowing where you want the ball to stop.

Soft 1, 2, 3 Speeds

For lesser than Soft 1 CB speeds, use the *Wrist Stroke*.

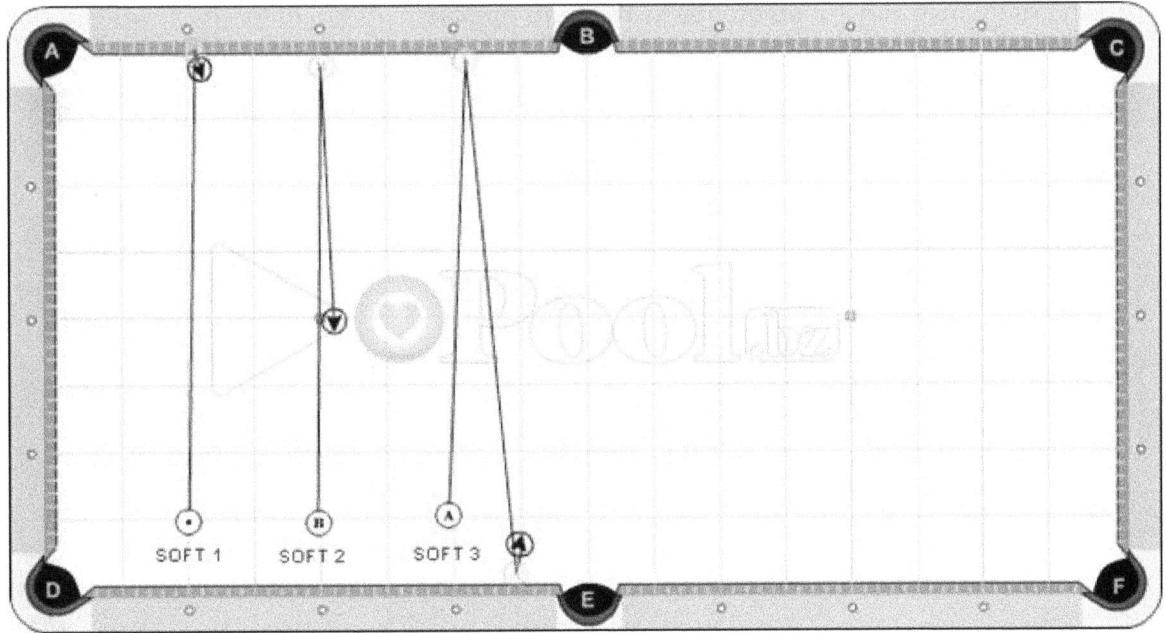

Medium 1, 2, 3 Speeds

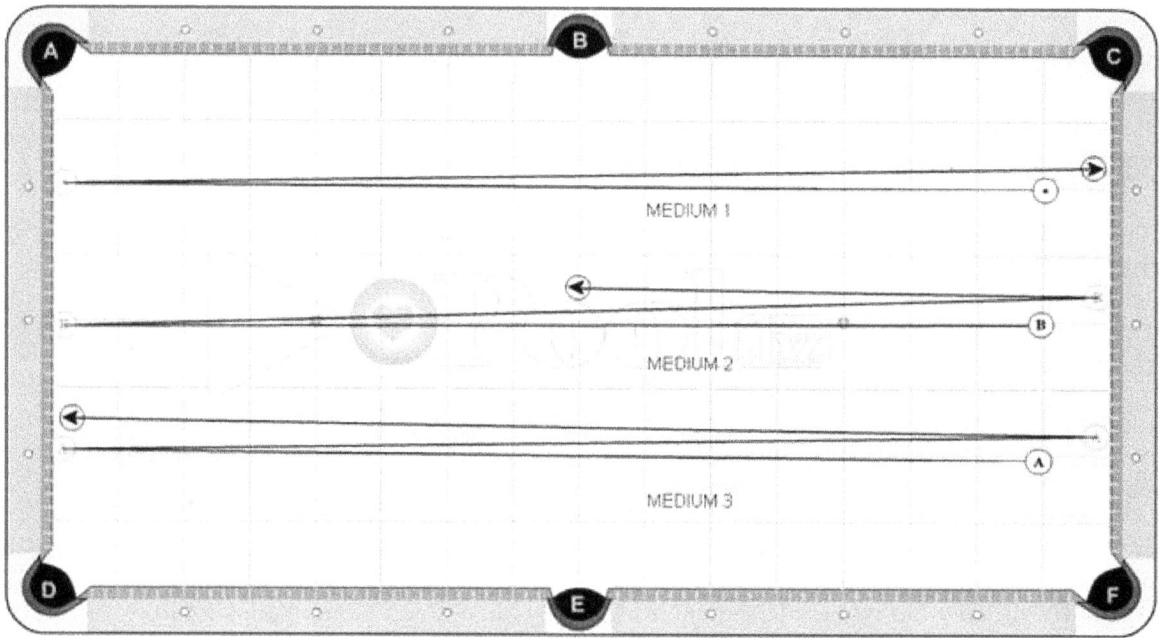

Hard 1 Speed

Only Hard 1 is shown. Hard 2 scratches in the side pocket.

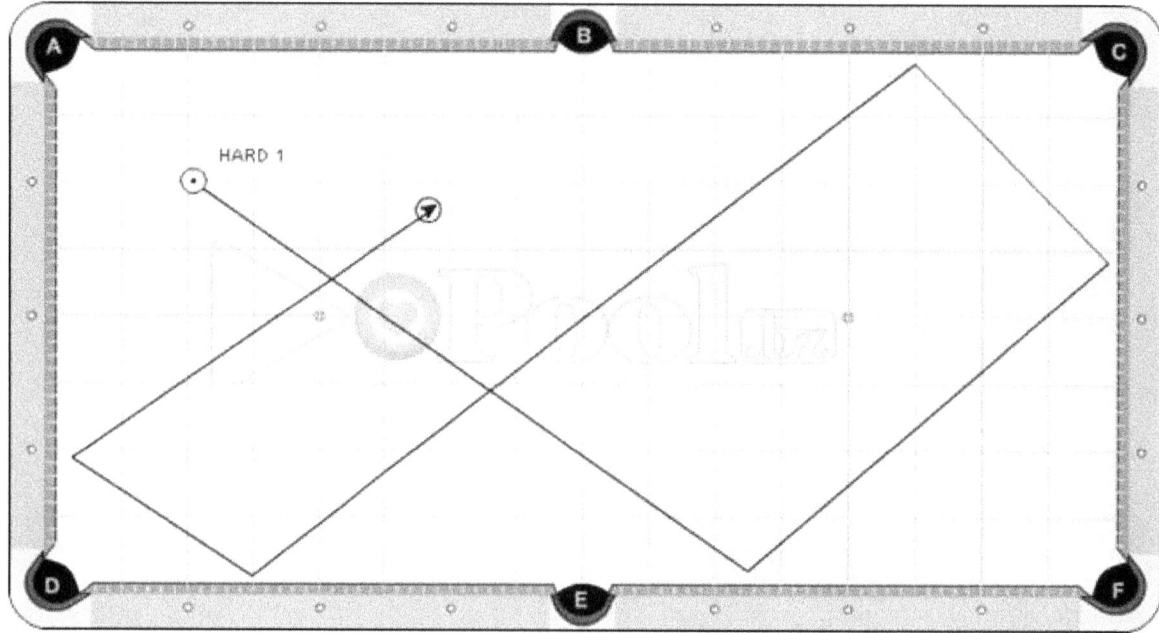

Wrist Stroke Mastery

Can you make the CB only travel an inch (2-3 cm)? When straight rail billiards and balkline billiards were international sports, a carefully mastered nudge shot could rack up thousands of points. The winners of these hours-long matches were determined by who had the best CB control within fractions of an inch (<2 cm).

There are safeties that call for VERY precise and small movements to be successful. Some of these movements require that the CB or object ball move a distance of a quarter ball roll or less. This level of ball roll mastery enables some very interesting opportunities in the right circumstances.

Your normal stroke with the forearm back and forth movement does not work. You just can't get the definite control necessary to make a short roll shot work. You must develop a movement that only uses your wrist to move the stick forward a fraction of an inch.

Here is how to make it work.

1. On the table, place the stick in your closed bridge fingers. Close your hand into a fist. Clench the cue so that the stick can barely slide back and forth.
2. Place your bridge hand about an inch (2 to 3 cm) from the CB. Keep the cue as level as possible.
3. With your stick hand in the normal position near the butt, grip the stick more firmly.
4. Move the stick back and forth using only your wrist. Get used to the resistance from the bridge grip.
5. When ready to trigger the shot, let the stick come forward a very short distance into the CB. The tip should barely penetrate the CB.

Remember, you are controlling the stick with your wrist movement. Do NOT move your forearm. This requires some serious practicing. You must get comfortable shooting with this limited movement. You can actually do lag shots using only the wrist stroke. Experiment – play several games, intentionally only using the wrist stroke.

Nudging Practice Procedure

Use the exercise below and learn to move the CB over precise distances.

1. Place a donut (paper reinforcement ring) where the CB starts.
2. Put the Post-It sheet about a diamond away from the CB.
3. Shoot the object ball onto the sheet. Repeat until mastered.
4. Move the sheet closer and master that distance.
5. Continue working on finer and finer control.

Repeat this once a week. Before a competition, a couple of slow roll practice strokes are all that is needed to remind your muscle memory.

Nudging

1 ball: CB into OB and both balls return to original position. **2 ball:** CB off the OB with the corner pocket blocked. **3 ball:** OB to the rail and up stop to block the corner pocket.

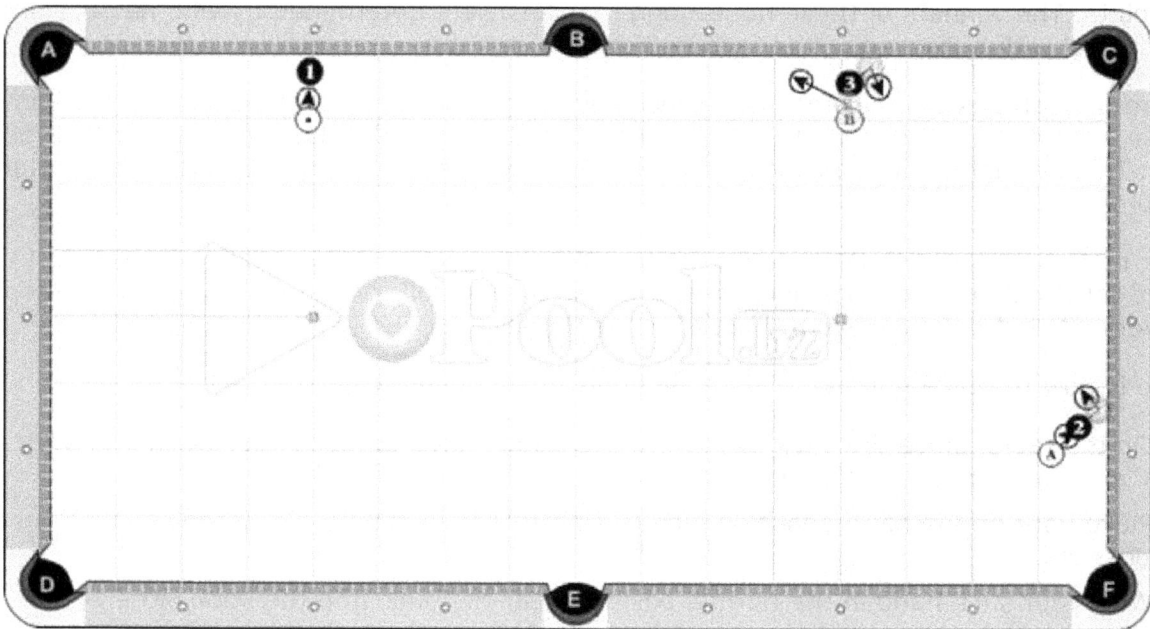

Back & Forth Nips

1 ball: Roll the CB across the top of the OB to push it to the rail with CB stopping within 1 ball width. Repeat in the other direction. **2-5 ball:** Move the CB across the top of the OB, back & forth, advancing a little as possible. *Count the number of successful consecutive shots.*

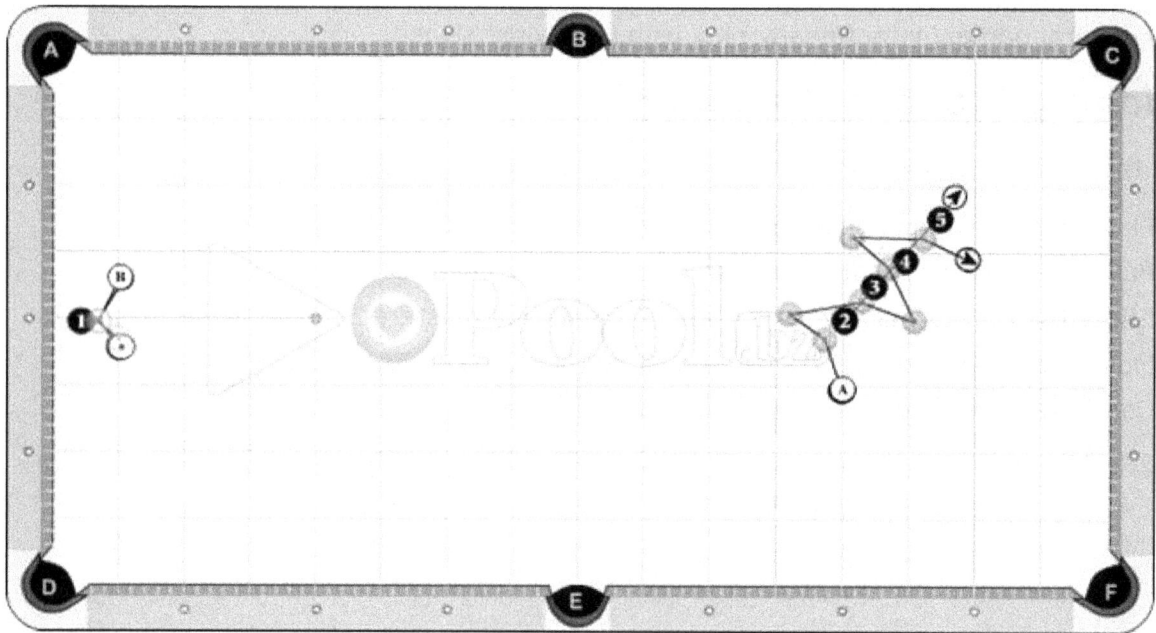

Come Back Home

Object: Shoot the CB at the indicated diamond target to the short rail and then return & hit the cue tip.

Cross Side

Object: Shoot the CB at the indicated diamond target to return & hit the cue tip.

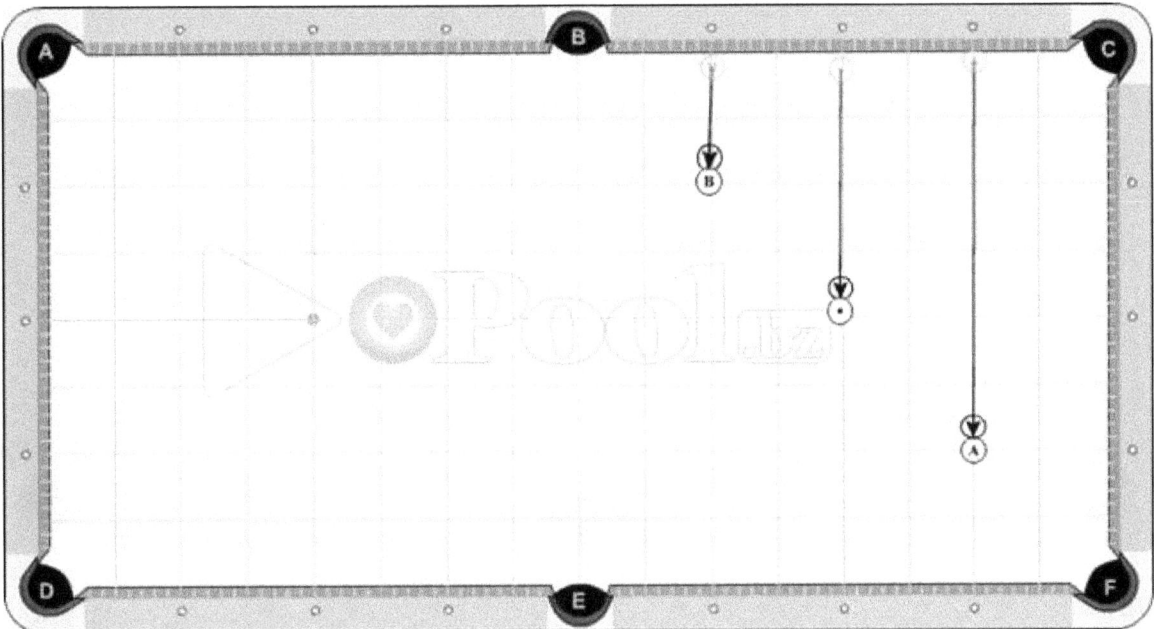

Long Table

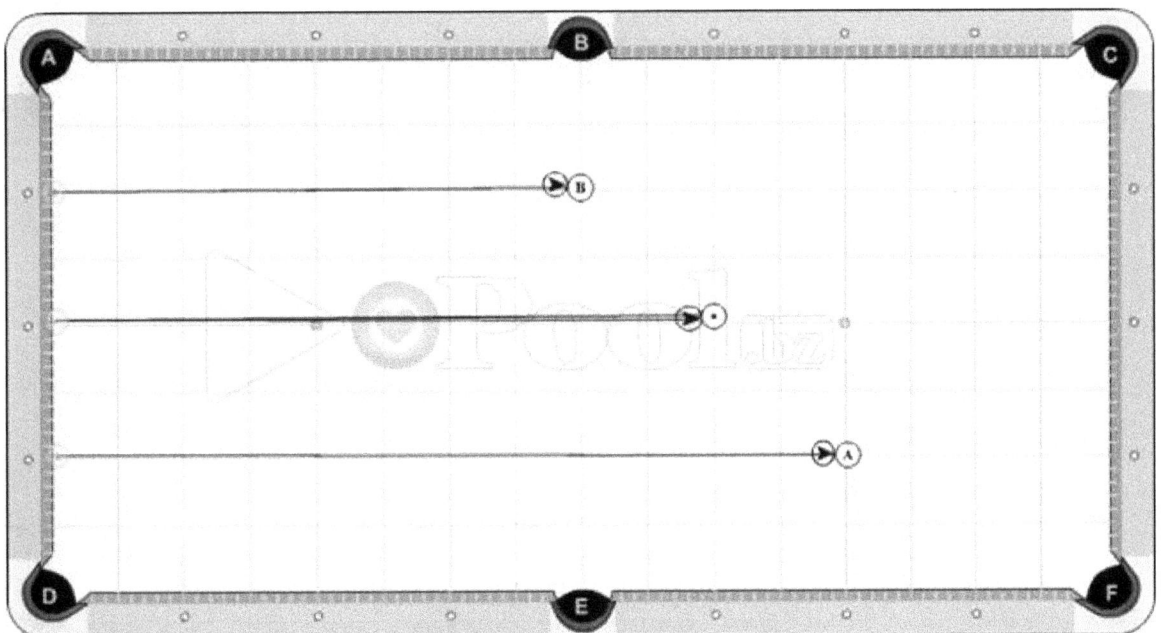

OB to the Rail & Back

Object: Shoot the CB into the OB. OB goes to the rail and comes back to hit the CB.

Set 1

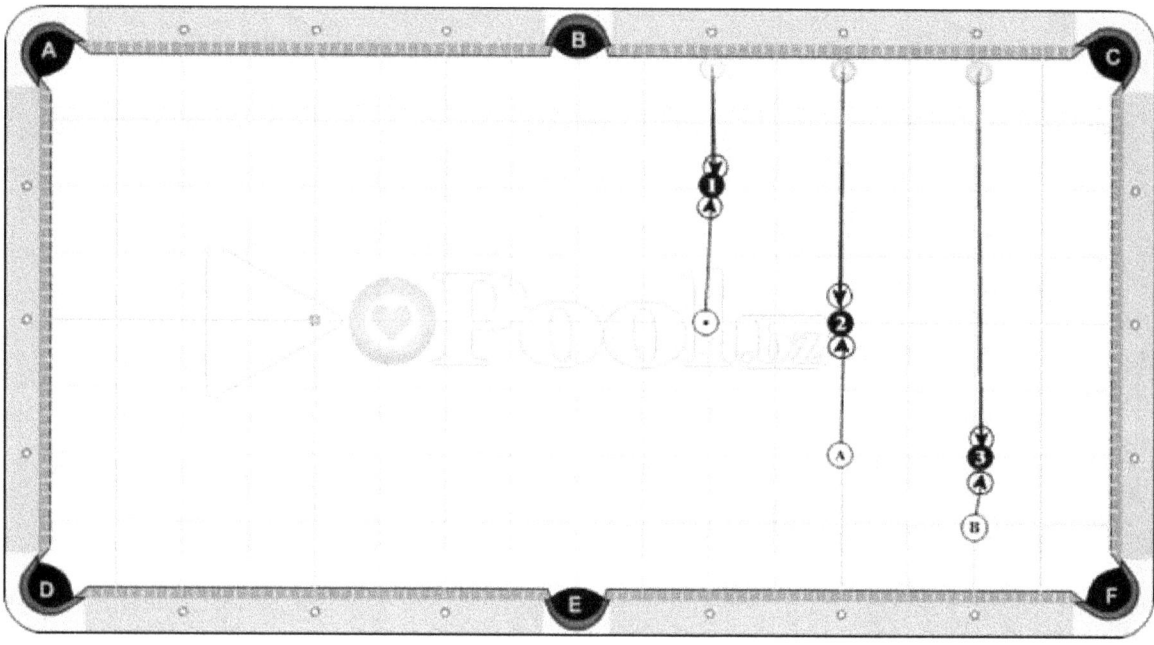

Set 2

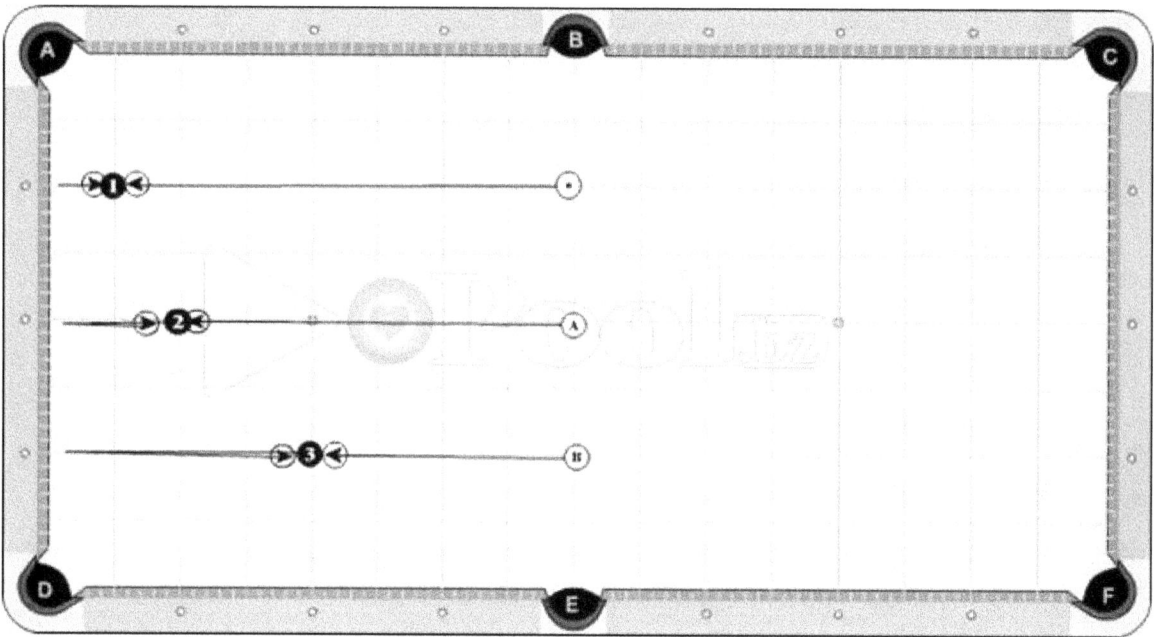

Set 3

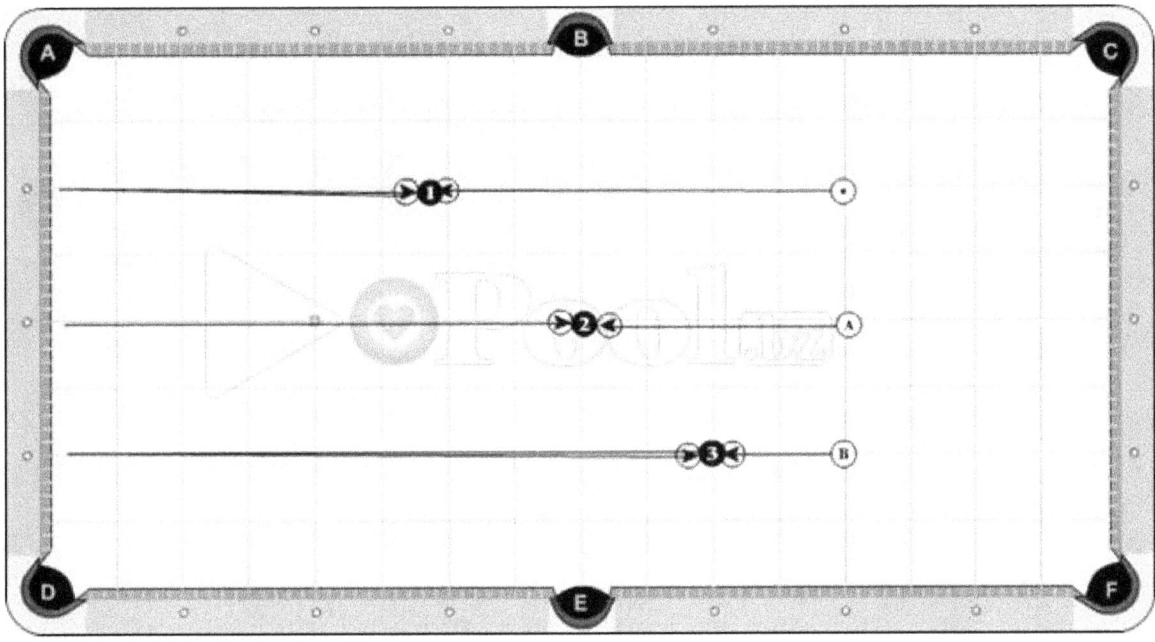

Set 3

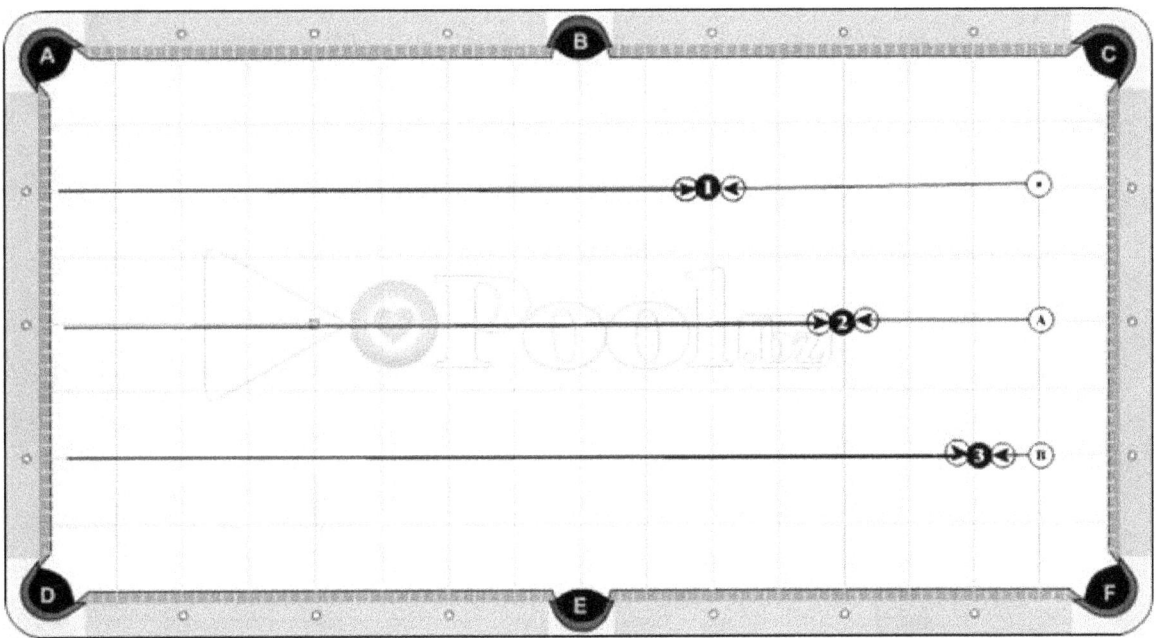

Stun the CB

Object: Pocket the OB and stop the CB dead (at all speeds).

Set 1

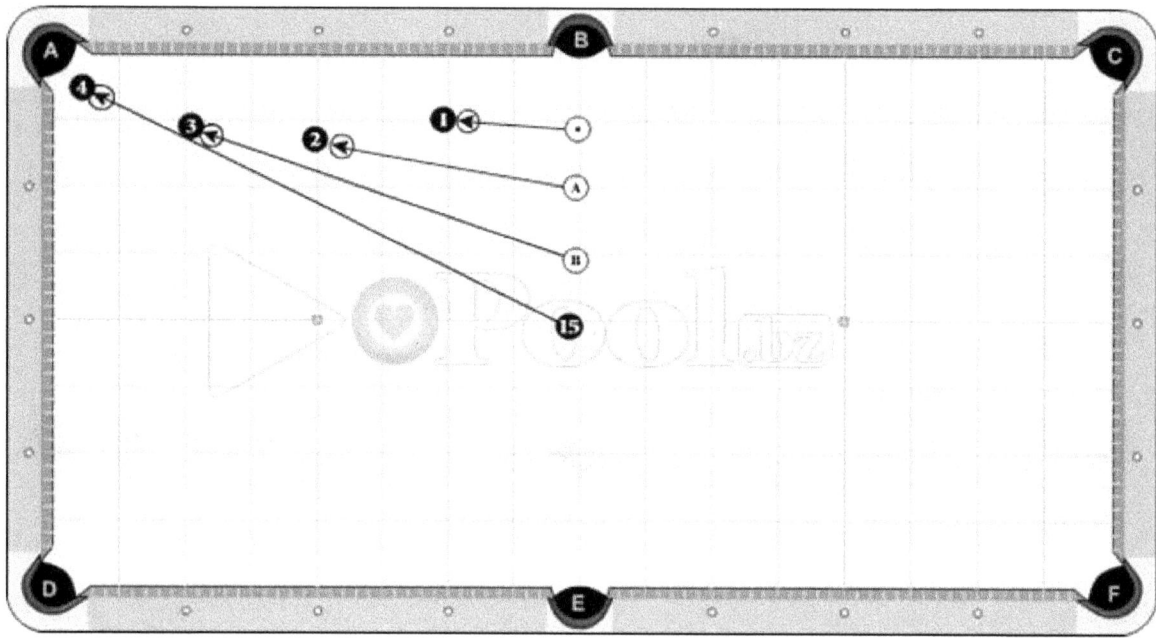

Set 2

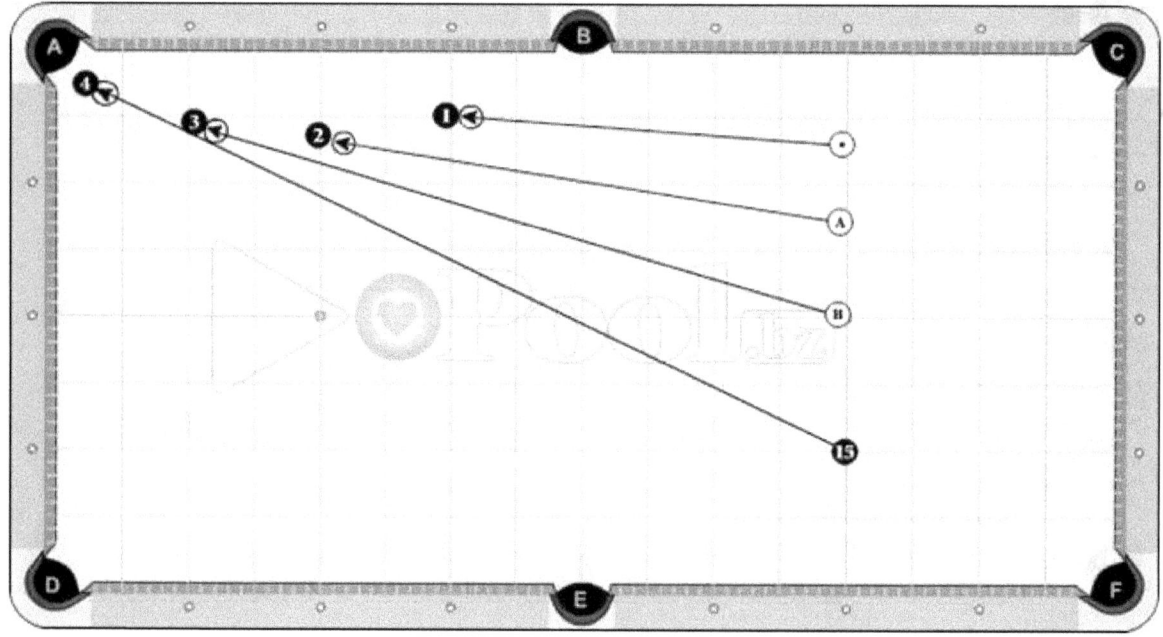

Set 3

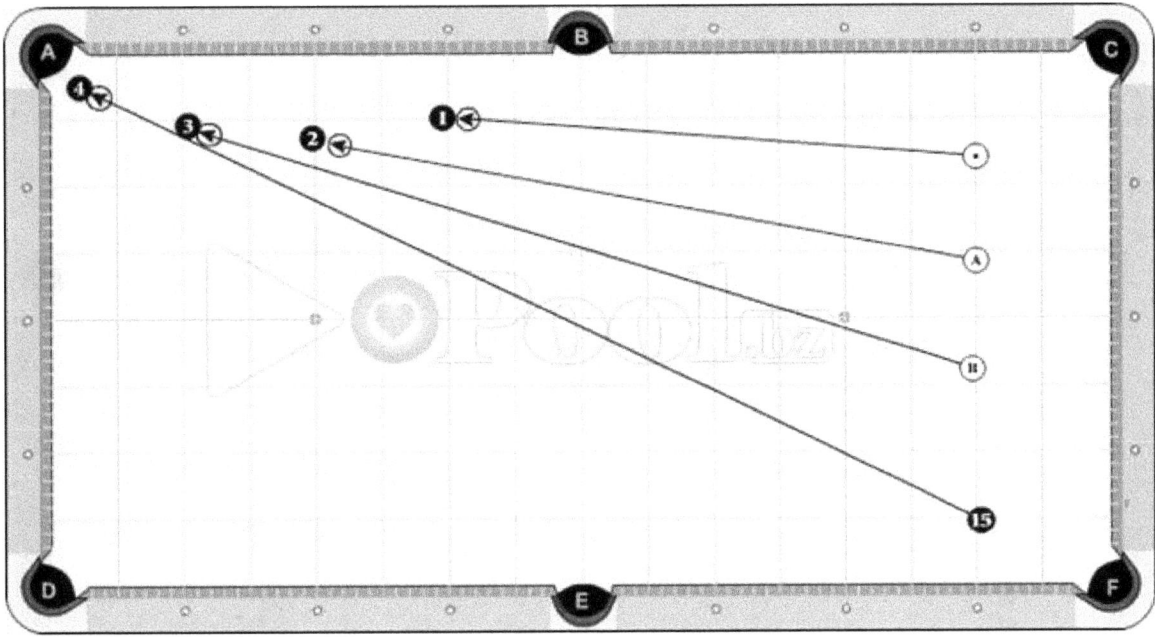

Set 4

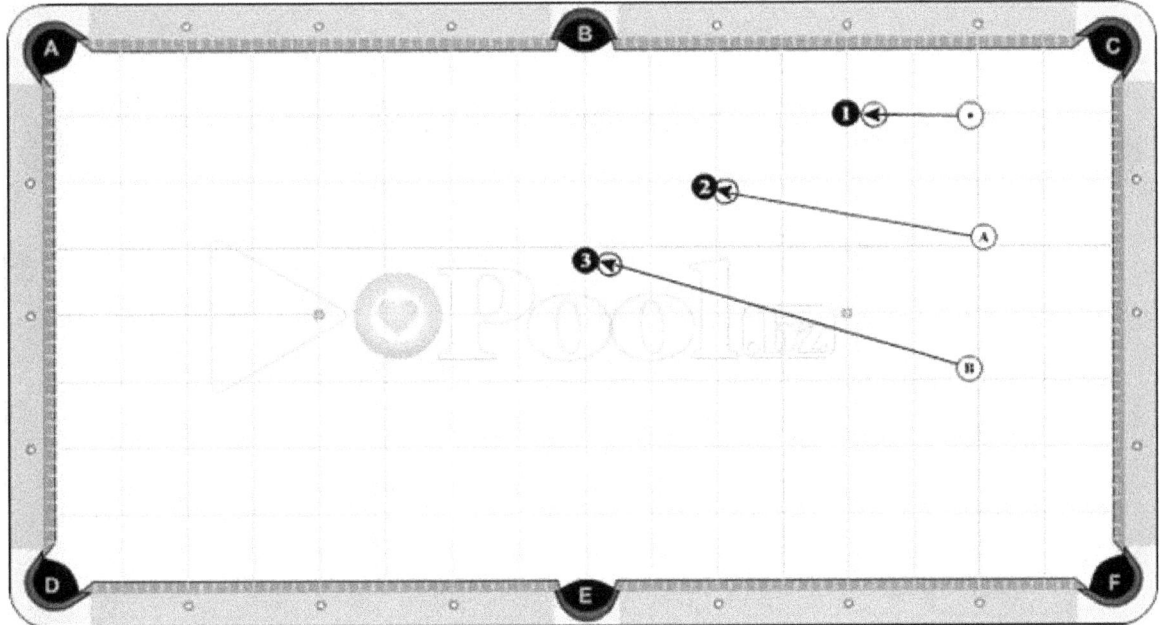

Follow It

1/2 D

Object: Pocket the OB and CB follows exactly 1/2 diamond.

Set 1

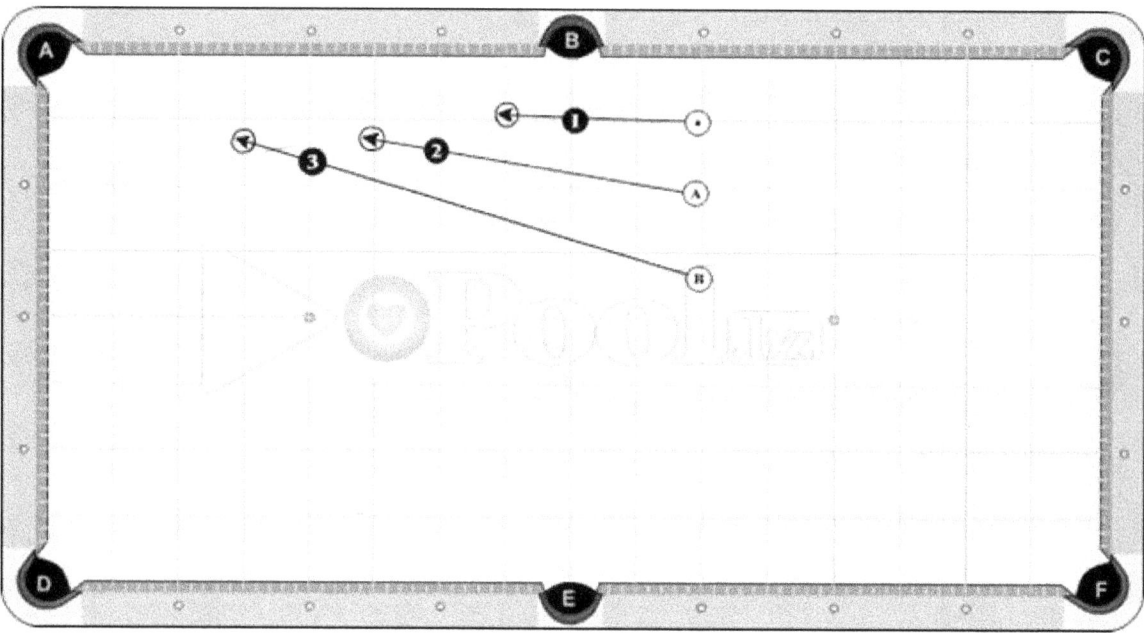

Set 2

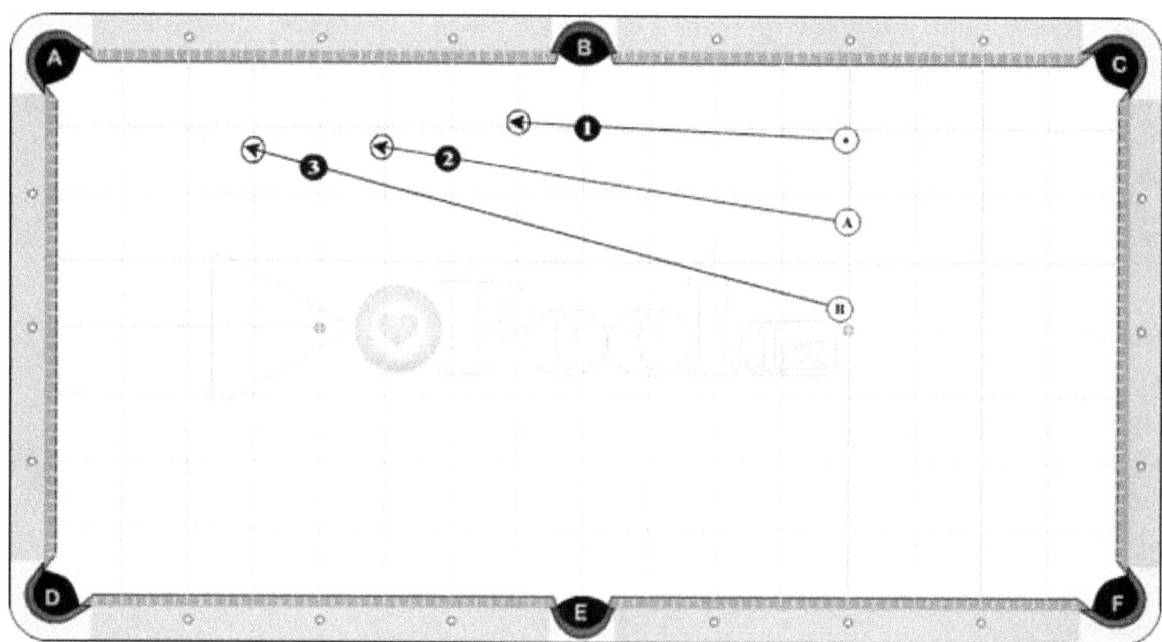

Set 3

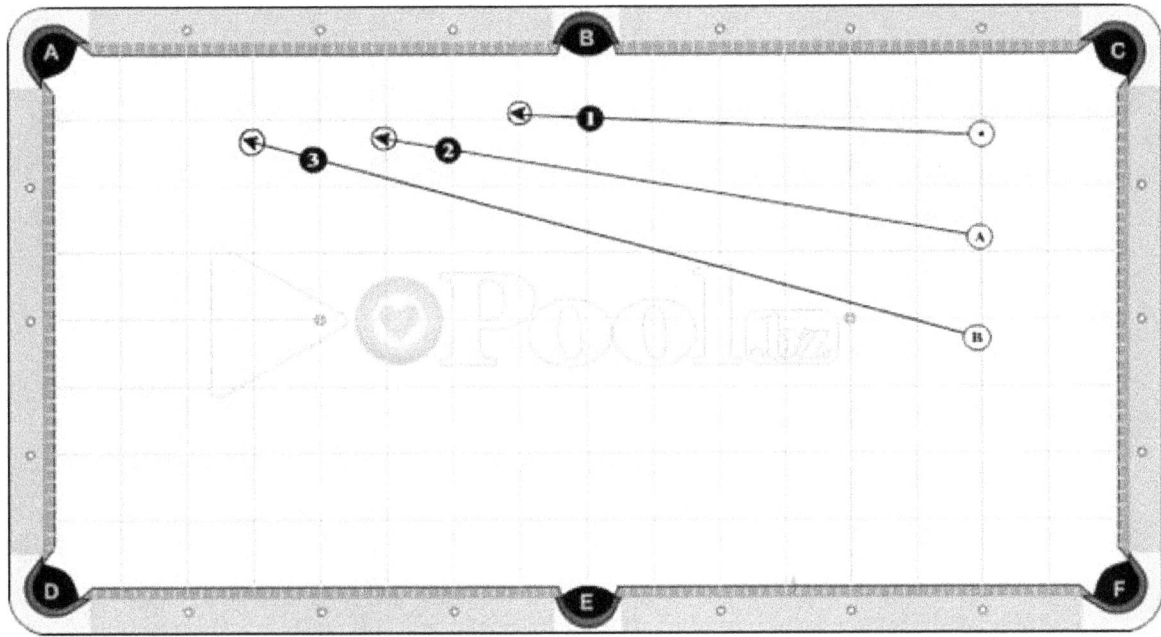

1 D

Object: Pocket the OB and CB follows exactly 1 diamond.

Set 1

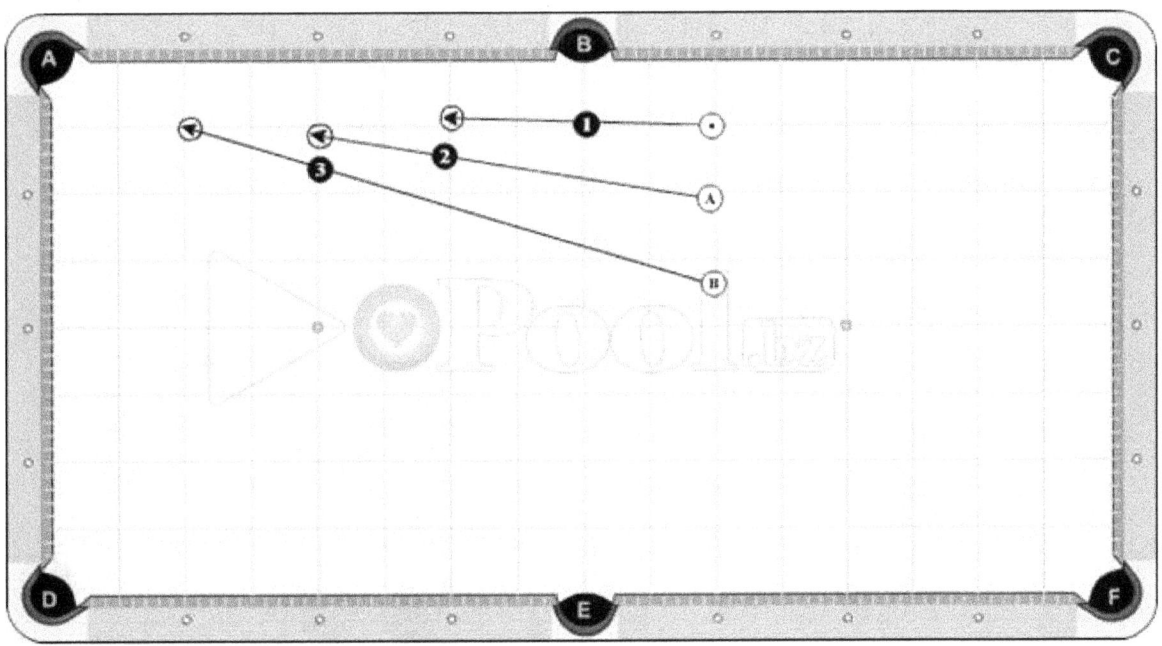

Set 2

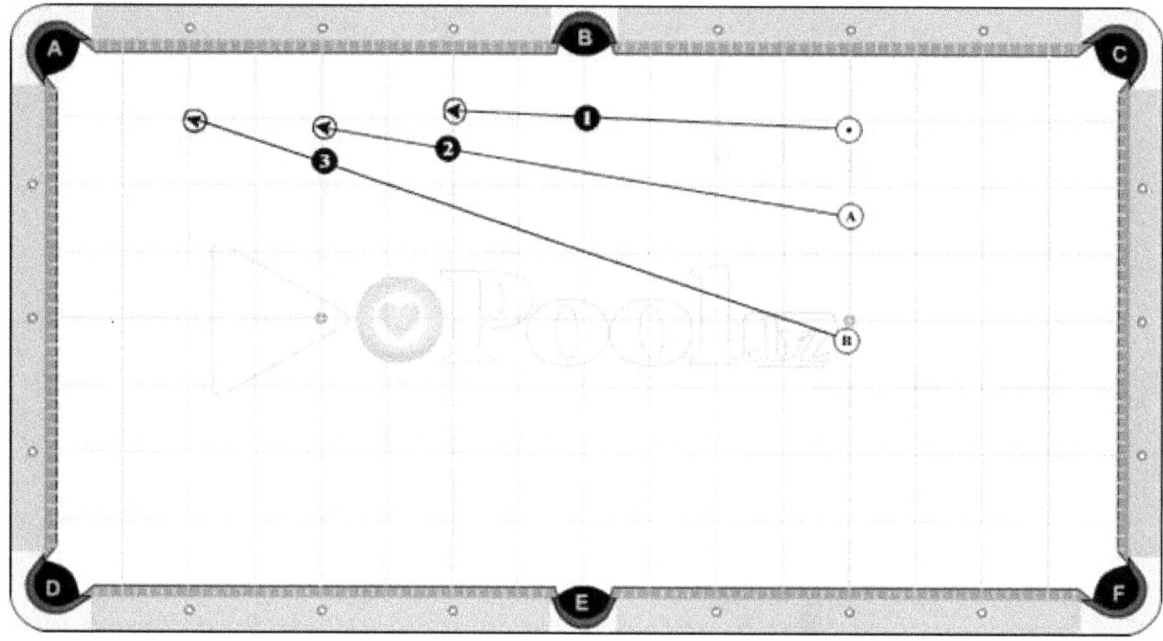

Set 3

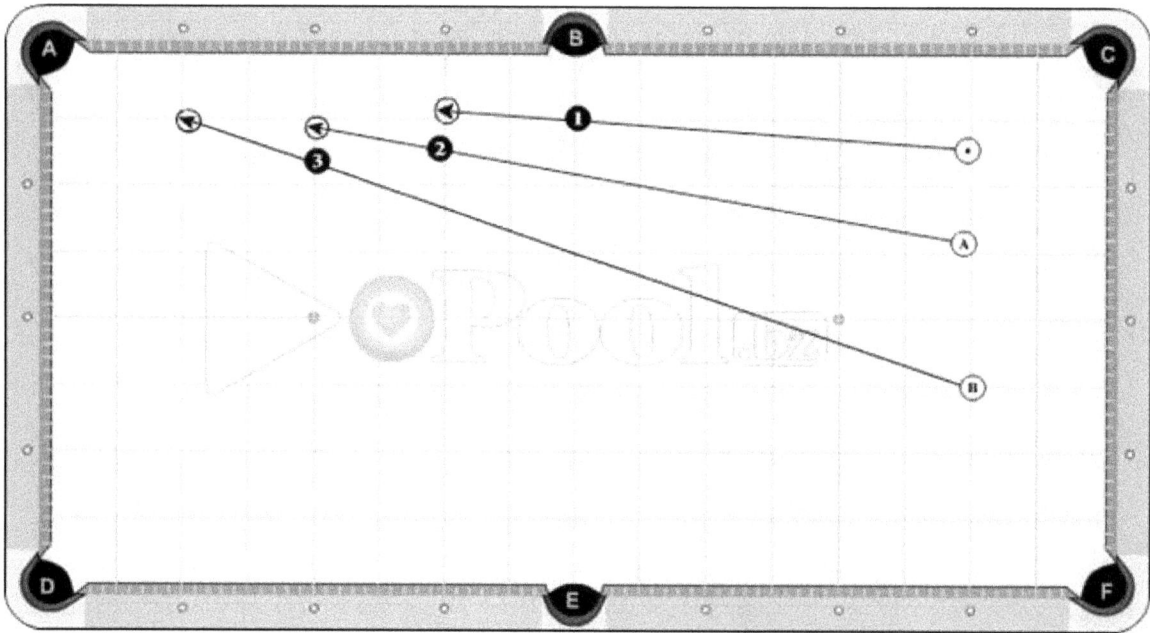

2 D

Object: Pocket the OB and CB follows exactly 2 diamonds.

Set 1

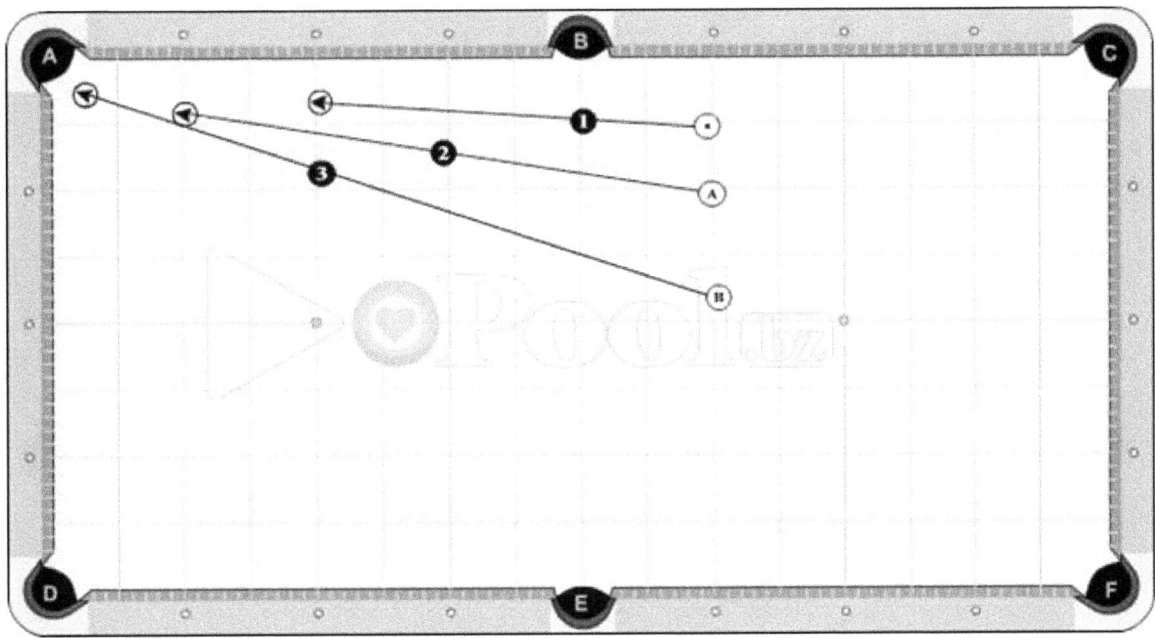

Set 2

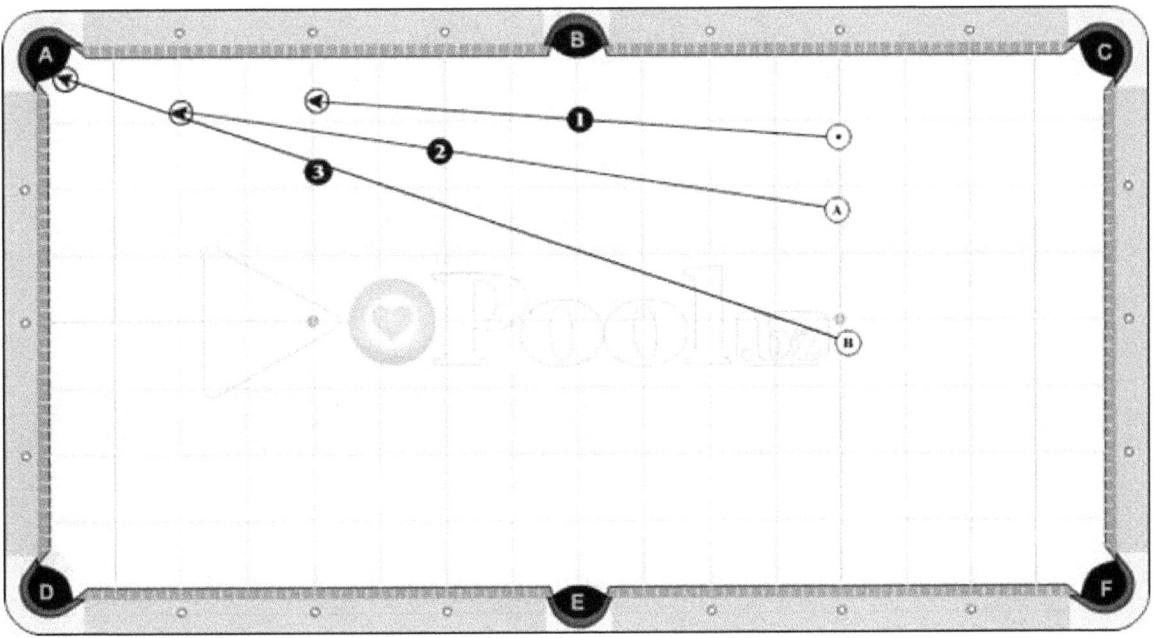

Set 3

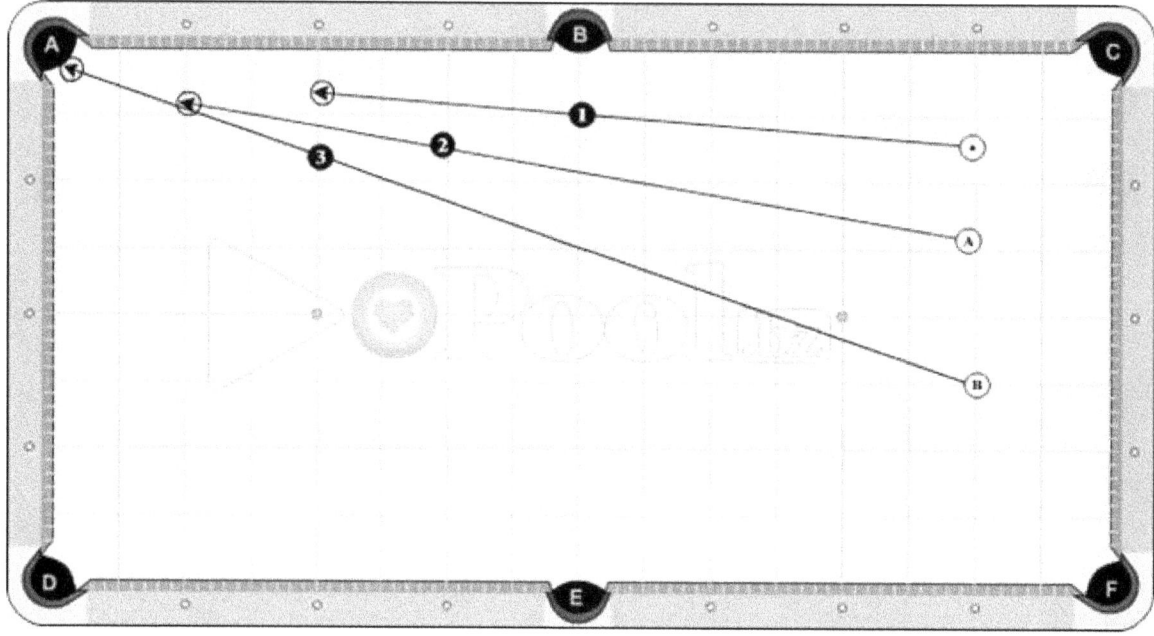

3 D

Object: Pocket the OB and CB follows exactly 3 diamonds.

Set 1

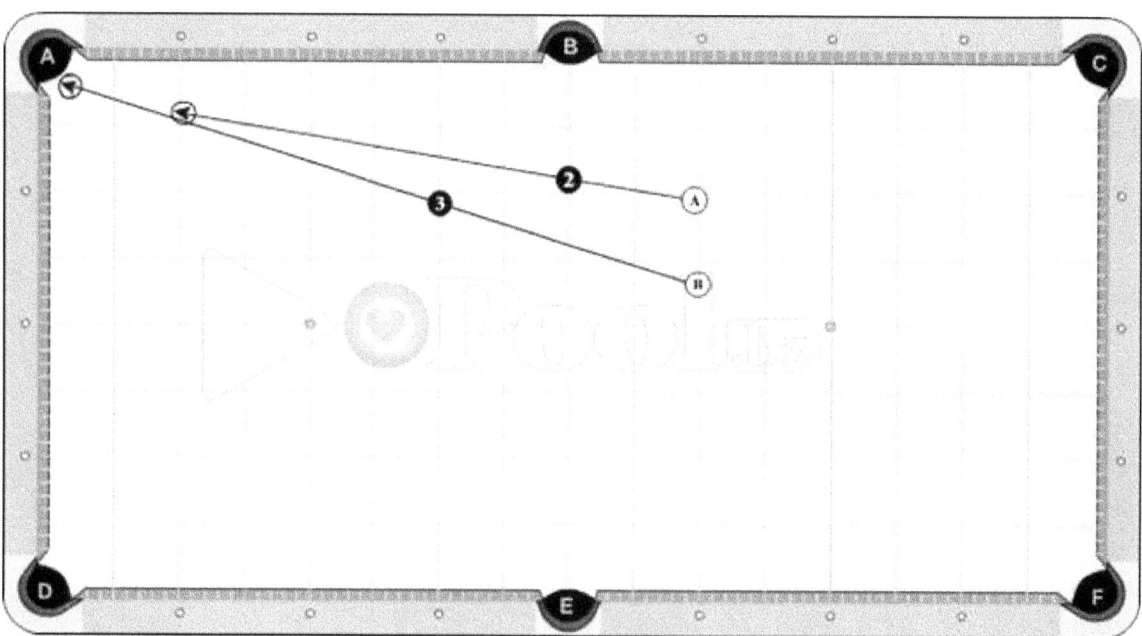

Set 2

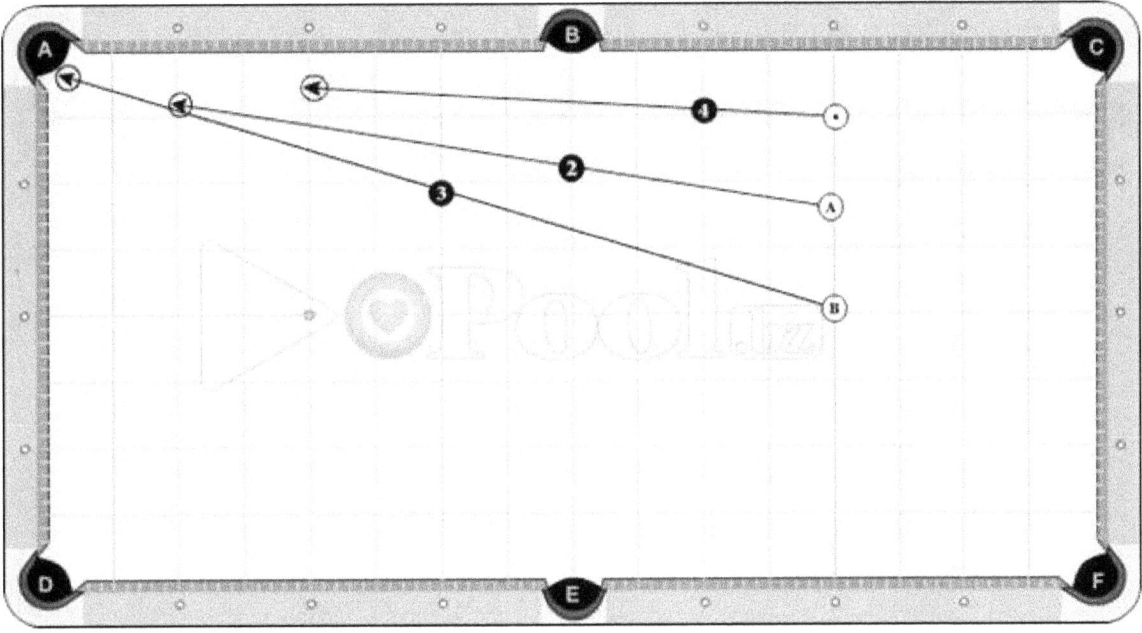

Set 3

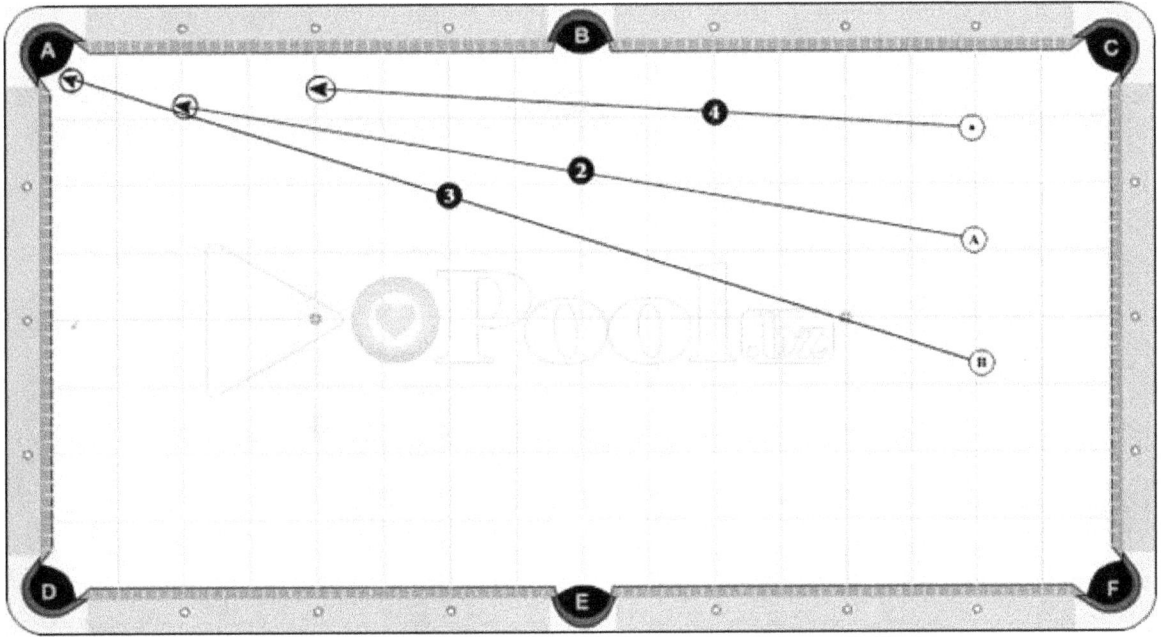

4 D

Object: Pocket the OB and CB follows exactly 4 diamonds.

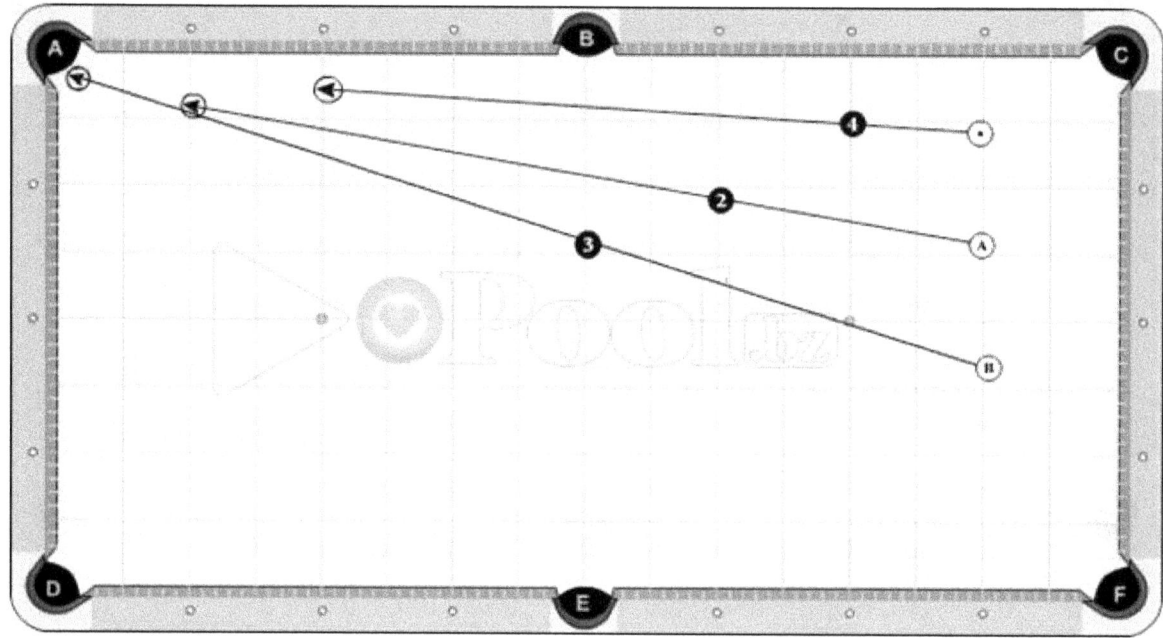

Progressive

Object: Pocket the OB and CB follows for indicated diamond distance (1, 2, 3 diamonds).

Set 1

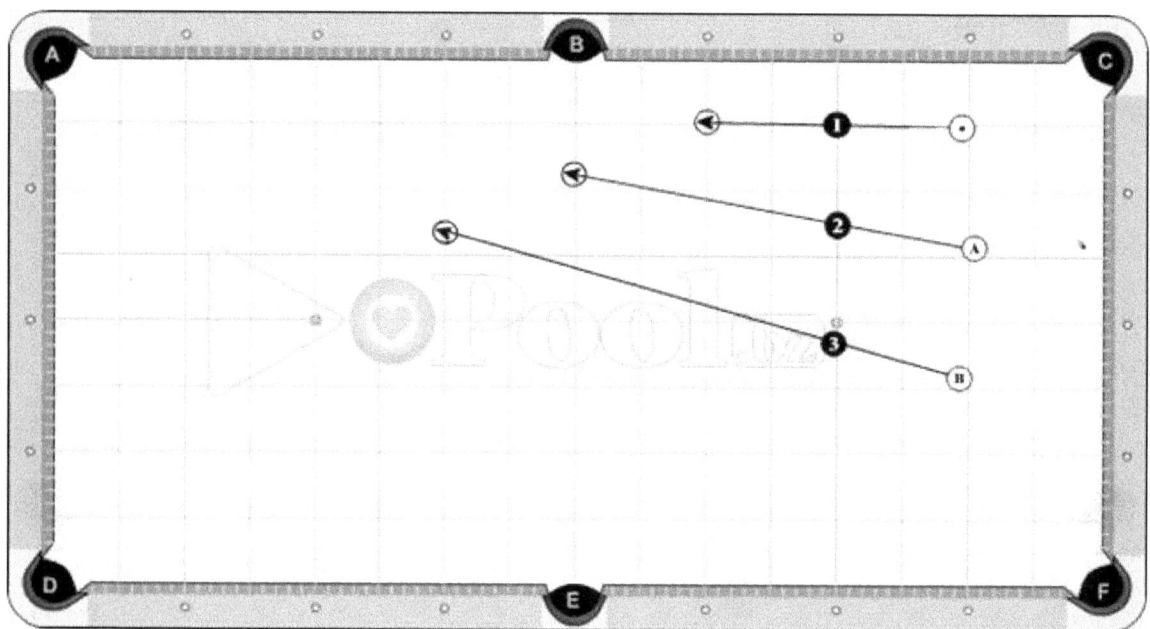

Set 2

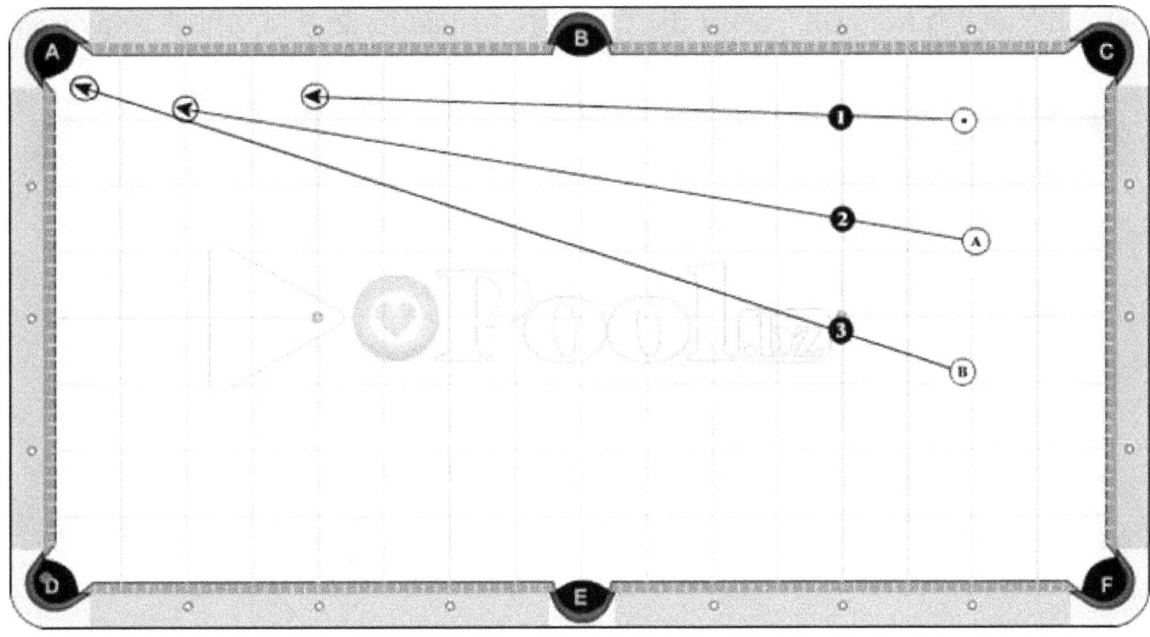

Follow To the Death

1 D

Object: Start at 1 D from OB, pocket the CB & OB. Repeat for 2, 3, 4, 5, 6, 7 D away from OB.

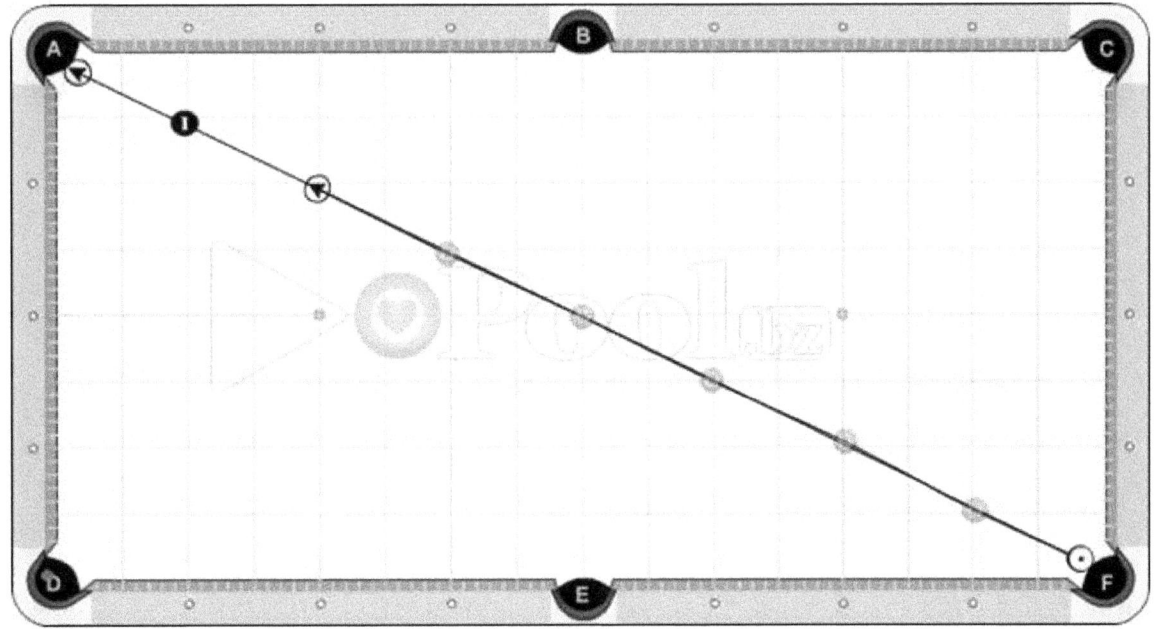

2 D

Object: Start at 1 D from OB, pocket the CB & OB. Repeat for 2, 3, 4, 5, 6 D away from OB.

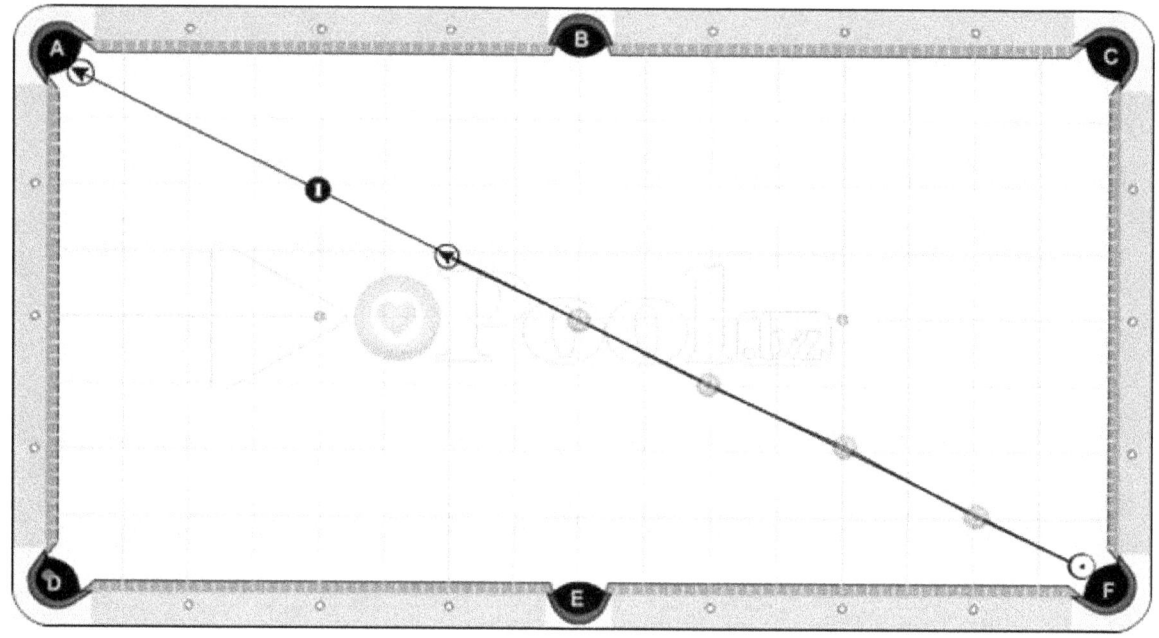

3D

Object: Start at 1 D from OB, pocket the CB & OB. Repeat for 2, 3, 4, 5 D away from OB.

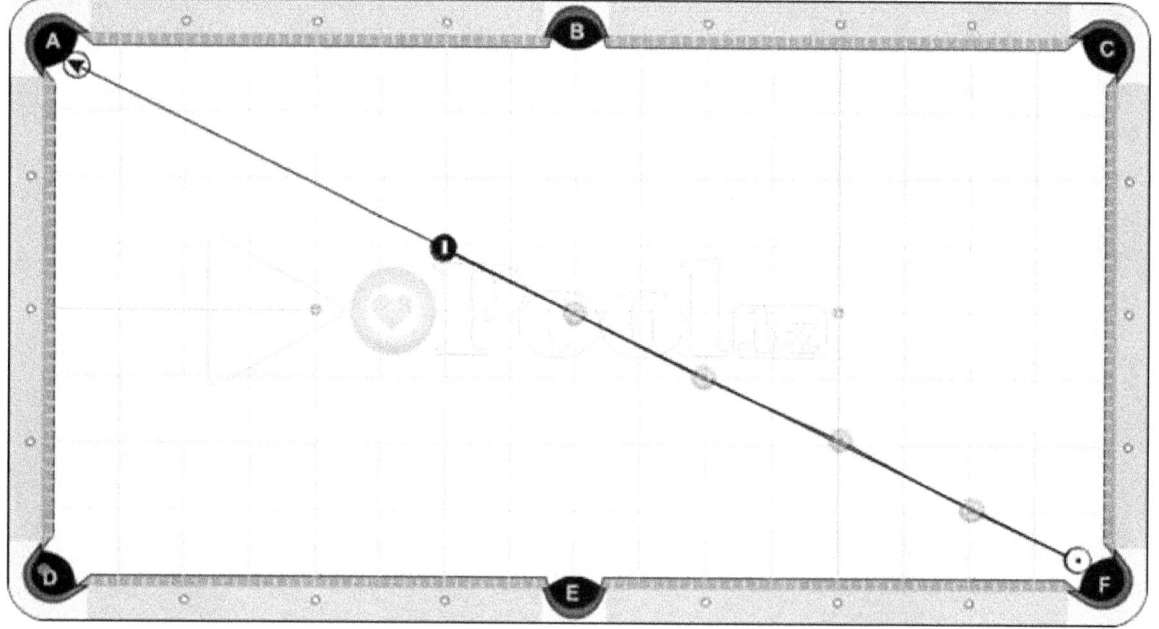

4 D

Object: Start at 1 D from OB, pocket the CB & OB. Repeat for 2, 3, 4 D away from OB.

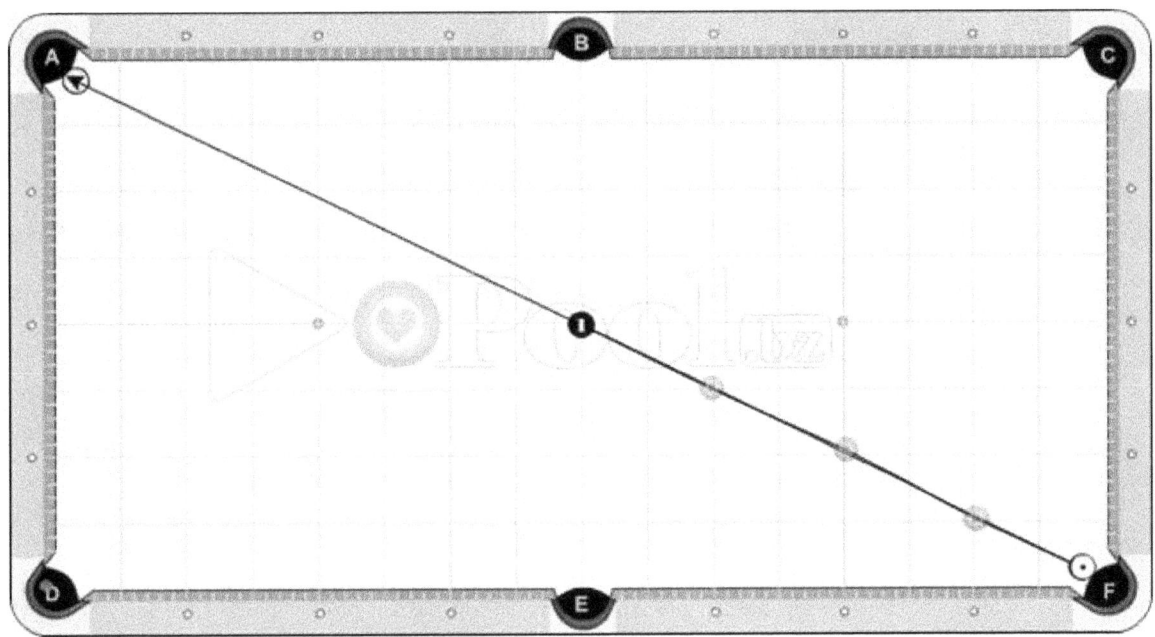

5 D

Object: Start at 1 D from OB, pocket the CB & OB. Repeat for 2, 3 D away from OB.

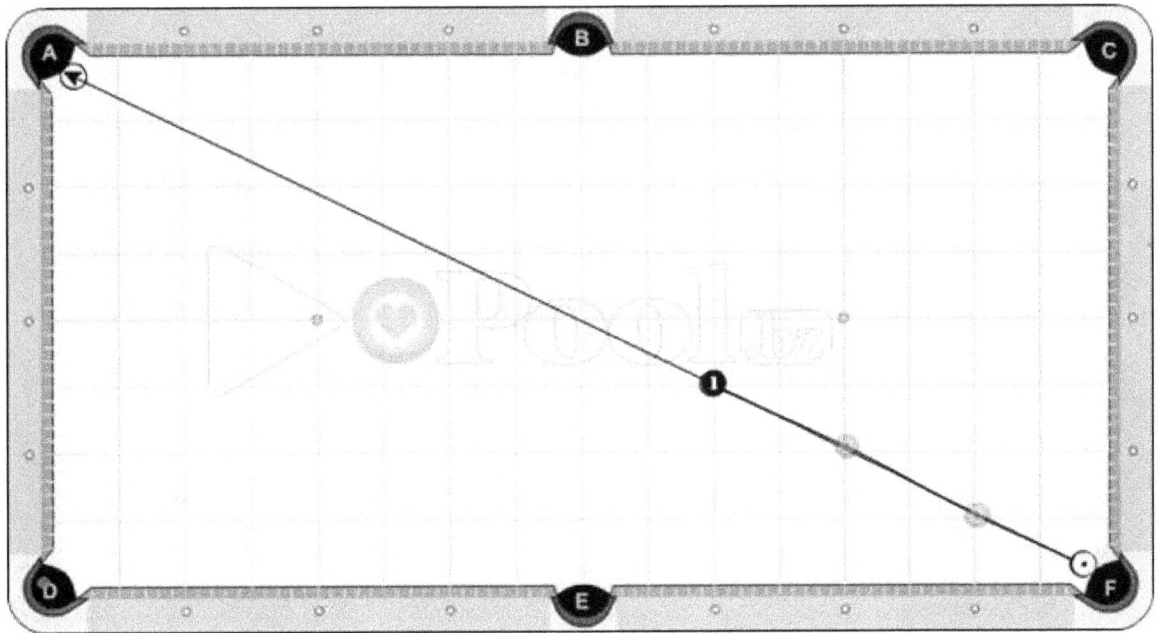

6 D

Object: Start at 1 D from OB, pocket the CB & OB. Repeat for 2 D away from OB.

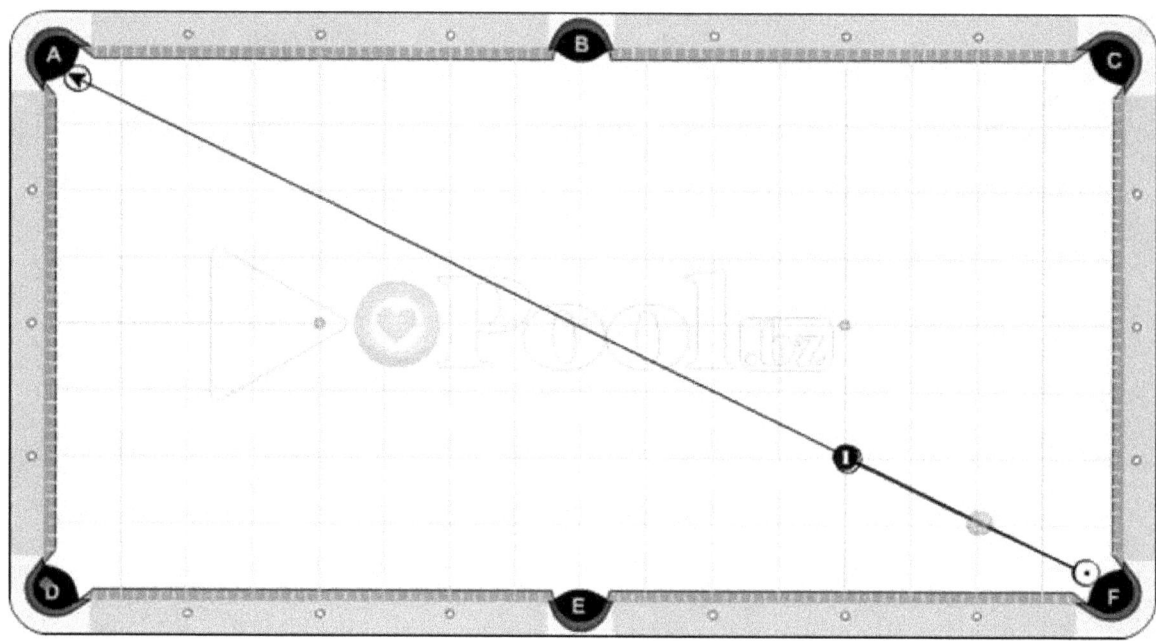

7 D

Object: Pocket the CB & OB.

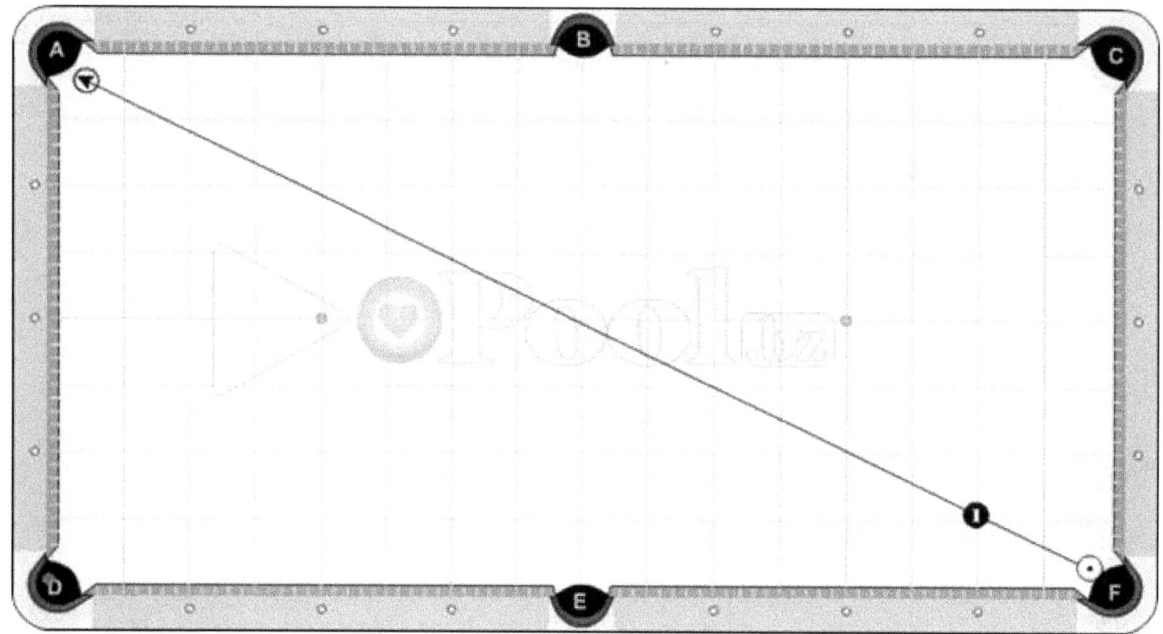

Draw to the Death

1 D

Object: Pocket the OB and draw the CB back into the pocket.

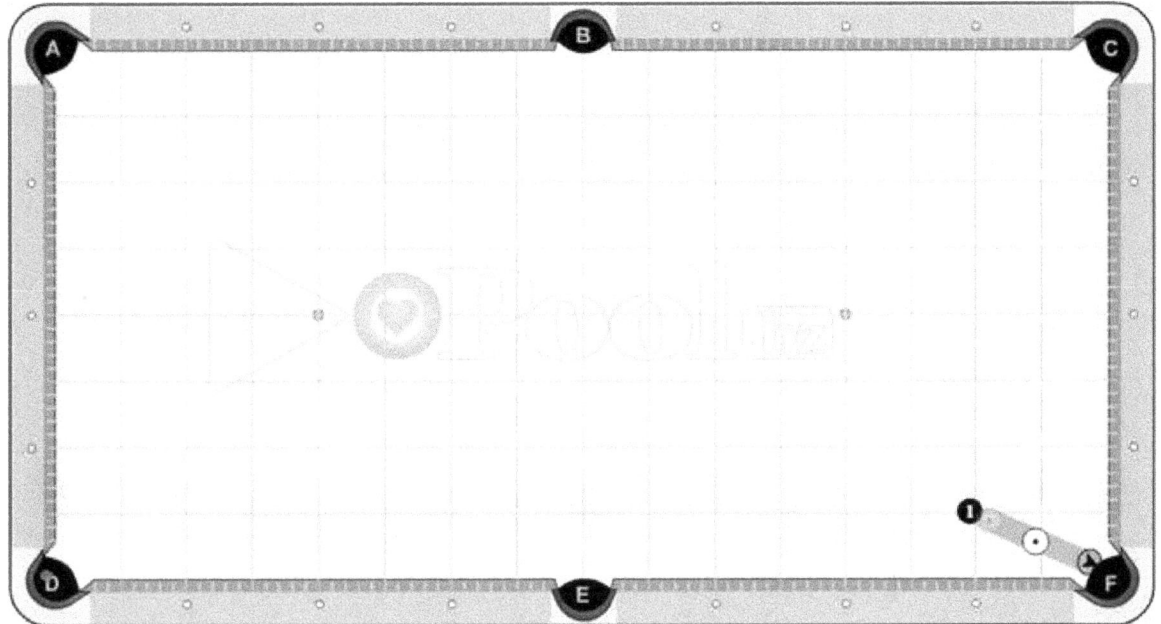

2 D

Object: Two positions (as shown)d - pocket the OB and draw the CB back into the pocket.

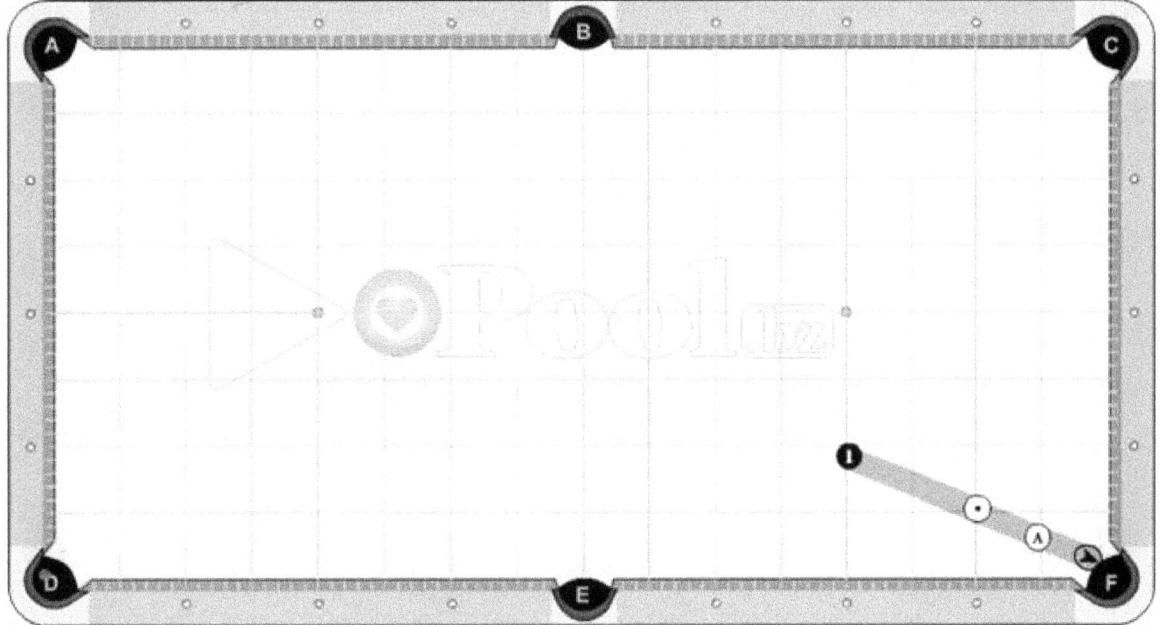

1 D

Object: Two positions (as shown) - pocket the OB and draw the CB back into the pocket.

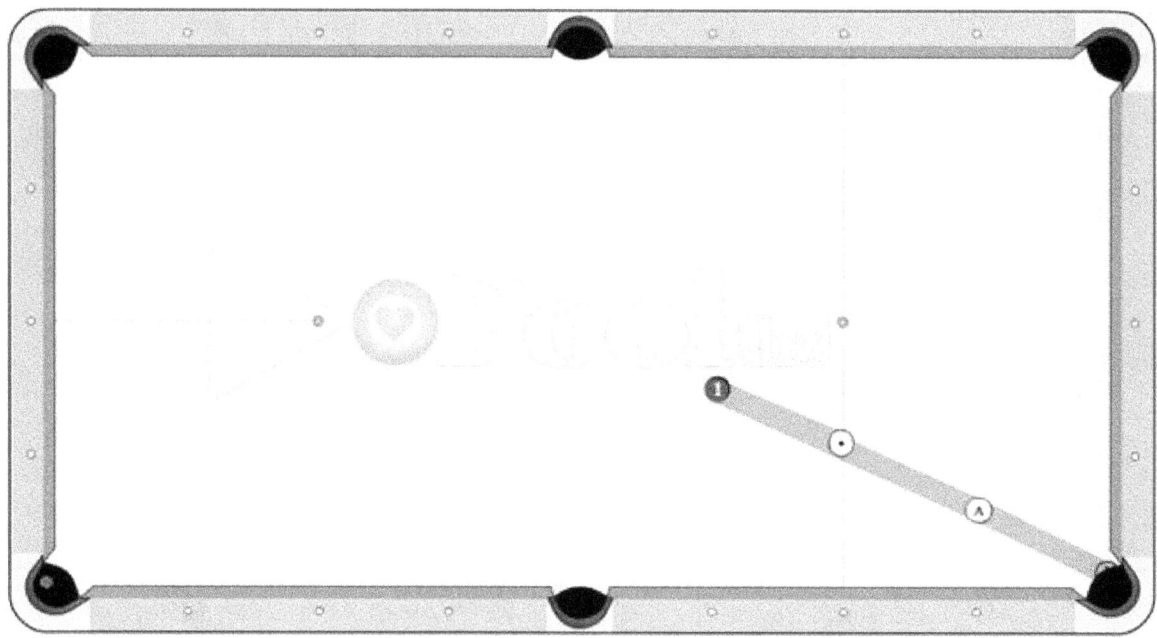

4 D

Object: Three positions (as shown) - pocket the OB and draw the CB back into the pocket.

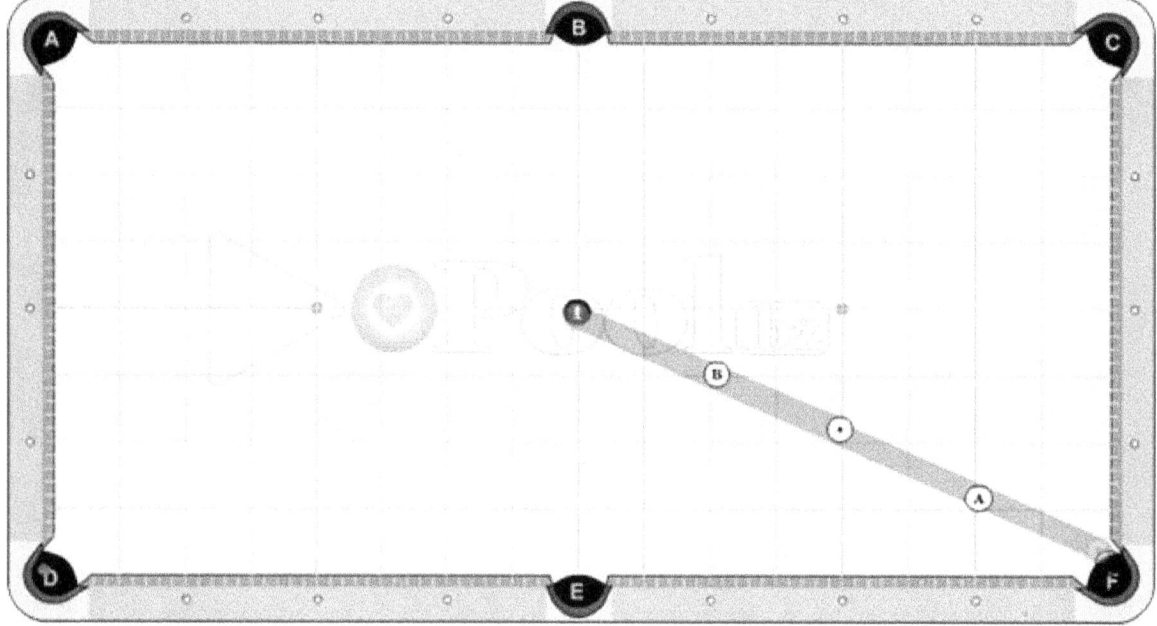

5 D

Object: Three positions (as shown) - pocket the OB and draw the CB back into the pocket.

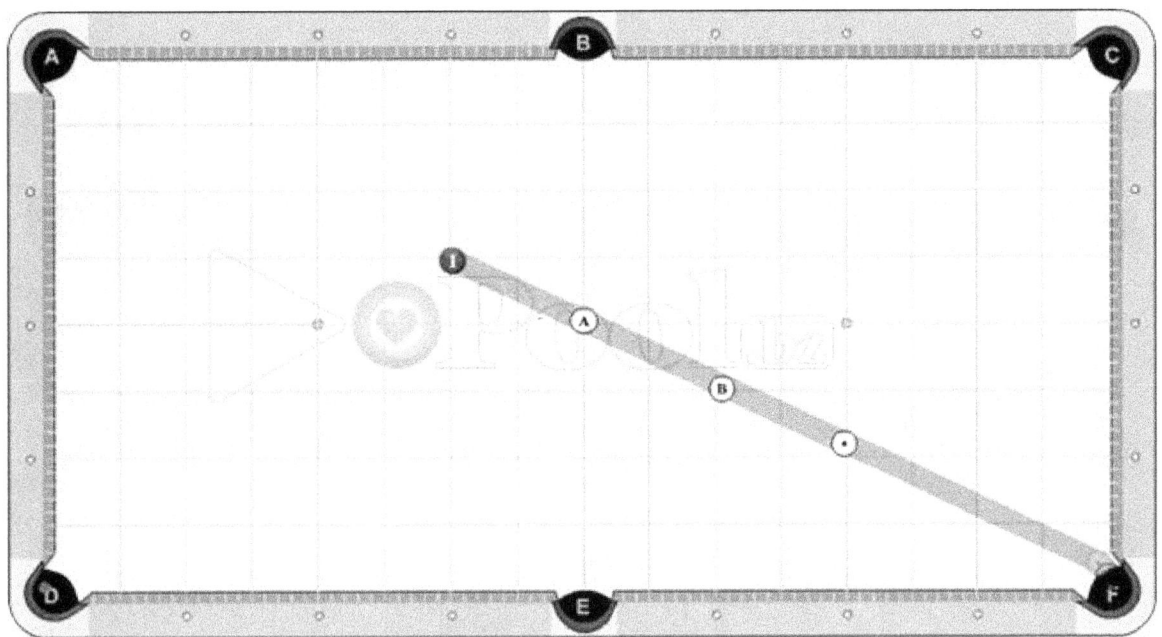

6 D

Object: Three positions (as shown) - pocket the OB and draw the CB back into the pocket.

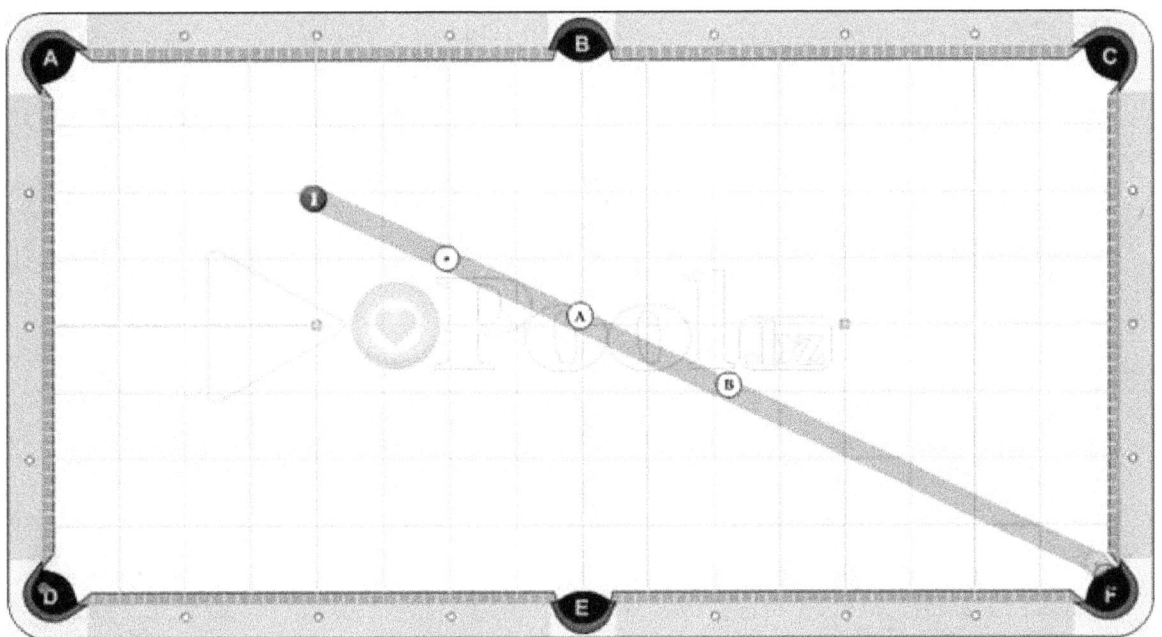

Draw to Me

1/2 Diamond CB Draw

Object: With CB 1/2 Diamond from OB, draw CB back to precise location (as shown)

Set 1

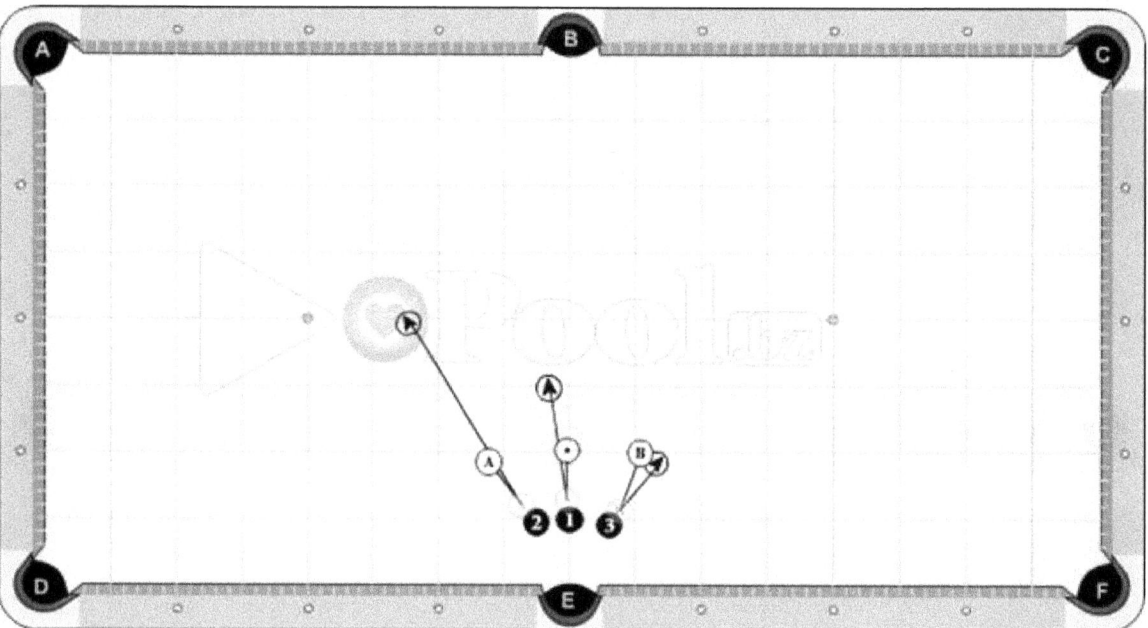

Set 2

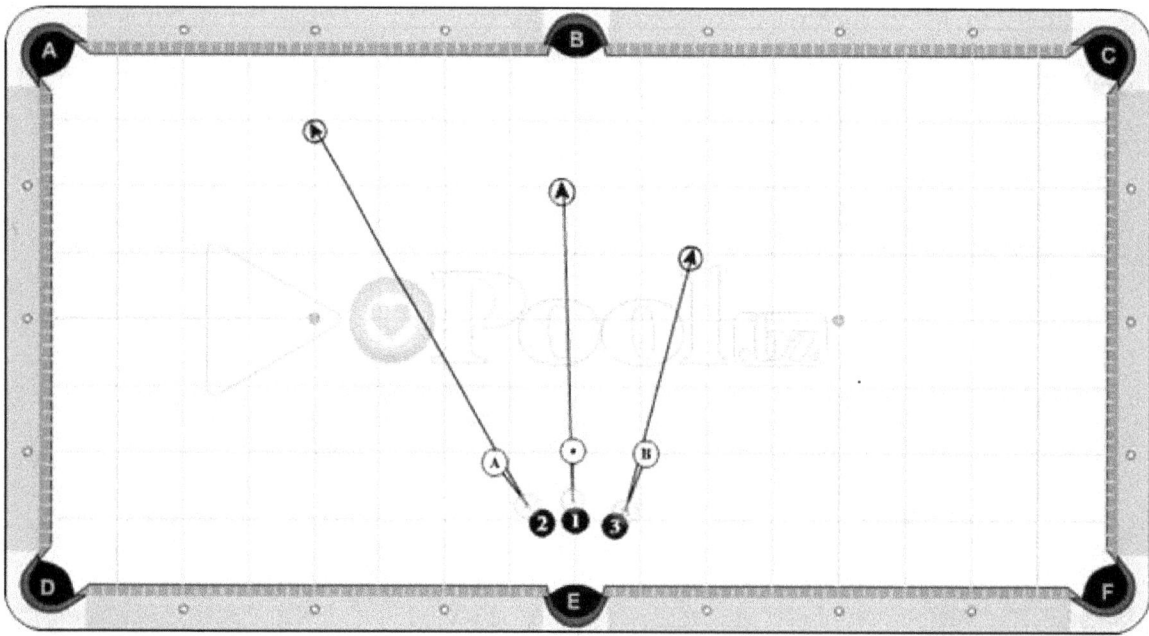

1 Diamond CB Draw

Object: With CB 1 Diamond from OB, draw CB back to precise location (as shown)

Set 1

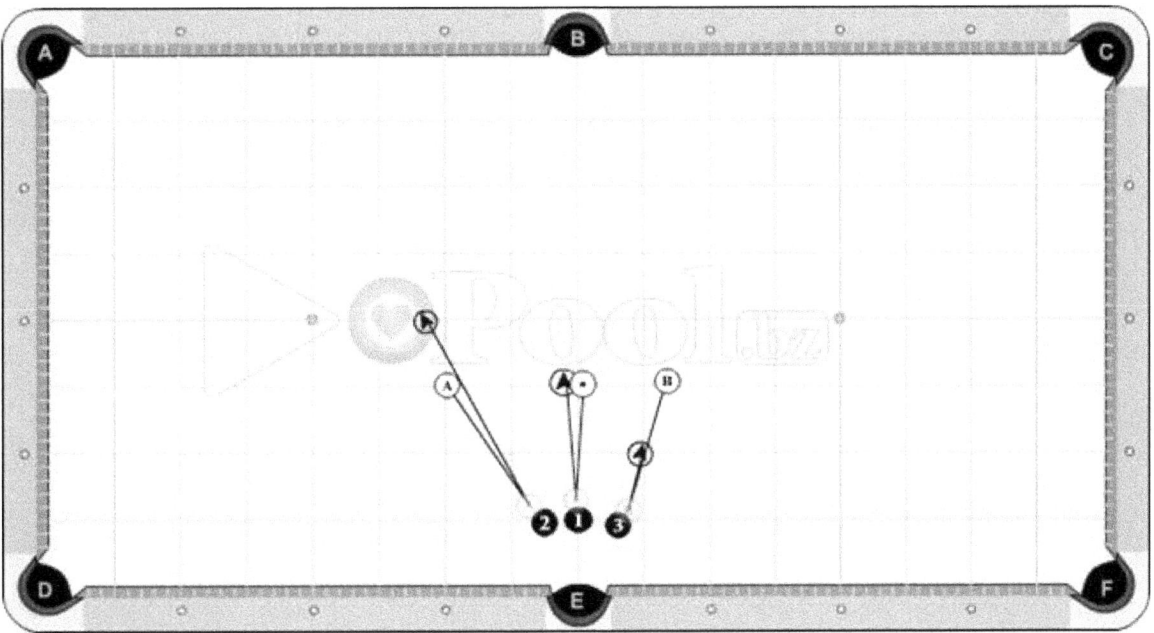

Set 2

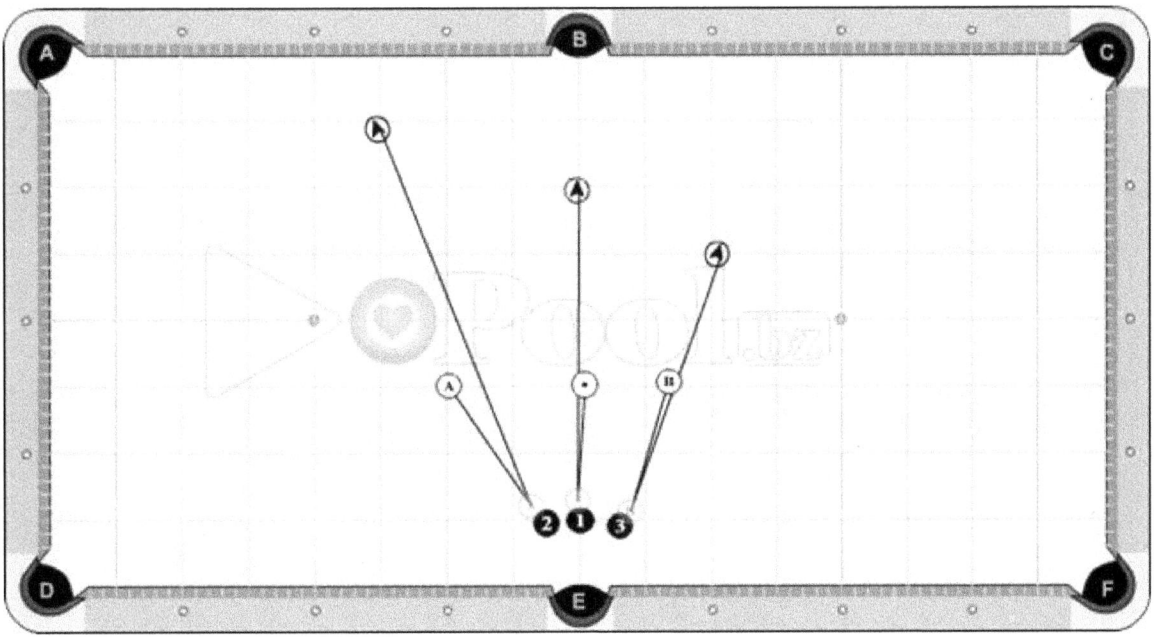

1-1/2 Diamond CB Draw

Object: With CB 1-1/2 Diamonds from OB, draw CB back to precise location (as shown)

Set 1

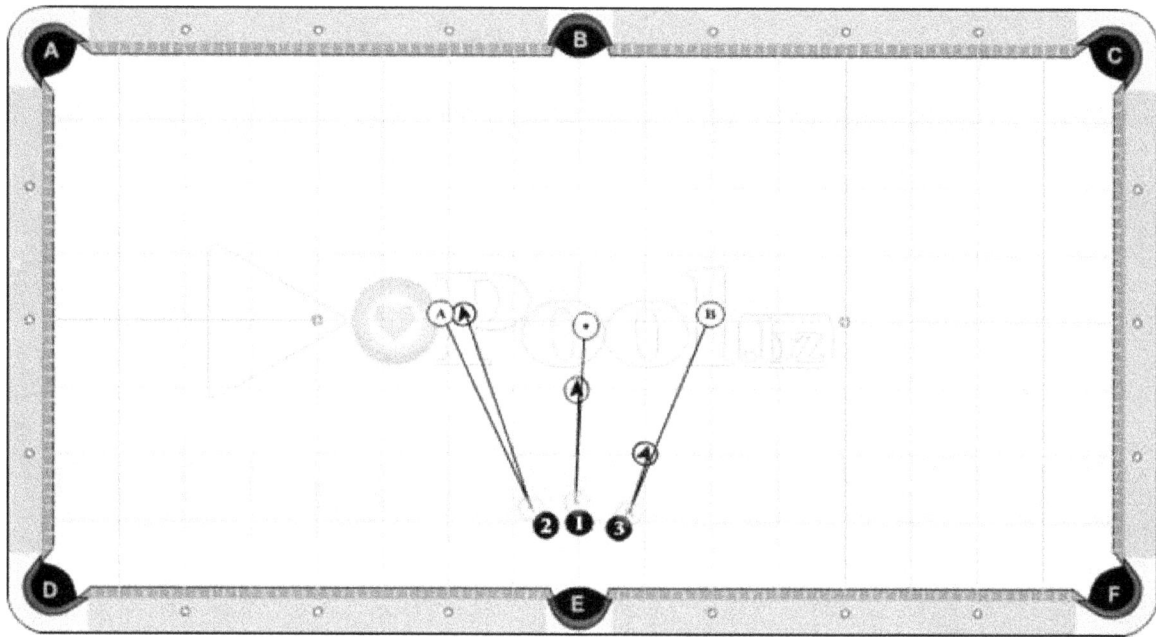

Set 2

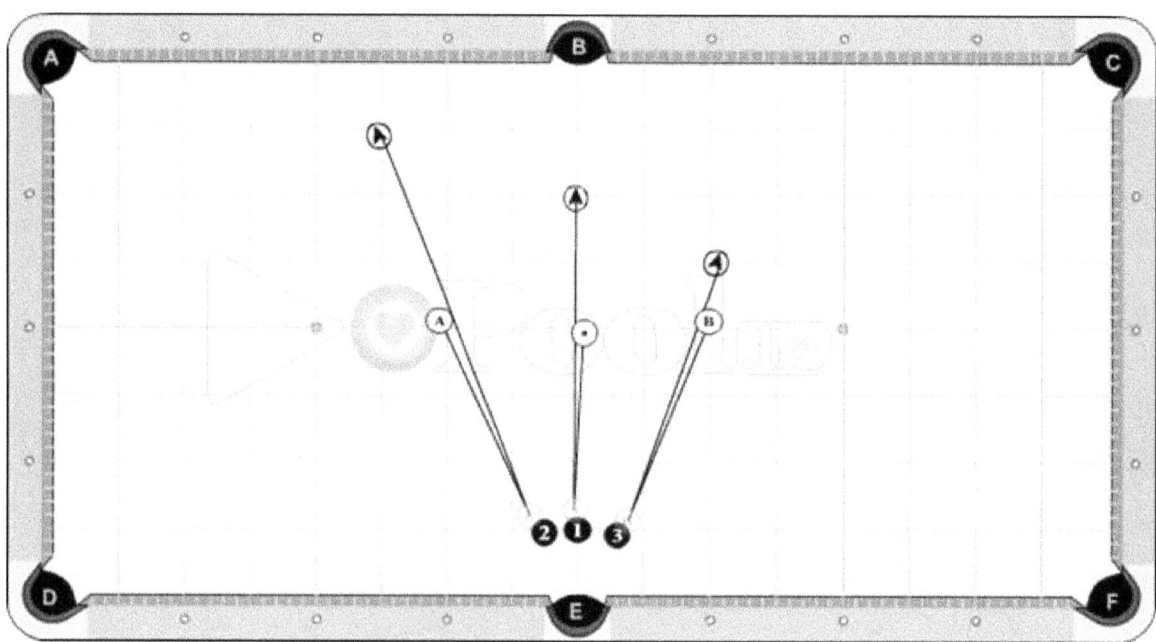

2 Diamond CB Draw

Object: With CB 2 Diamonds from OB, draw CB back to precise location (as shown)

Set 1

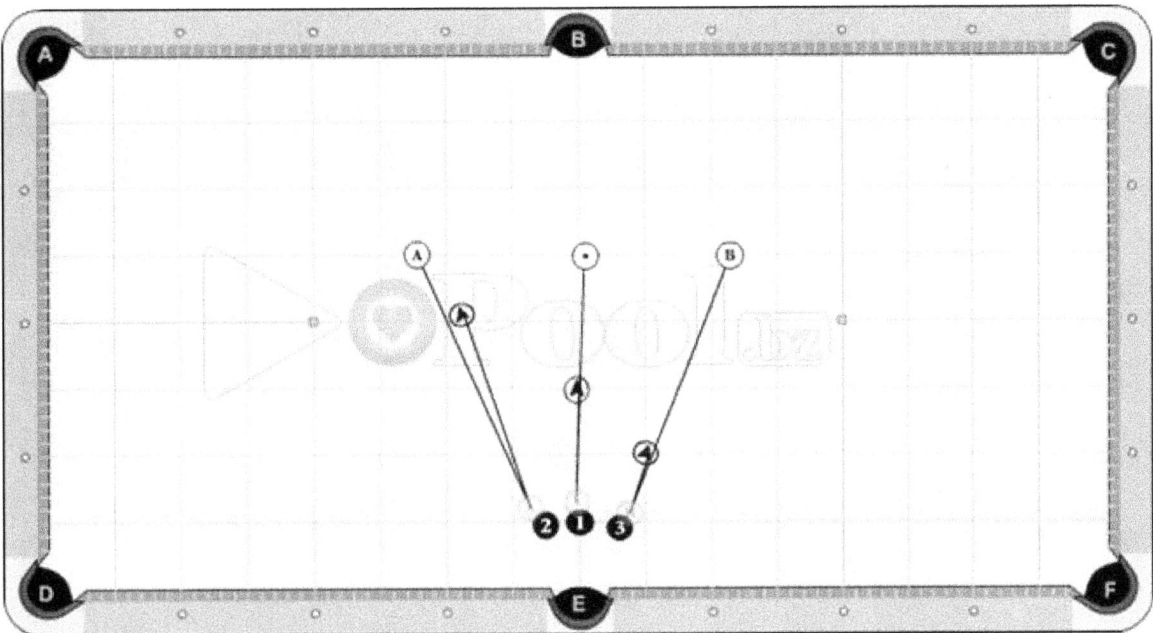

Set 2

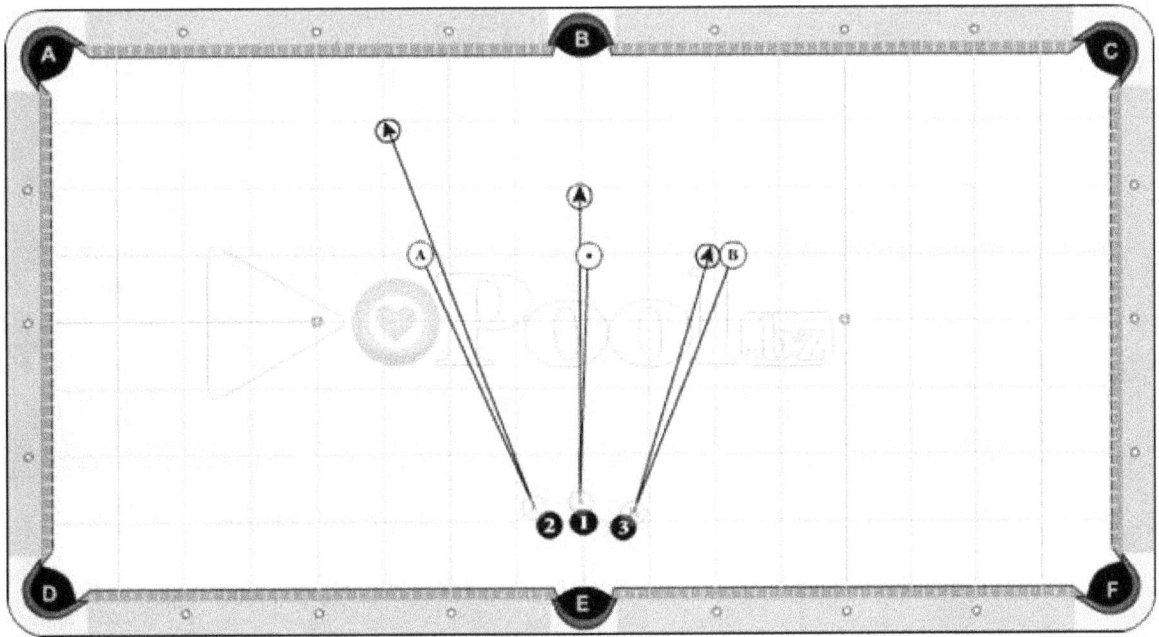

3 Diamond CB Draw

Object: With CB 3 Diamonds from OB, draw CB back to precise location (as shown)

Set 1

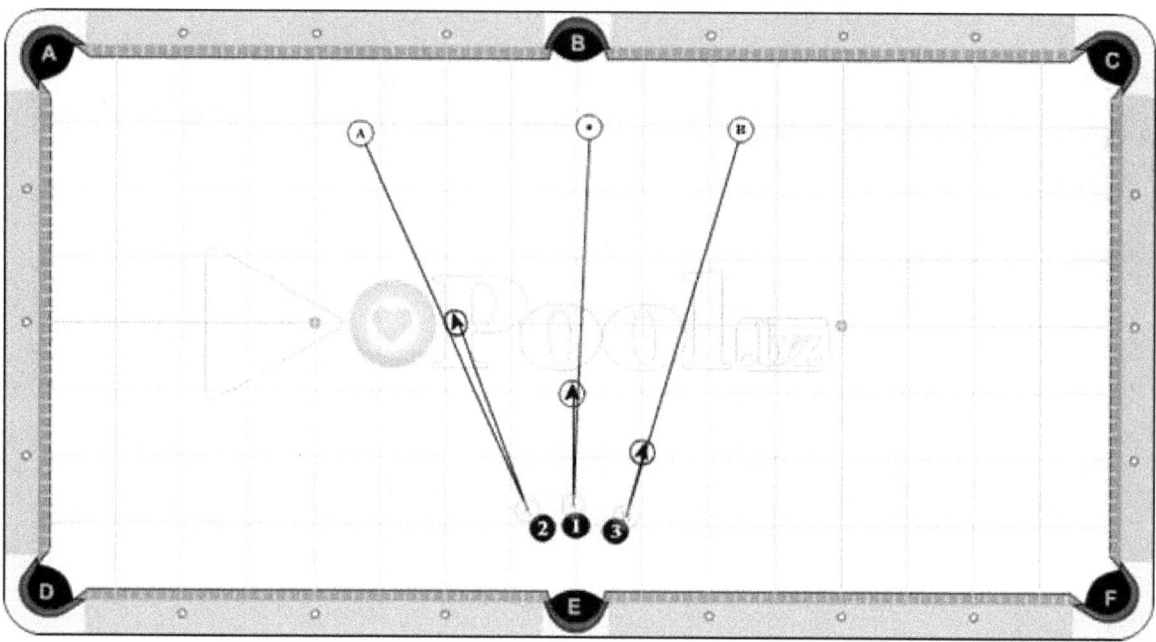

Set 2

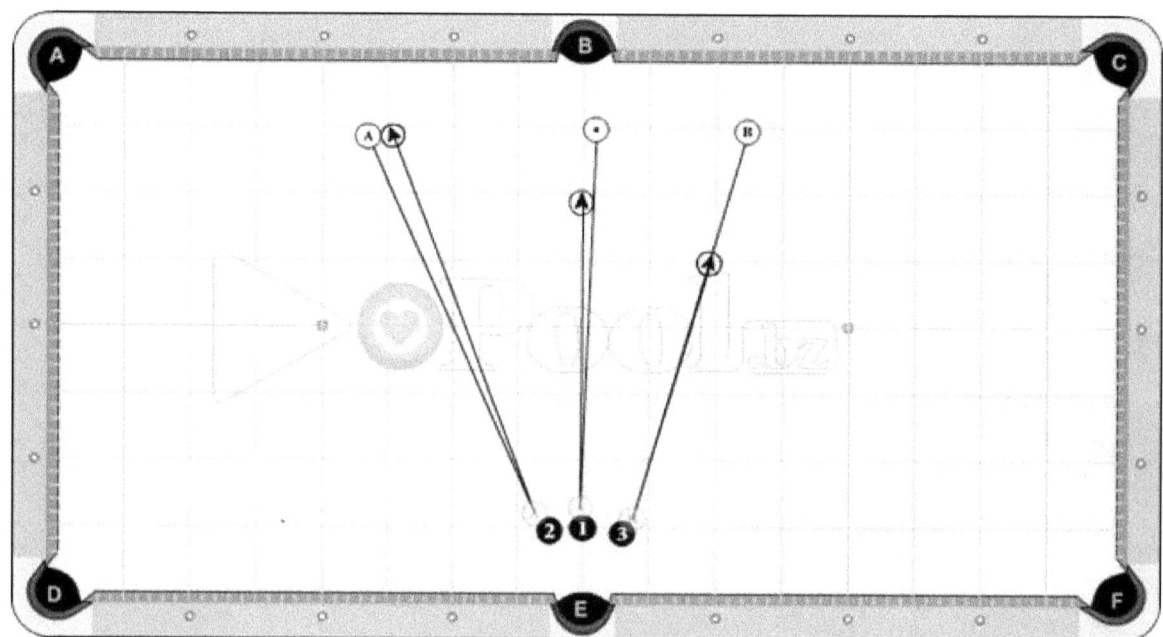

4 Diamond CB Draw

Object: With CB 4 Diamonds from OB, draw CB back to precise location (as shown)

Set 1

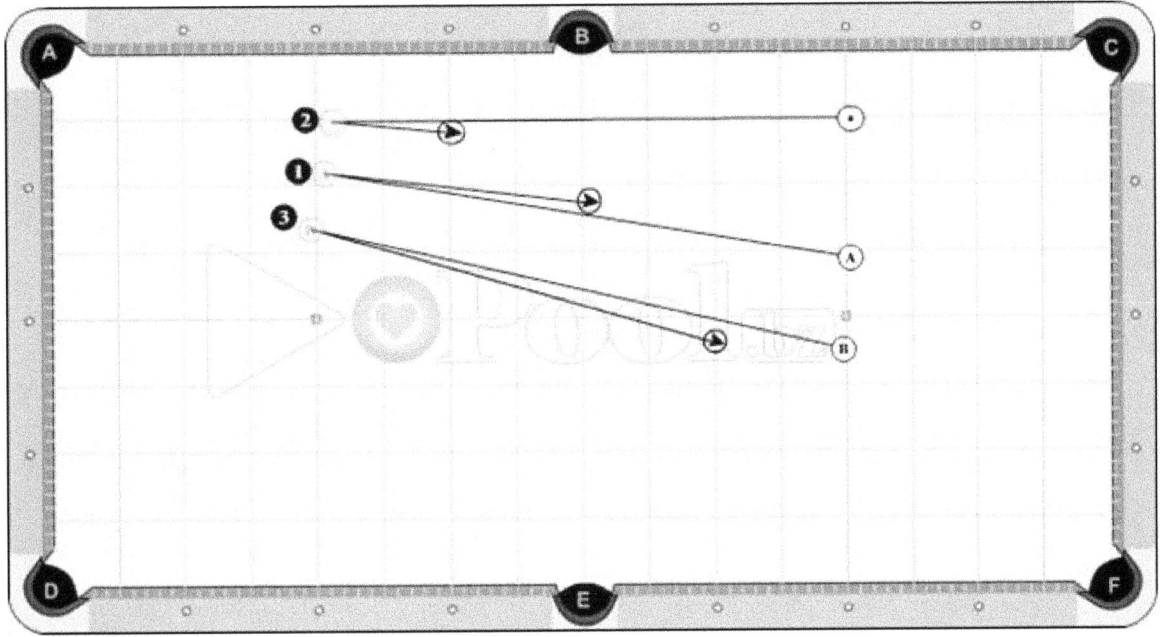

Set 2

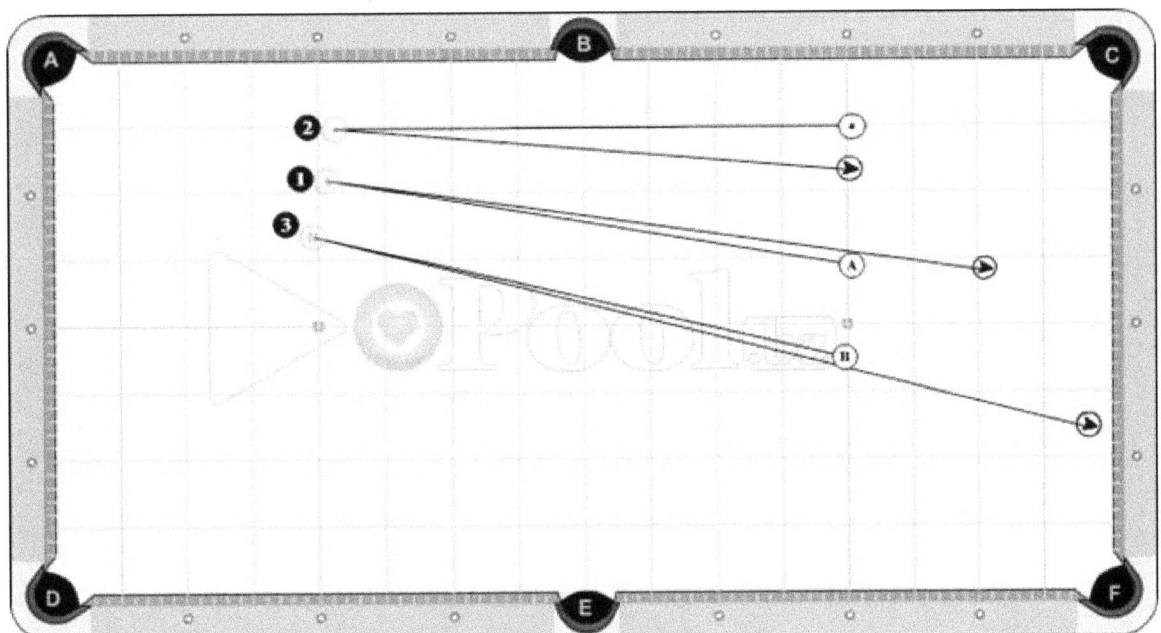

Progressive Draw

Object: With CB and OB in position, draw CB back, precisely as shown.

Set 1

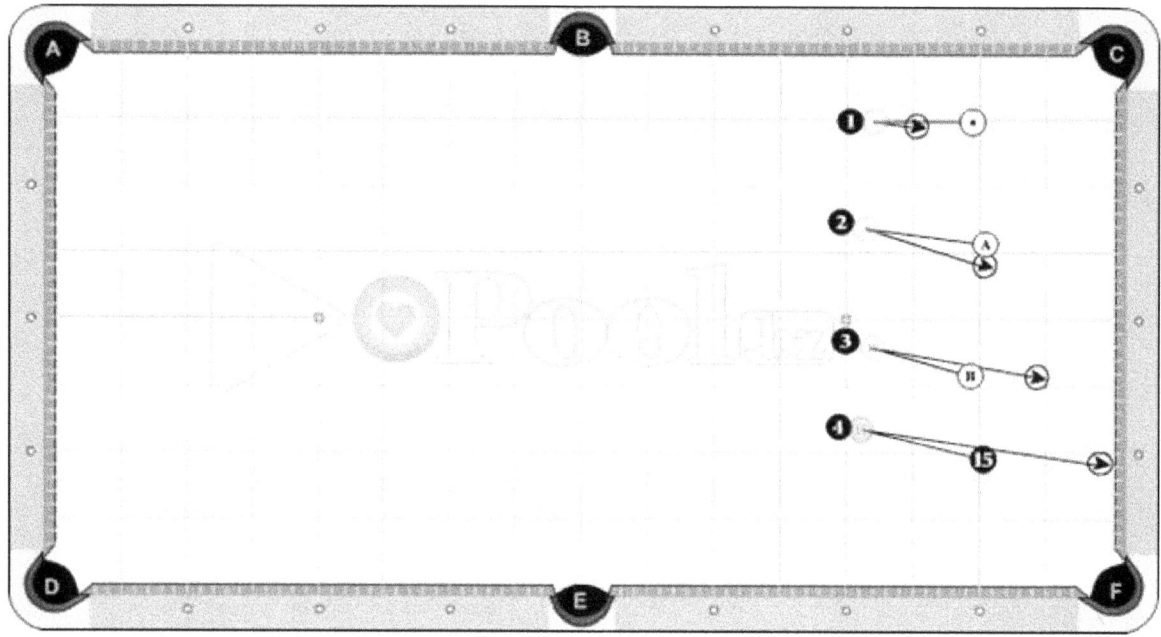

Set 2

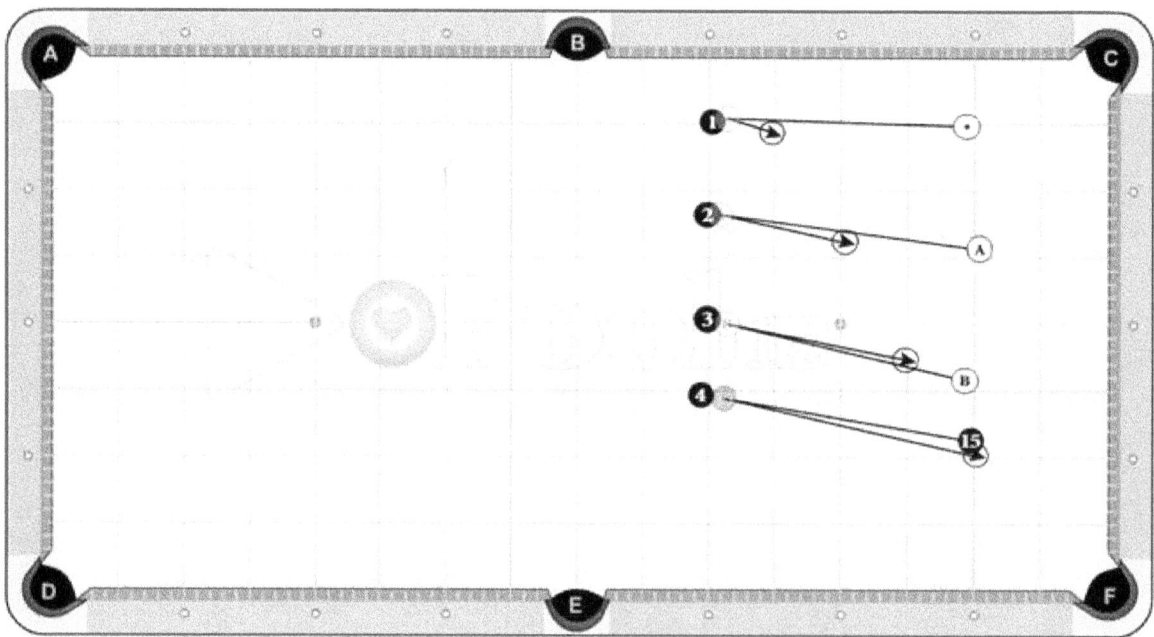

Set 3

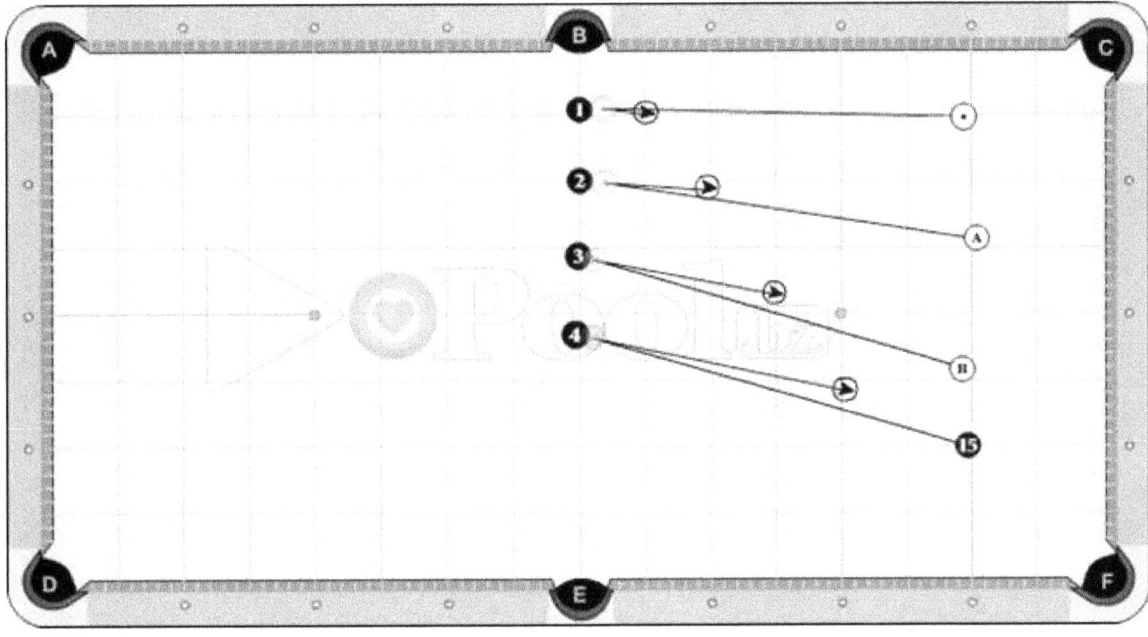

Set 4

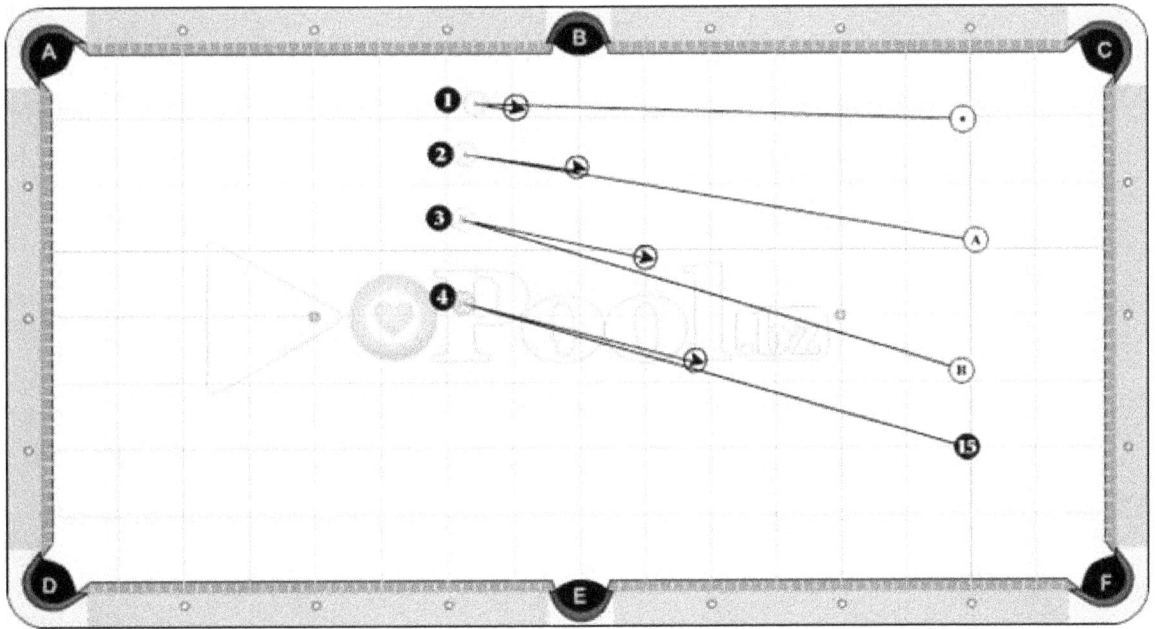

Set 5

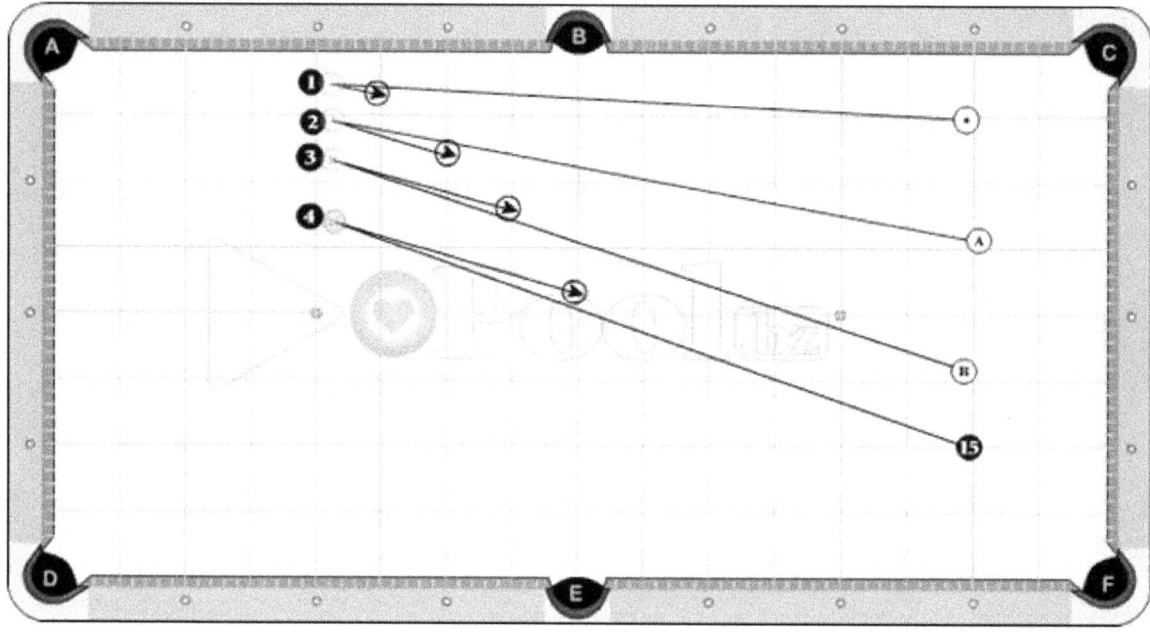

Set 6

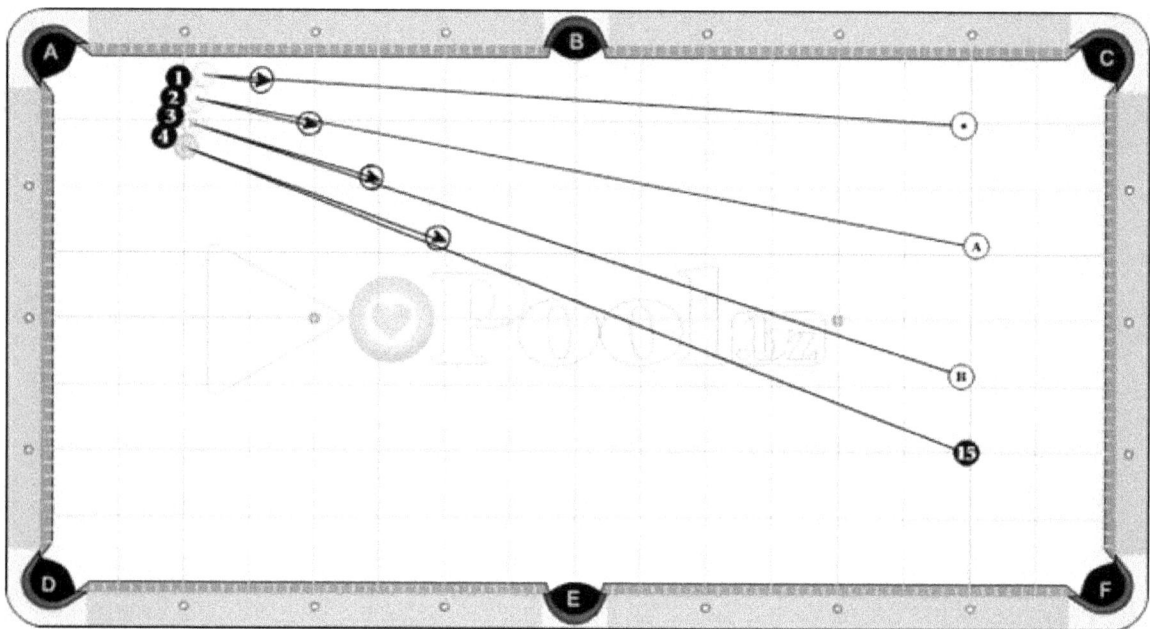

Repetitive Draw

Start with ball in hand. Pocket the OB and draw the CB back for the next shot. Turn ends on a miss. This drills requires that you overdraw the CB and bring it back to approximatley 1 – 2 diamonds from the object ball. It won't take long to dial the correct speed/spin combinations. Pocket as many balls in one turn as possible.

Set 1

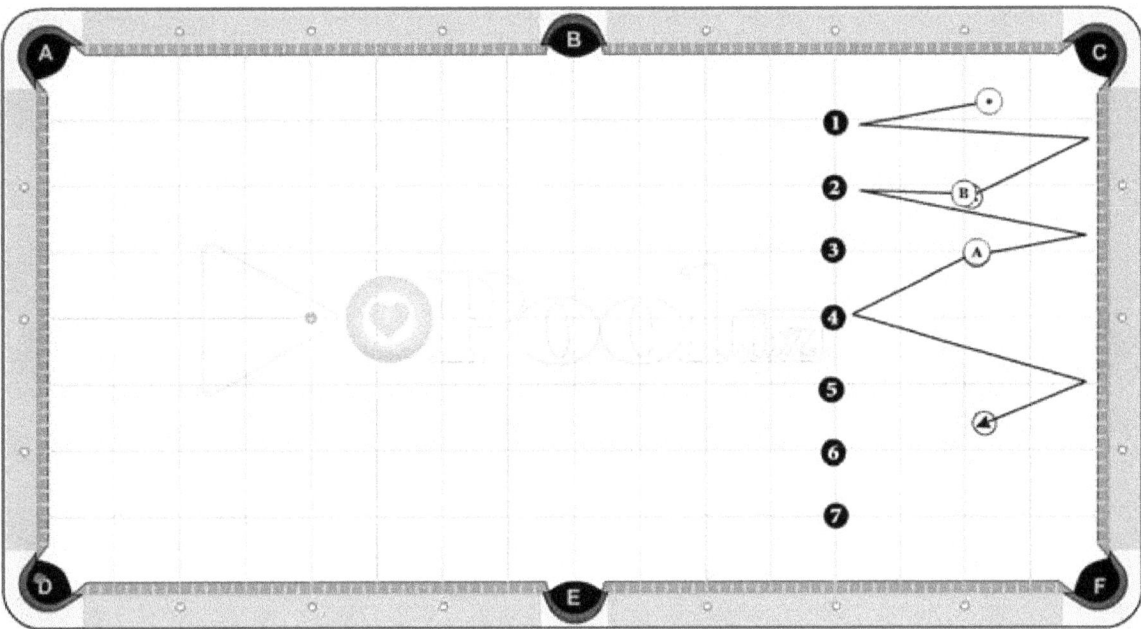

Set 2

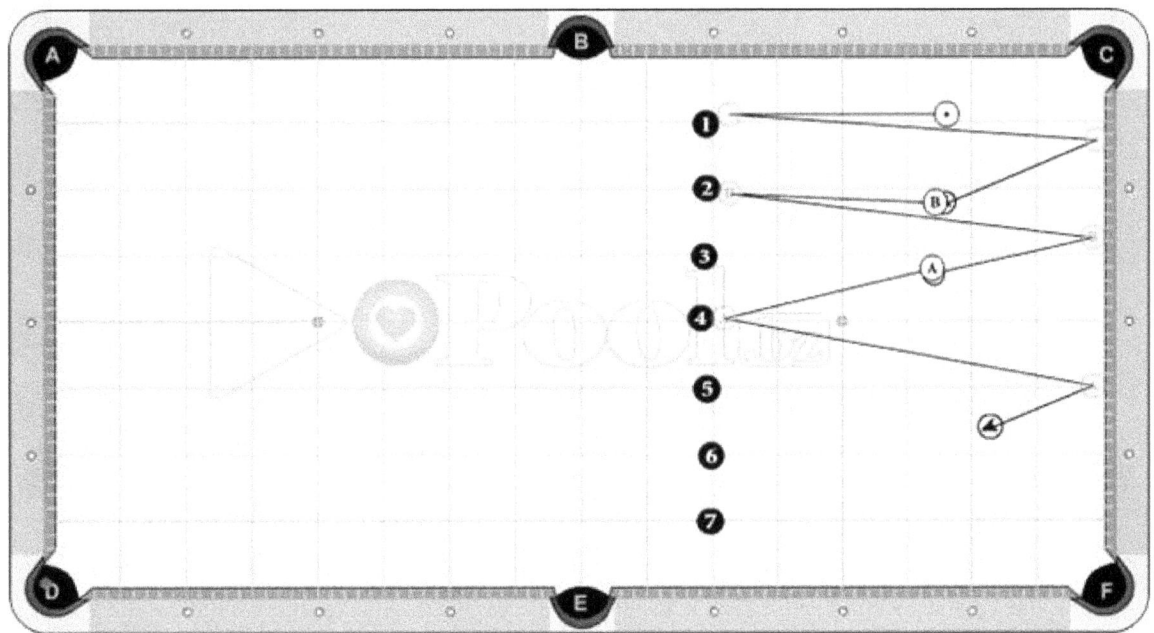

Set 3

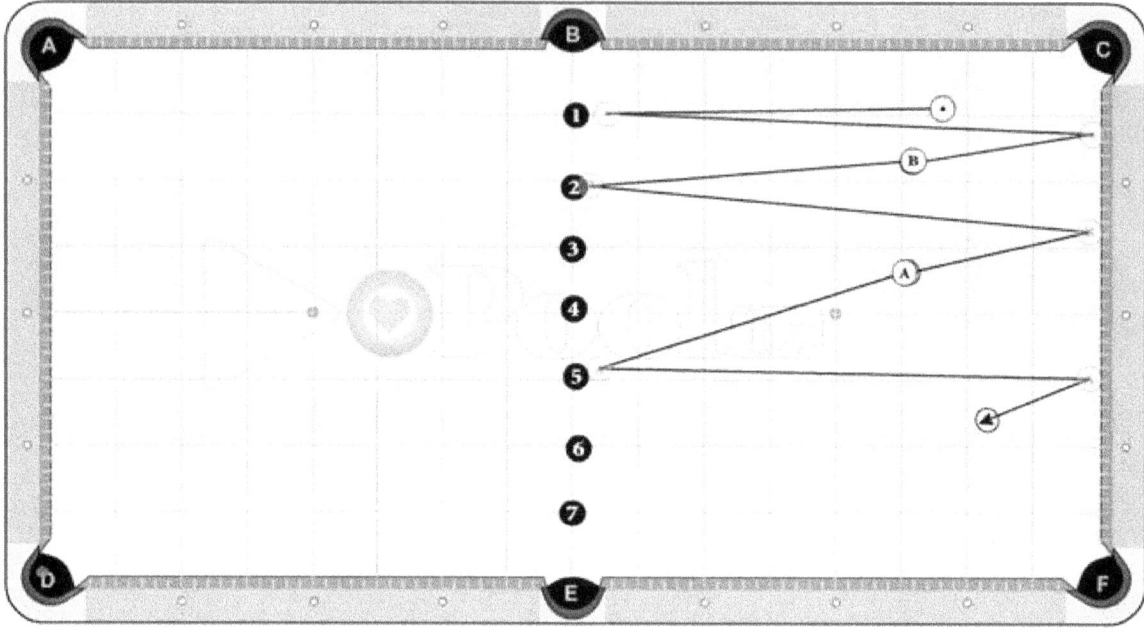

Set 4

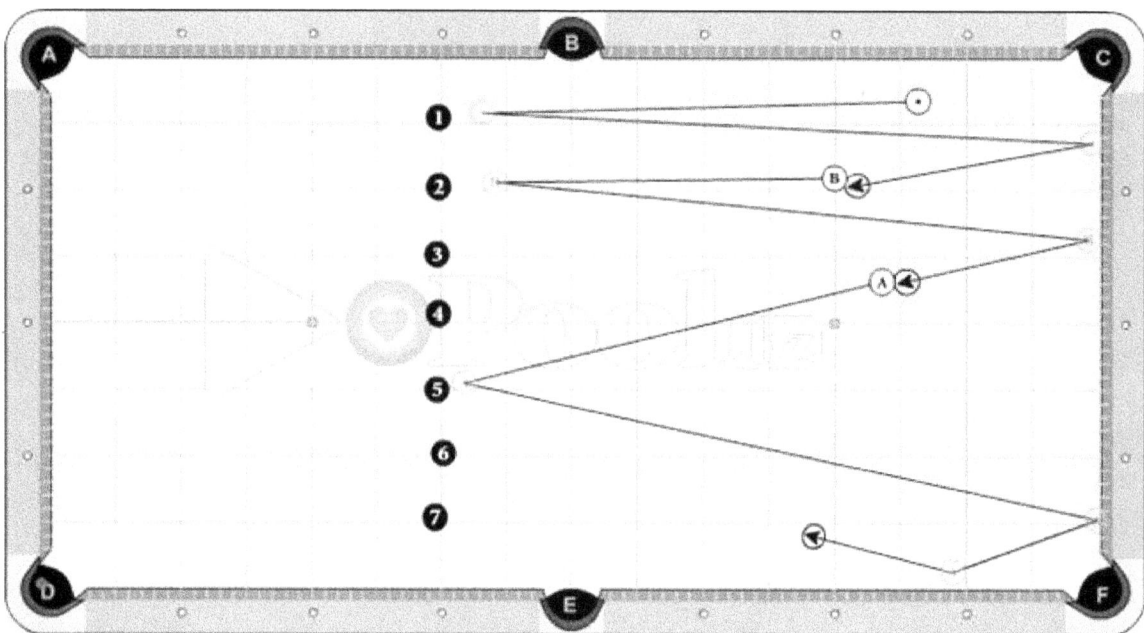

CB Management

Other drills will improve your skills in CB control. However, there is far more to getting the CB to move around at your command and will. Getting position

These are an excellent selection of exercises that will focus on CB control over short, medium, and long table distances. Some are designed to help you select a precise path, other exercises help you master where the CB stops.

When you have started to gain control of the CB, your self-confidence improves significantly. Situations that used to confuse and confound you become routine circumstances that are easily handled.

It is well worth the effort to put some serious practice effort into these exercises. The surprise you observe on your opponent's face as you get out of a difficult layout is worth the effort. After observing a few of your escapes, your opponent will treat you with greater respect.

Control Path of the Cue Ball (Easy)

Object: Draw or spin the CB back from the OB in the paths (as shown).

Set 1

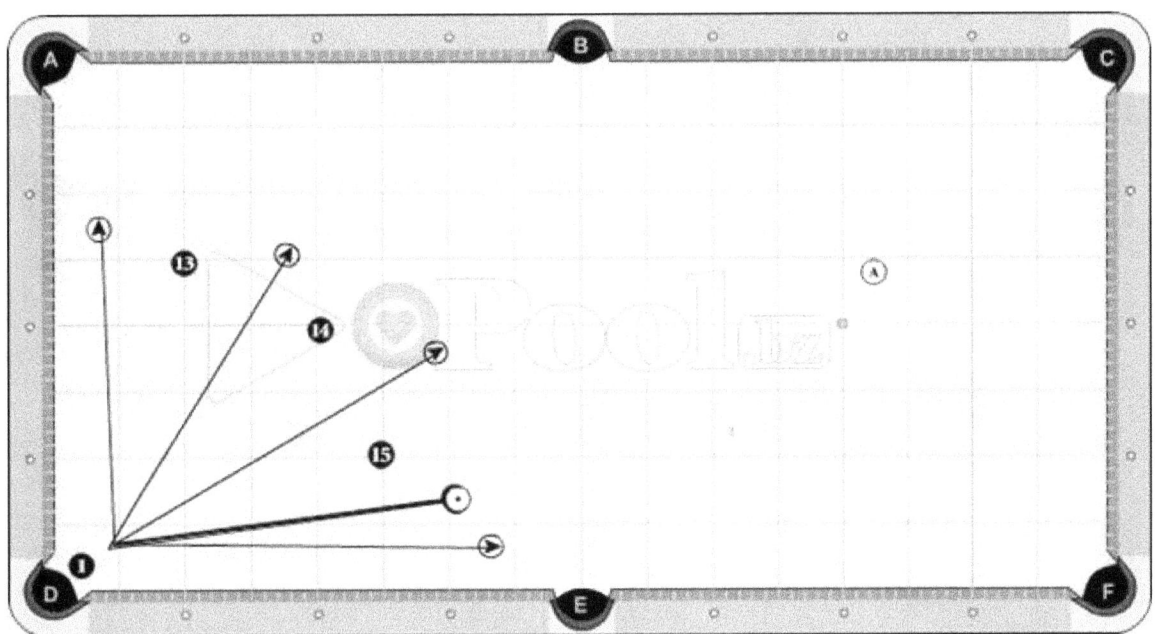

Set 2

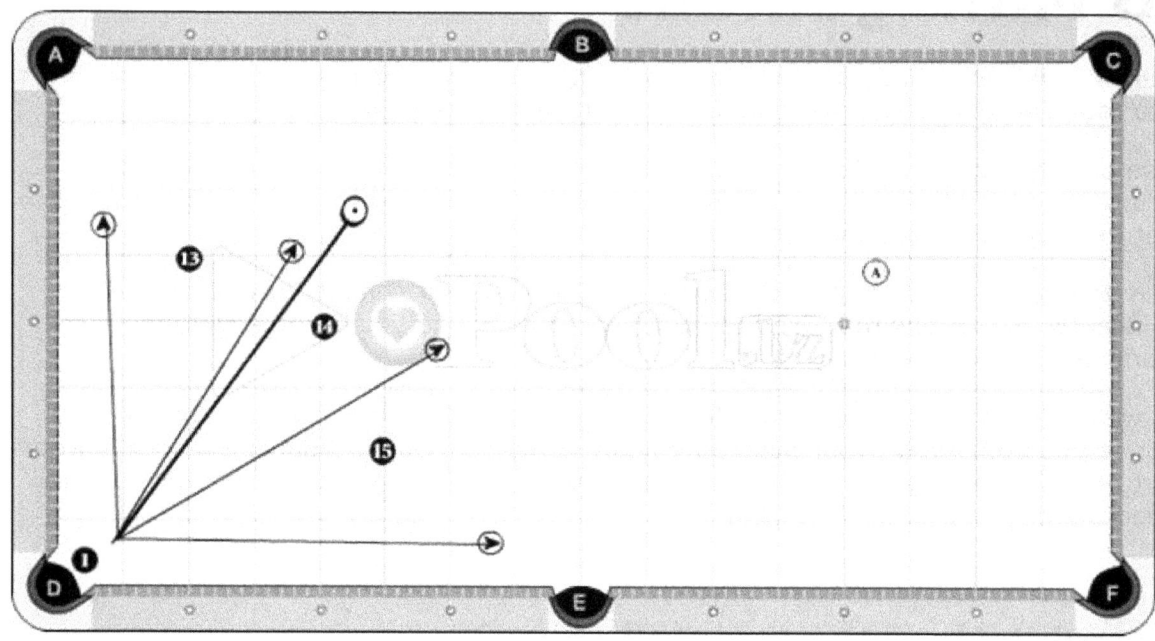

Set 3

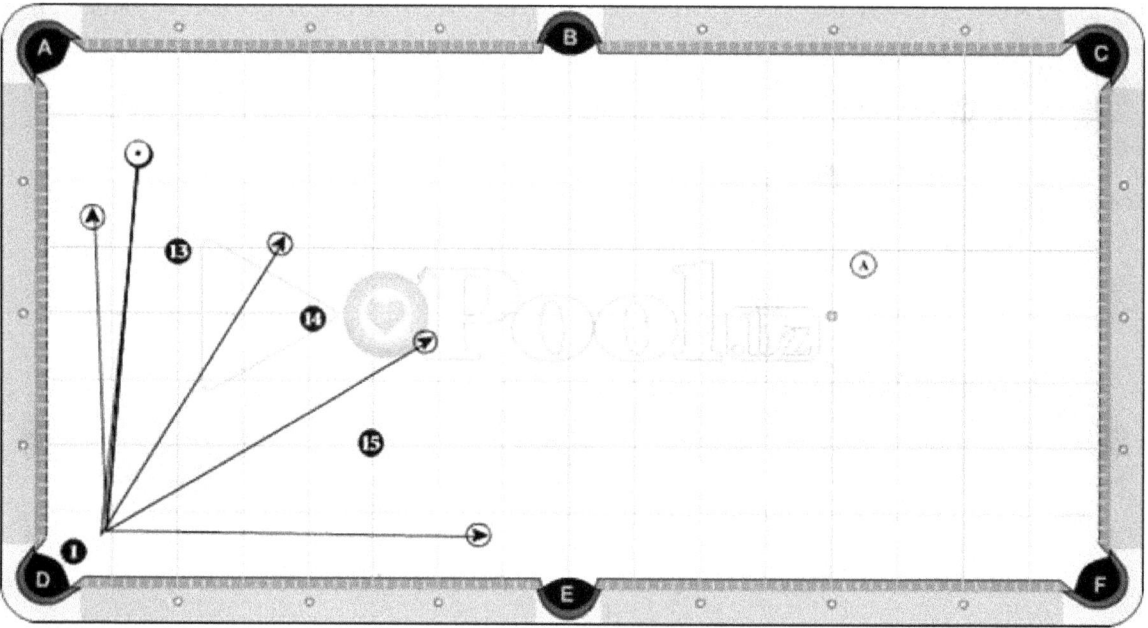

Control Path of the Cue Ball (Intermediate)

Object: Draw or spin the CB back from the OB in the paths (as shown).

Set 1

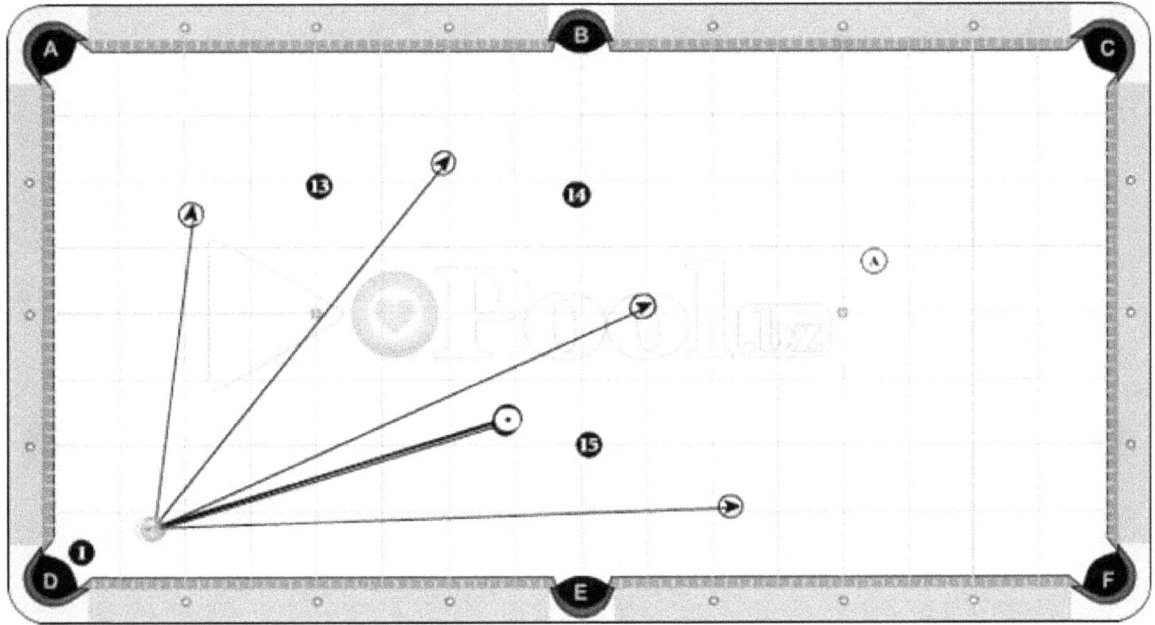

Set 2

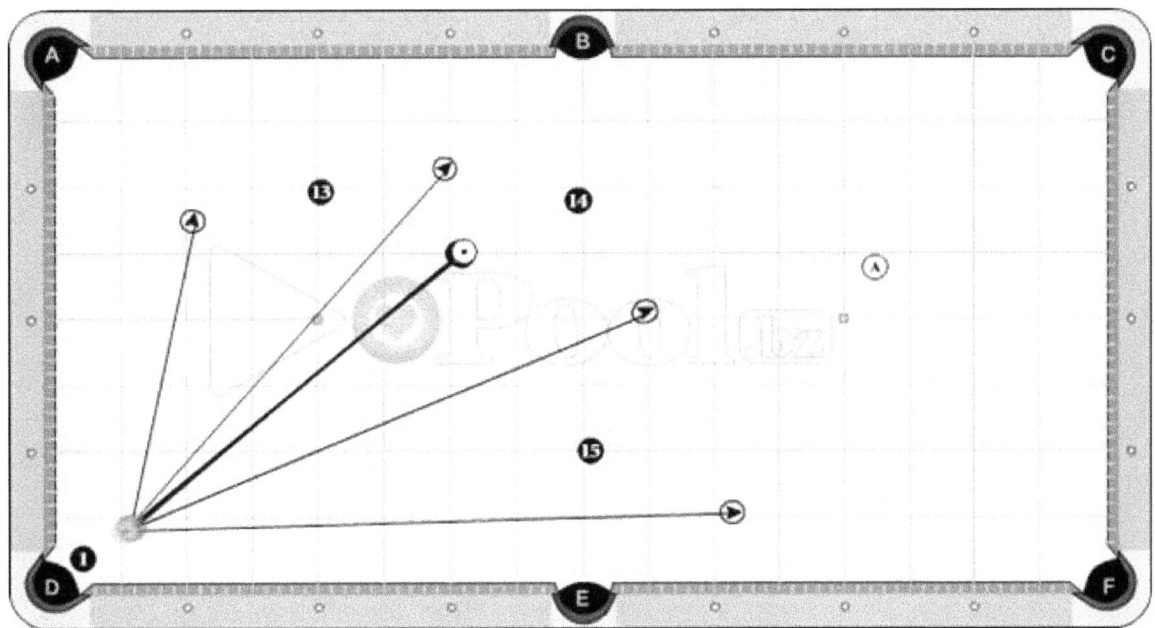

Set 3

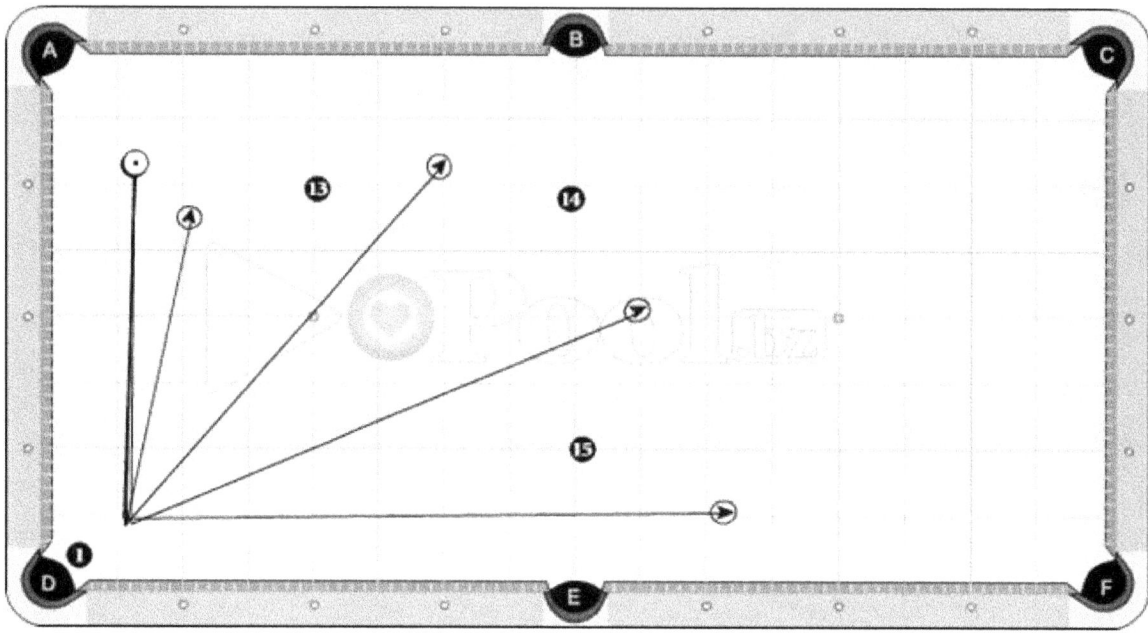

Control Path of the Cue Ball (Advanced)

Object: Draw or spin the CB back from the OB in the paths (as shown).

Set 1

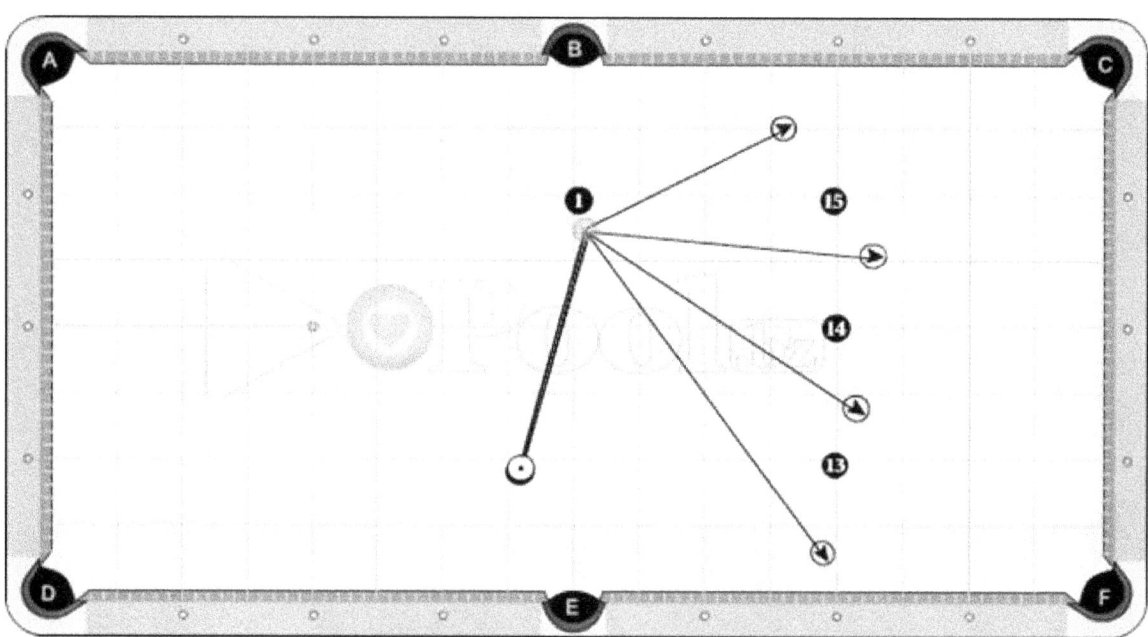

Set 2

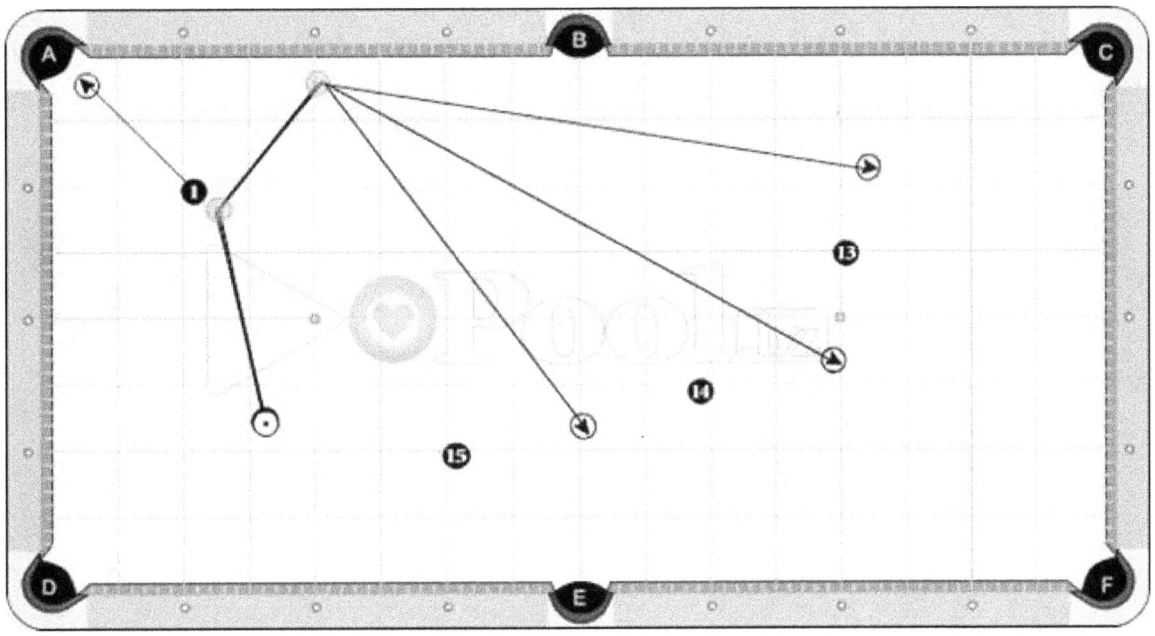

Set 3

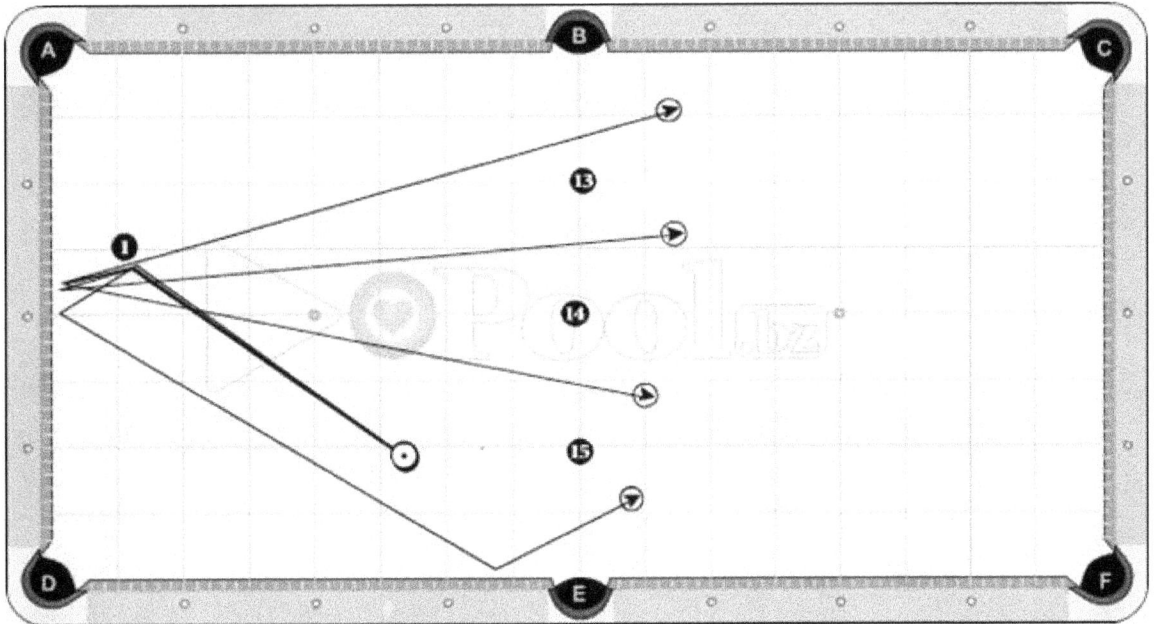

CB Location Positioning

Object: Select one OB to be your target (any position as shown). Pocket the 1 ball, then move the CB within a half diamond of the target object ball.

Set 1

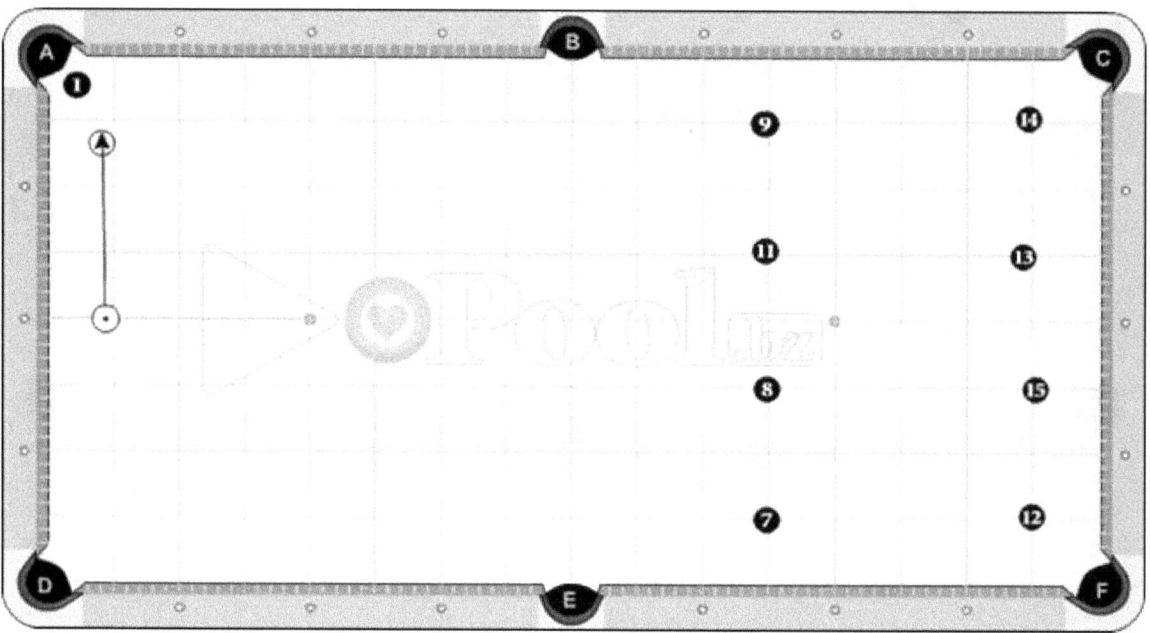

Set 2

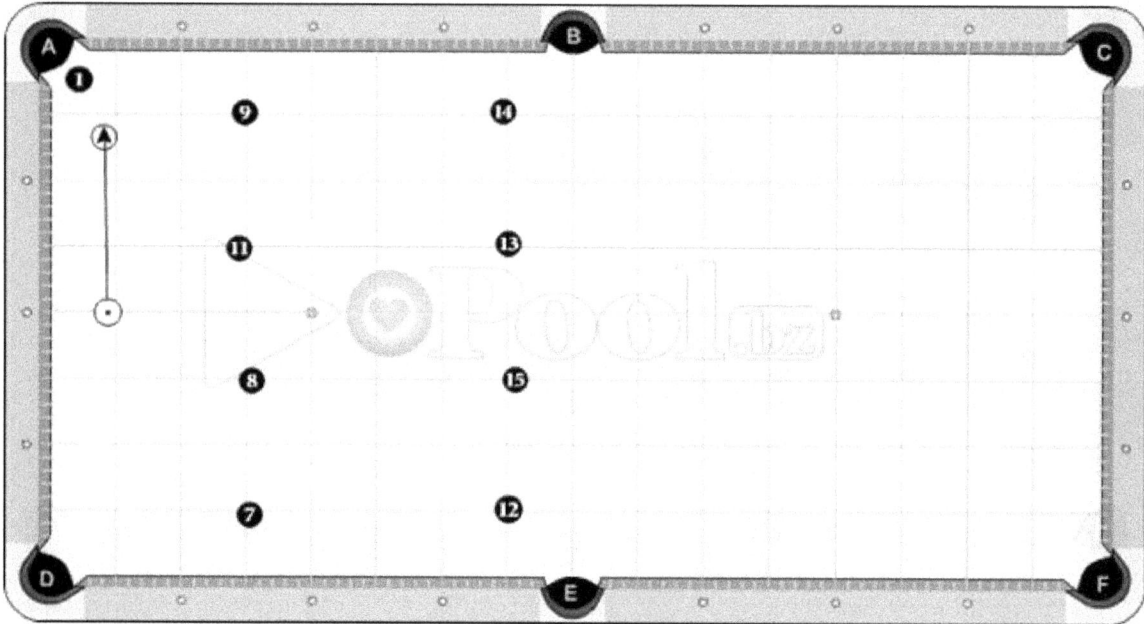

Set 3

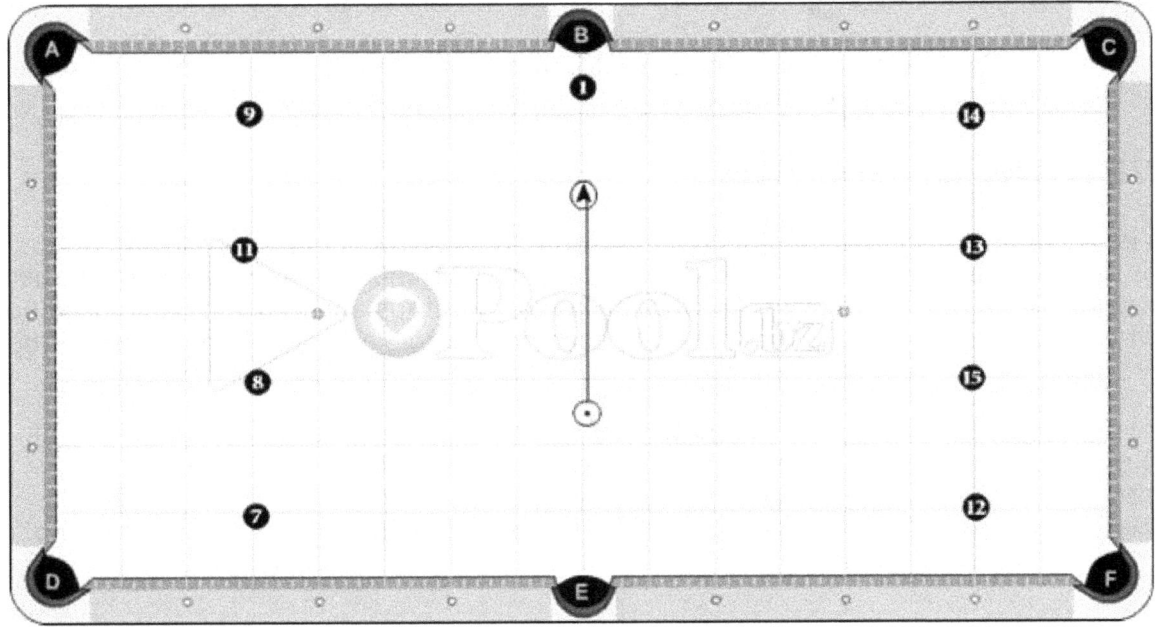

Set 4

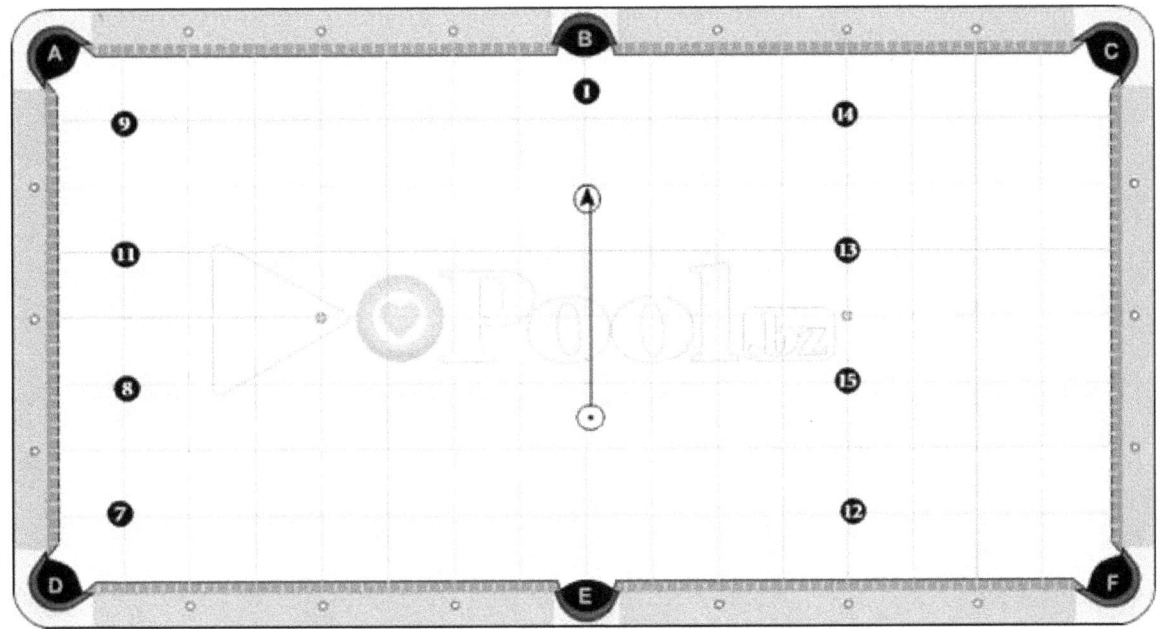

Positioning Skill Development

This section provides drills and exercises that improve and develop your skills. You are expected to use all of the as many of the 39 different CB speeds/spins as possible.

Triangle Exercises

This is the first time this set of drills has appeared in publication anywhere in the world. All of my students learn these drills and have rapidly made significant improvements in their CB control skills. Spend a few weeks working on these setups and you will be amazed how much your game gets better. There is no expectation to pocket any ball, only control the CB.

To keep things interesting, the very nature of these drills provides an infinite variety of starting setups. You must figure out the correct CB speed/spin to make the shot work. There are more than one speed/spin shots to make this work. For example, 6:00/half tip/medium and 6:00/full tip/soft and 4:30/full tip/soft can all work for the same setup.

Instructions: Shoot the CB into the first OB and roll the CB up to the second OB. The second OB must not roll more than two ball widths. A particular shot is mastered when you succeeds 4 out of 5 times.

Simple Triangles

Set 1

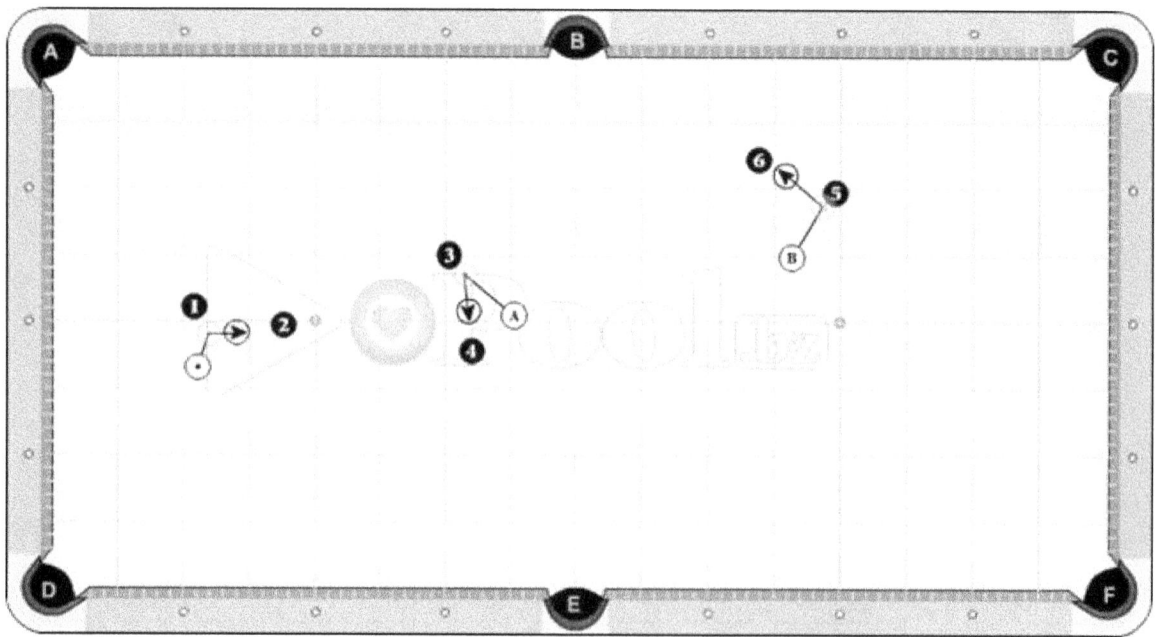

Set 2

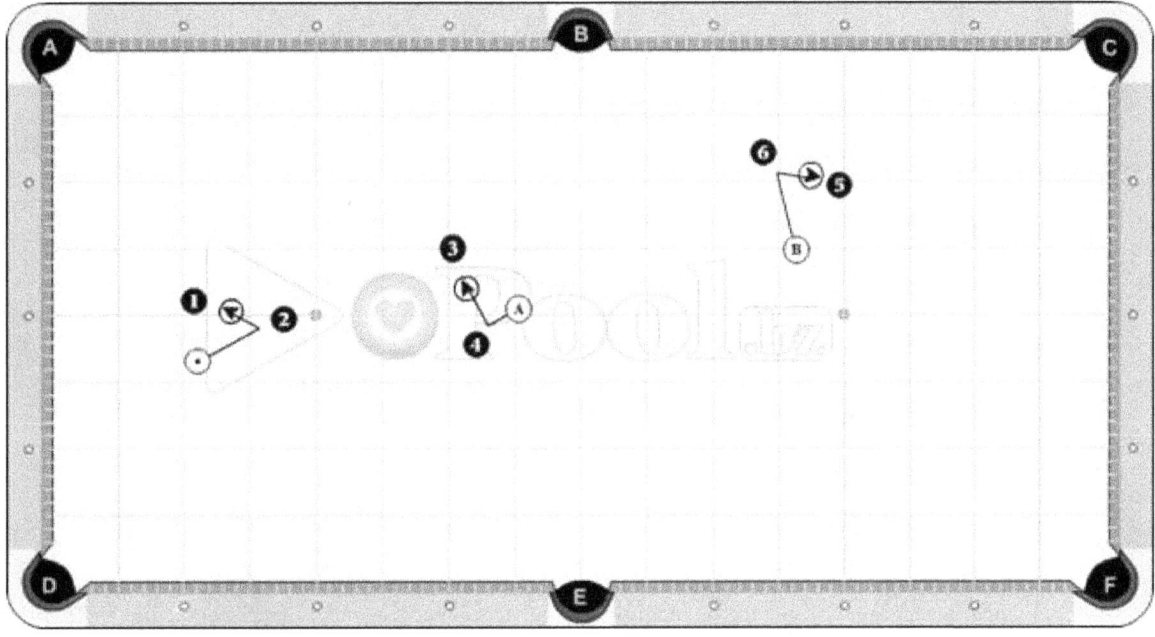

Set 3

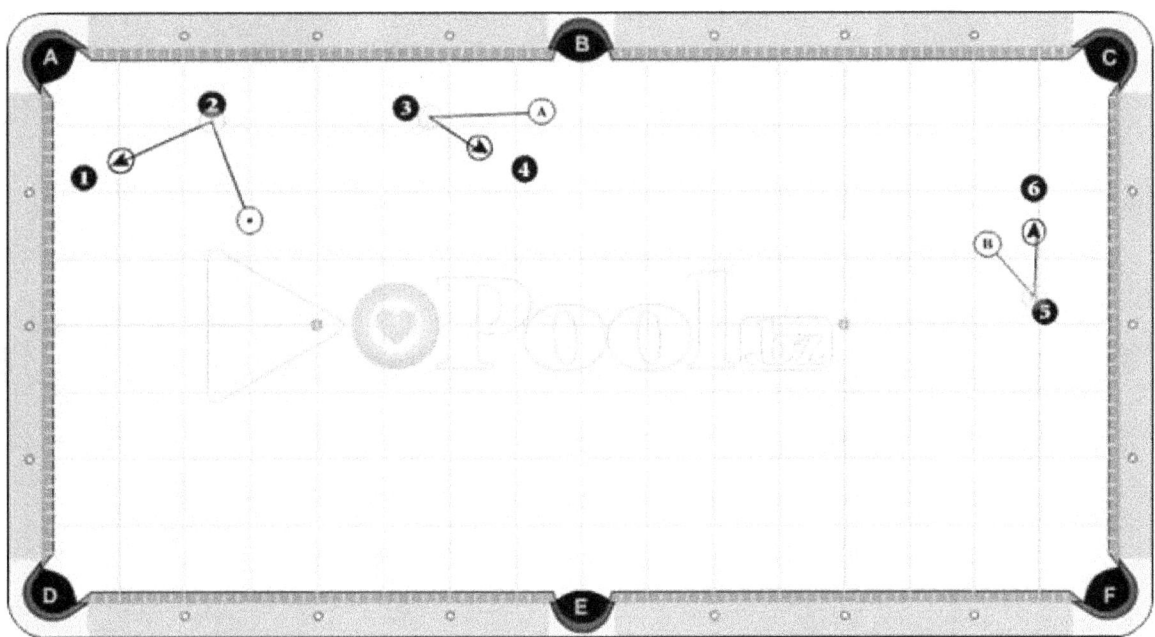

Set 4

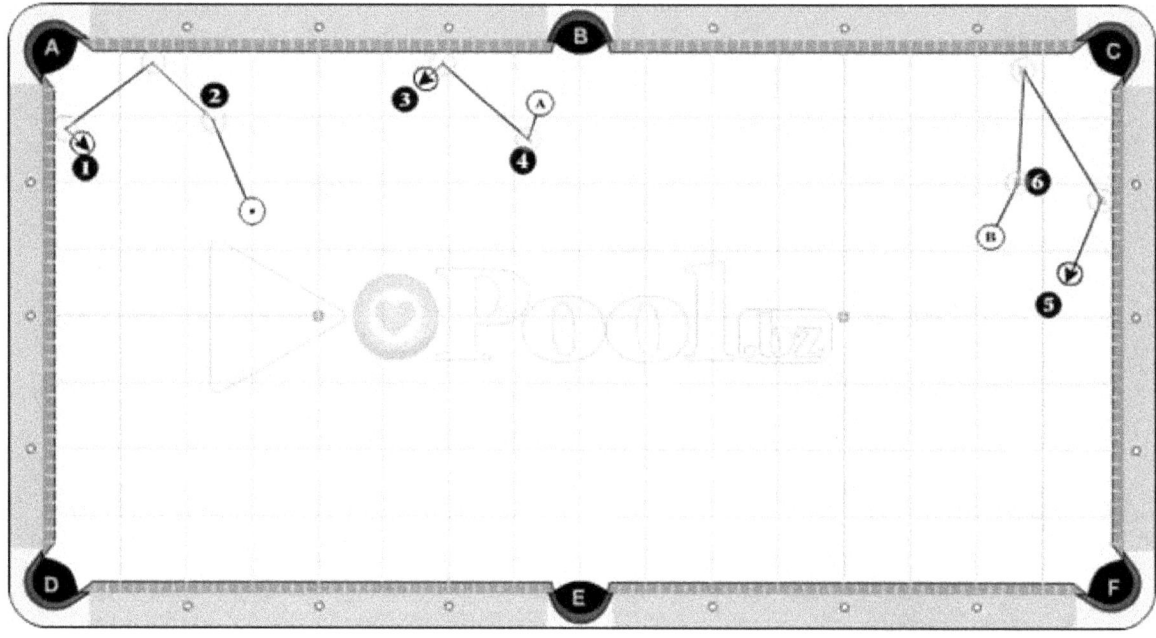

Set 5

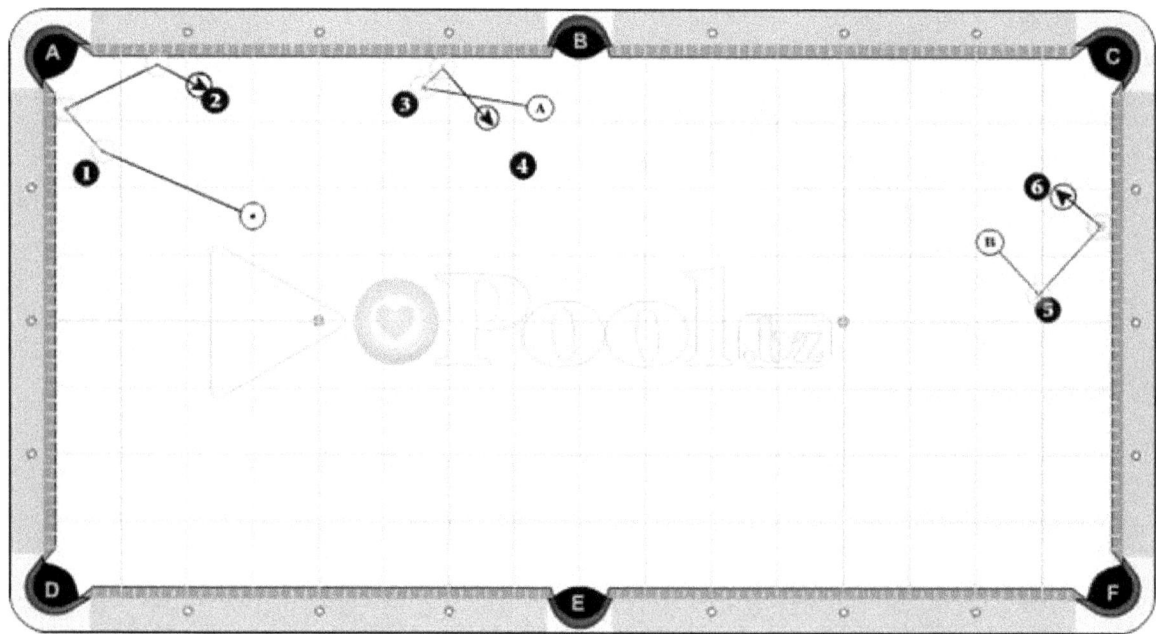

Intermediate Triangles

Extend the difficulty factor (as shown).

Set 1

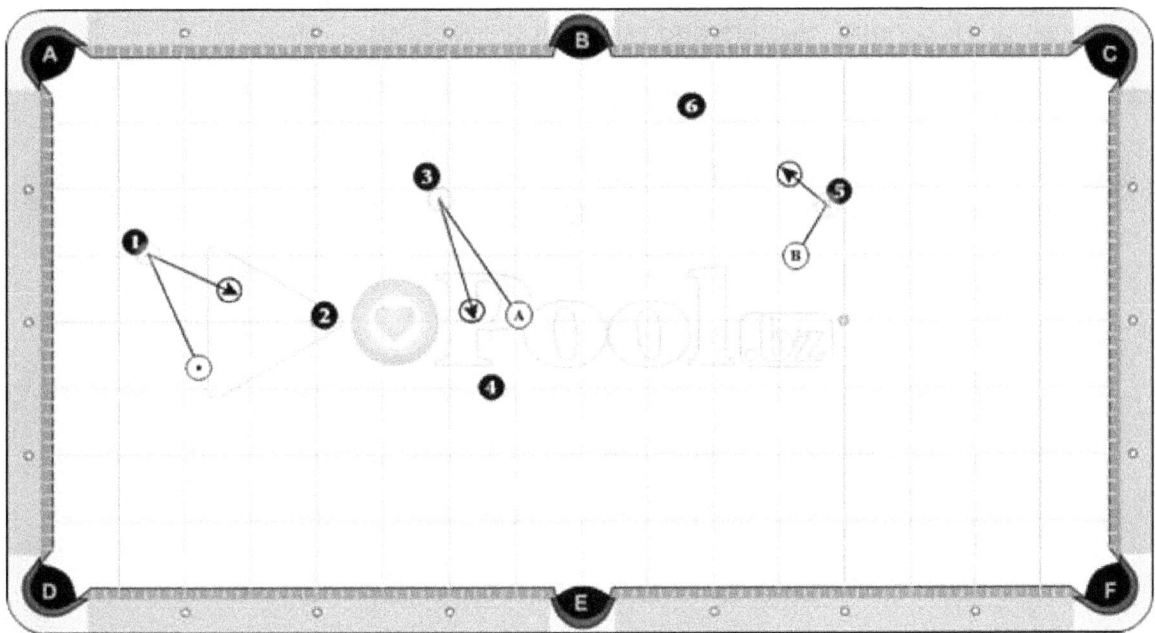

Set 2

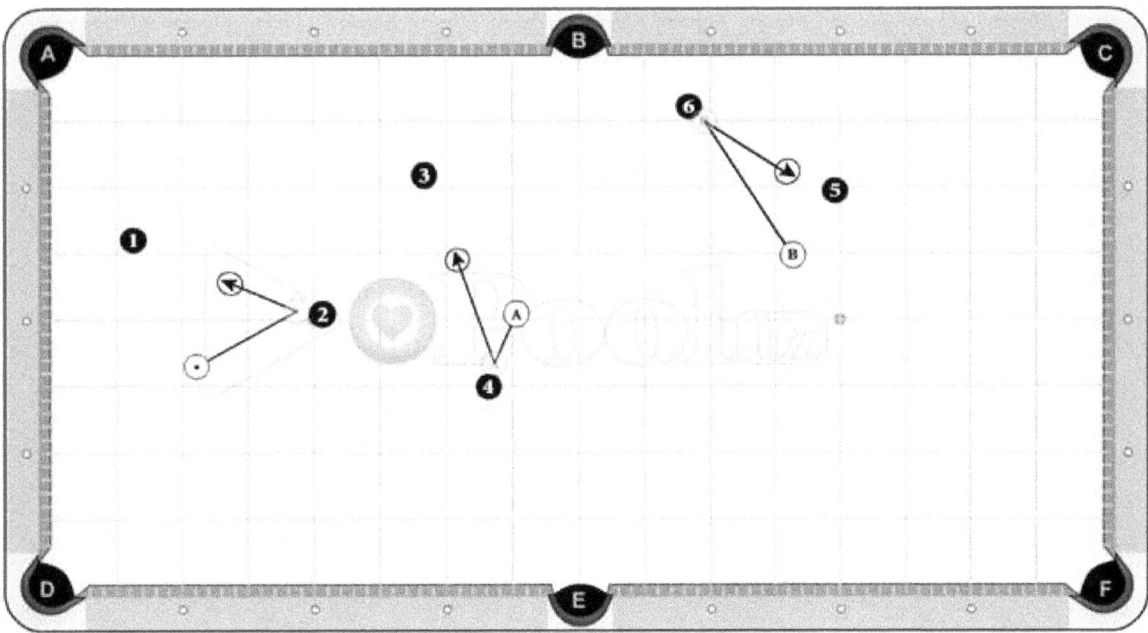

Advanced Triangles

For these drills, you have to make the CB travel much further. The chances of success place these shots outside of your Comfort Zone. However, practicing these setups and gaining some control over the results will enhance your reputation (when successful). Plus, these exercises significantly improve your abilities to shoot into killer safeties. These shots are also very useful for opening clusters and other problem balls.

Set 1

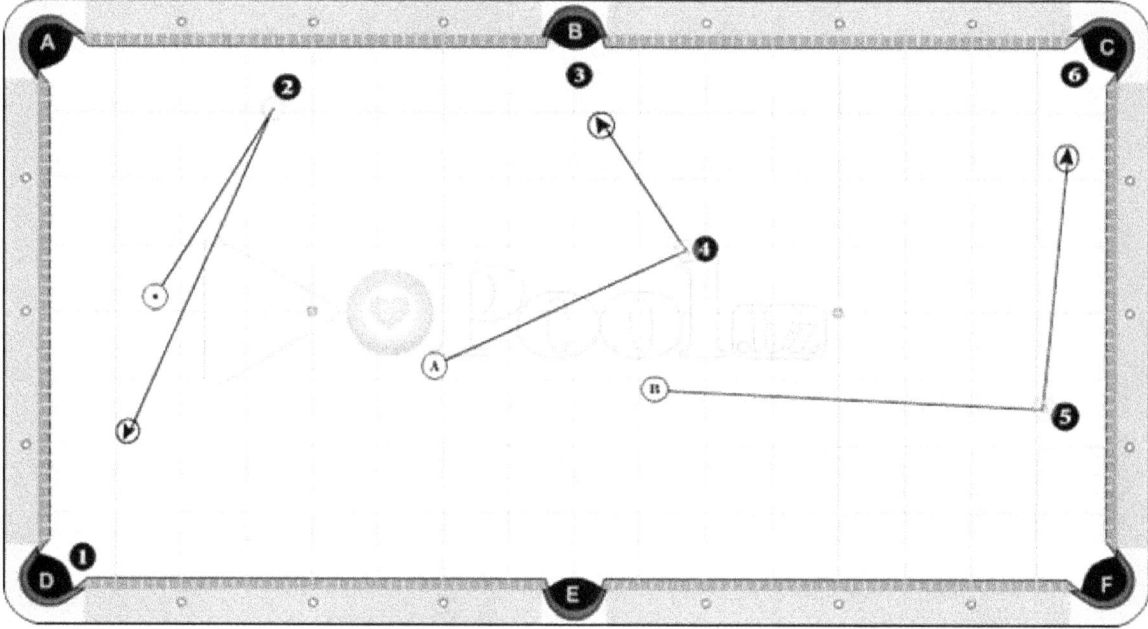

Set 2

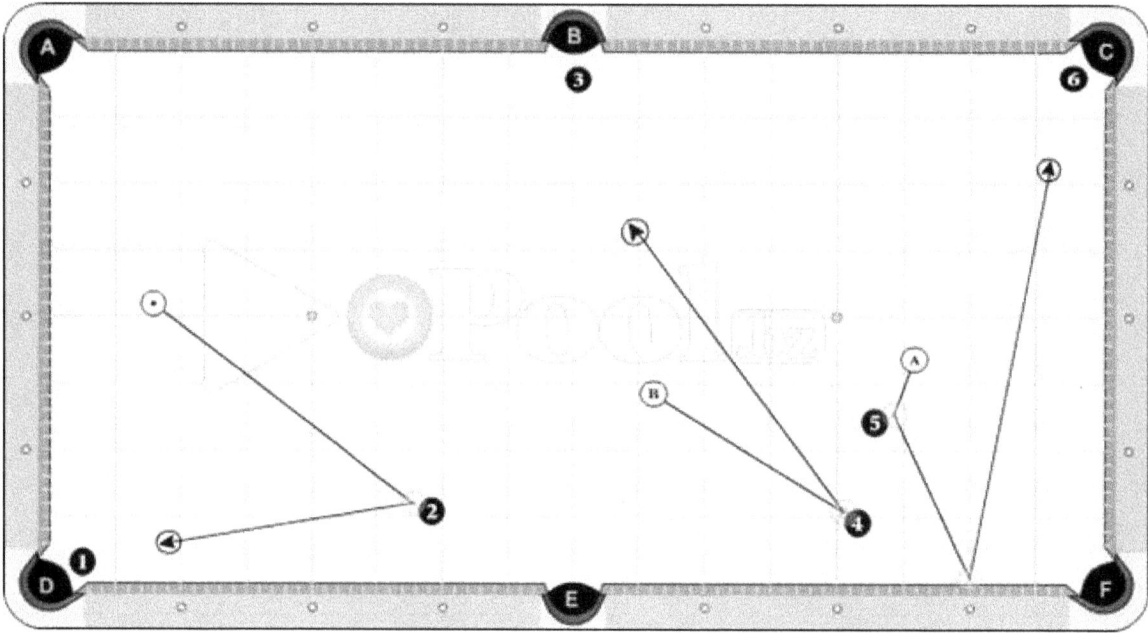

Set 3

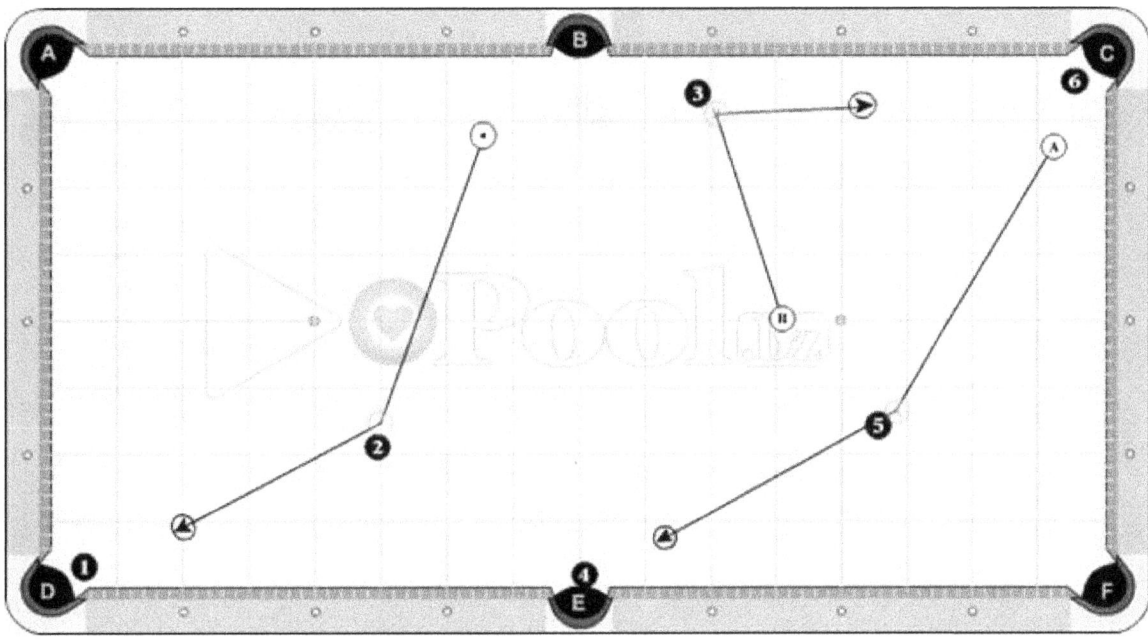

Set 4

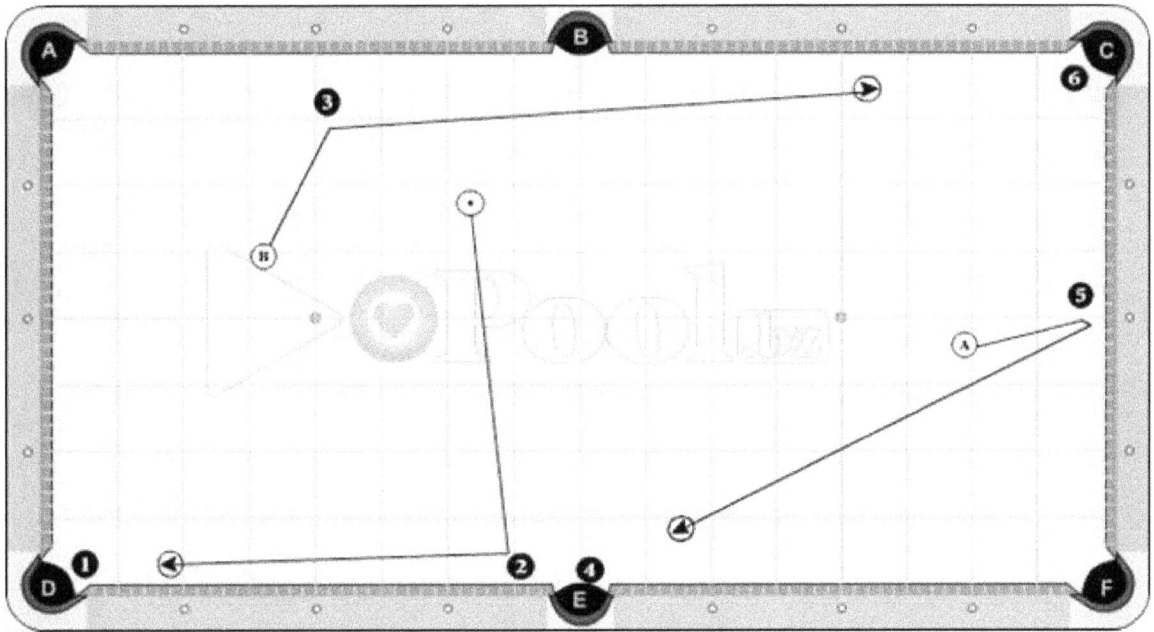

Cluster Clearing Triangles

Set 1

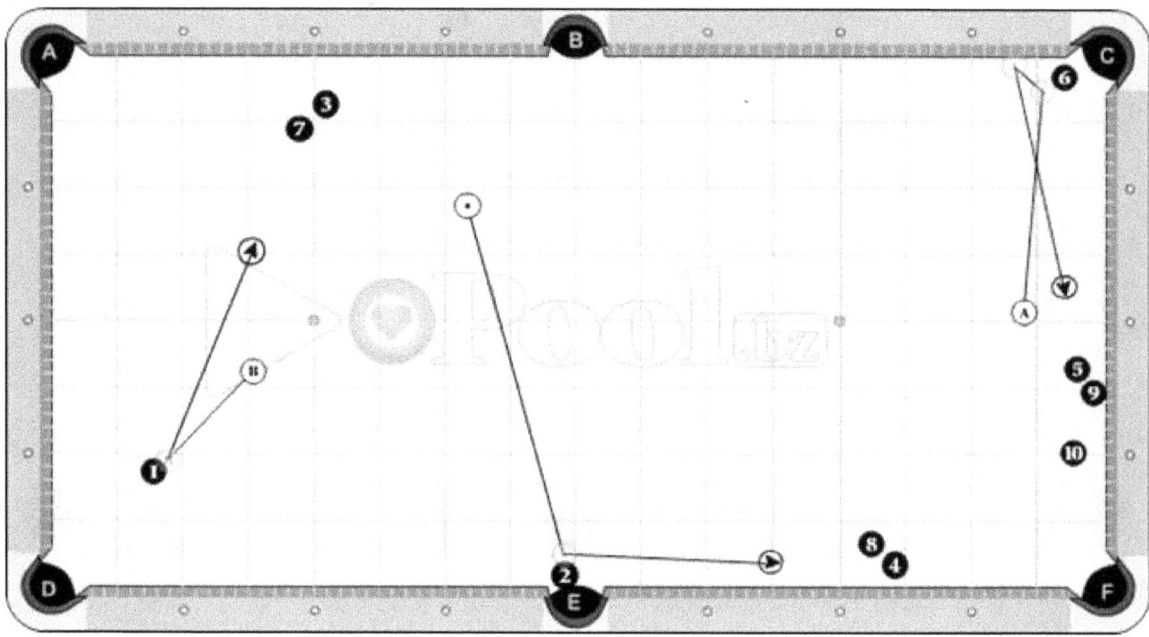

Set 2

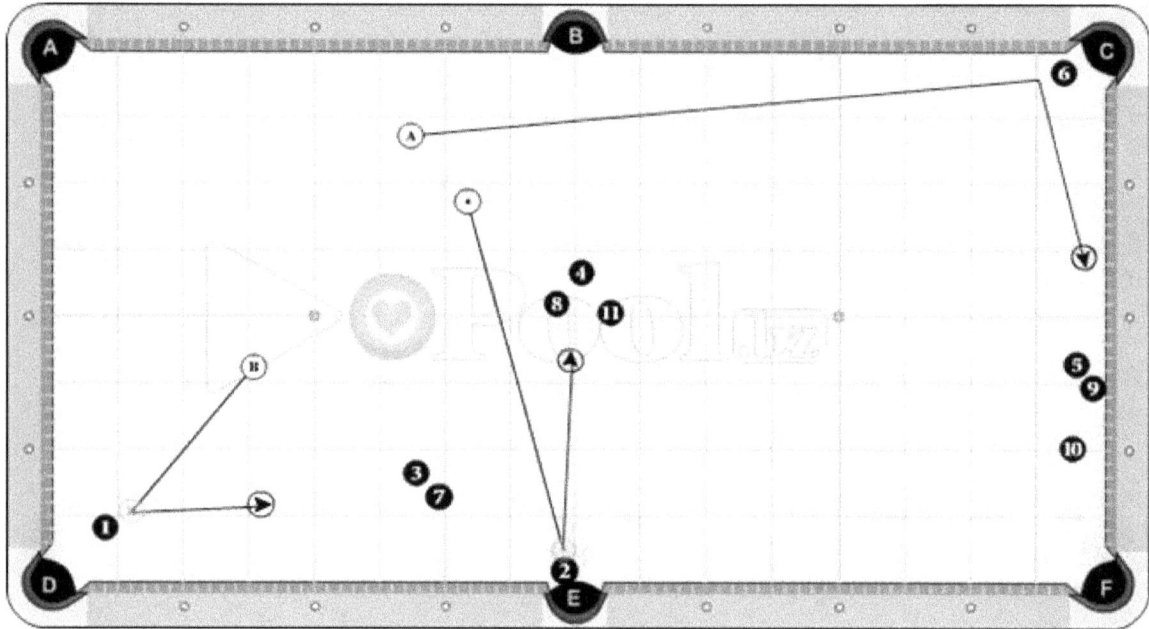

Turn the Corner

3 Ball Groups

Object: Pocket the balls. Chose any ball, left to right, right to left sequences.

Set 1

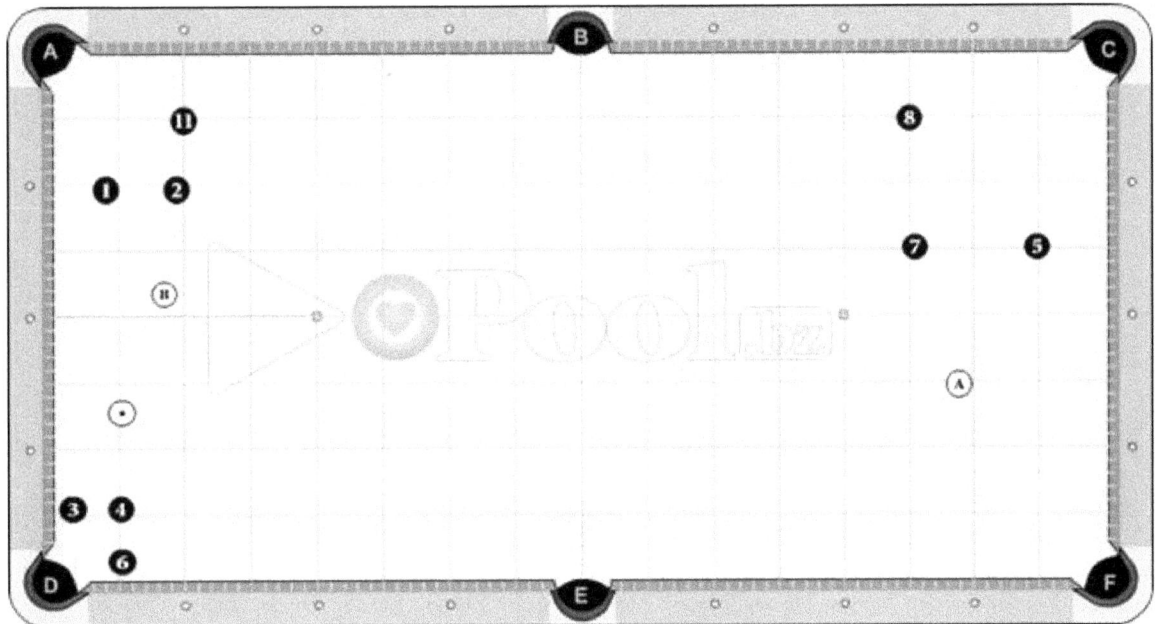

Set 2

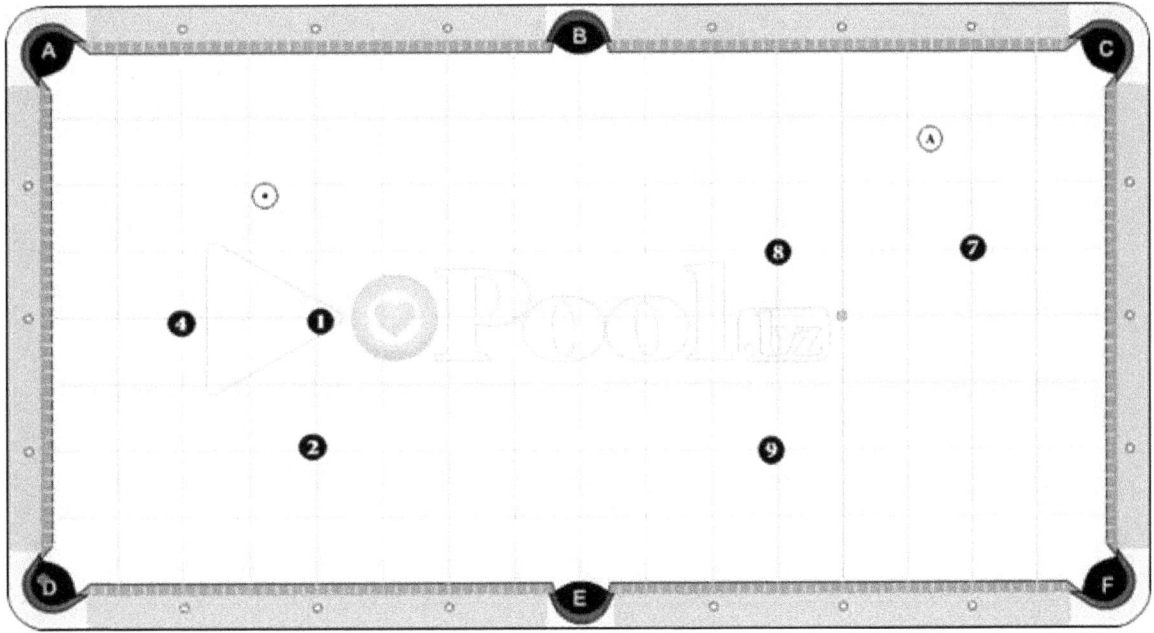

5 Ball Groups

Options: Pocket the balls. Chose any ball, left to right, right to left sequences.

Set 1

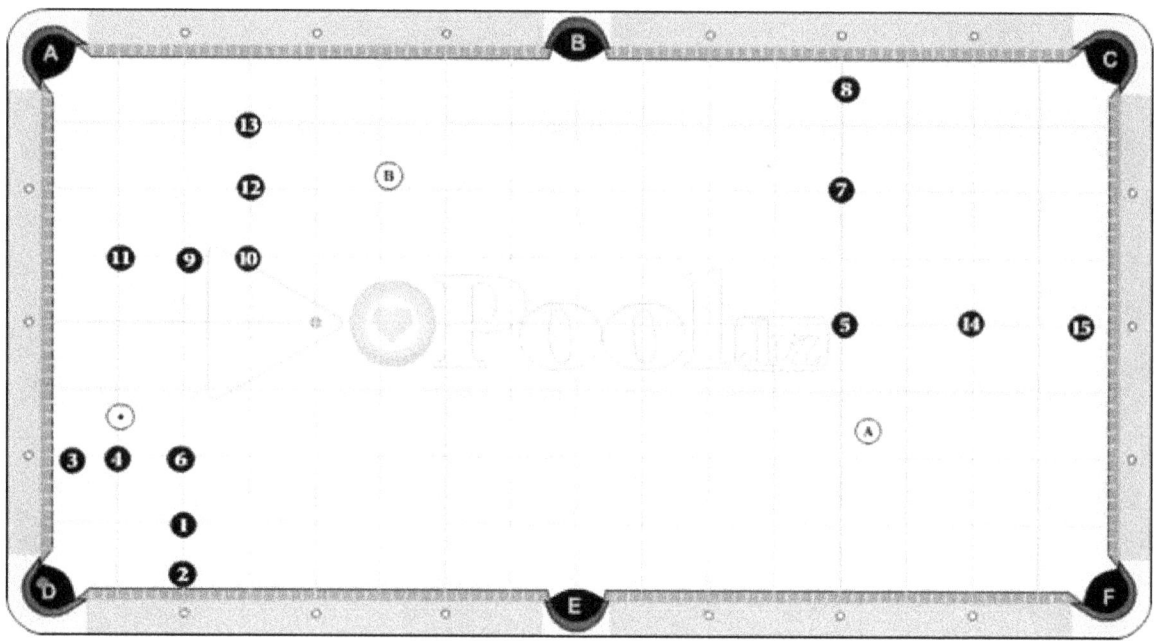

Set 2

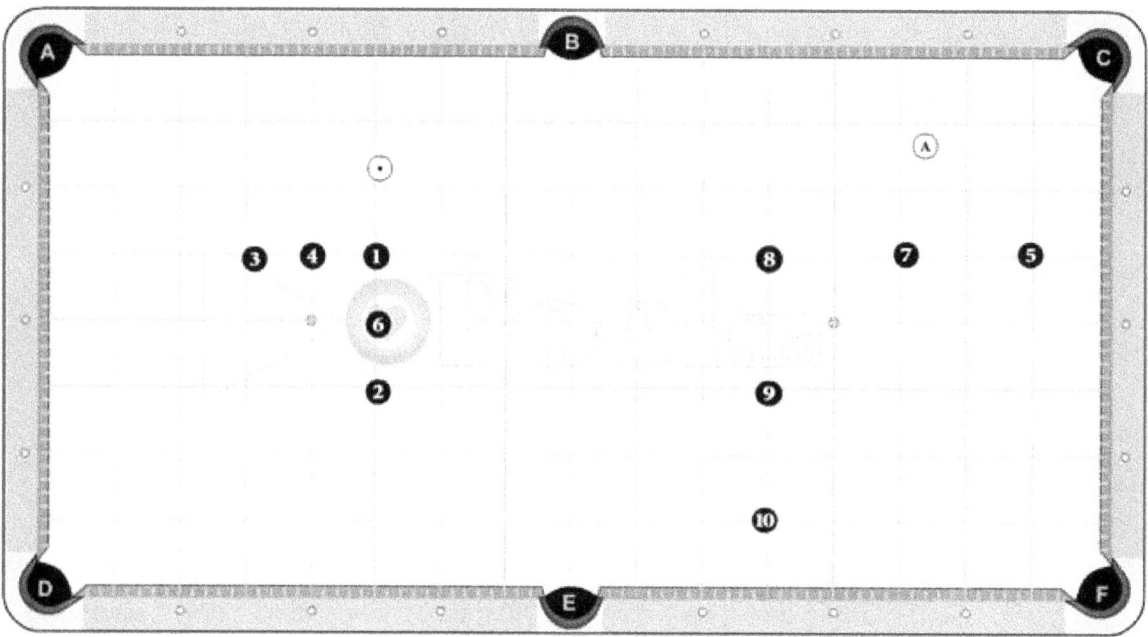

Advanced Groups

Object: Pocket the balls. Chose any ball, left to right, right to left sequences.

Set 1

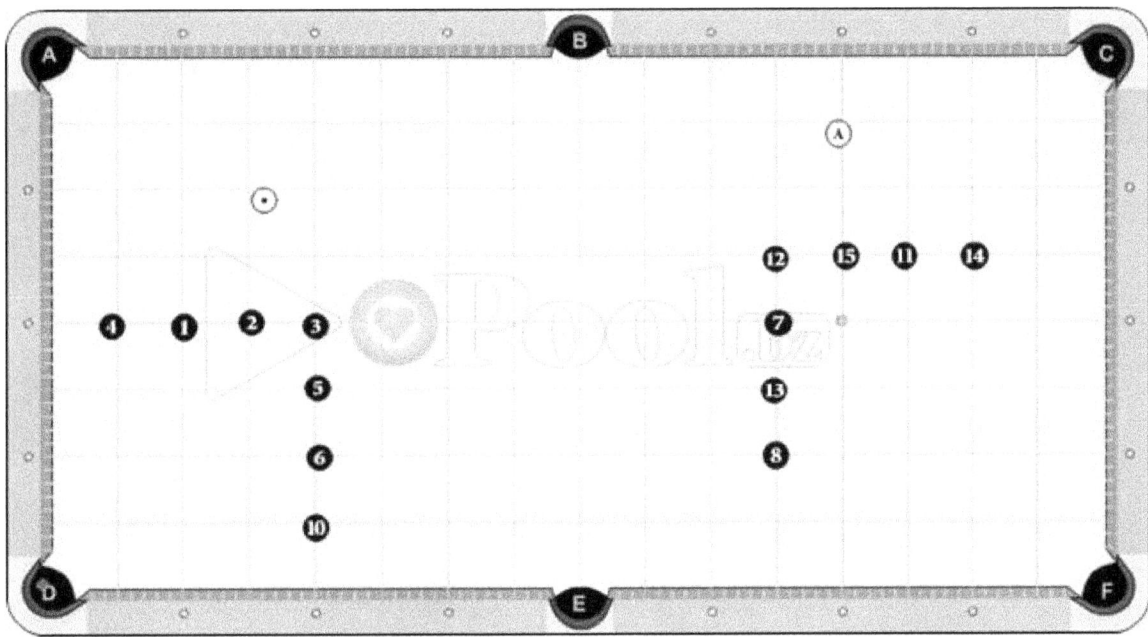

Set 2

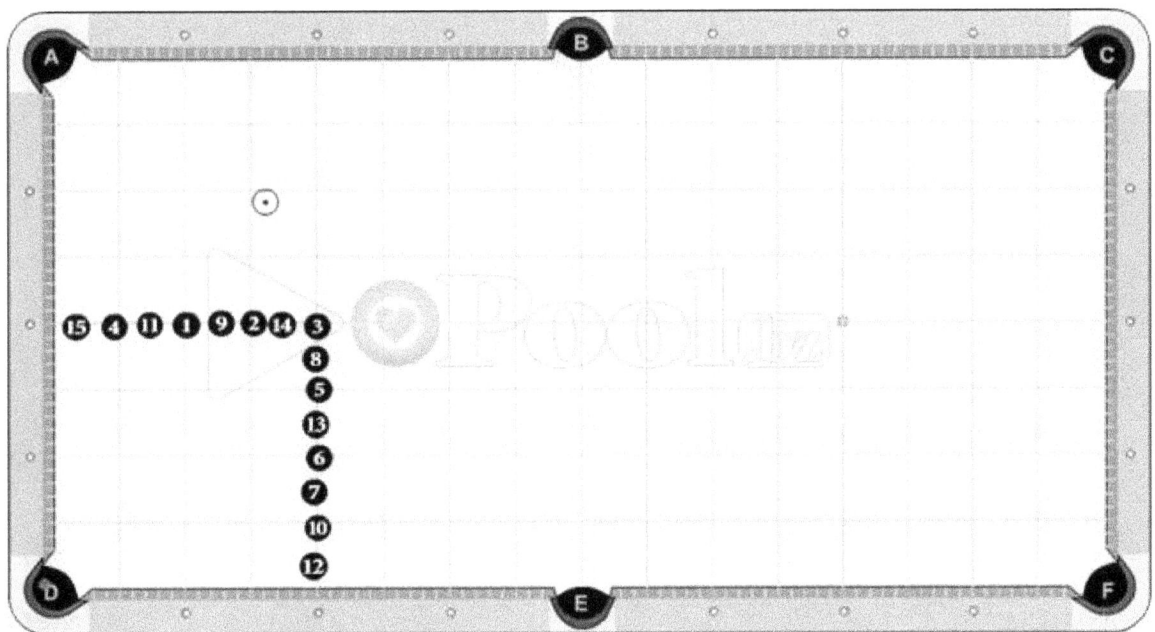

Short Stacks

Object: Pocket the balls. Chose any ball, in sequence, reverse sequence.

Set 1

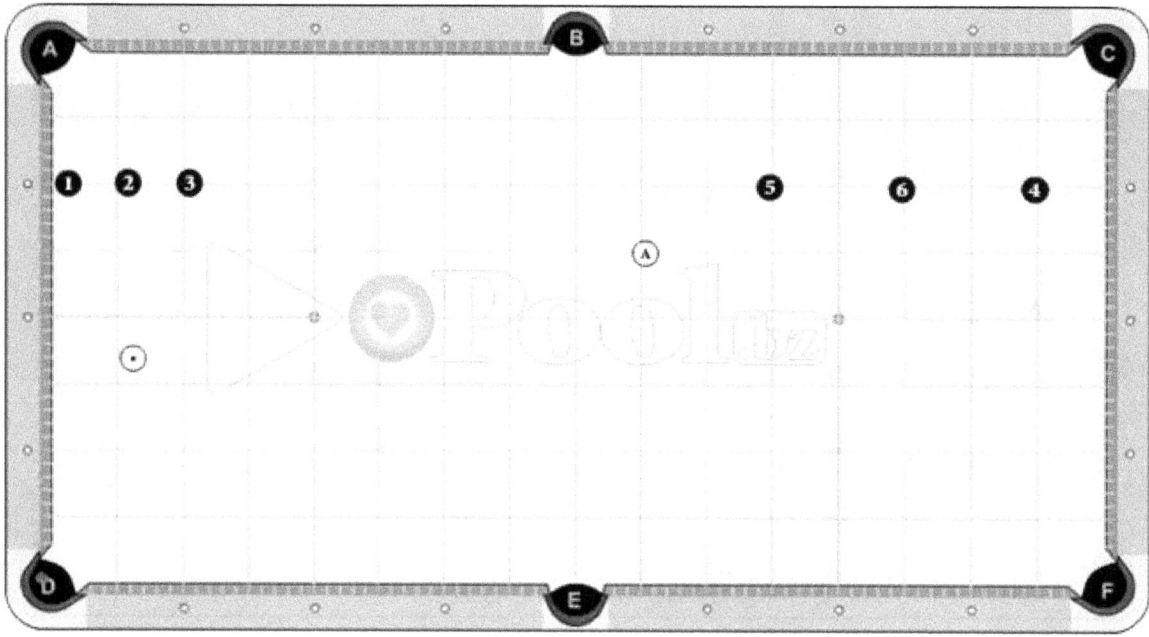

Set 2

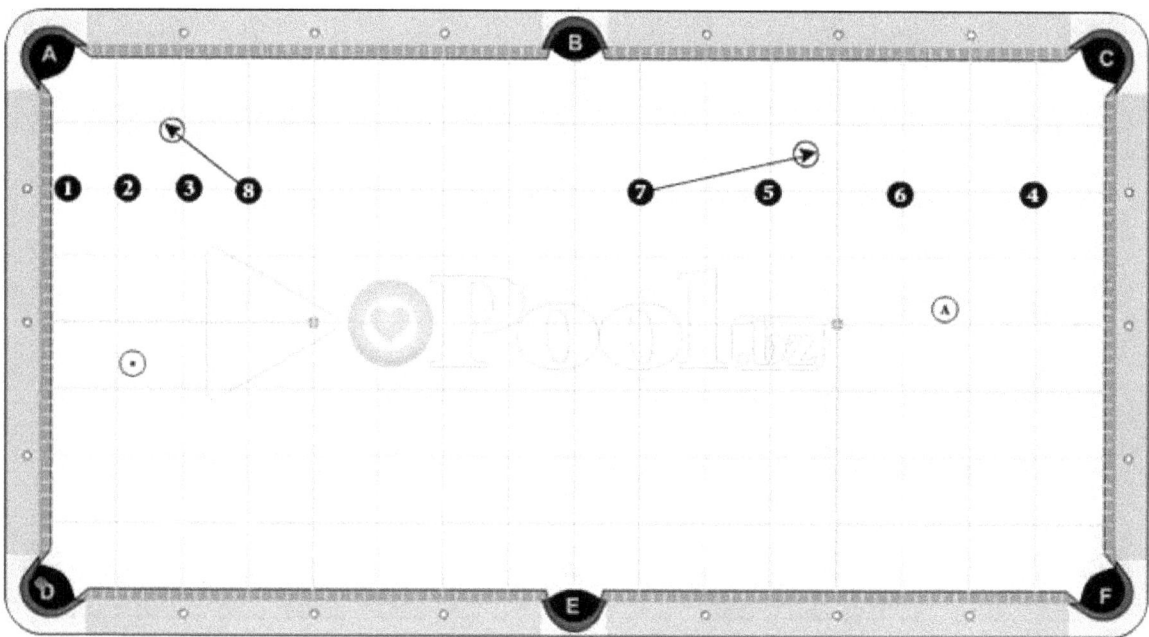

Set 3

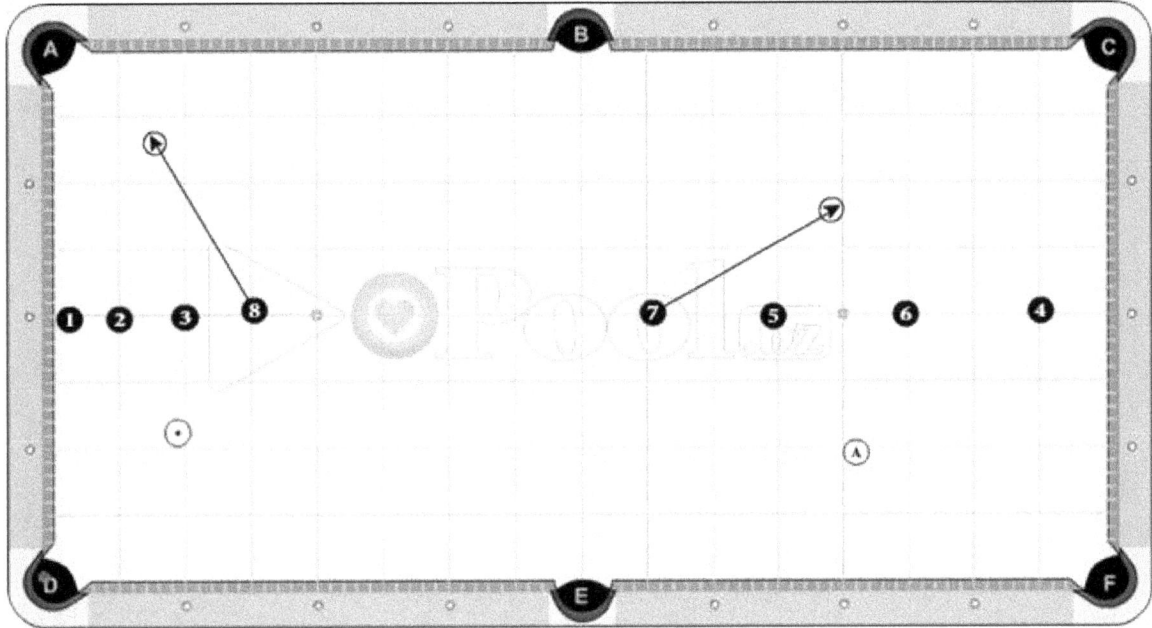

Down the Line

Object: Pocket the balls. Chose any ball into any pocket, only one side, down the line, or every other ball, etc.

Set 1

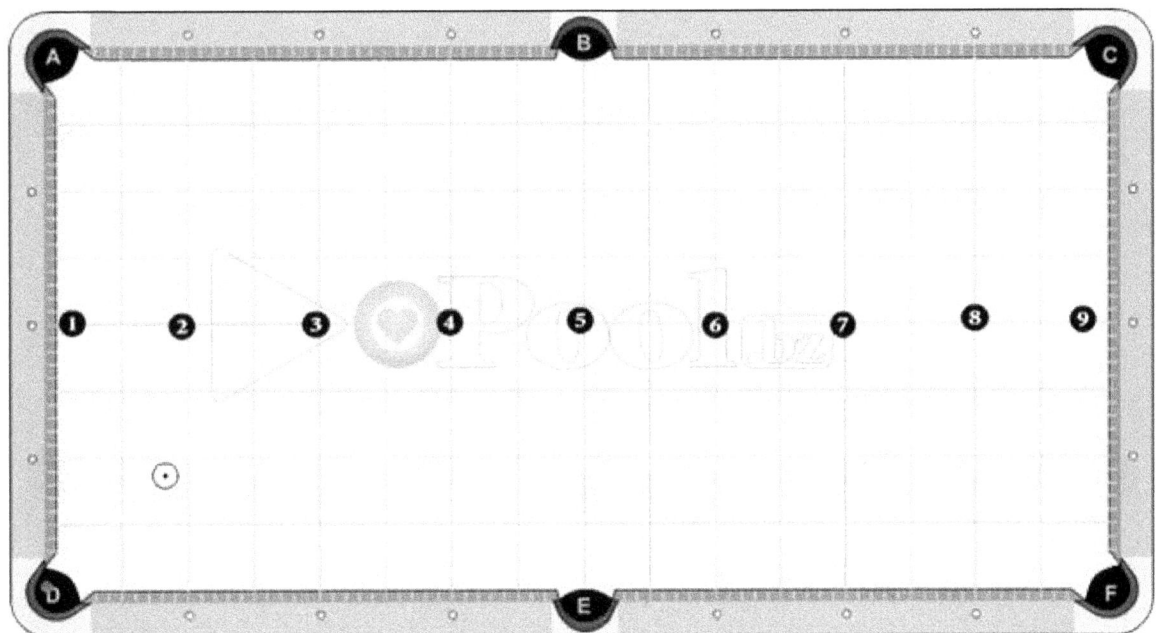

Set 2

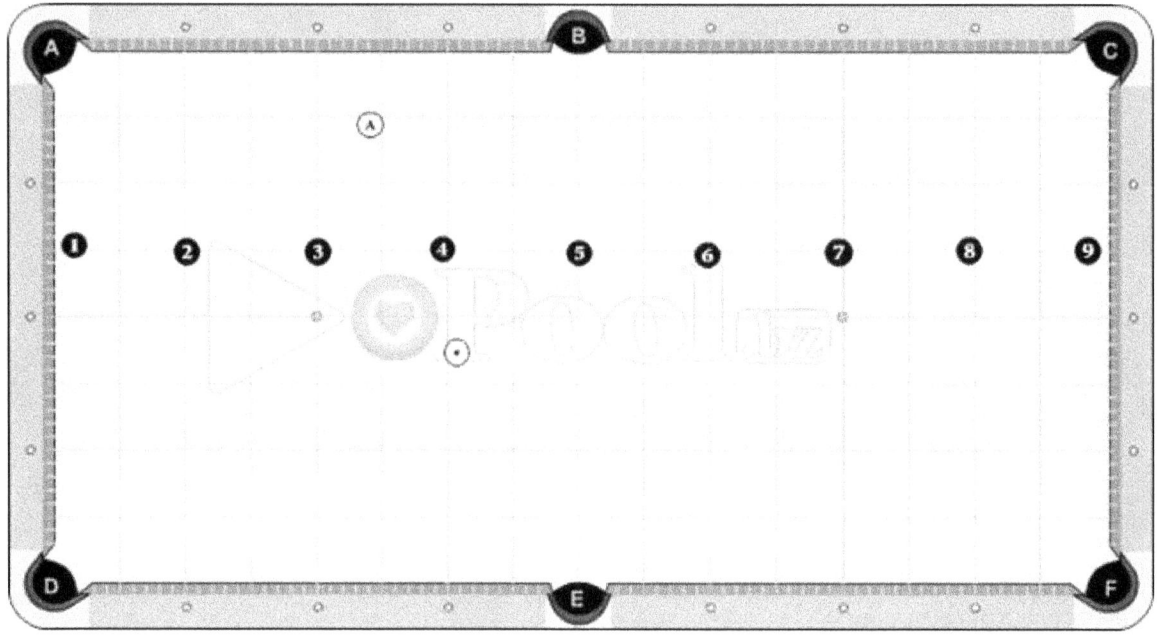

Set 3

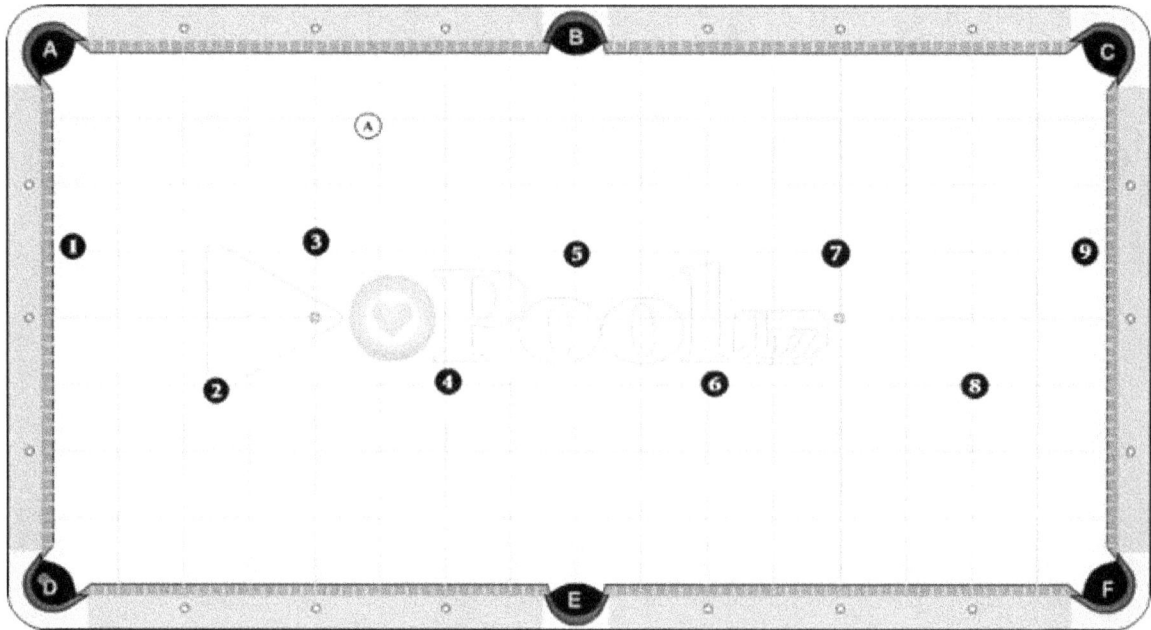

Side Pocket – Single Groups

Object: Pocket the balls. Chose any ball, sequential, reverse sequence.

Set 1

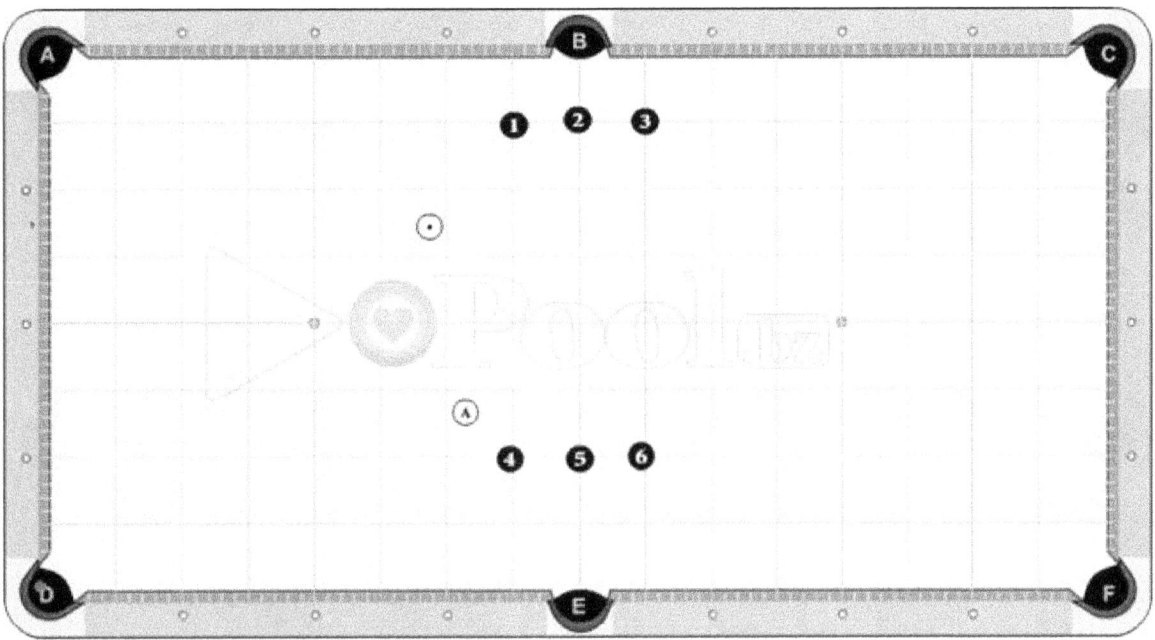

Set 2

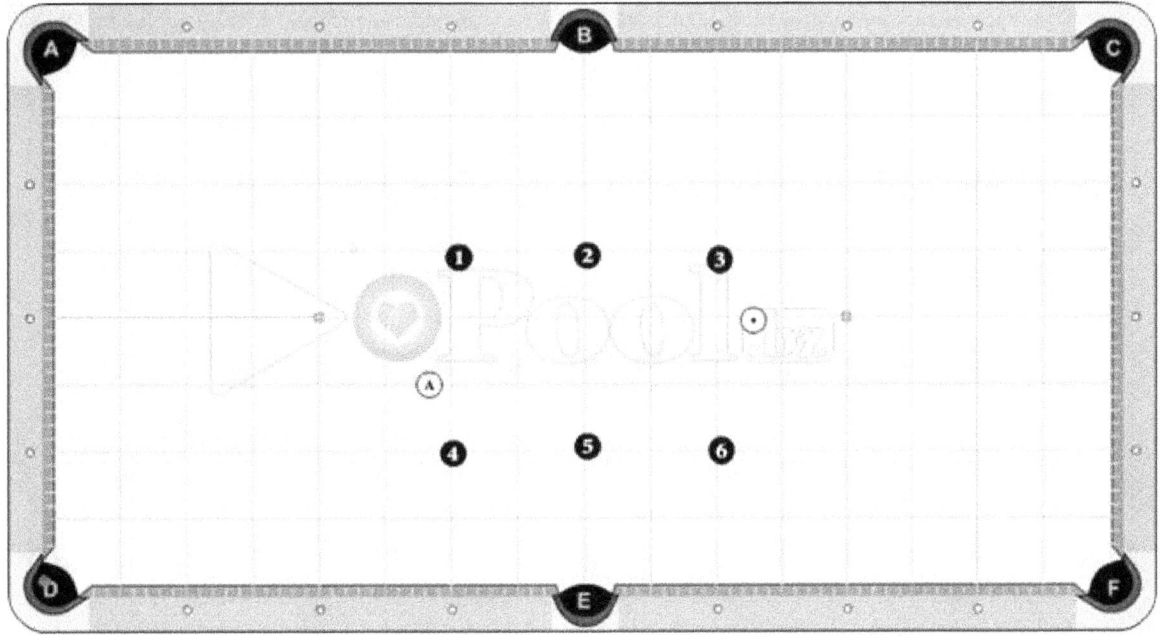

Set 3

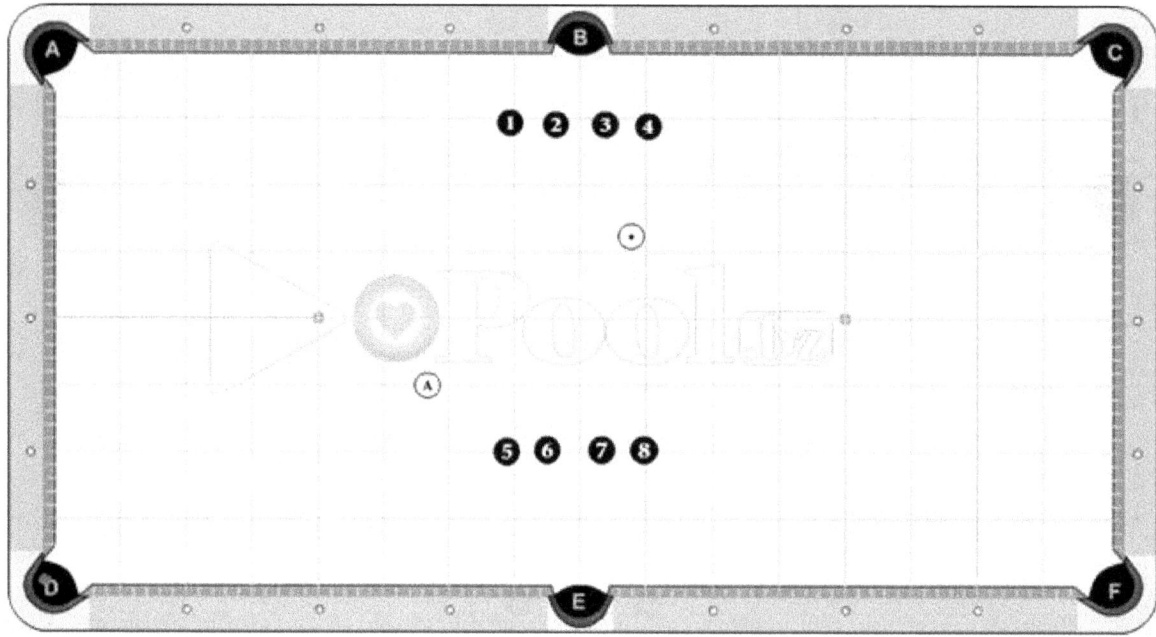

Set 4

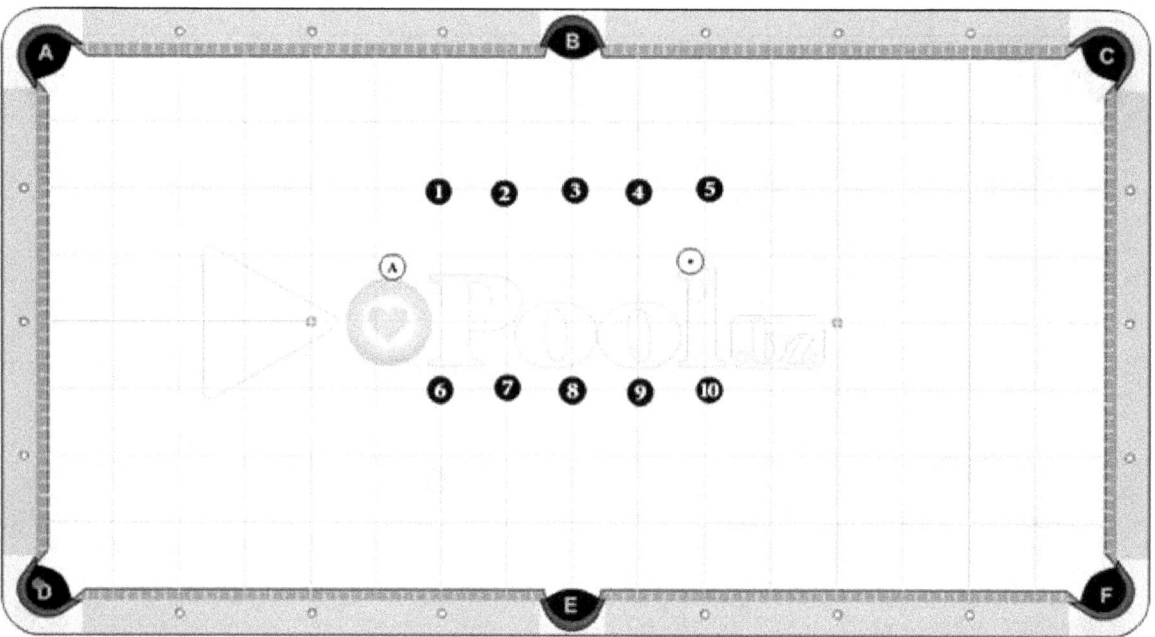

Side Pocket – Double Groups

Object: Pocket the balls. Chose any ball, one side first, sequential, reverse sequence.

Set 1

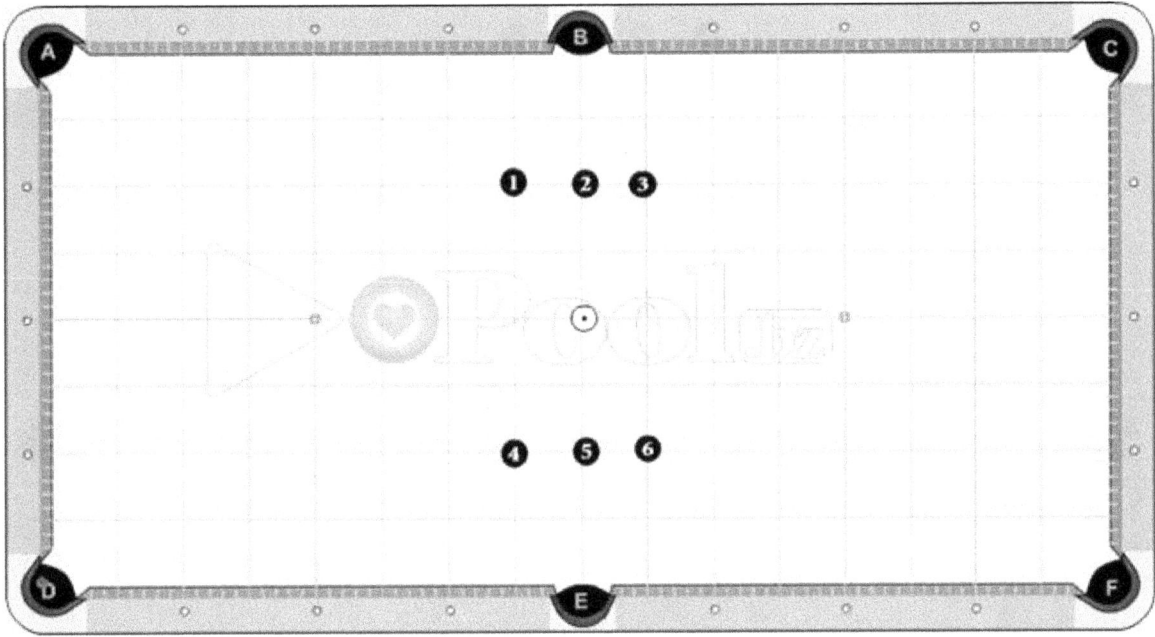

Set 2

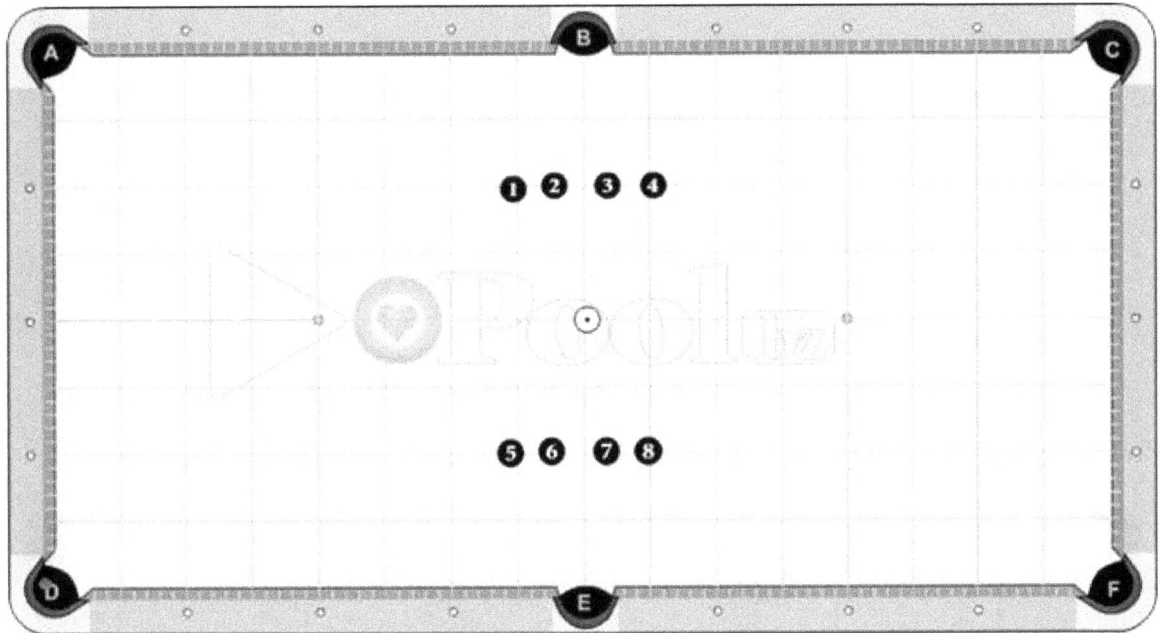

Set 3

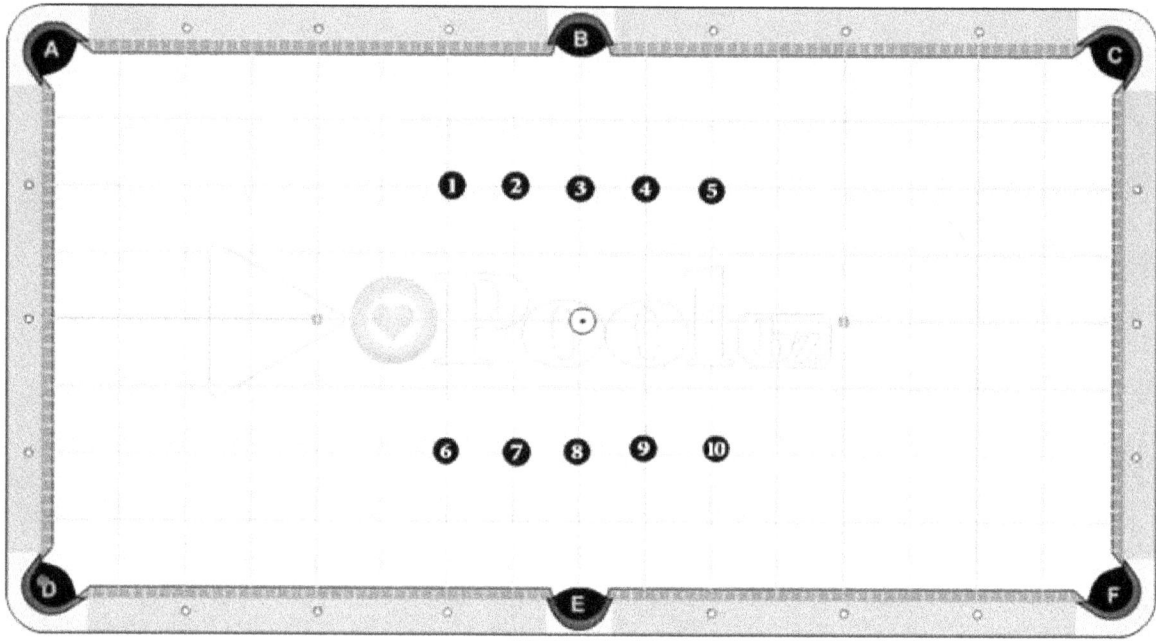

Set 4

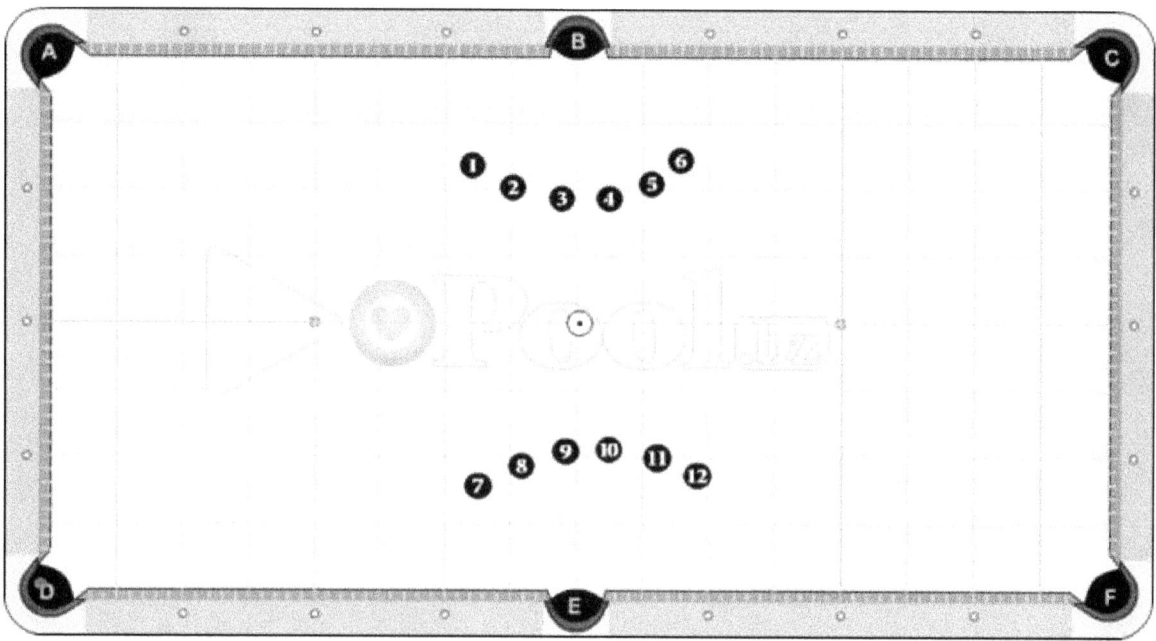

Double 3 Ball Groups #1

Object: Pocket the balls. Chose any ball, one side first, sequential, reverse sequence.

Set 1

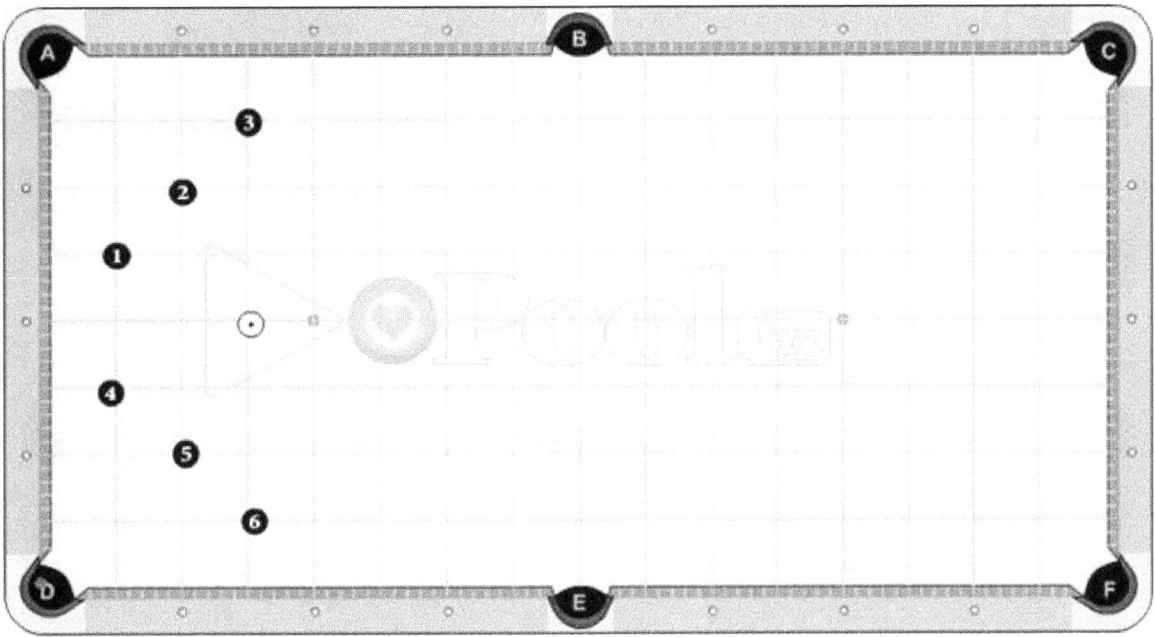

Set 2

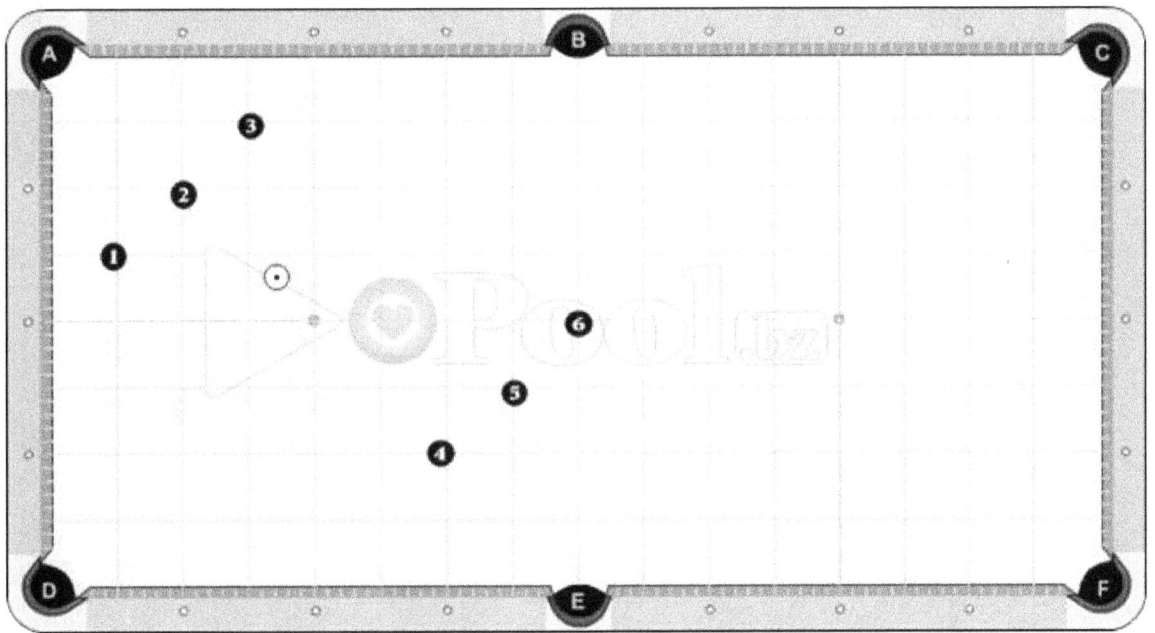

Set 3

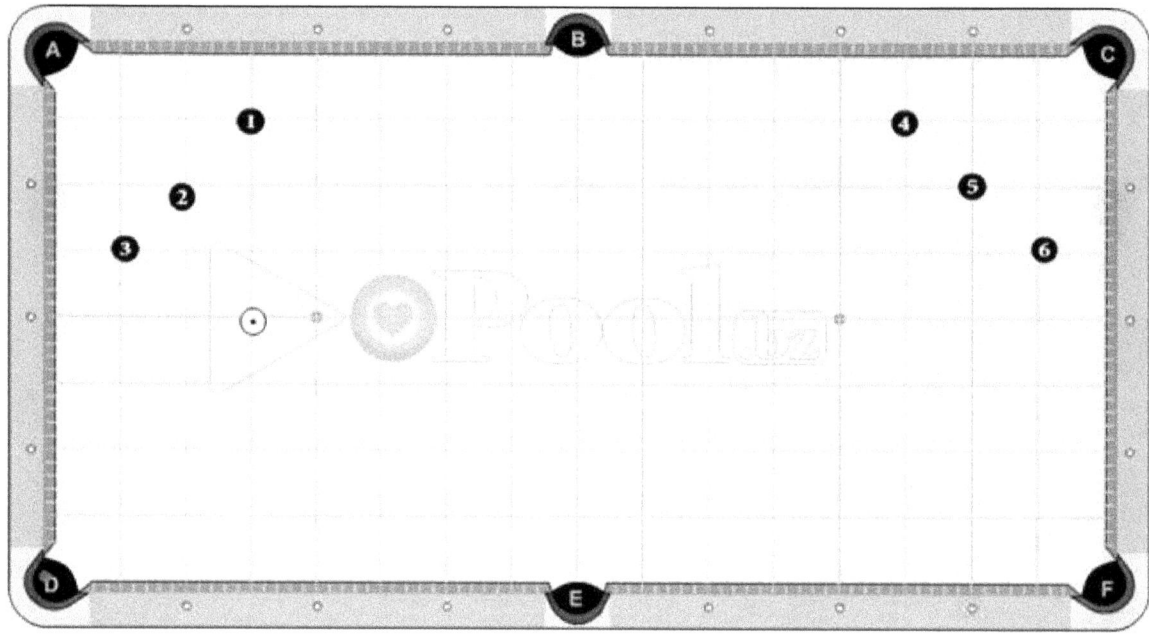

Set 4

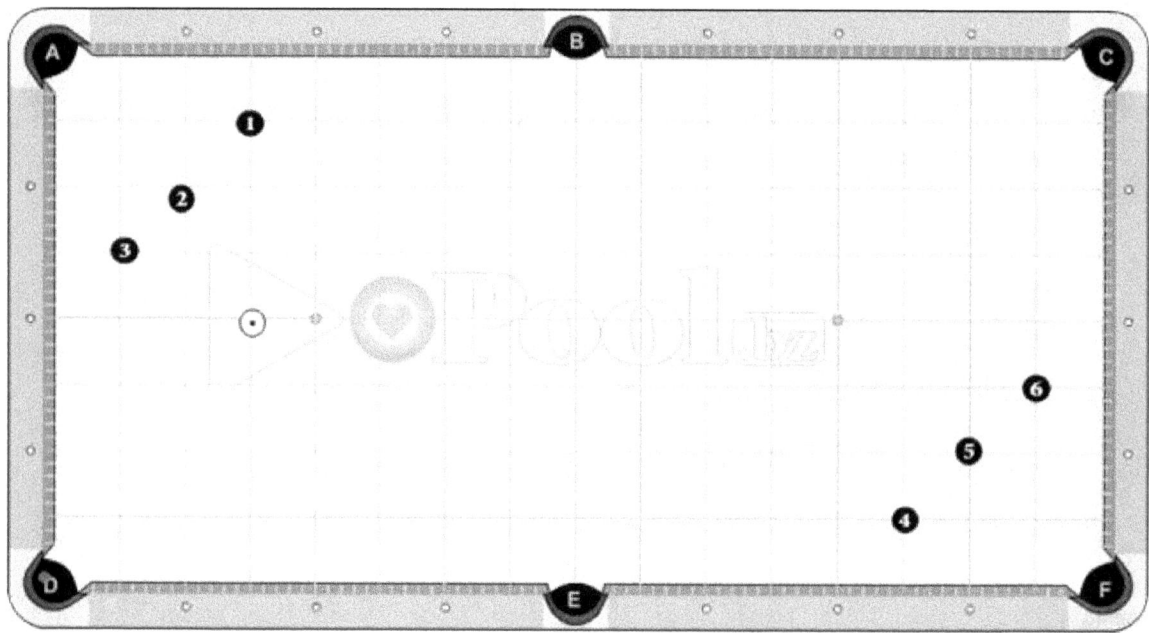

Double 3 Ball Groups #2

Object: Pocket the balls. Chose any ball, one side first, sequential, reverse sequence.

Set 1

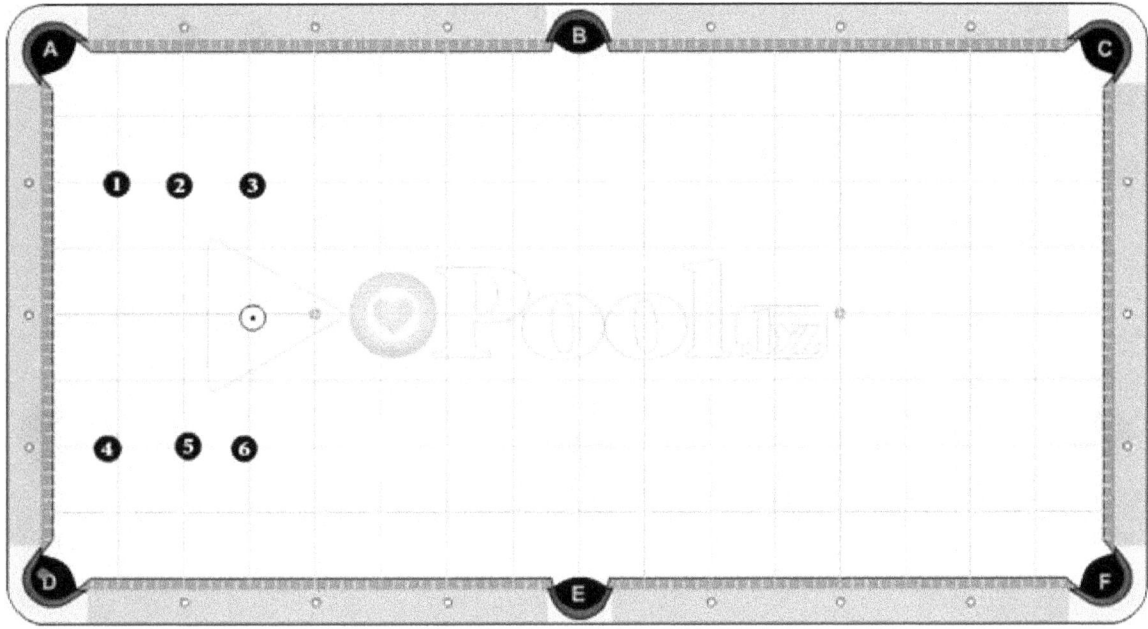

Set 2

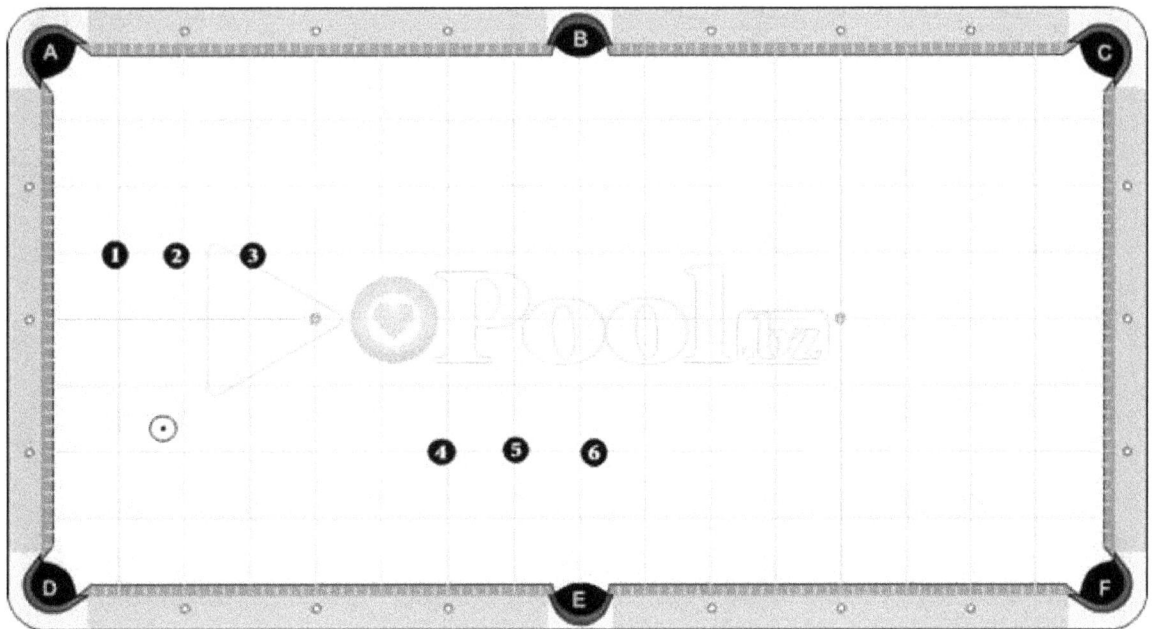

Set 3

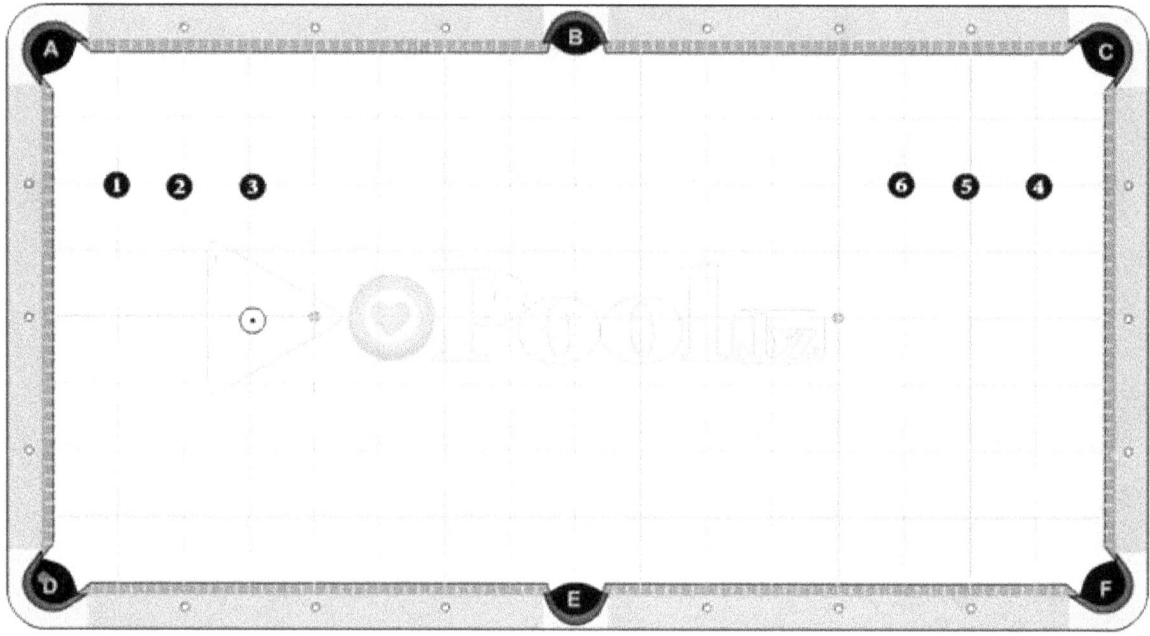

Set 4

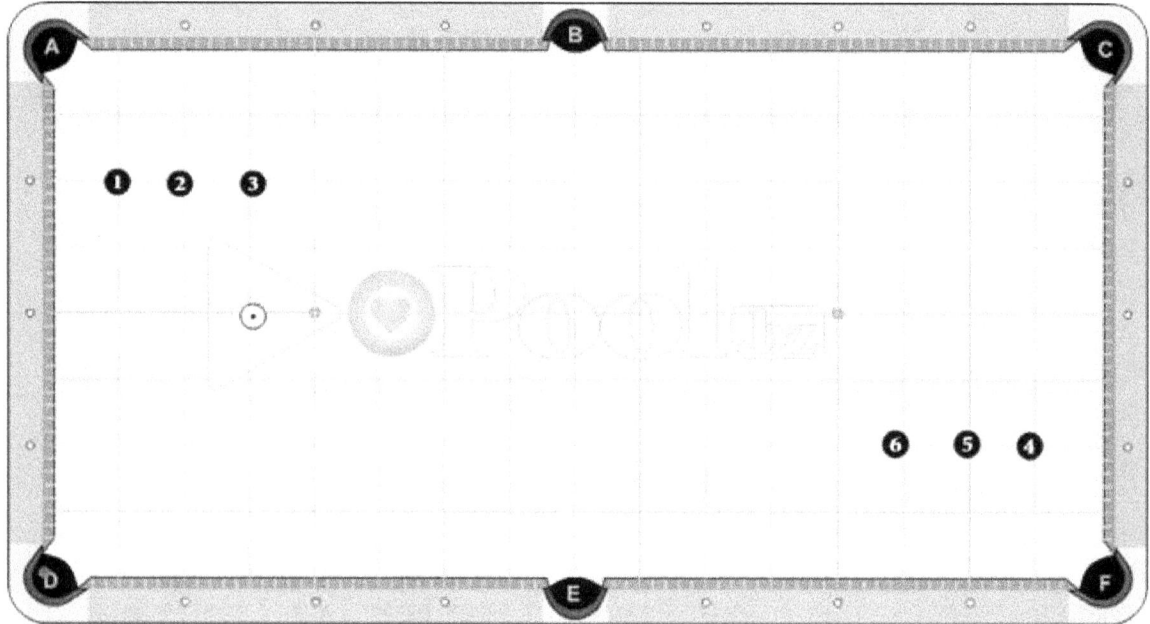

Double 3 Ball Groups #3

Object: Pocket the balls. Chose any ball, one side first, sequential, reverse sequence.

Set 1

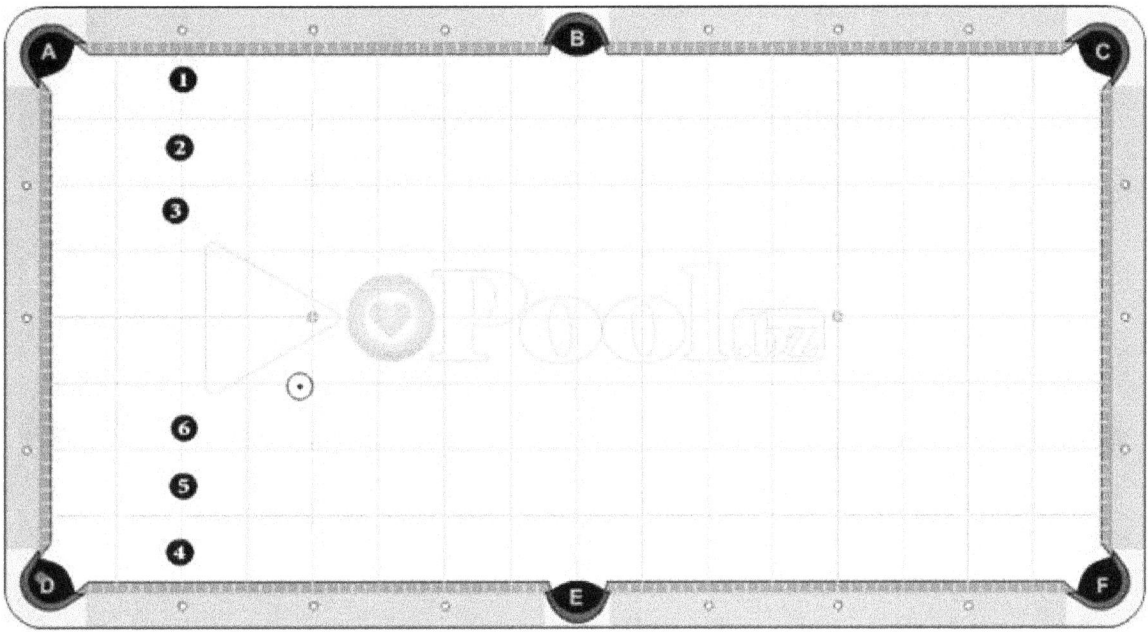

Set 2

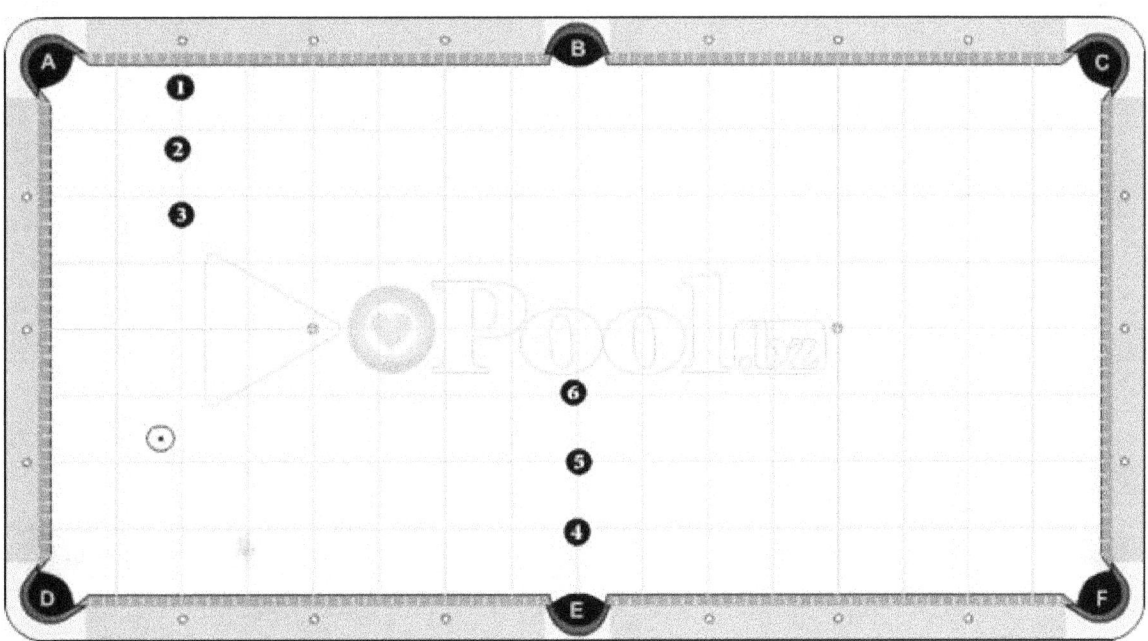

Set 3

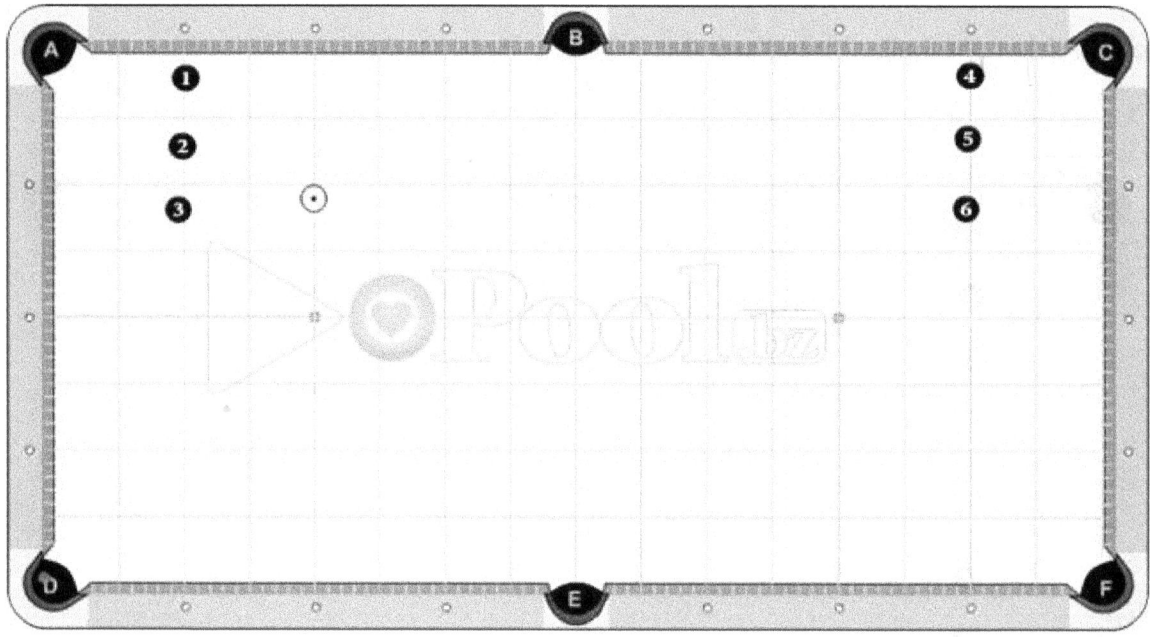

Set 4

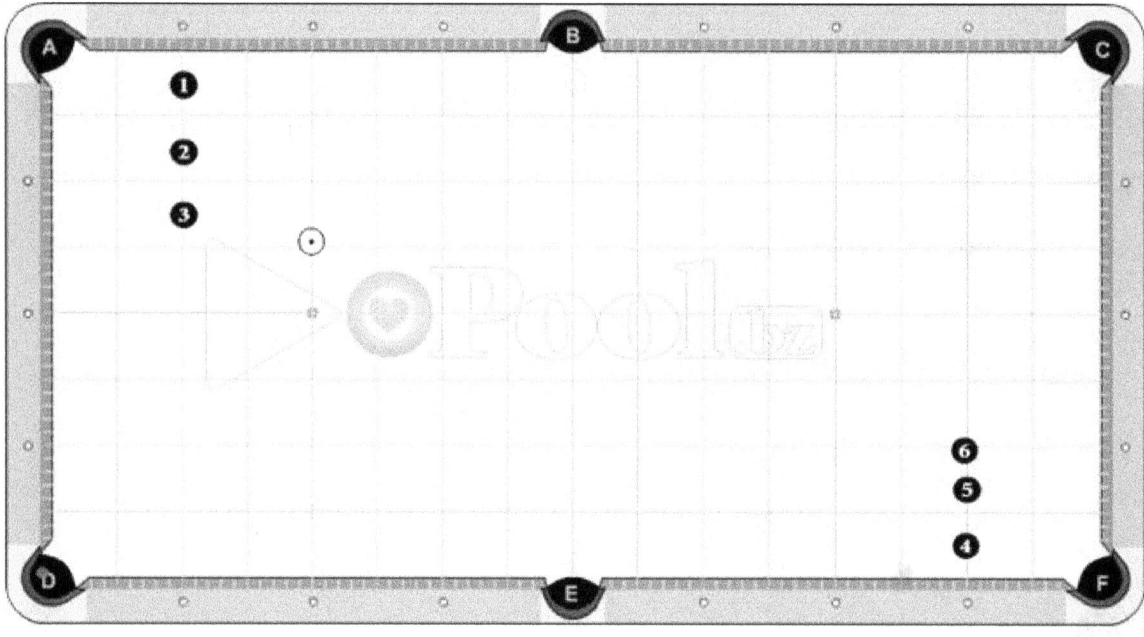

Around the Table

Single Ball Setups

Object: Pocket the balls. Chose any ball, round the table, in-sequence, reverse sequence.

Set 1

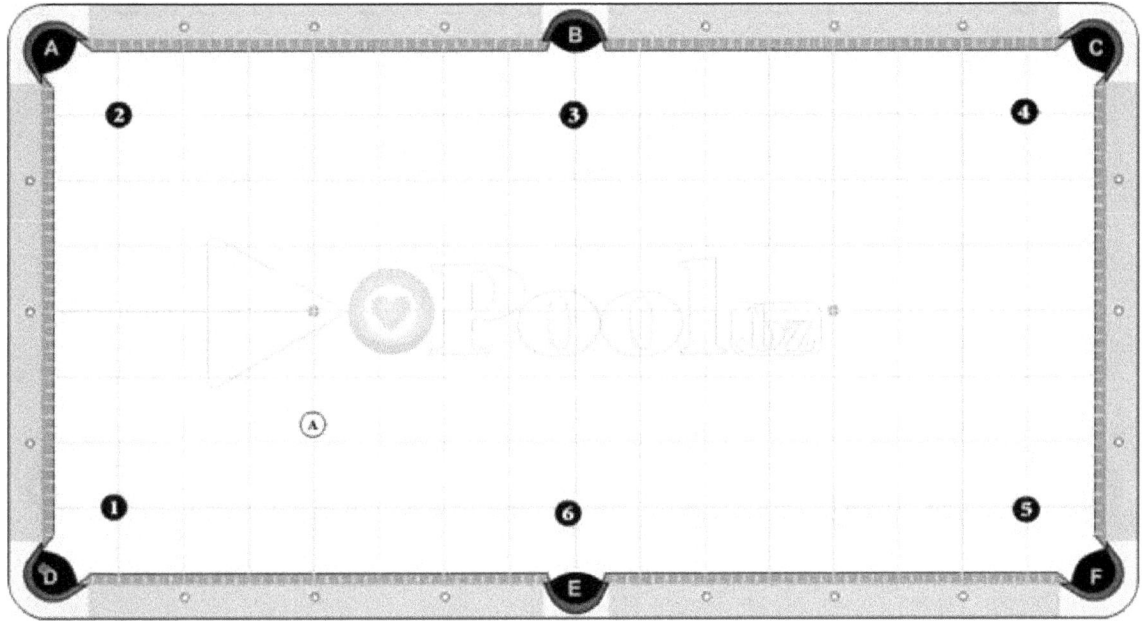

Set 2

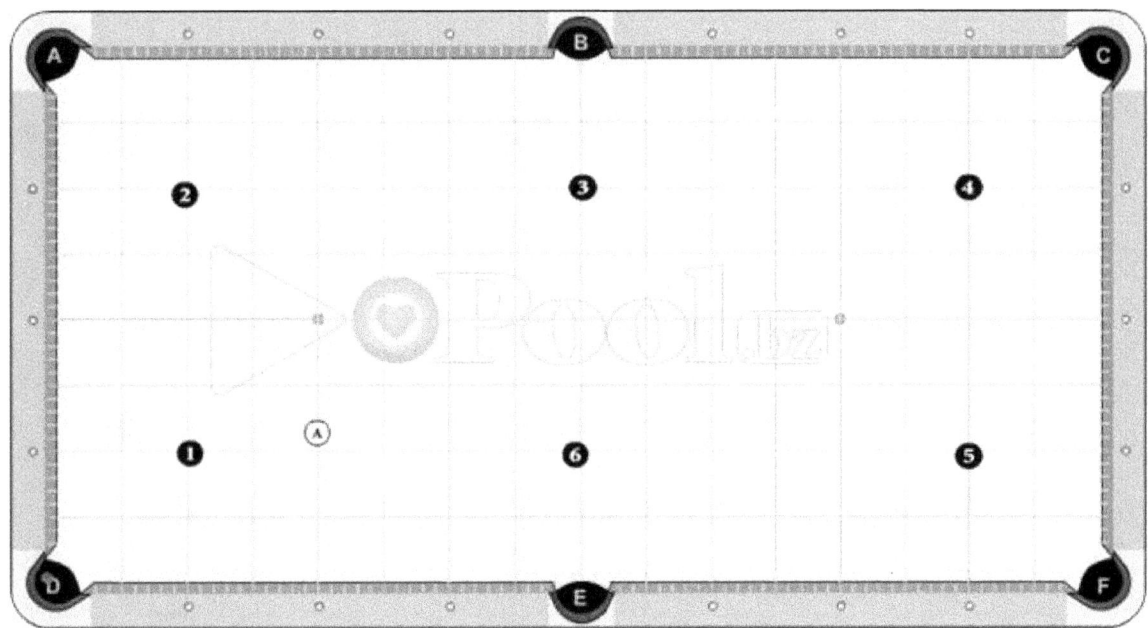

Double Ball Setups

Object: Pocket the balls. Chose any ball, round the table, in-sequence, reverse sequence.

Set 1

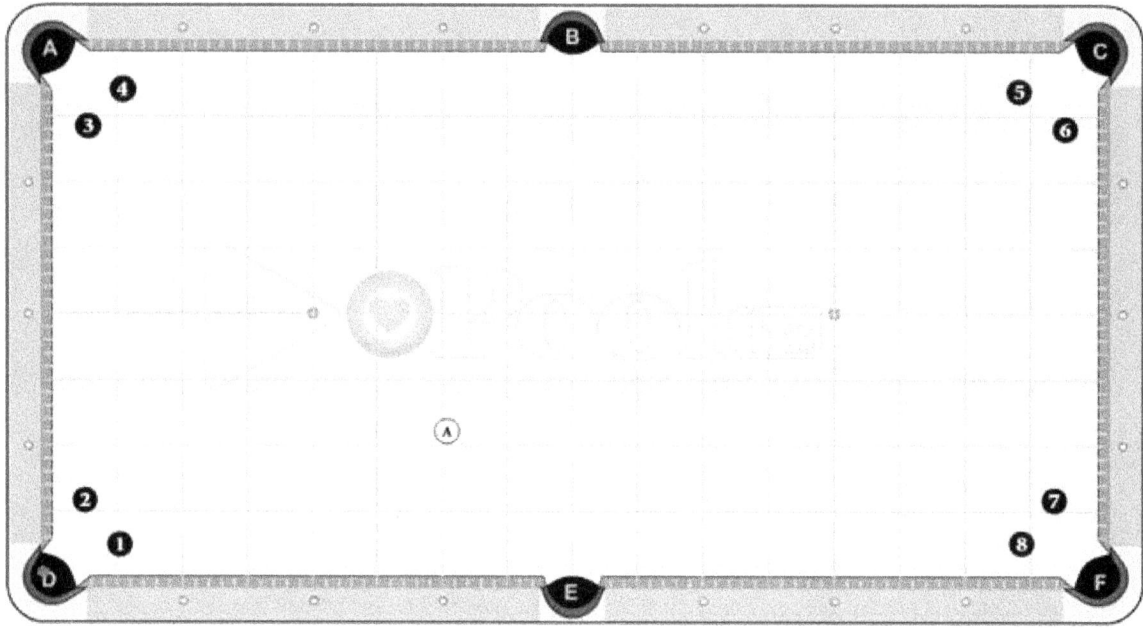

Set 2

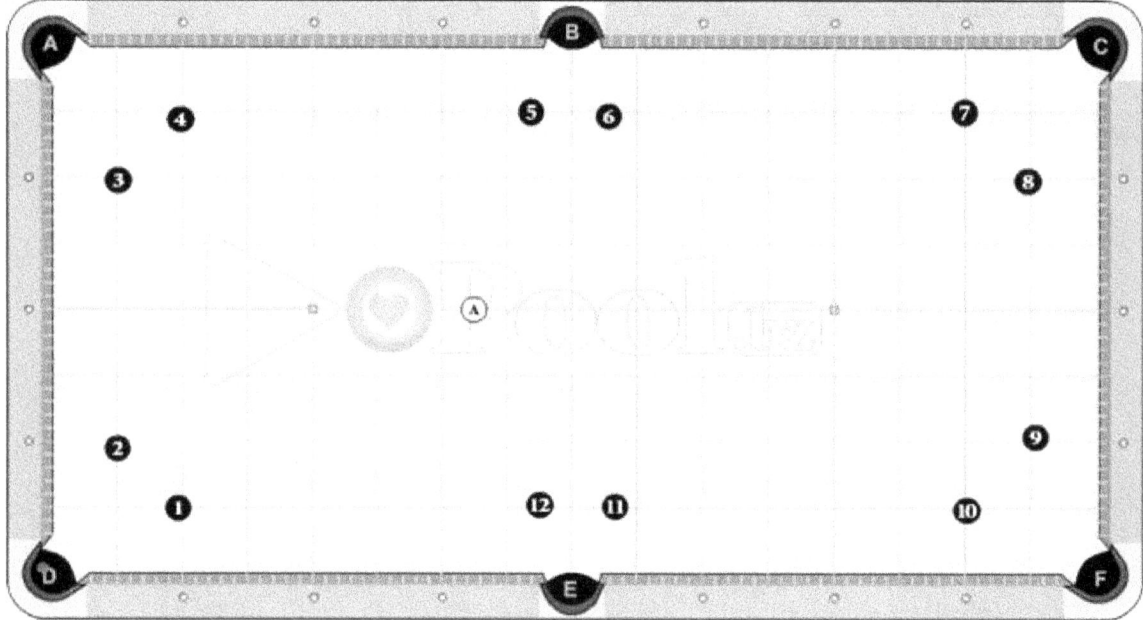

Set 3

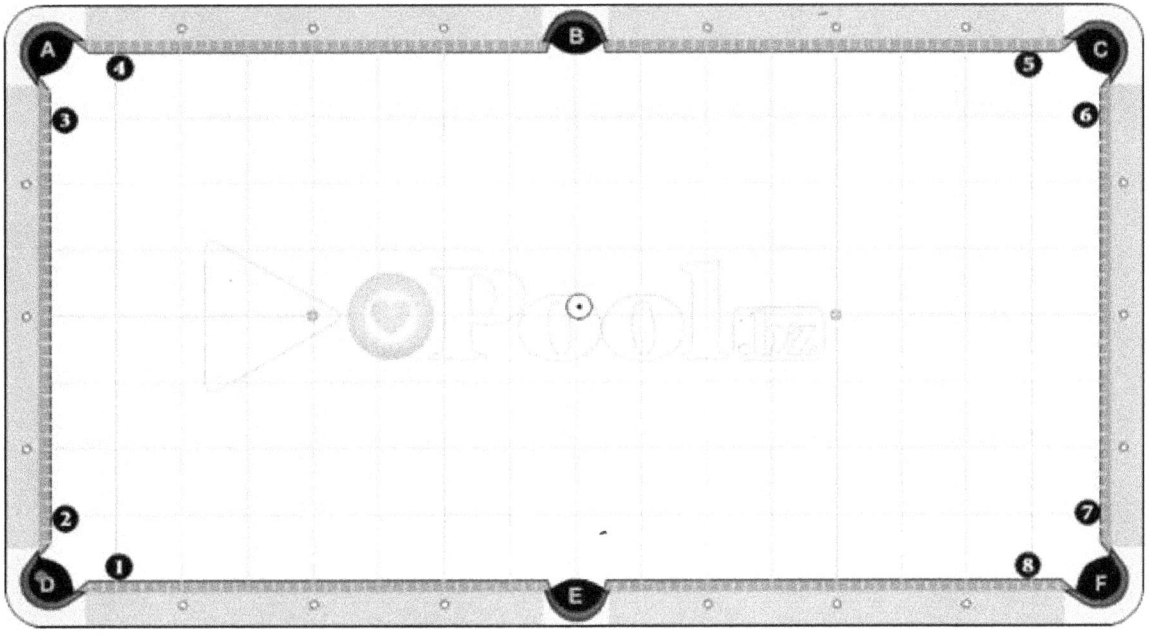

Set 4

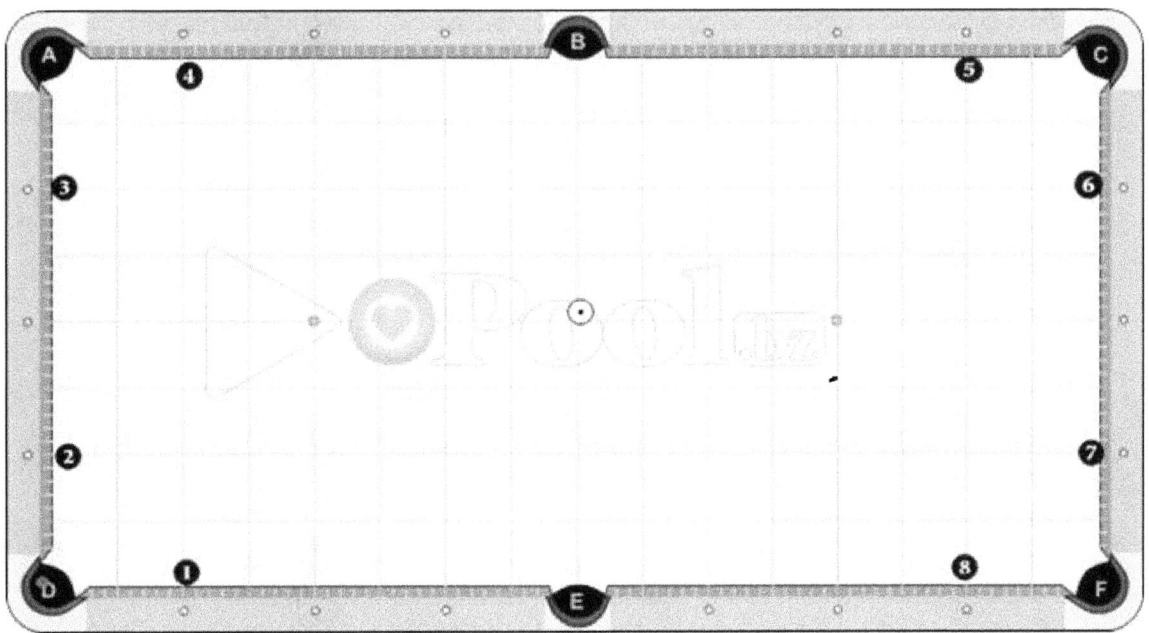

Set 5

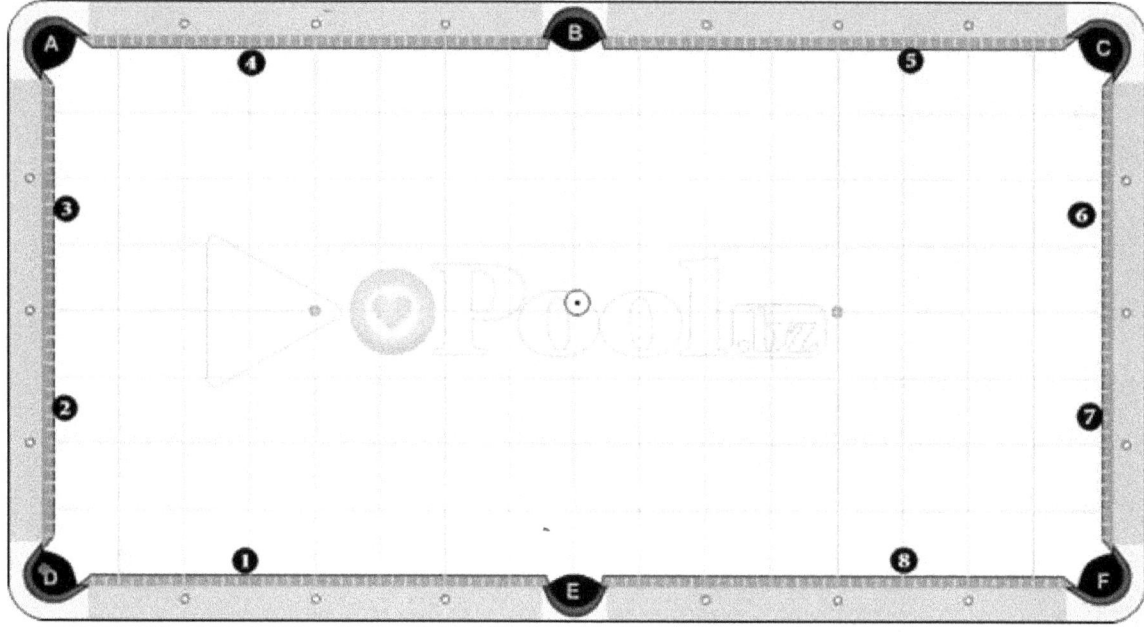

Set 6

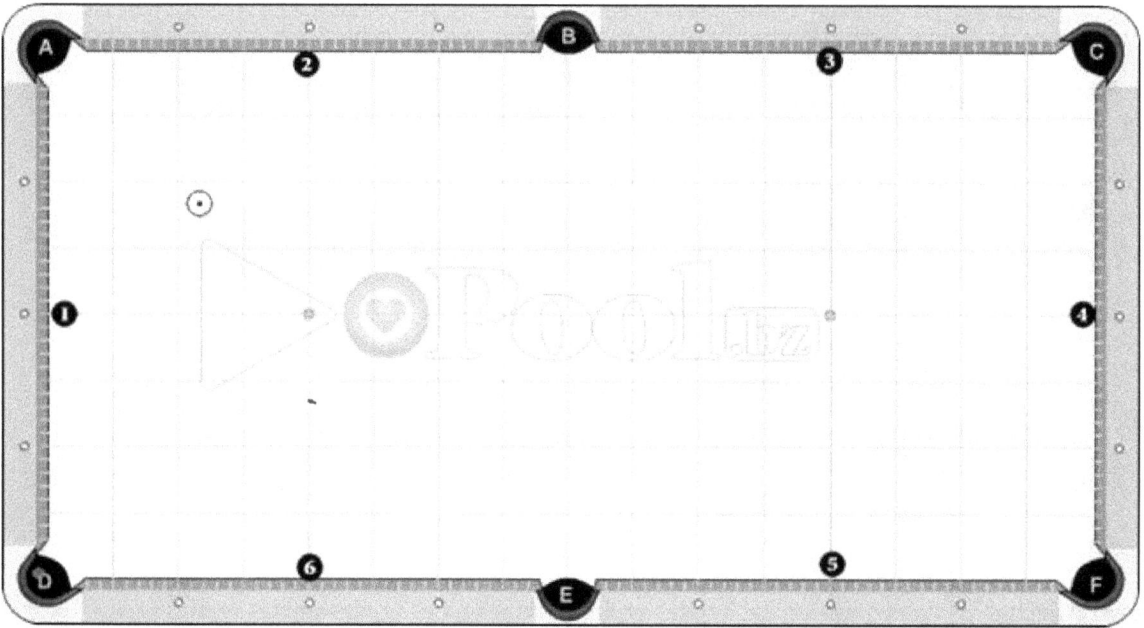

Inside Out

Circle

Object: Pocket the balls. Any sequence, in-sequence, reverse sequence. (Don't leave the center.)

Set 1

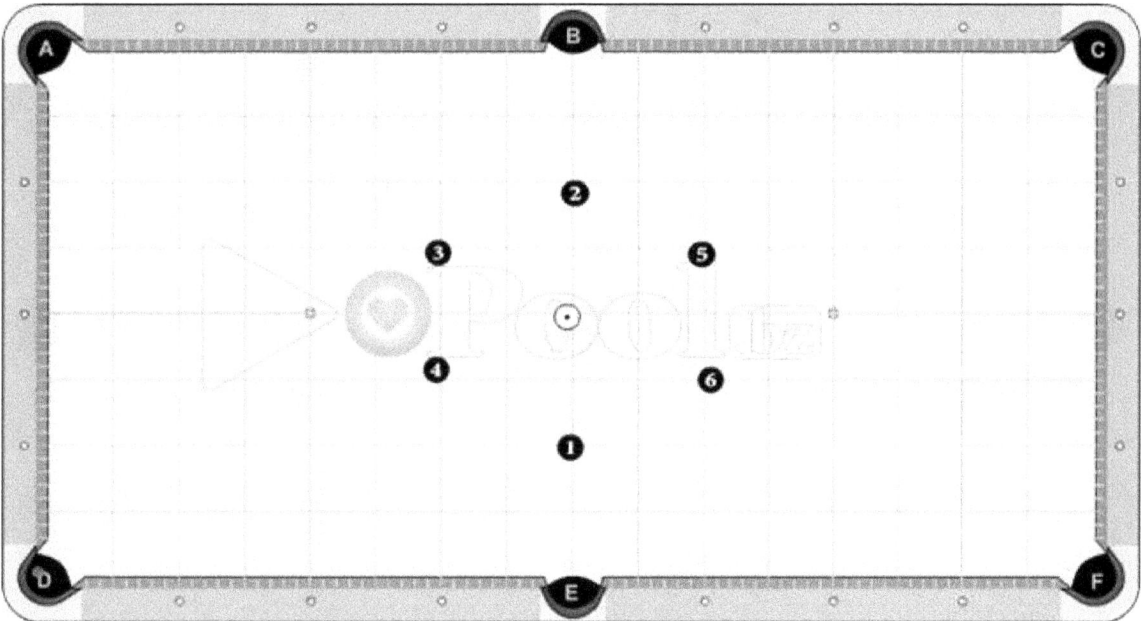

Set 2

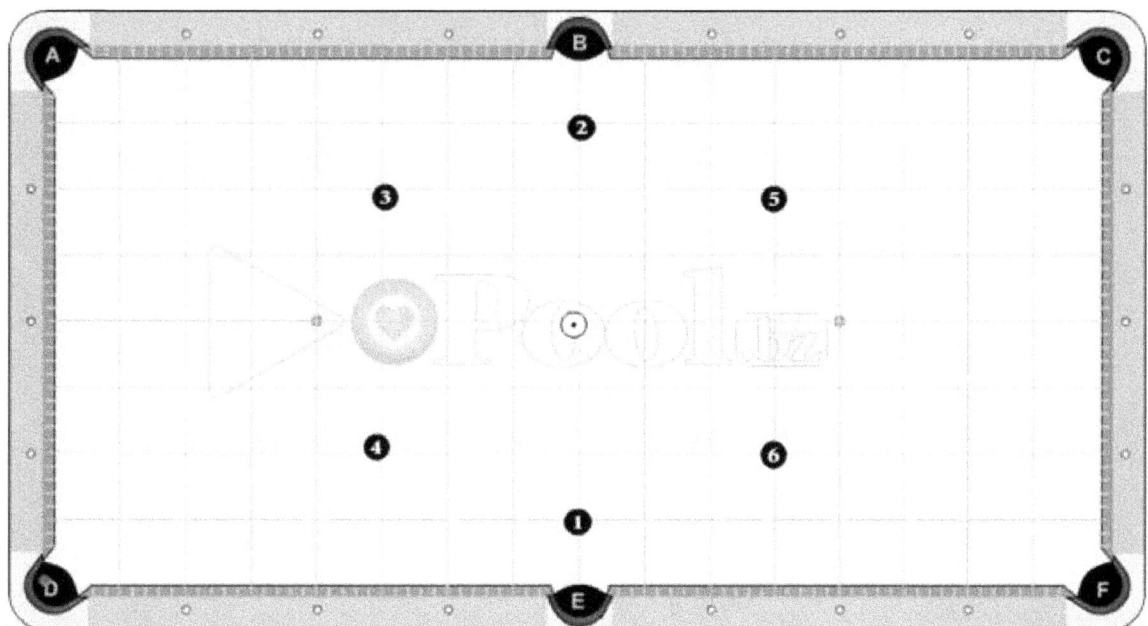

Set 3

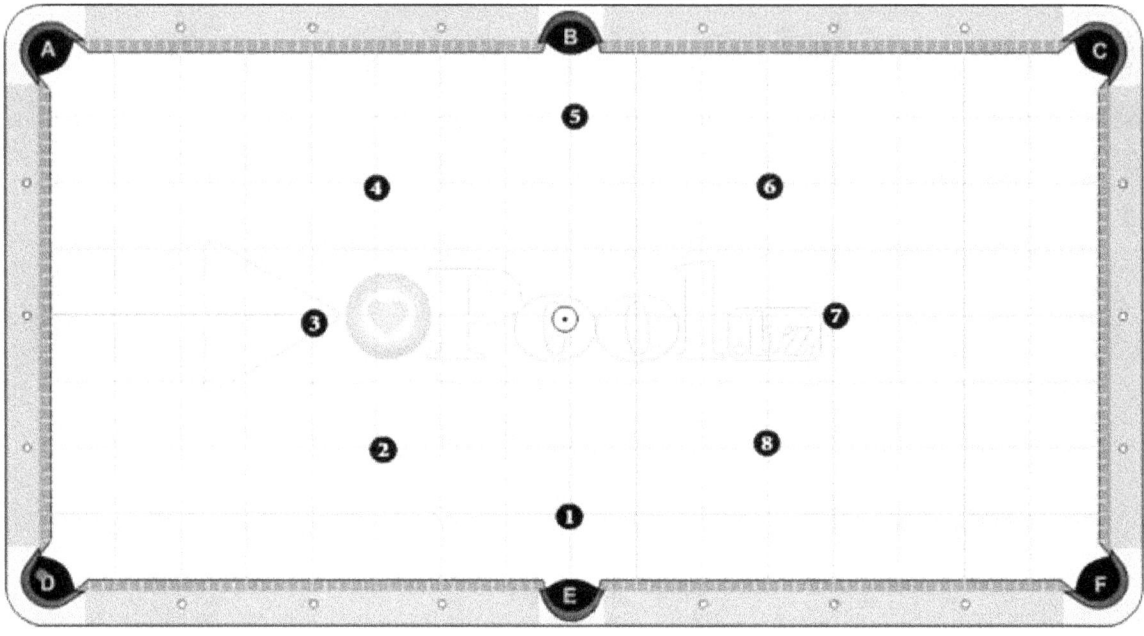

Set 4

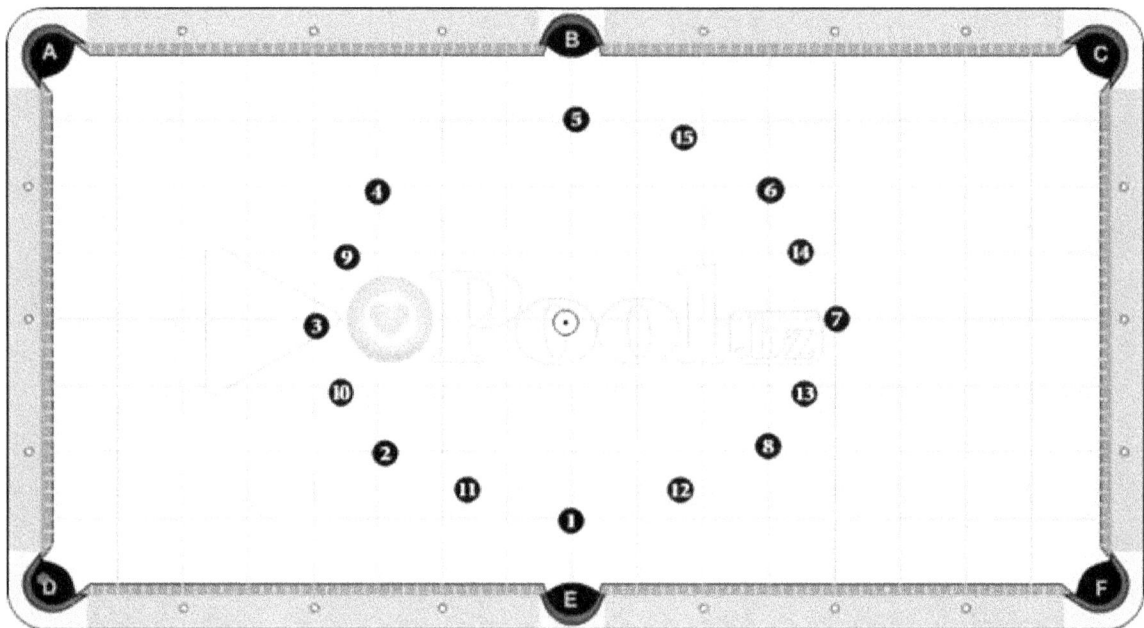

Box

Object: Pocket the balls. Any sequence, in-sequence, reverse sequence. (Don't leave the center.)

Set 1

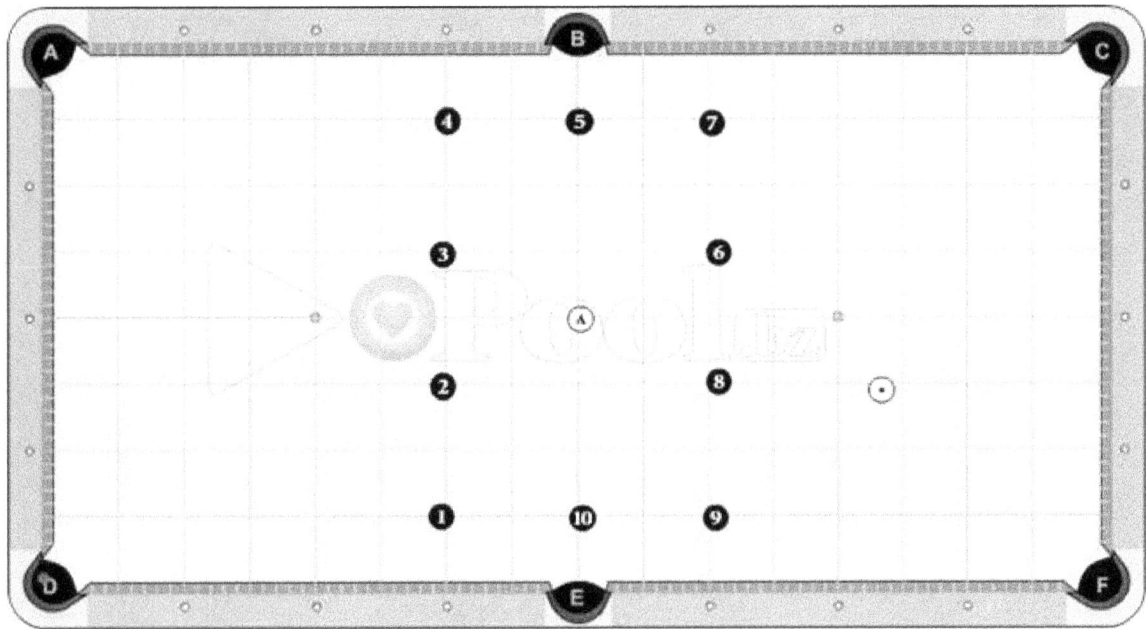

Set 2

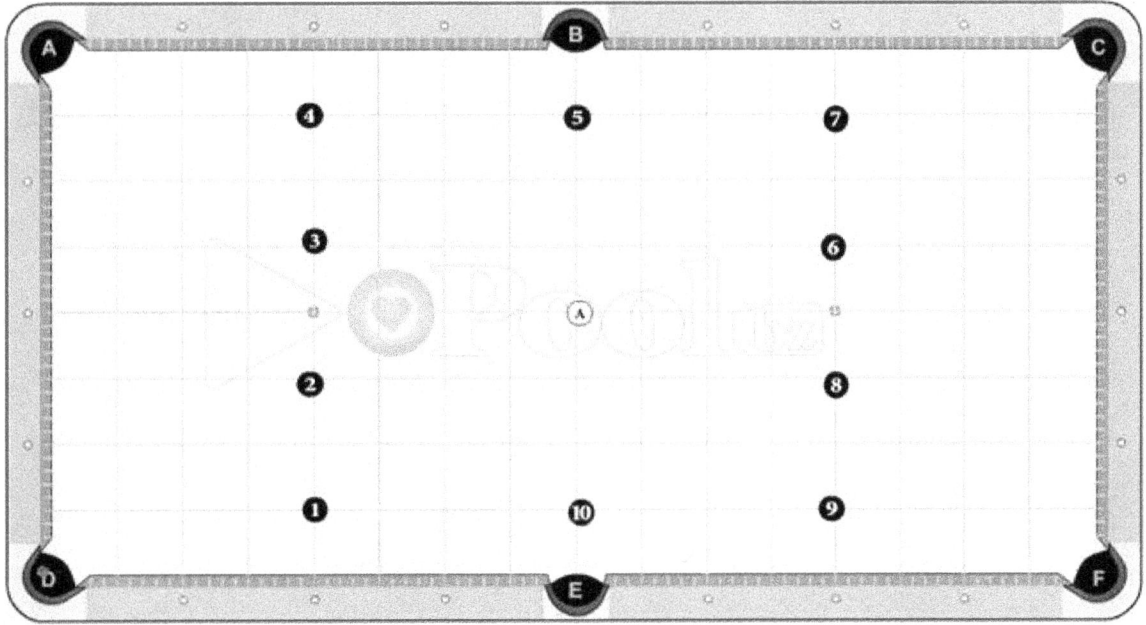

"V" Setups

Object: Pocket the balls. Any sequence, in-sequence, reverse sequence. Stay inside the "V" or outside the "V".

Set 1

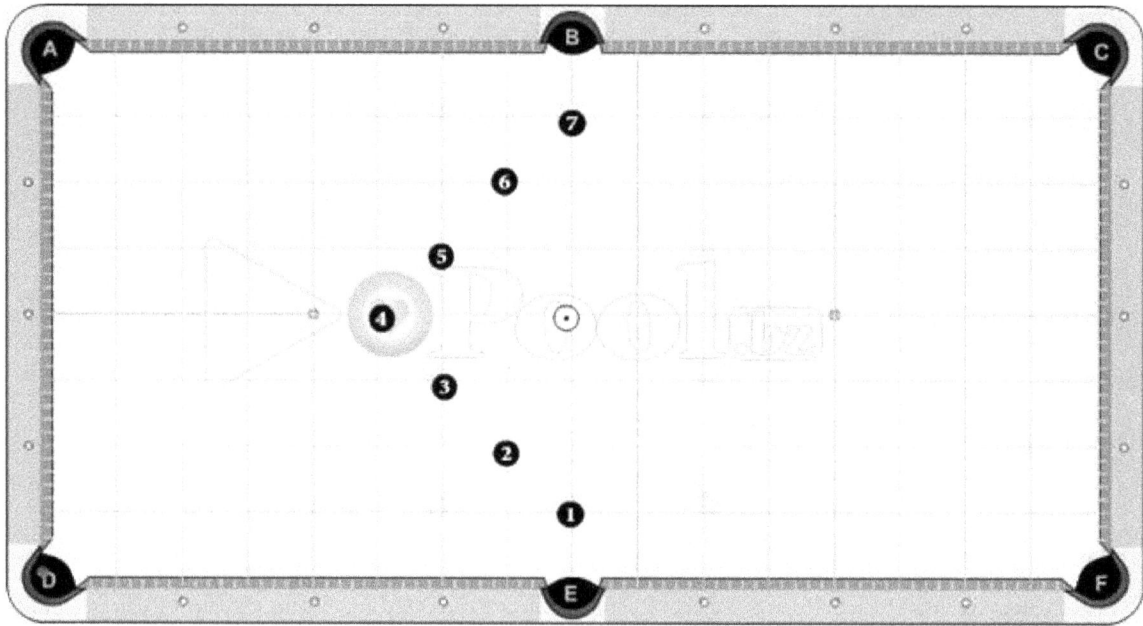

Set 2

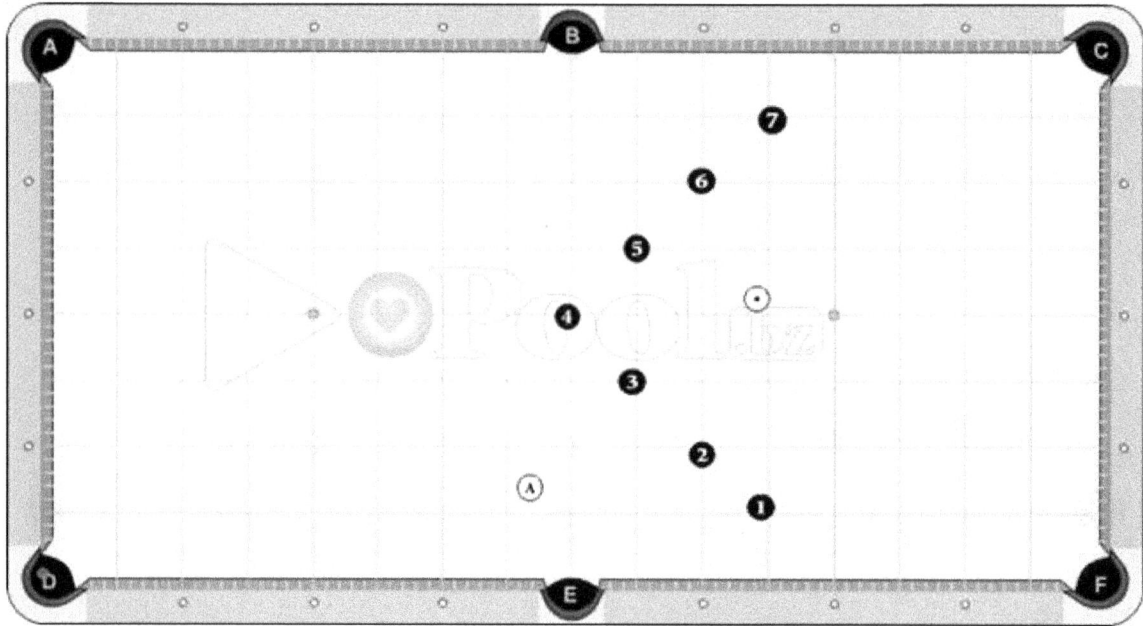

Set 3

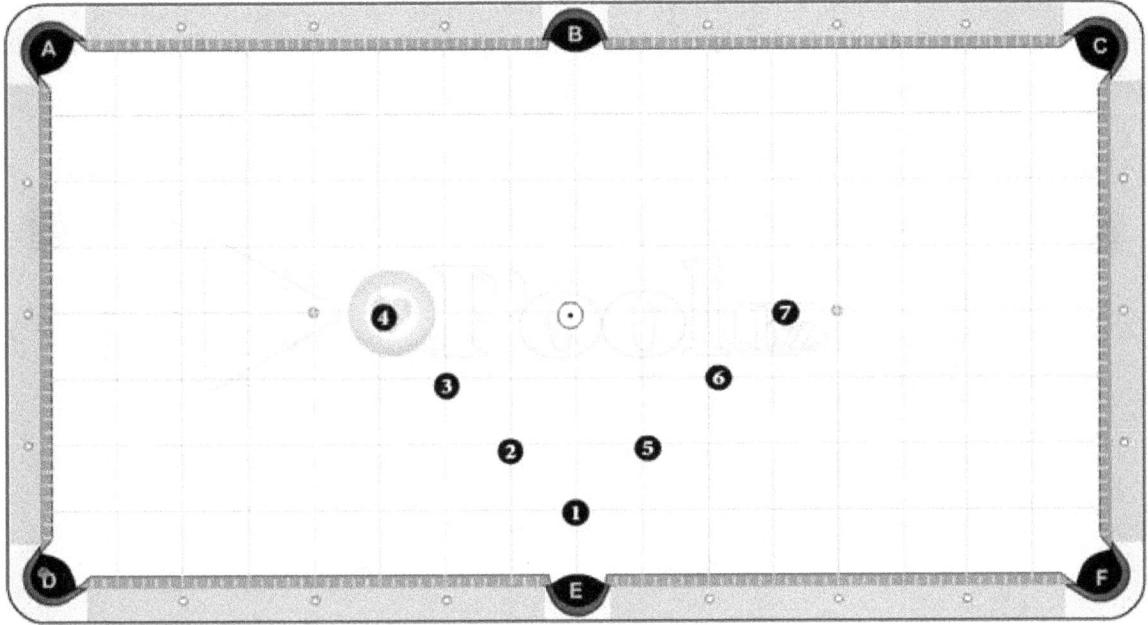

Set 4

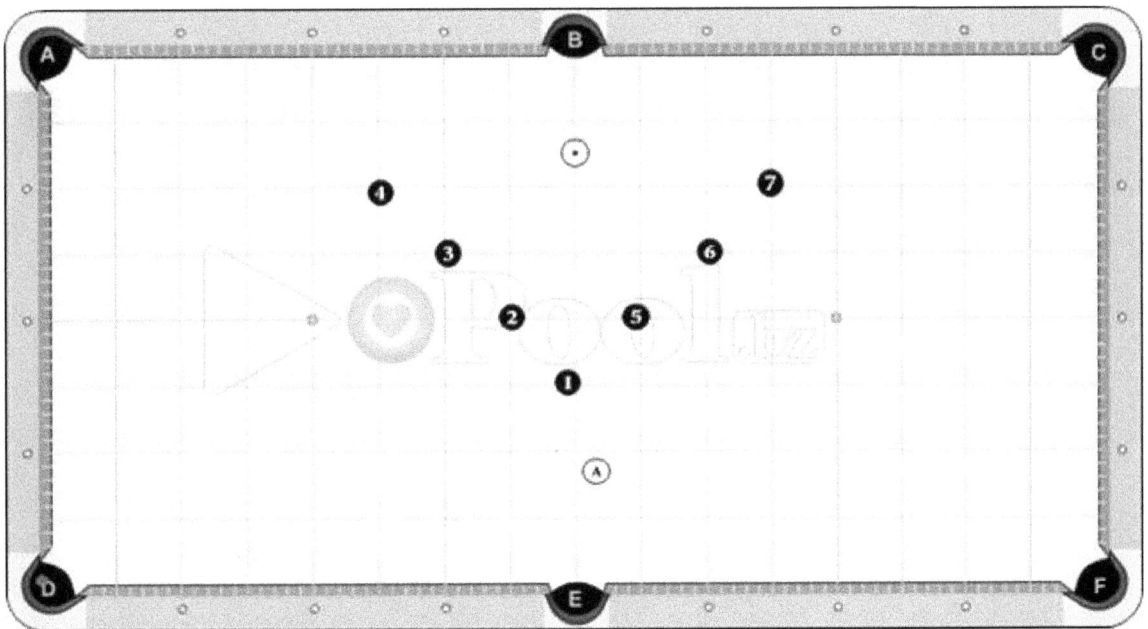

Long Line Setups

Object: Pocket the balls. Any sequence, in-sequence, reverse sequence. Stay on one side of the line.

Set 1

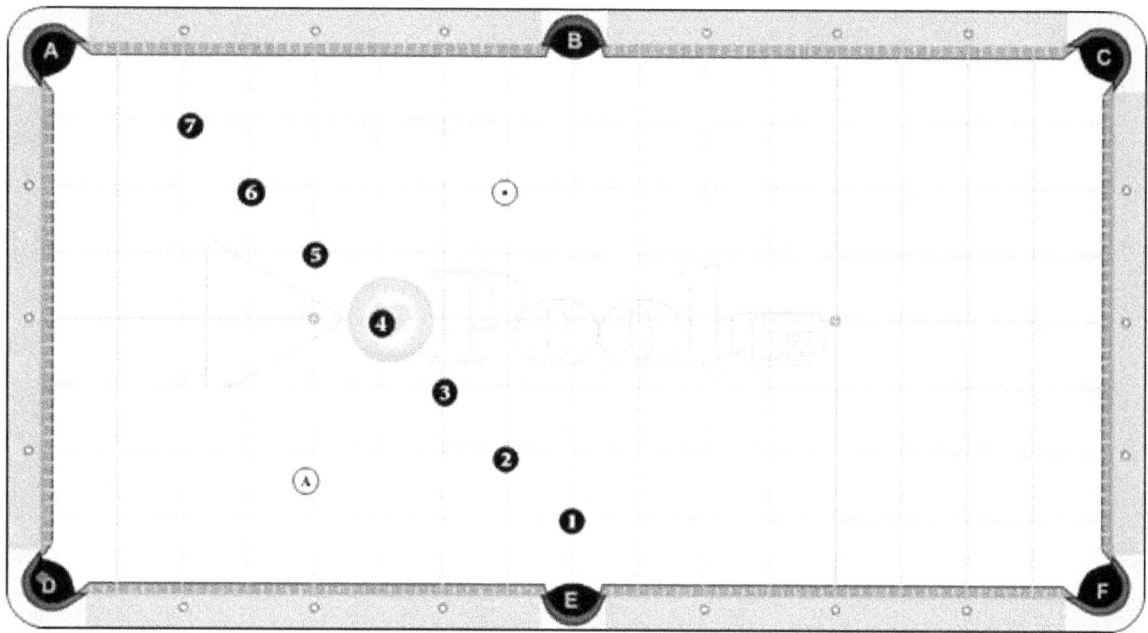

Set 2

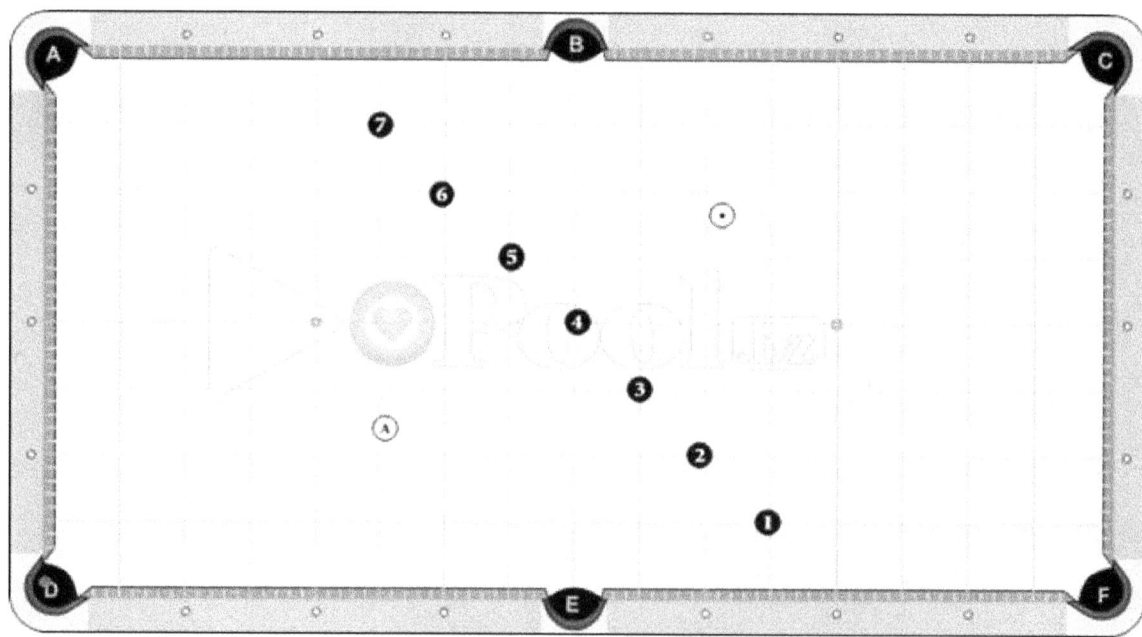

Set 3

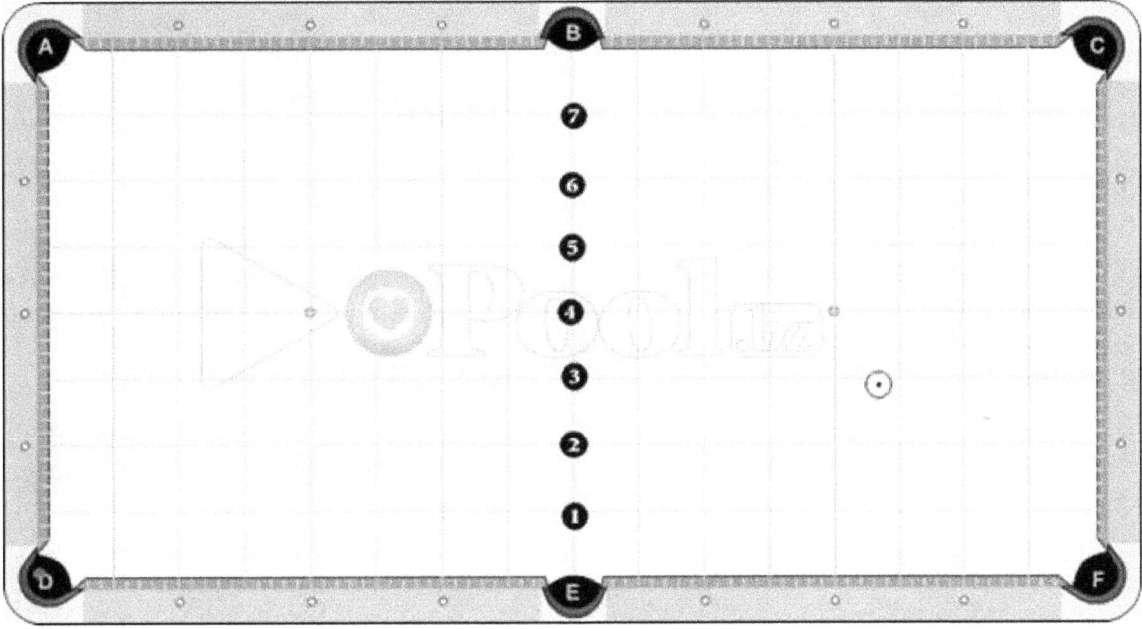

Set 4

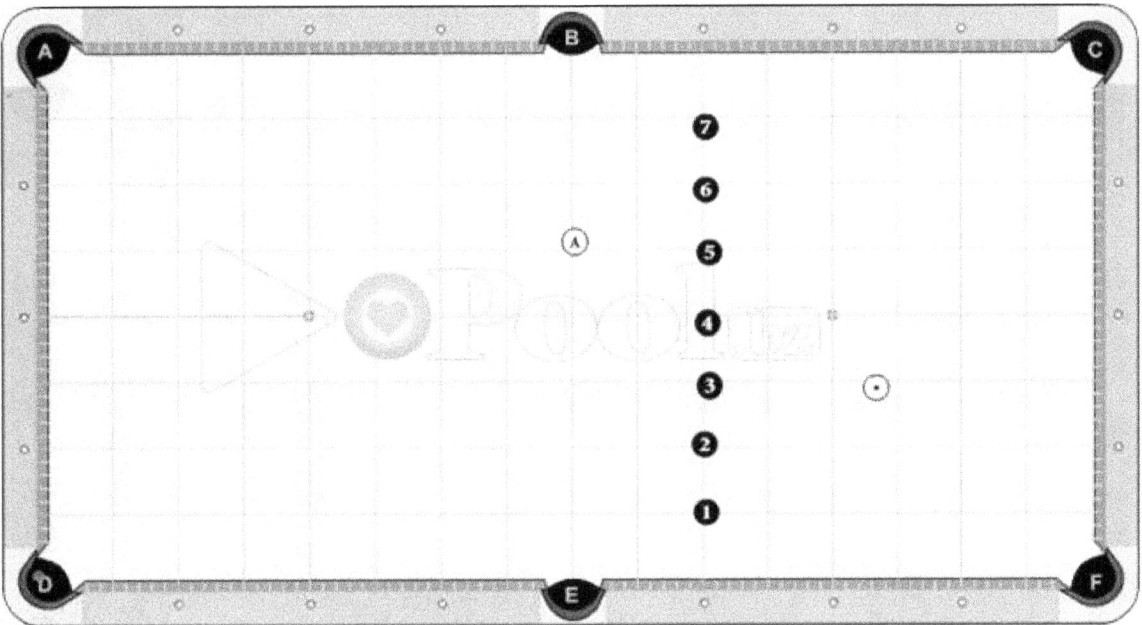

Banking

All of the banking exercises and drills shown here are one rail only.

Multi-rail Banks: There are simply too many variables to consider when calculating two, three, and more rail banks. This unpredictable variety means that multi-rail banks can never be trustworthy (85-100%). At best, with extensive table experience, a successful percentage can be reached of 35-50 percent success.

Most players consider themselves lucky to get 25-35% success on banks. Even for these exercises and drills, if you can achieve 50-65 percent success you are getting pretty good. These banking exercises are designed to increase your success percentage to 50-75 percent.

Experiment around with these shots so that you know the furthest angle from the CB into the OB that gets the OB into the pocket. Pay attention to each shot and make adjustments until your experience is enough to consistently make the bank shot.

Cross Corner Banks

Each of these positions must be mastered using the 26 primary 36 CB shots from the **CB Speed/Spin Matrix**. Some of the CB spins will "throw" the object ball and you must know when and how much reaction you get off the OB.

On Rail Banks

Object: Place CB on grey line. Bank OB into corner pocket.

Set 1

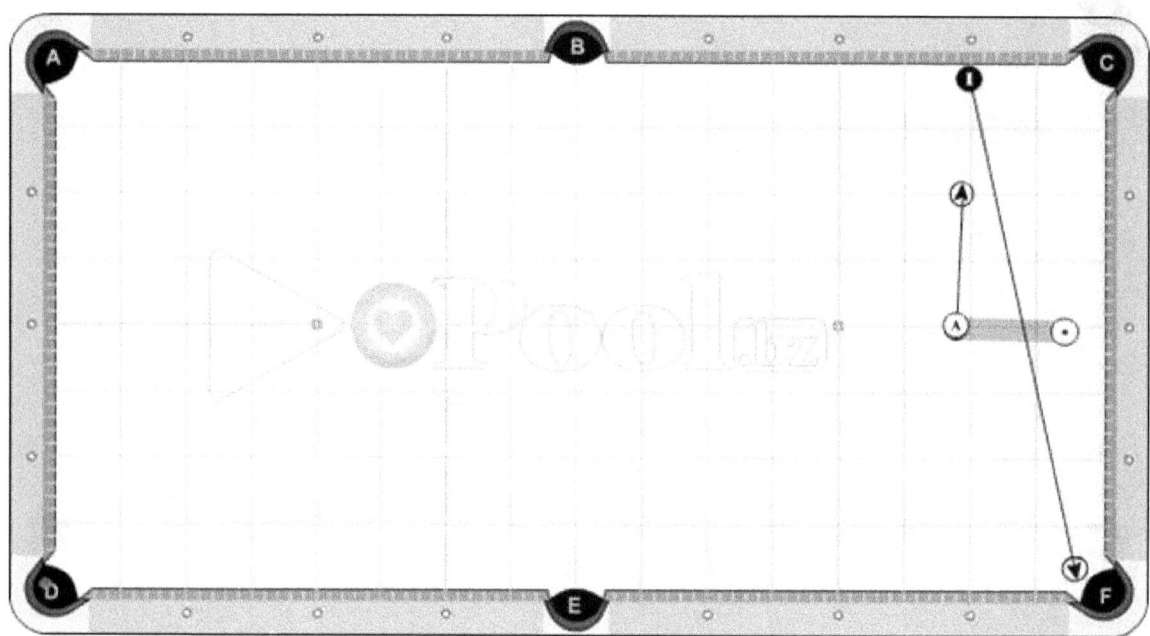

Set 2

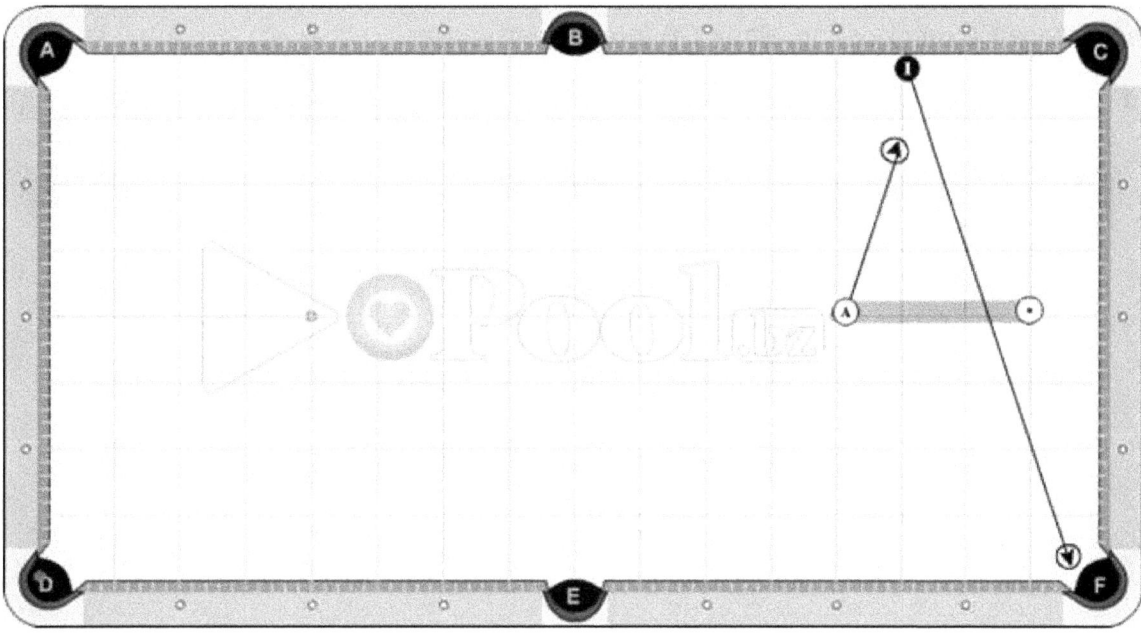

Set 3

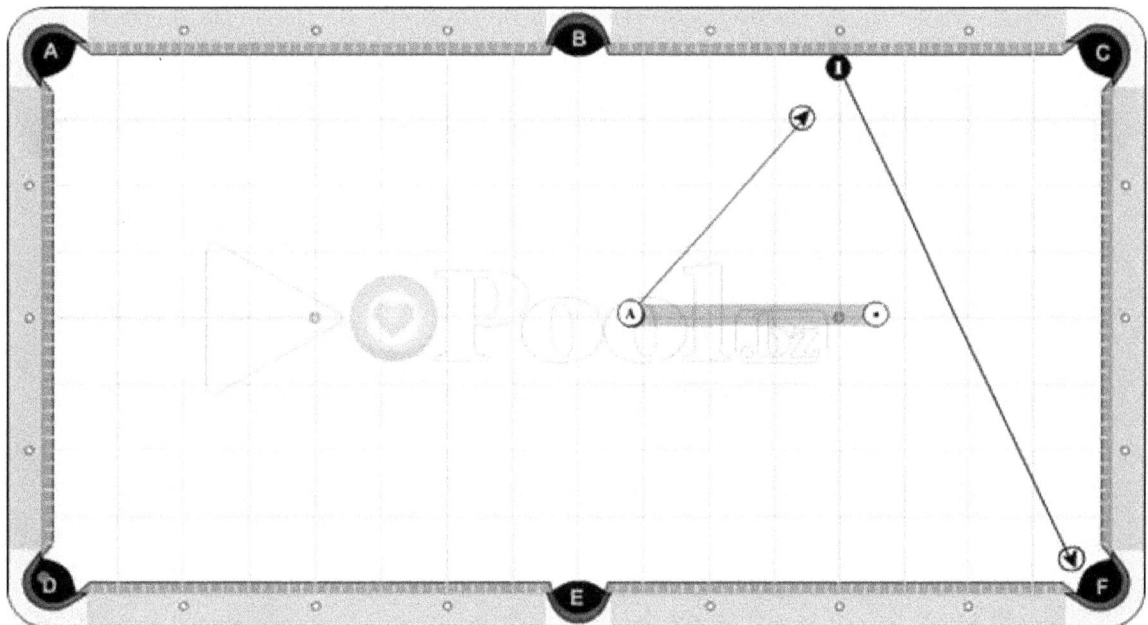

Near Rail Banks

Object: Place CB on grey line. Bank OB into corner pocket.

Set 1

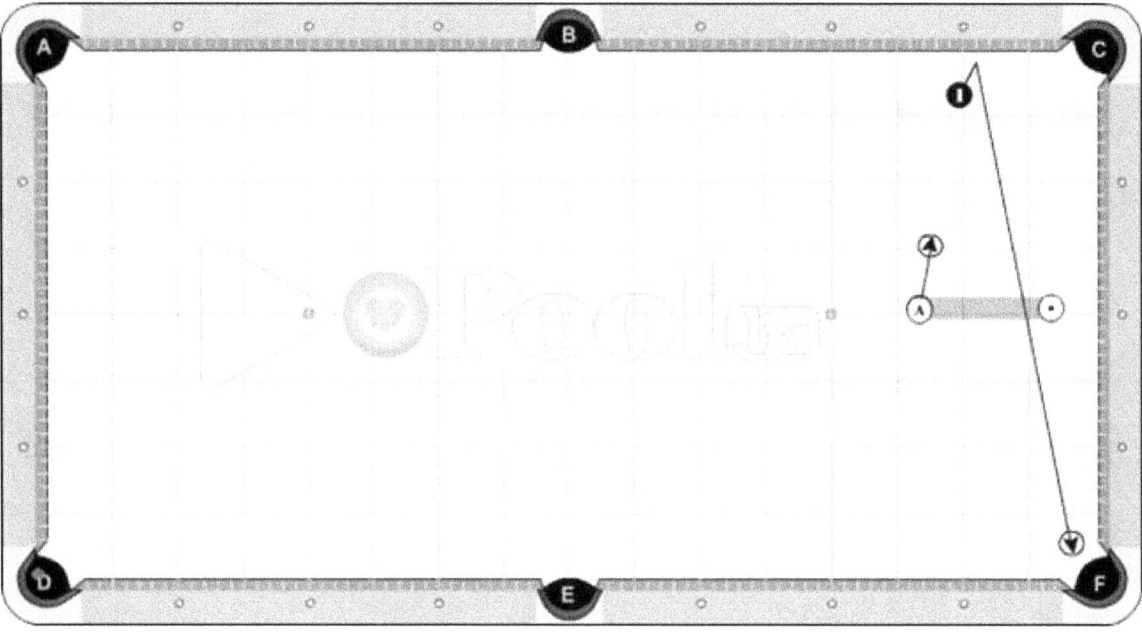

Set 2

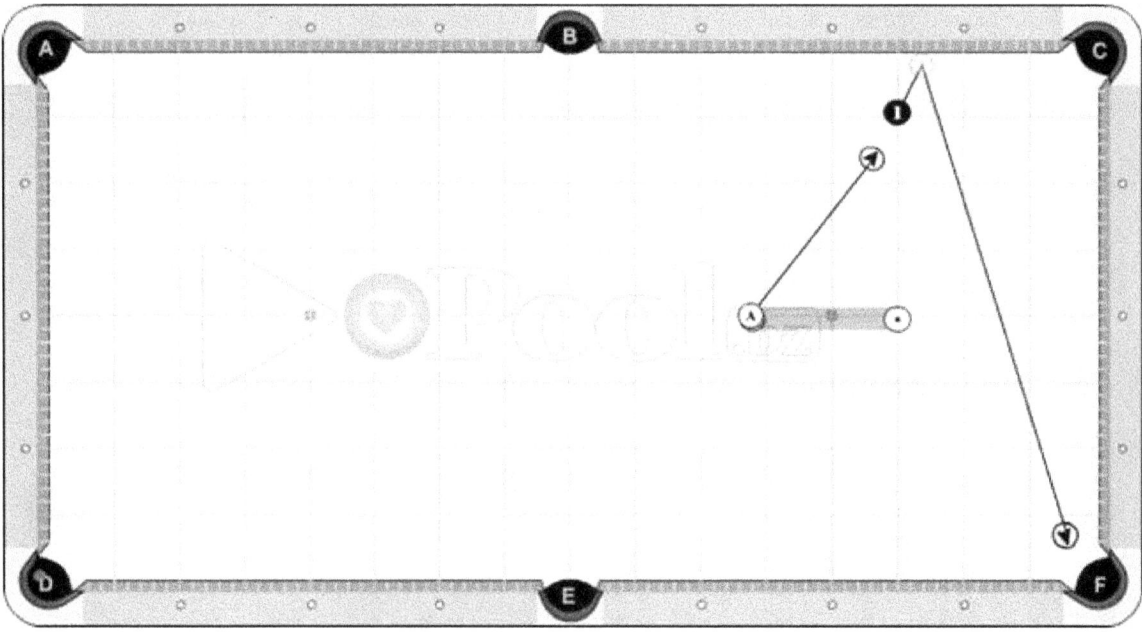

Set 3

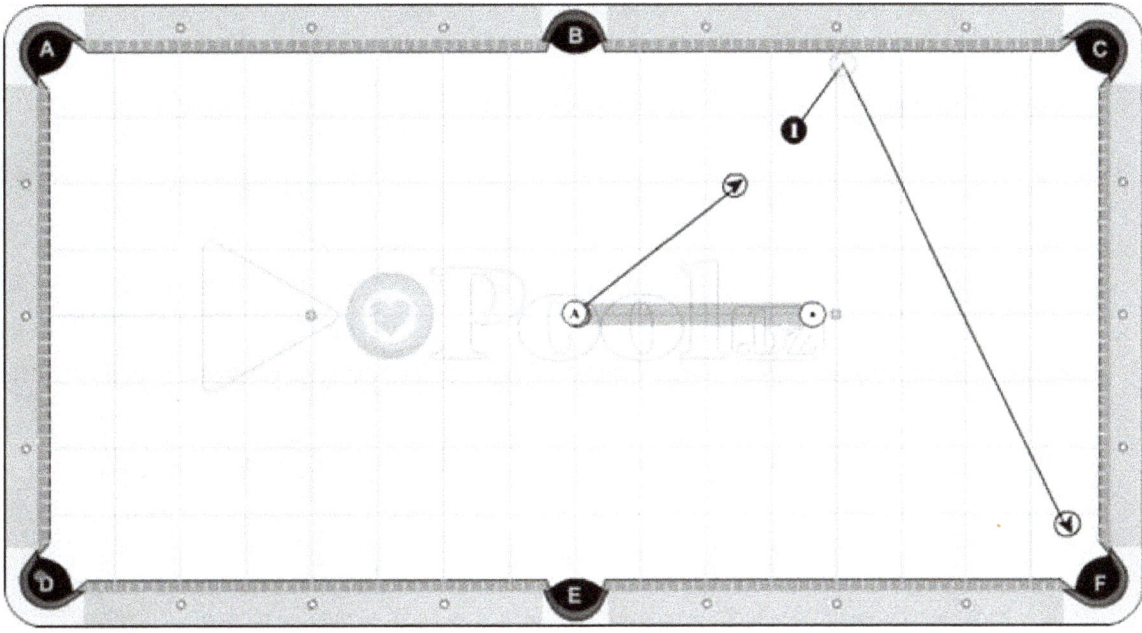

1 D Away Banks

Object: Place CB on grey line. Bank OB into corner pocket.

Set 1

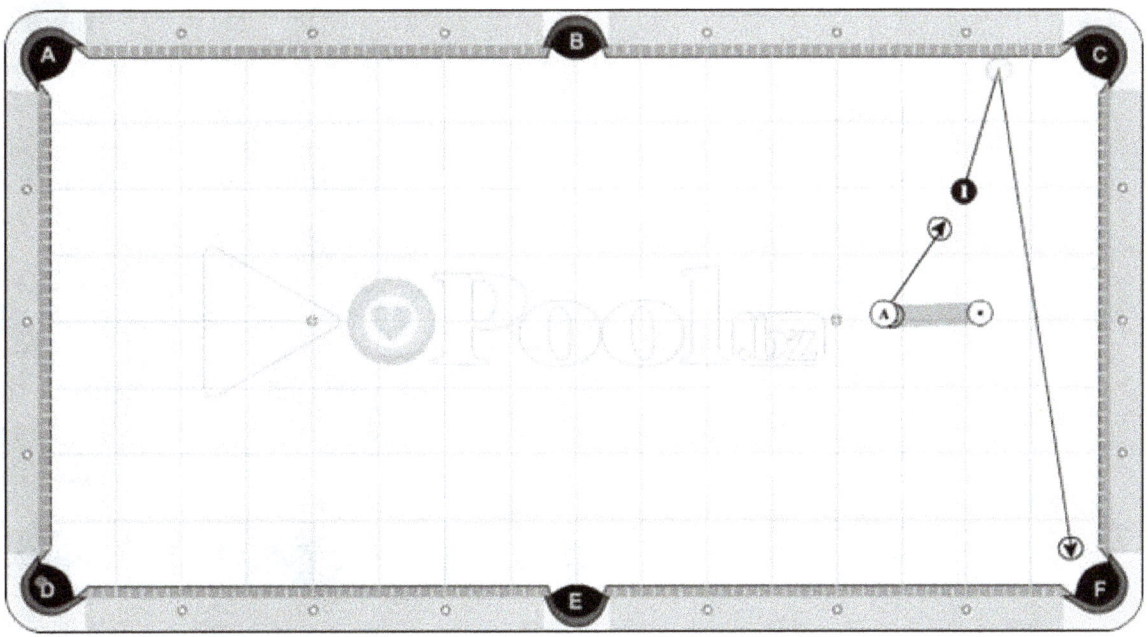

Set 2

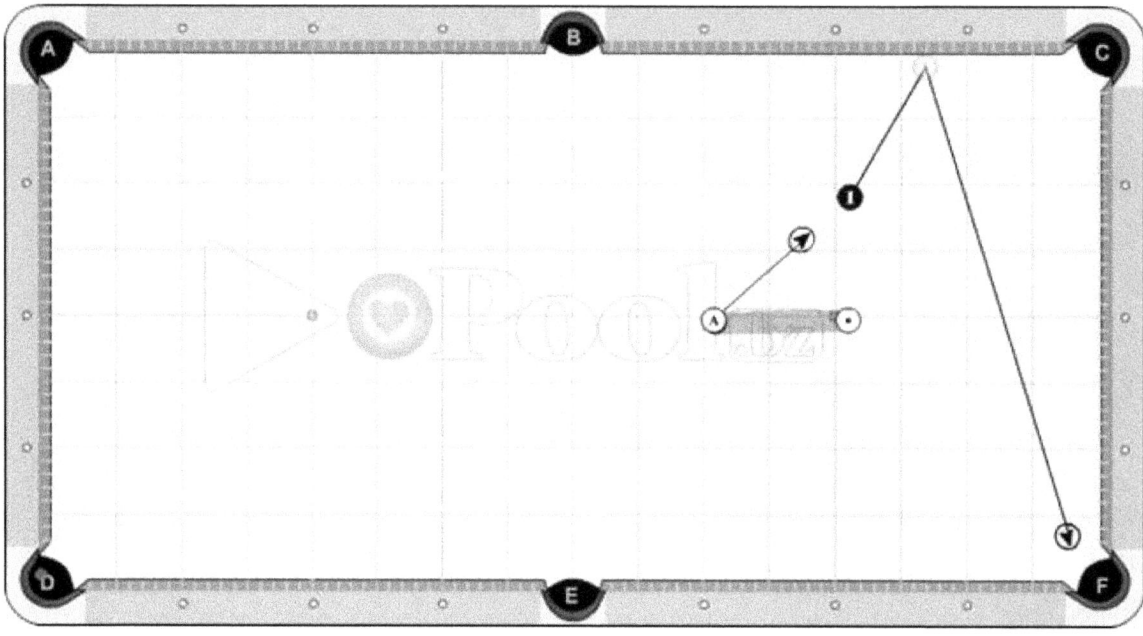

Set 3

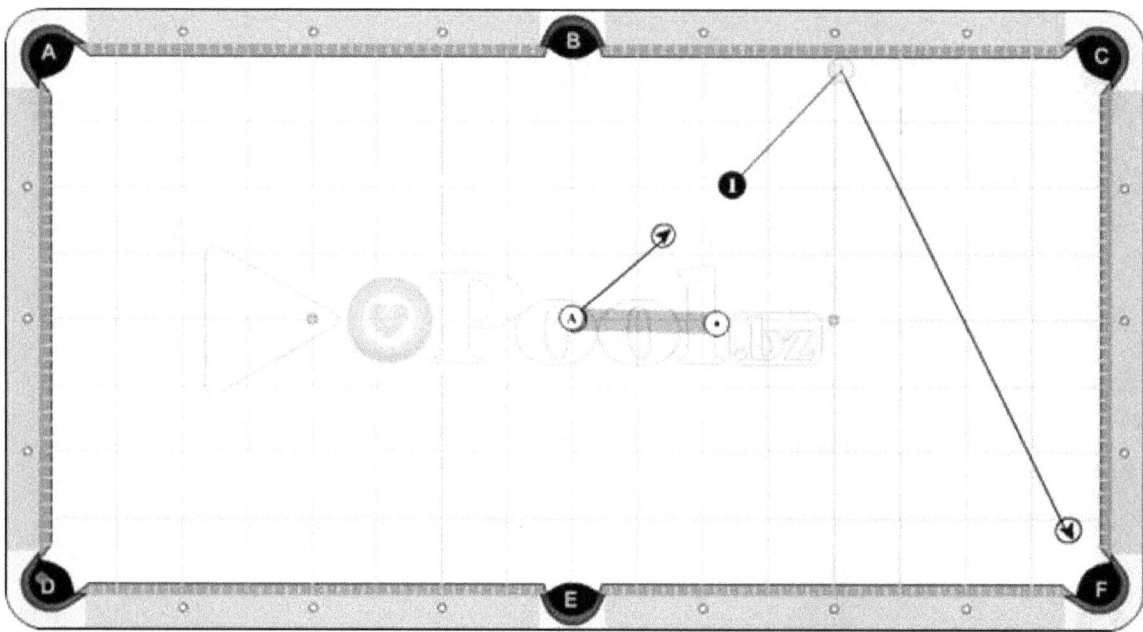

2 D Away Banks

Object: Place CB on grey line. Bank OB into corner pocket.

Set 1

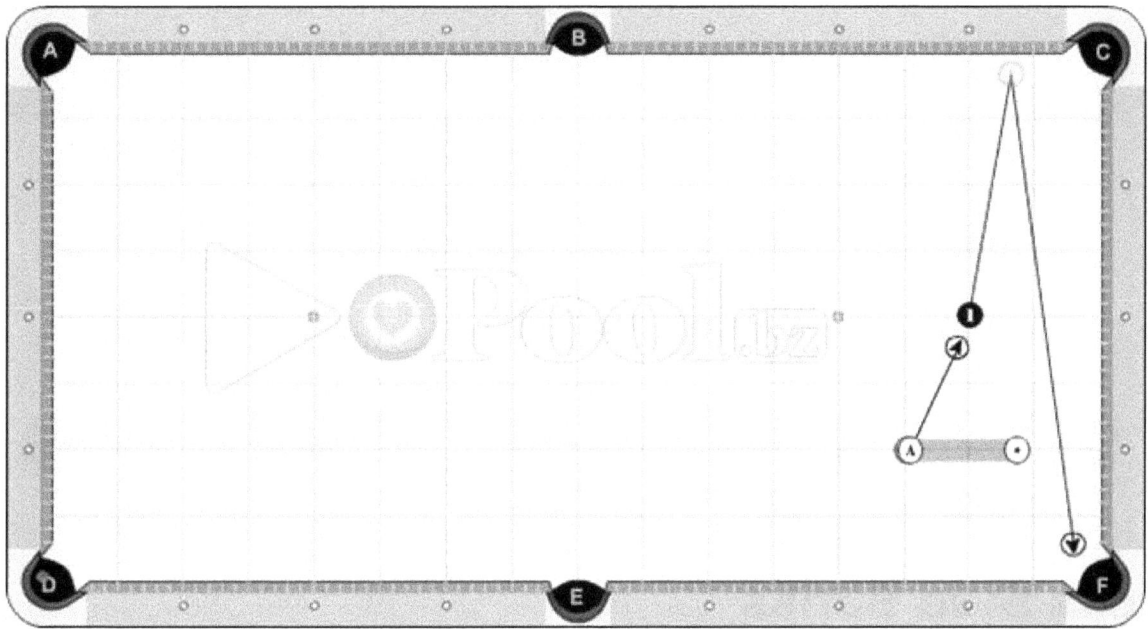

Set 2

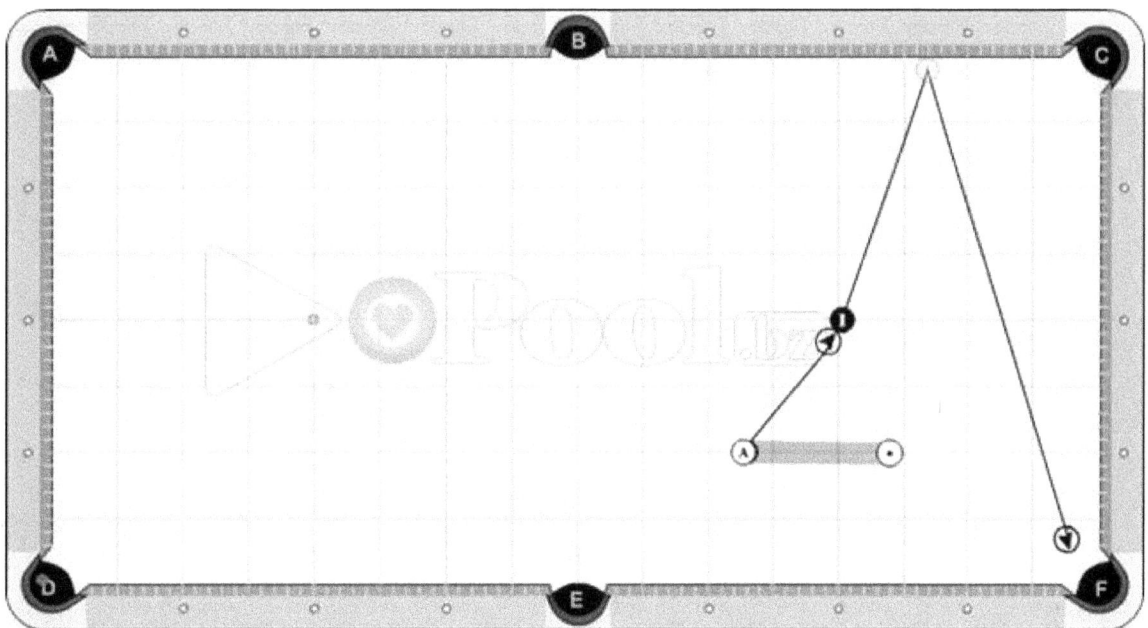

Set 3

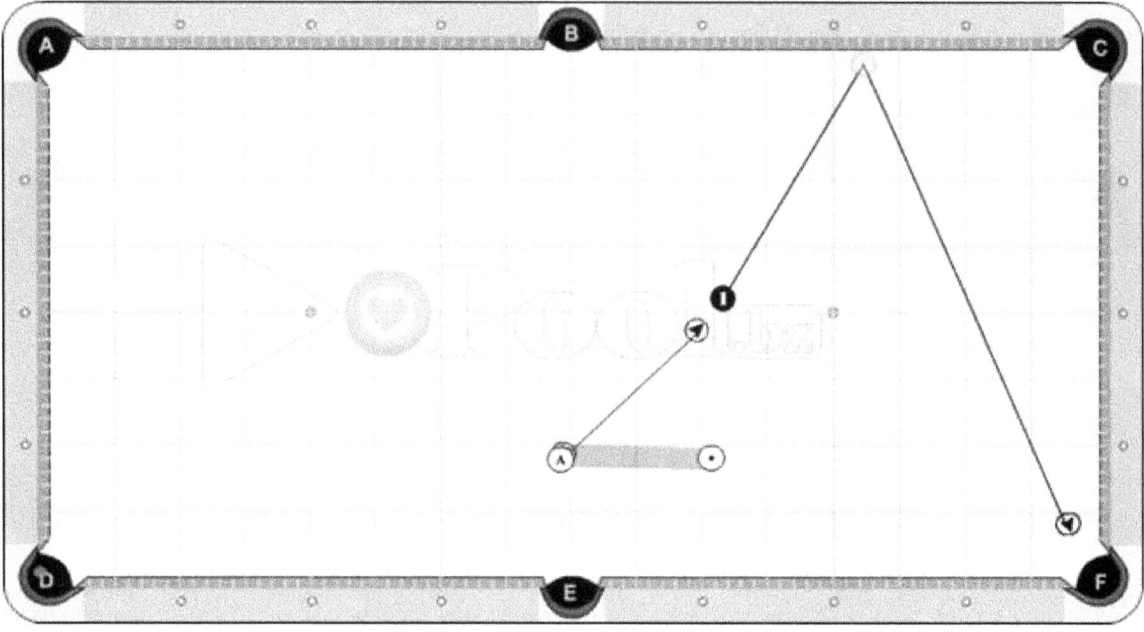

Cross Side Banks

On Rail Banks

Object: Place CB on grey line. Bank OB into side pocket.

Set 1

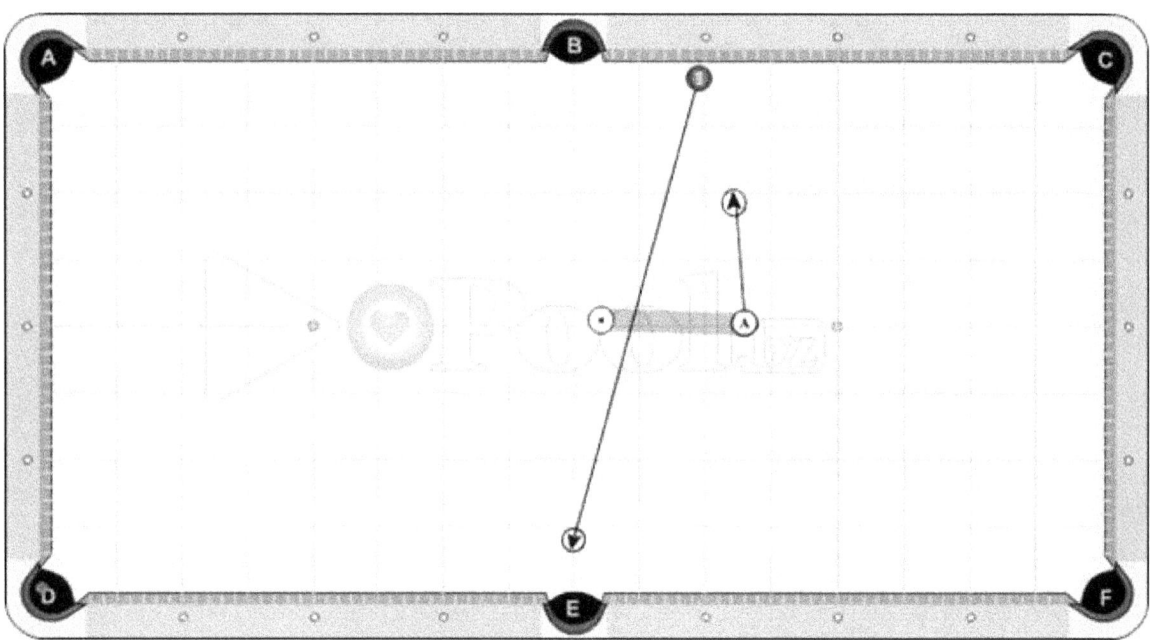

Set 2

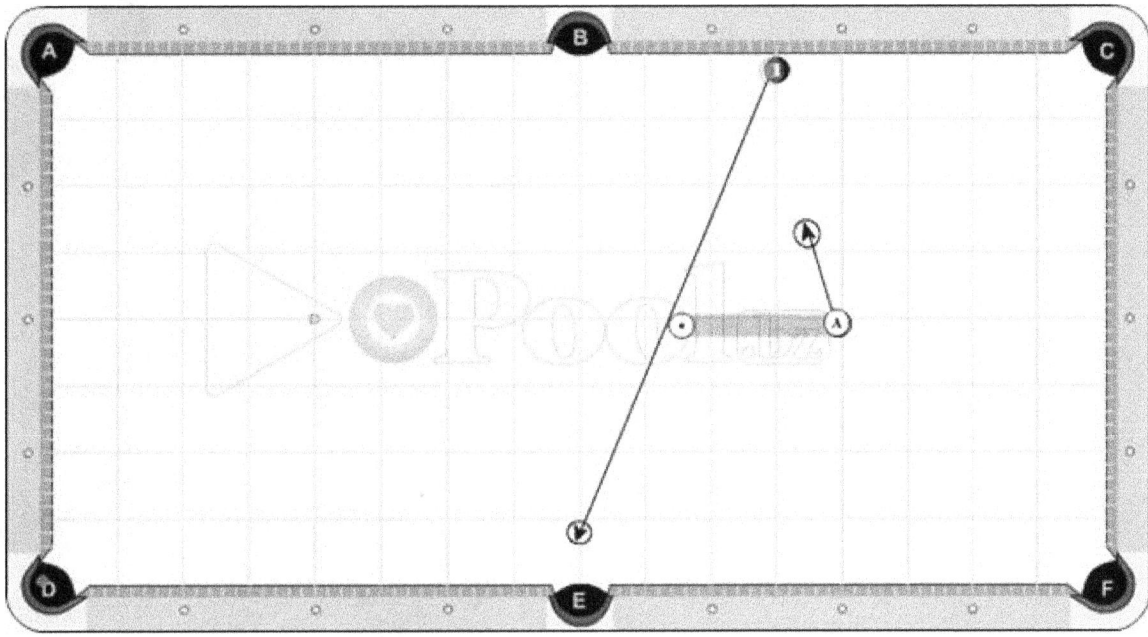

Set 3

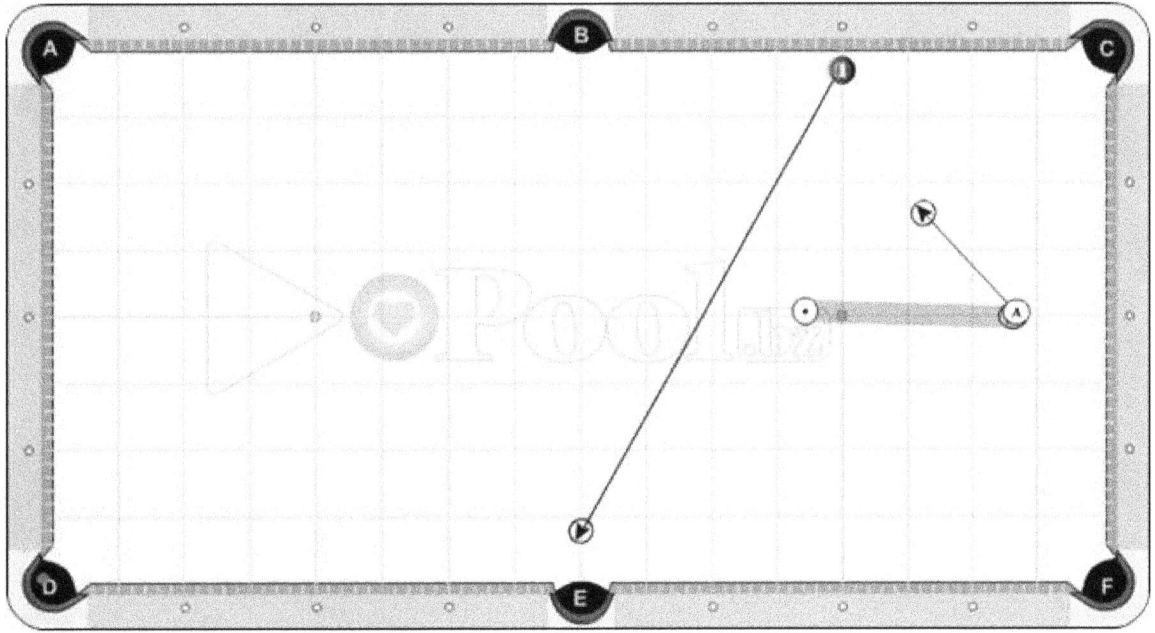

Set 4

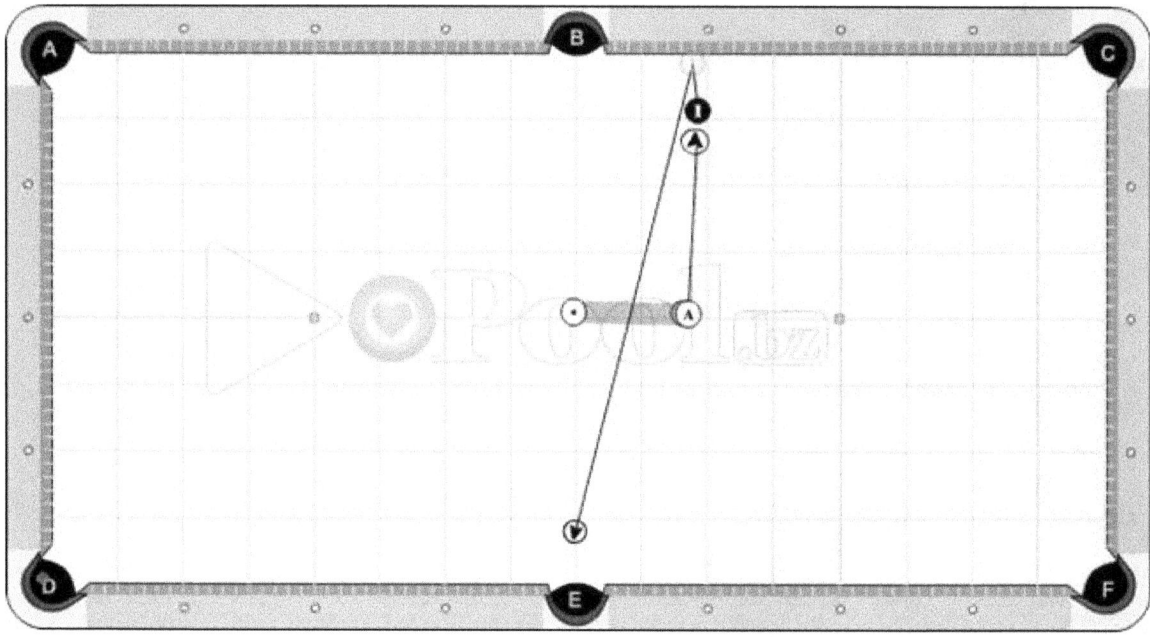

Set 5

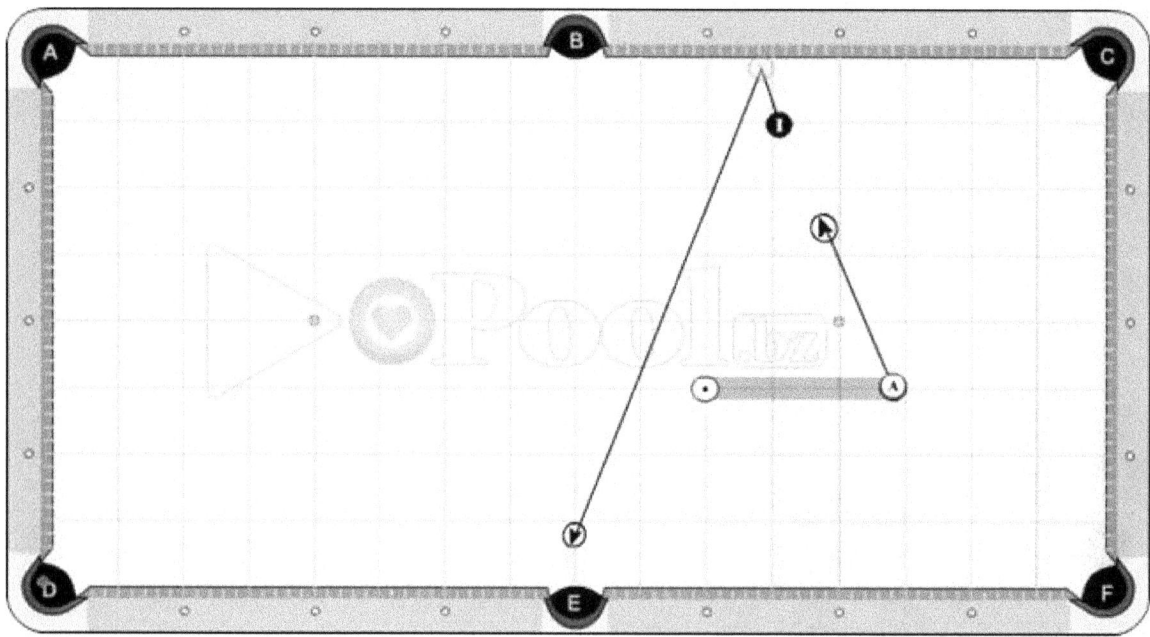

Near Rail Banks

Object: Place CB on grey line. Bank OB into side pocket.

Set 1

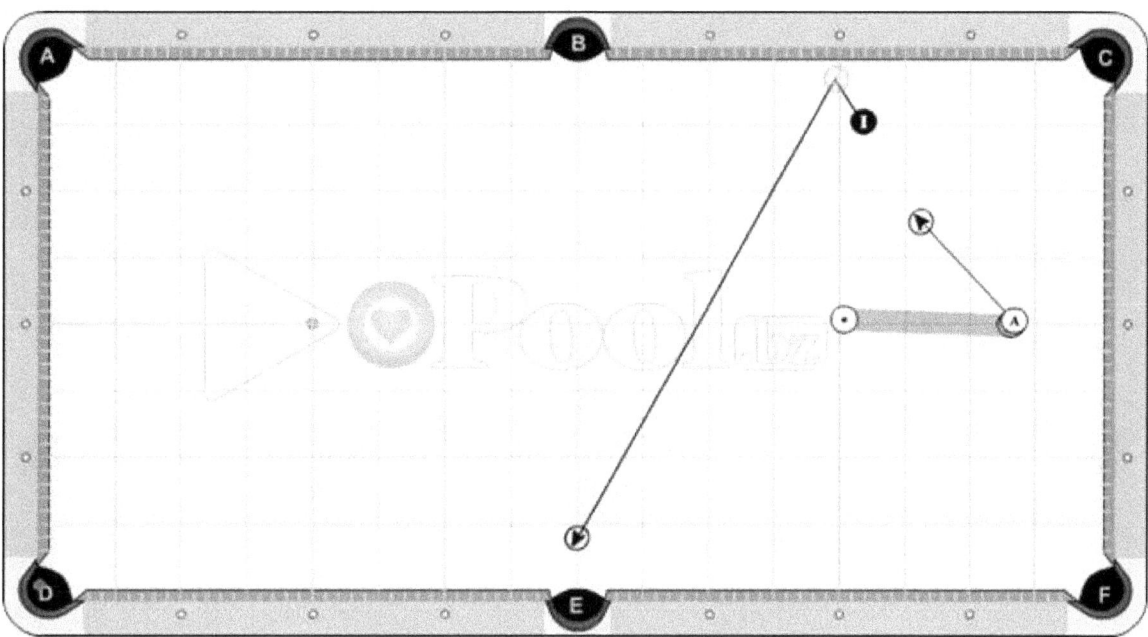

Set 2

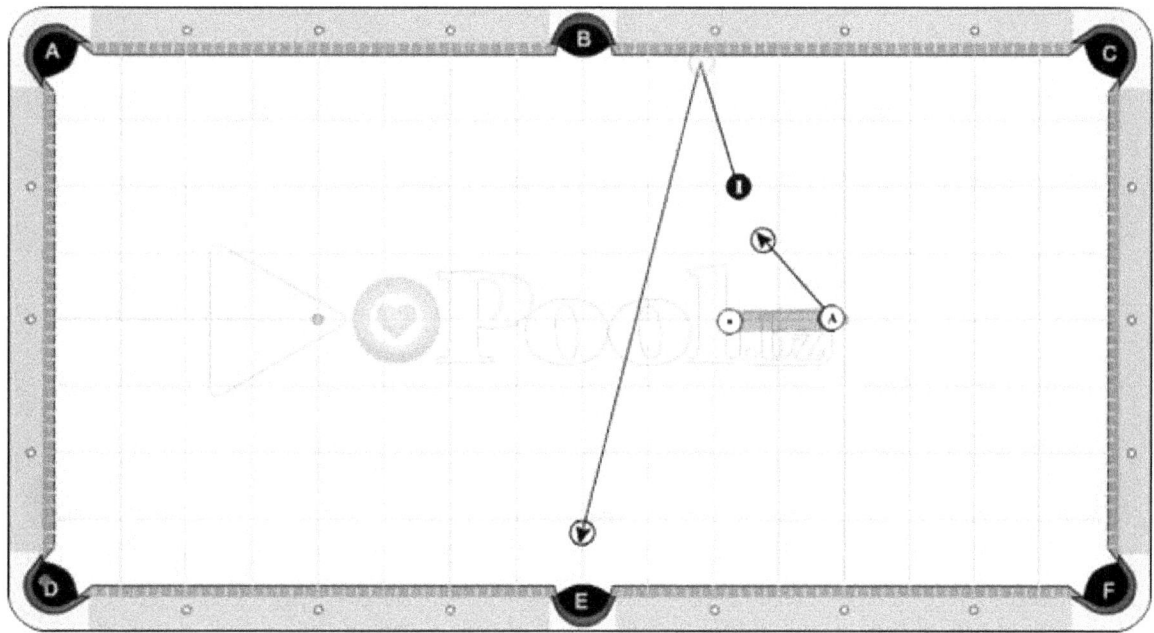

Set 3

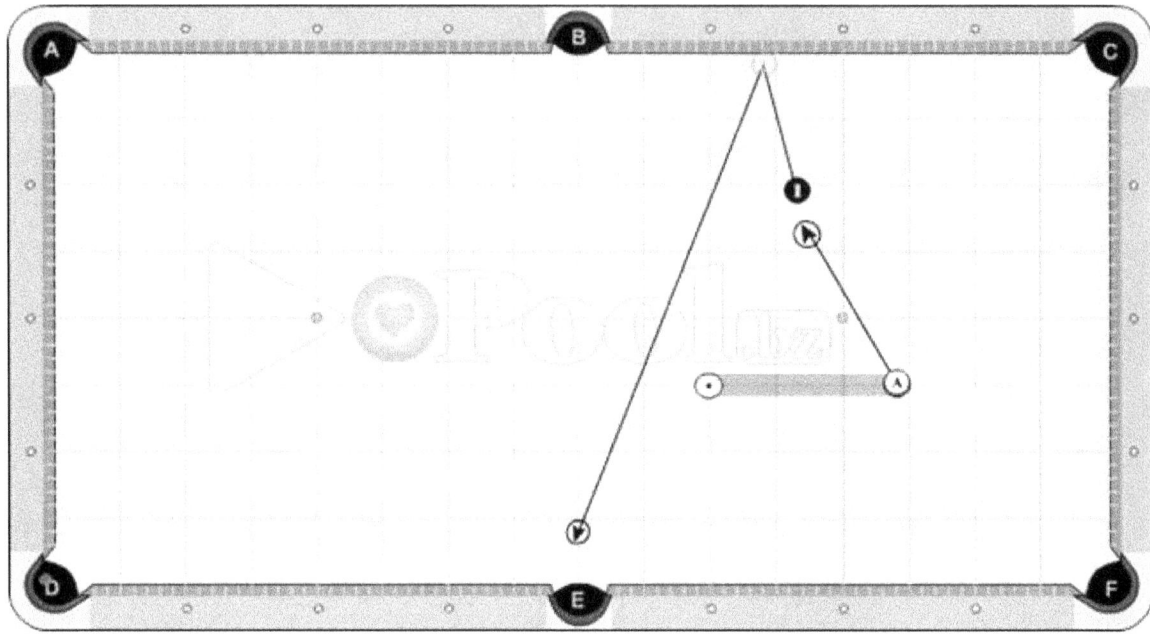

Set 4

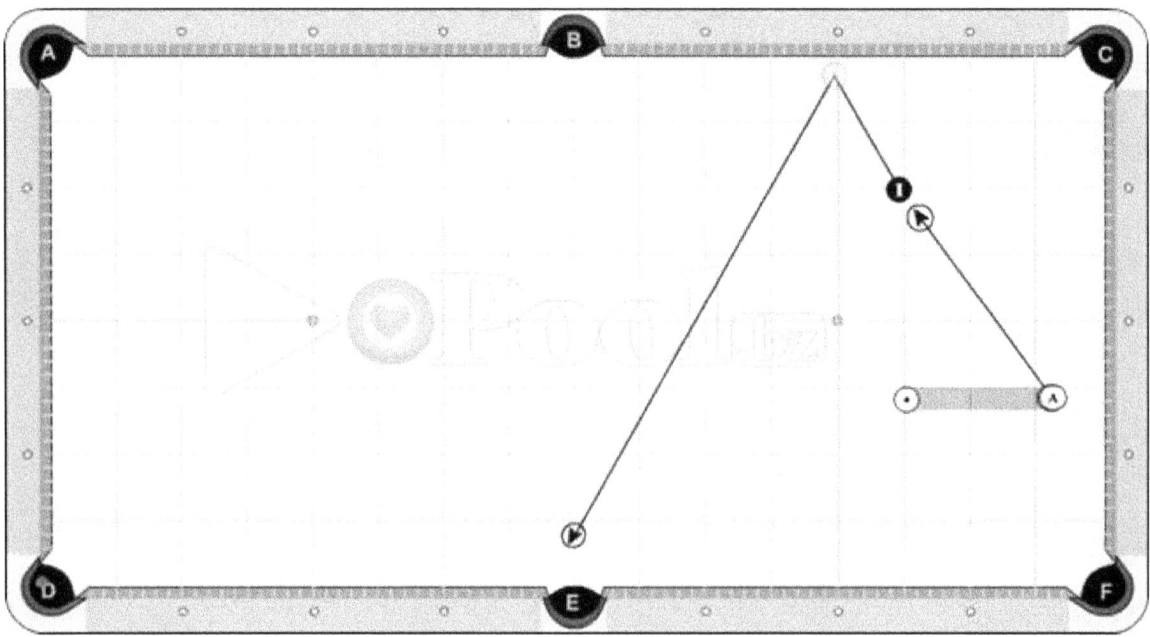

2 D Away Banks

Object: Place CB on grey line. Bank OB into side pocket.

Set 1

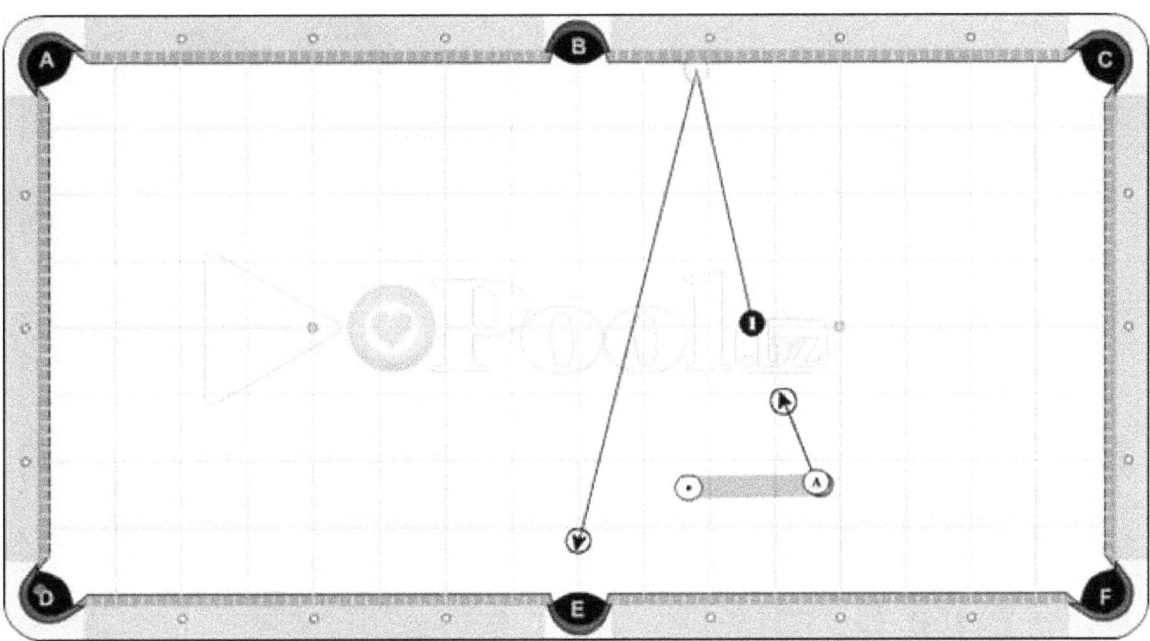

Set 2

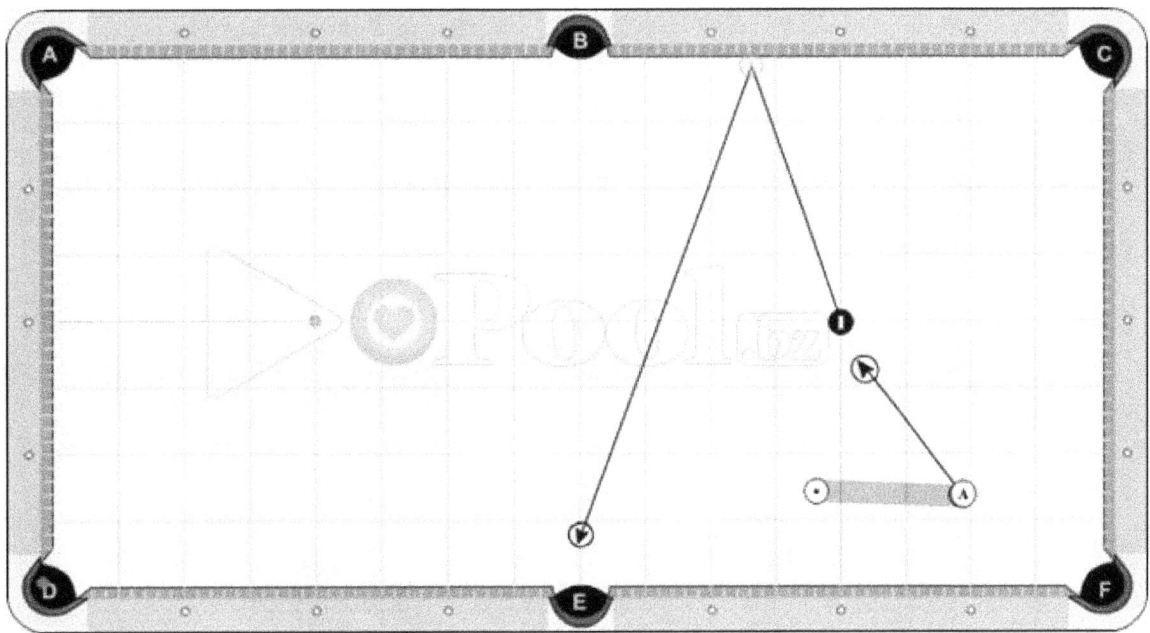

Set 3

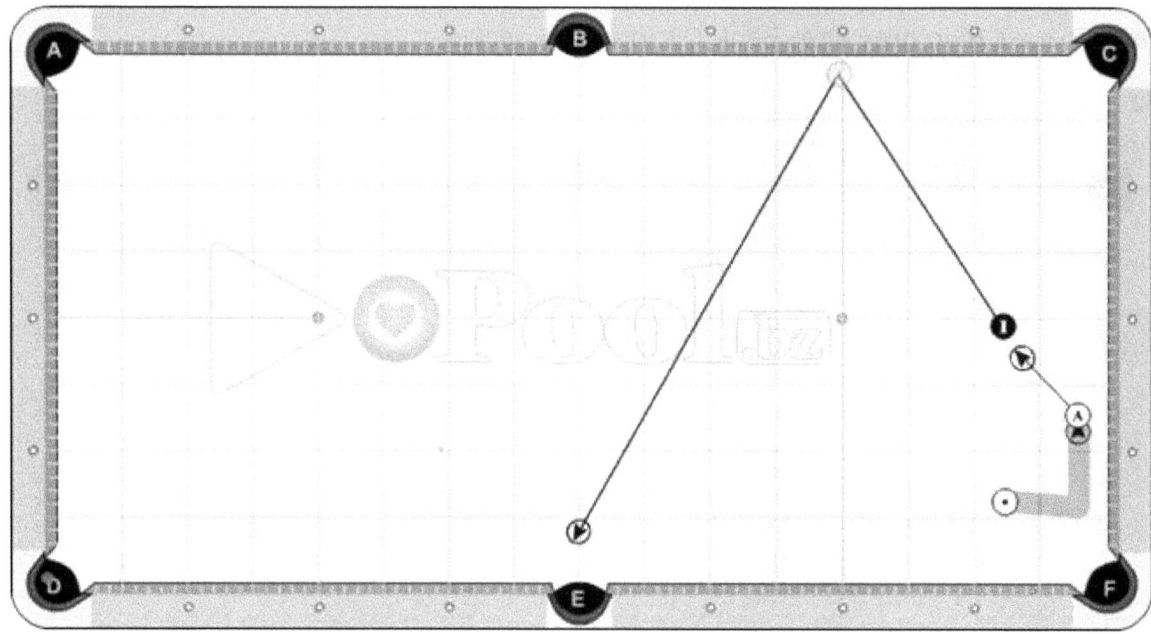

Long Table Banks

On Rail Long Banks

Object: Place CB on grey line. Bank OB into side pocket.

Set 1

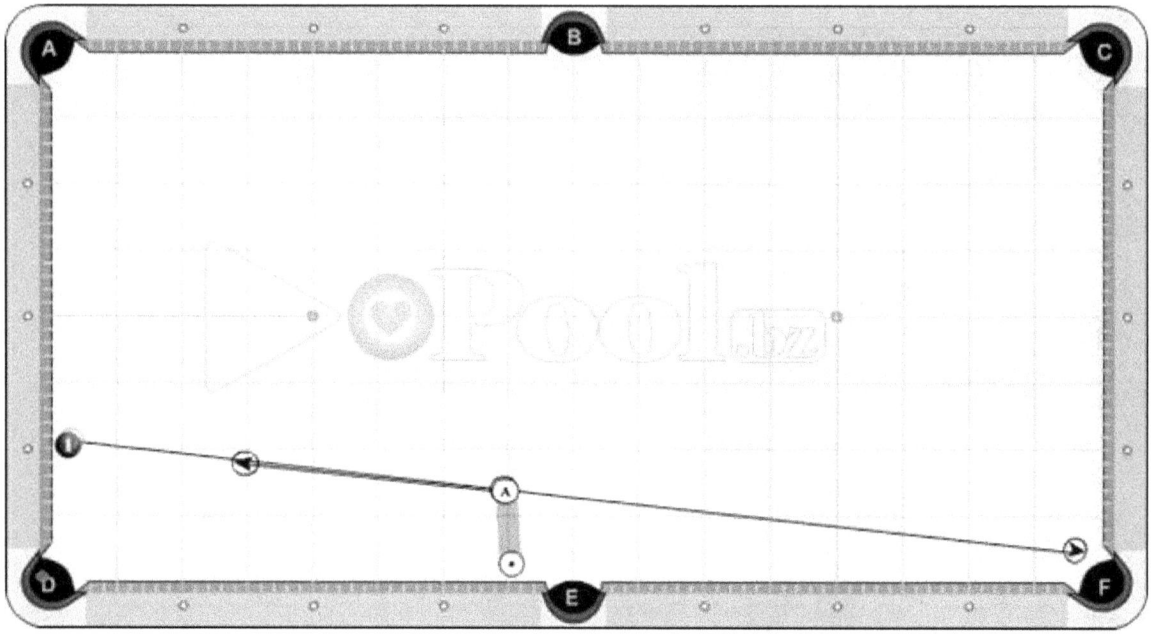

Set 2

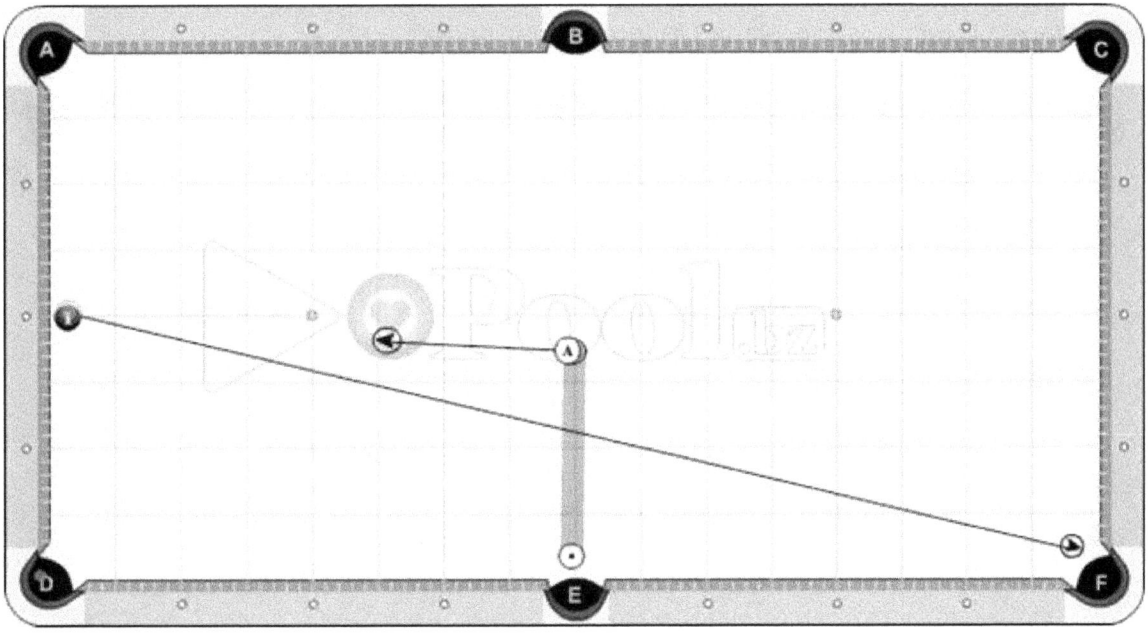

Set 3

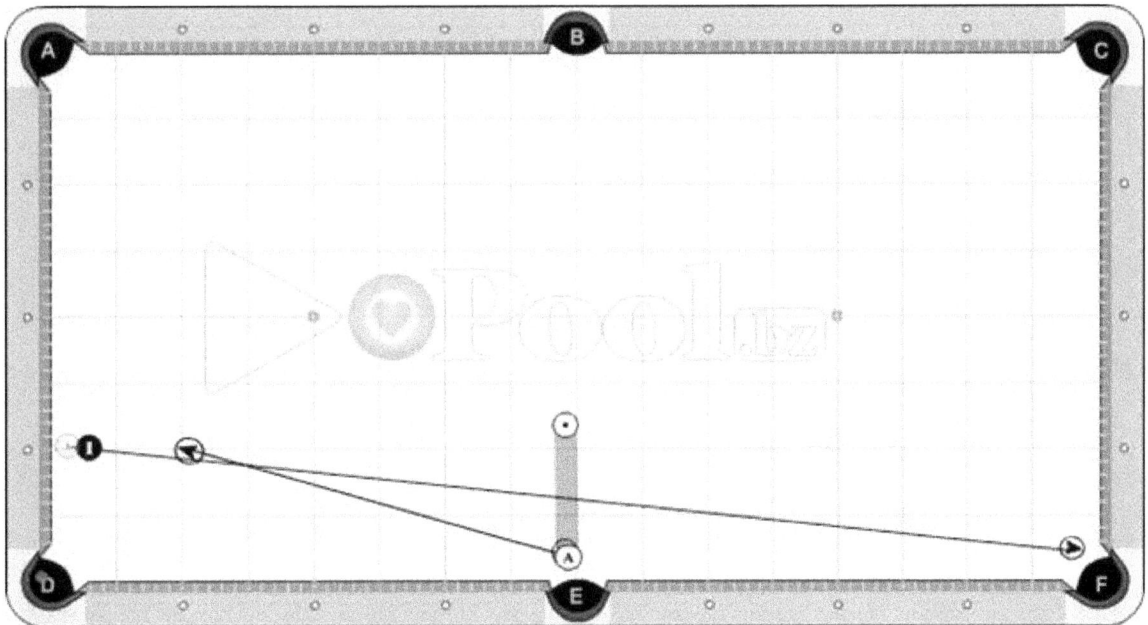

Near Rail Long Banks

Object: Place CB on grey line. Bank OB into corner pocket.

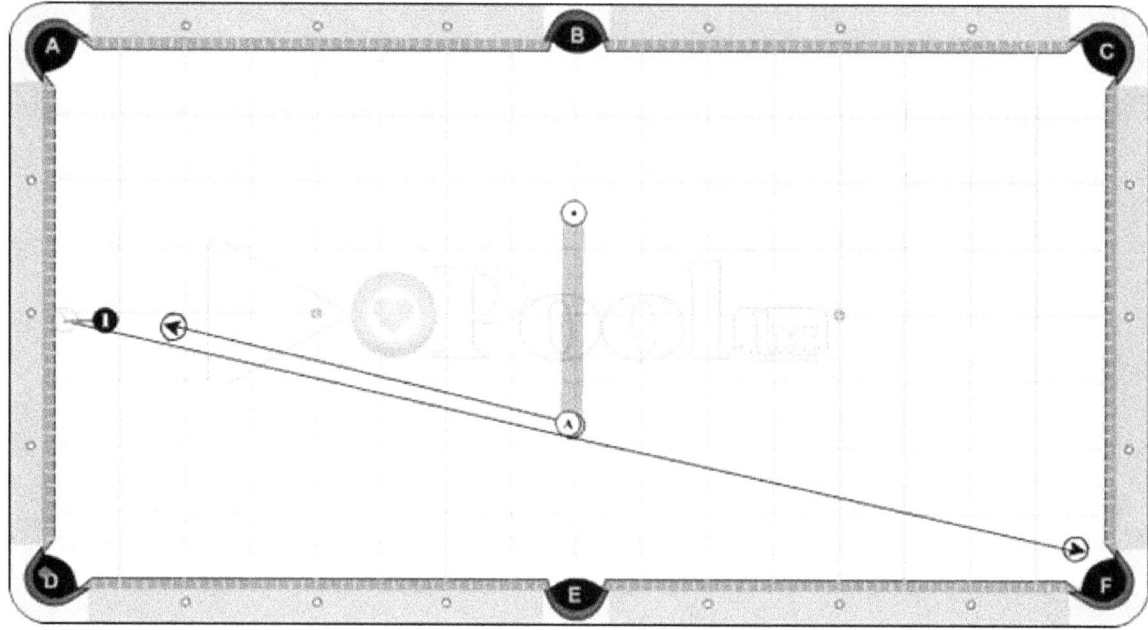

2 D Away Long Banks

Object: Place CB on grey line. Bank OB into corner pocket.

Set 1

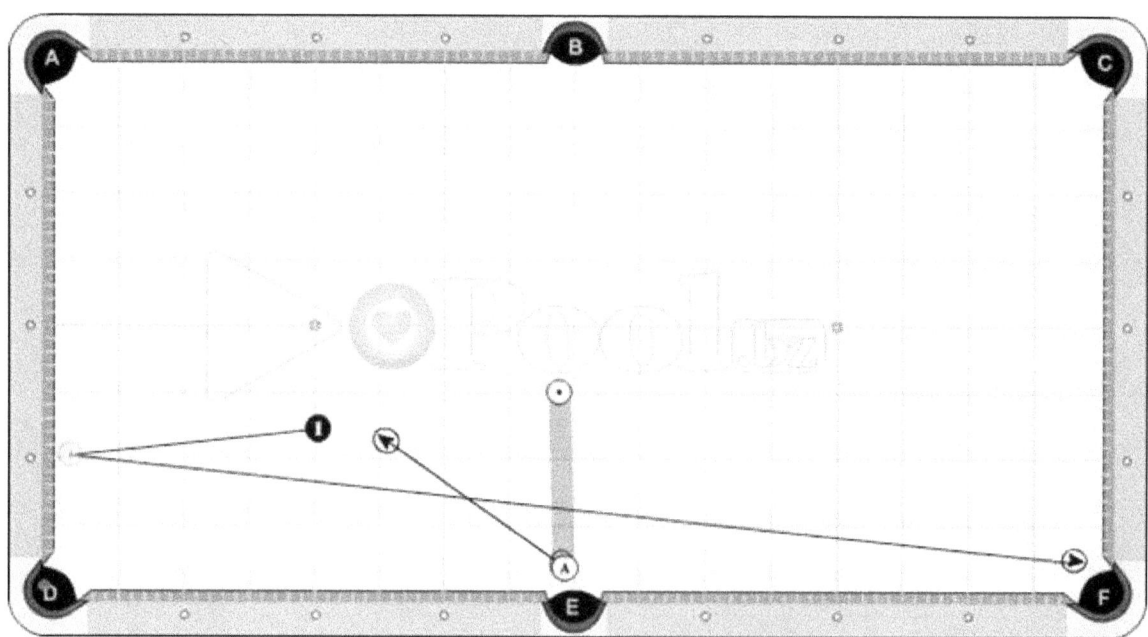

Set 2

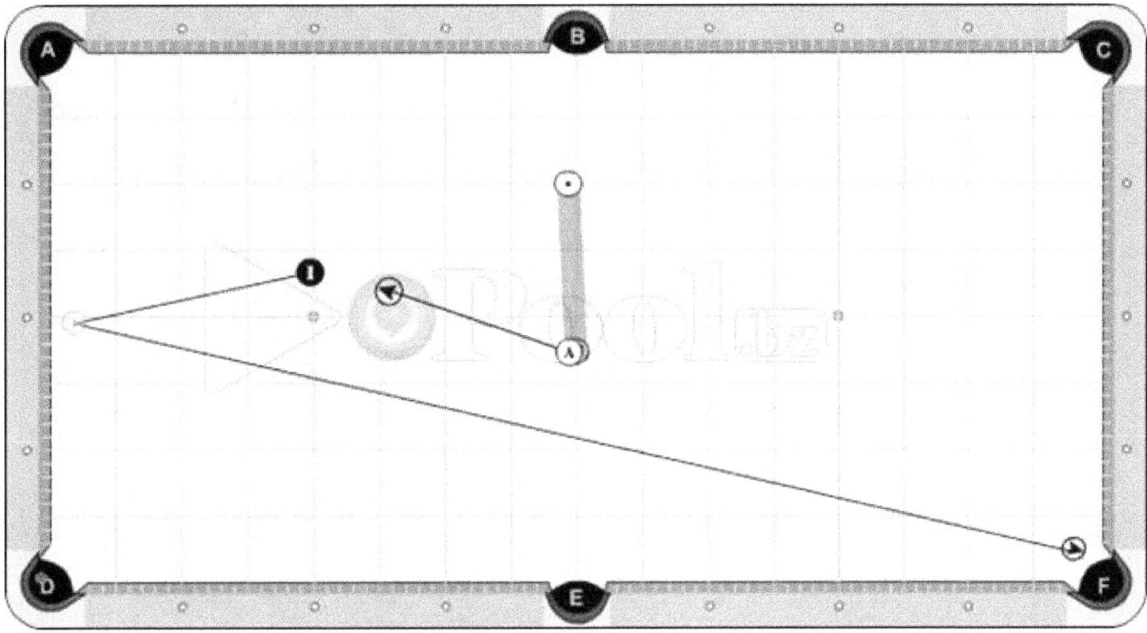

4 D Away Long Banks

Object: Place CB on grey line. Bank OB into corner pocket.

Set 1

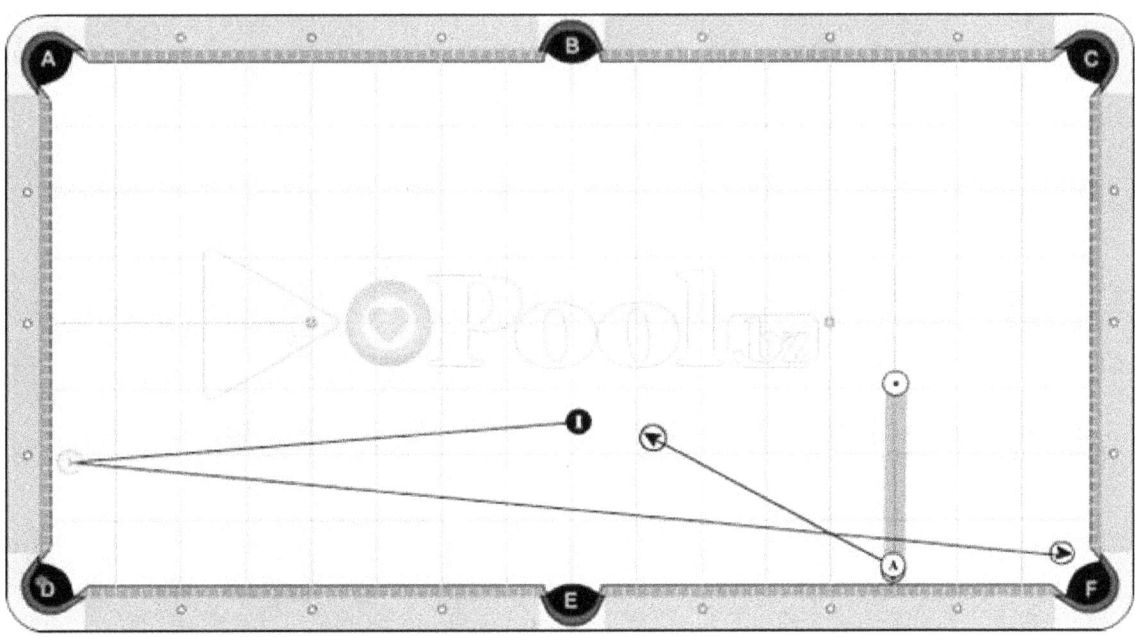

Set 2

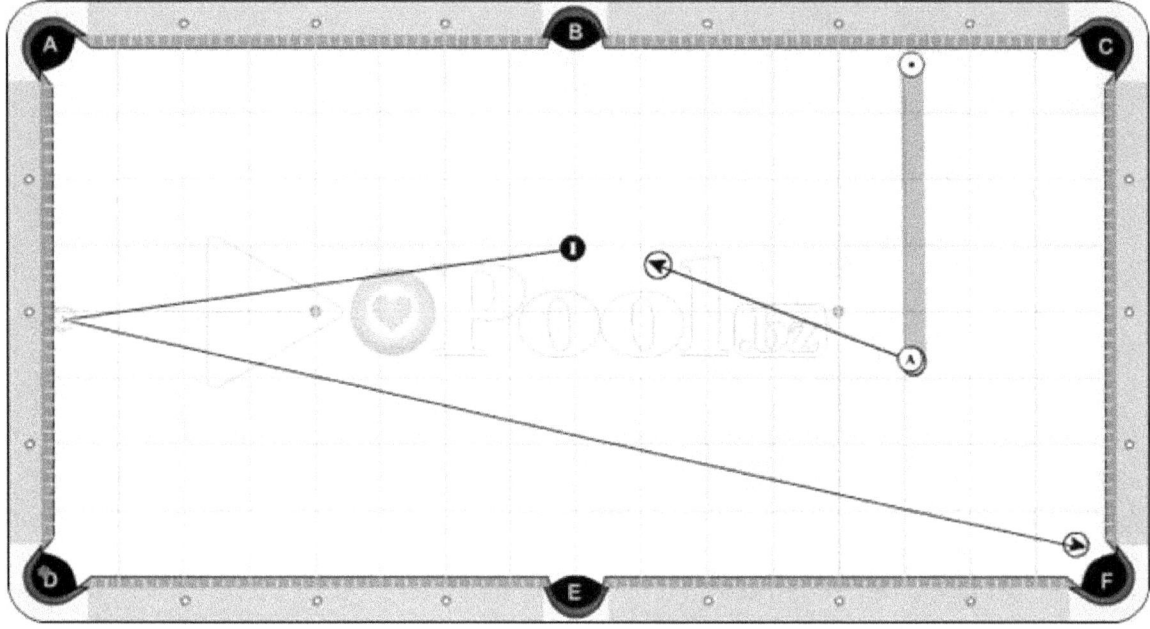

6 D Away Long Banks

Object: Place CB on grey line. Bank OB into corner pocket.

Set 1

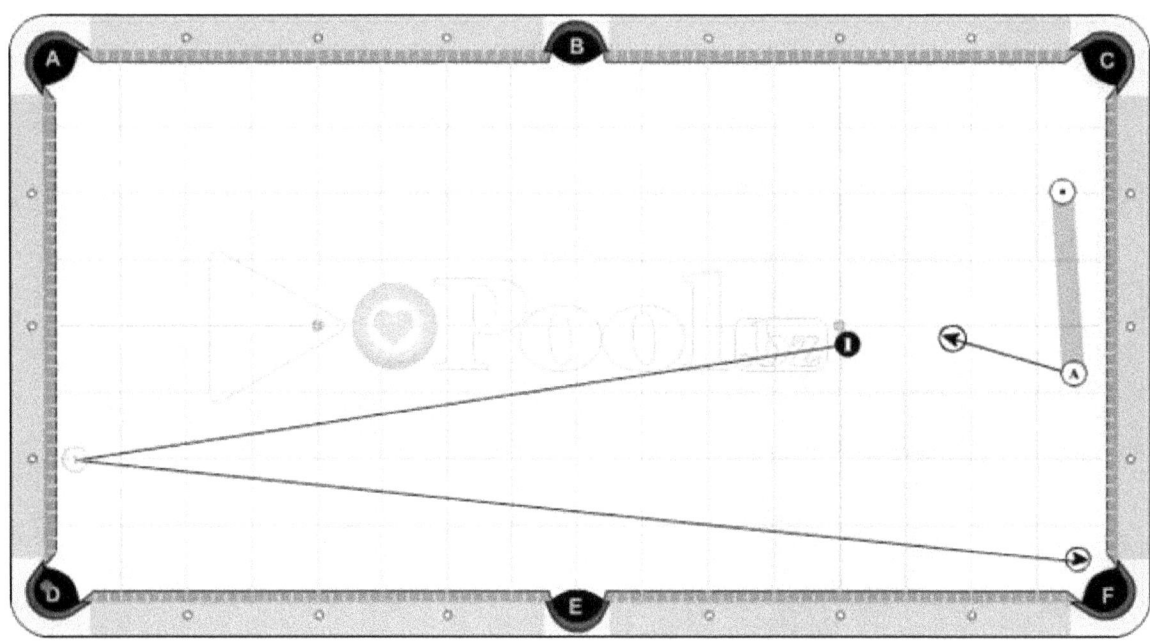

Combinations & Caroms

Combination shots require the CB to hit an OB which then contacts another OB which is pocketed. Carom shots require the CB to contact an OB, after which the CB contacts another OB which then moves to an intended location (pocket or table position).

These shots are not common because of the extreme precision required for a successful result. Because of that, players will often select alternative shots of any other kind. However, these types of shots do come up and sometimes there simply isn't any other alternative. This can occur, even when you have considered the various defensive options.

The only options that will be displayed for you to practice are those that are fairly simple in setup. This book is not going to consider some of the wilder accidental lucky combination/carom shots that occur when the billiard gods decide to interfere with your game.

Dead-on Combo & Carom Examples

Here are some examples of easy combos and caroms. These are obvious when you see them, and sometimes irresistible, even though that might not be the right shot at the time.

Easy Combos

These combination examples are essentially fool-proof. Well, maybe. Players can find ways to mess up even the most fool-proof setups. Study the shot and select the correct CB speed.

Object: Contact the first OB to pocket the second OB.

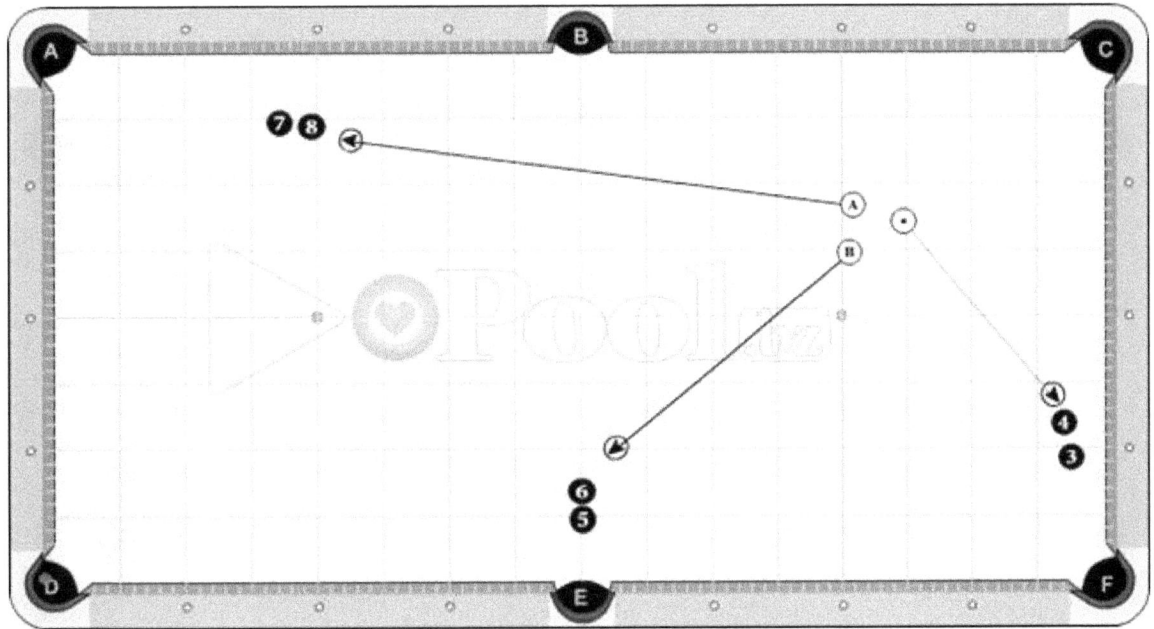

Easy Caroms

Object: Carom off first ball and pocket the second ball.

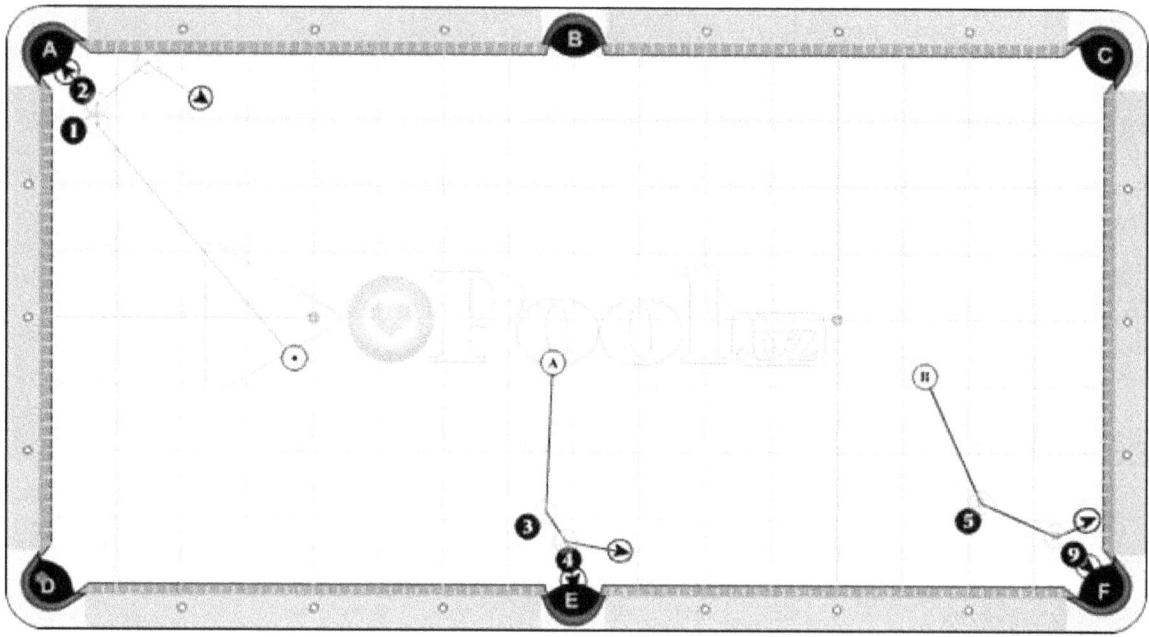

Combination Exercises

Easy Combinations

Object: Pocket the second ball. Place CB on grey line and first OB on its grey line.

Set 1

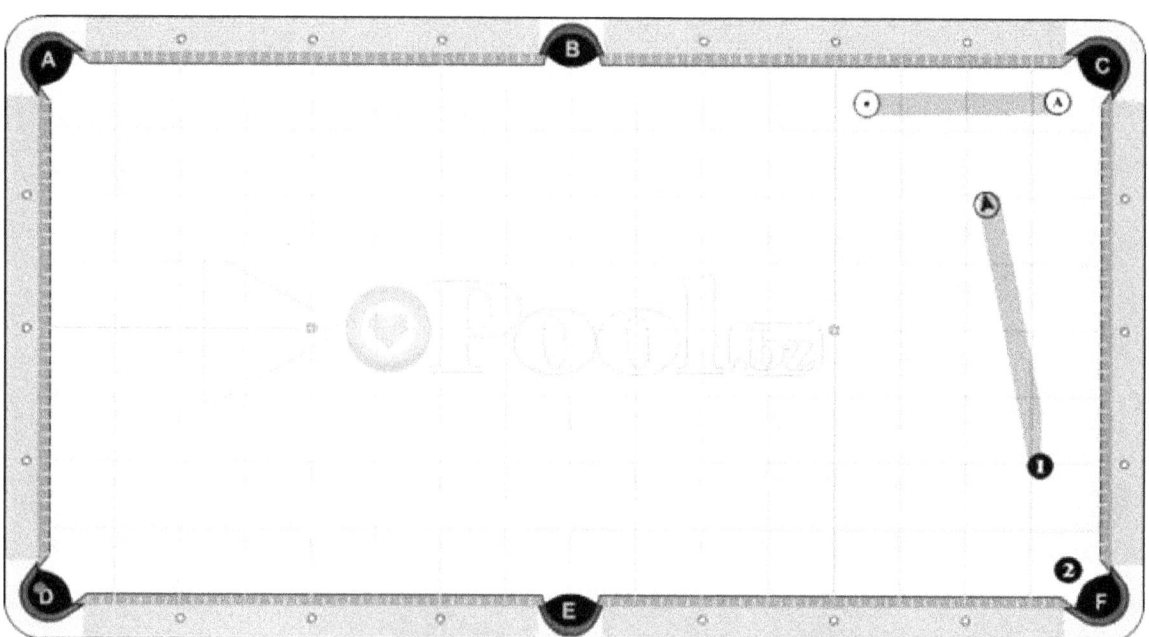

Set 2

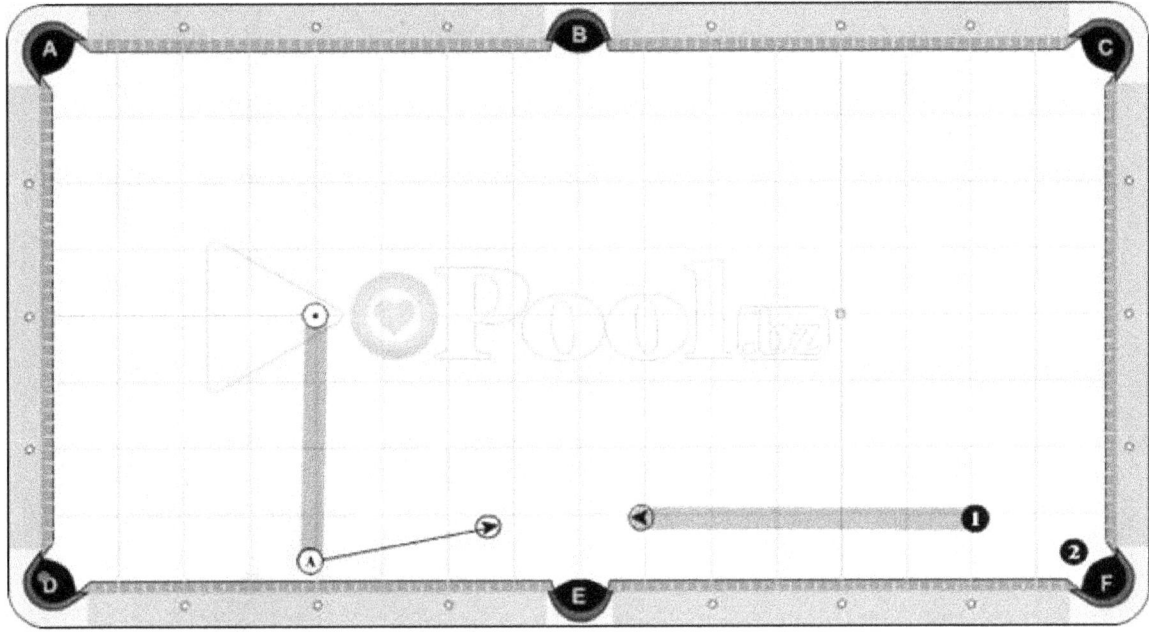

Set 3

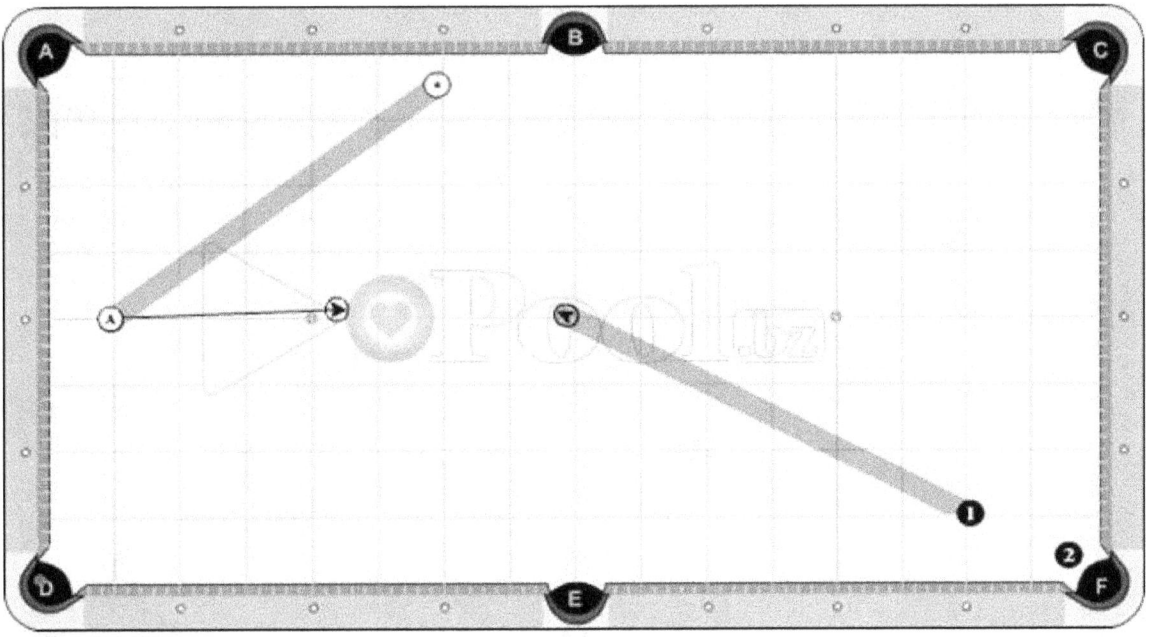

Easy Side Combinations

Object: Pocket the second ball. Place CB on grey line and first OB on its grey line.

Set 1

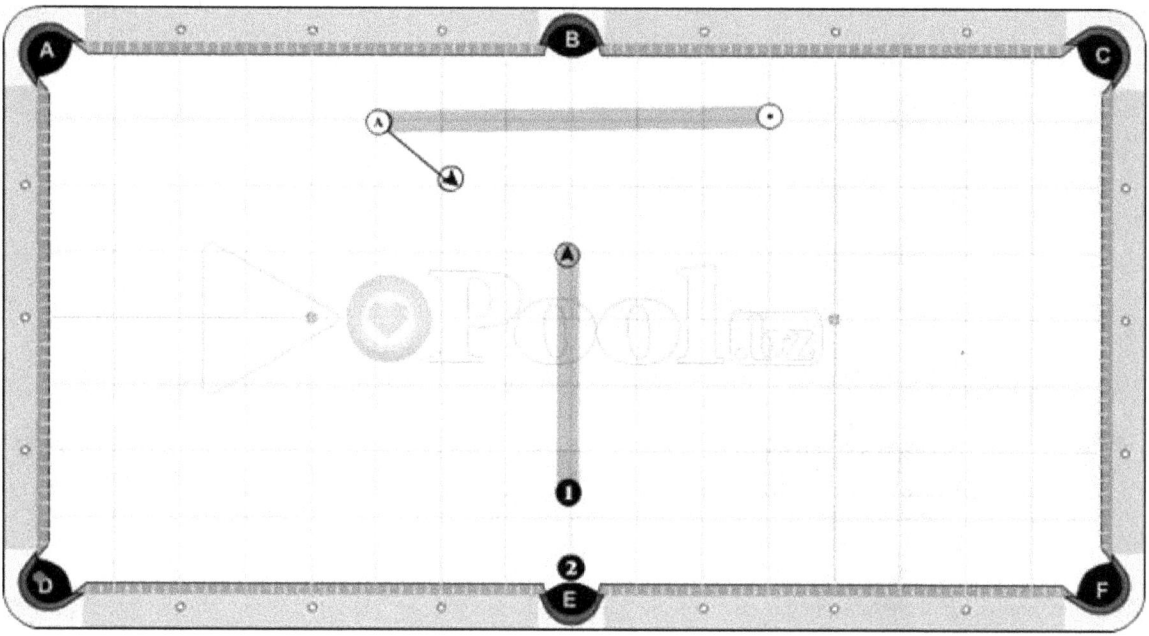

Set 2

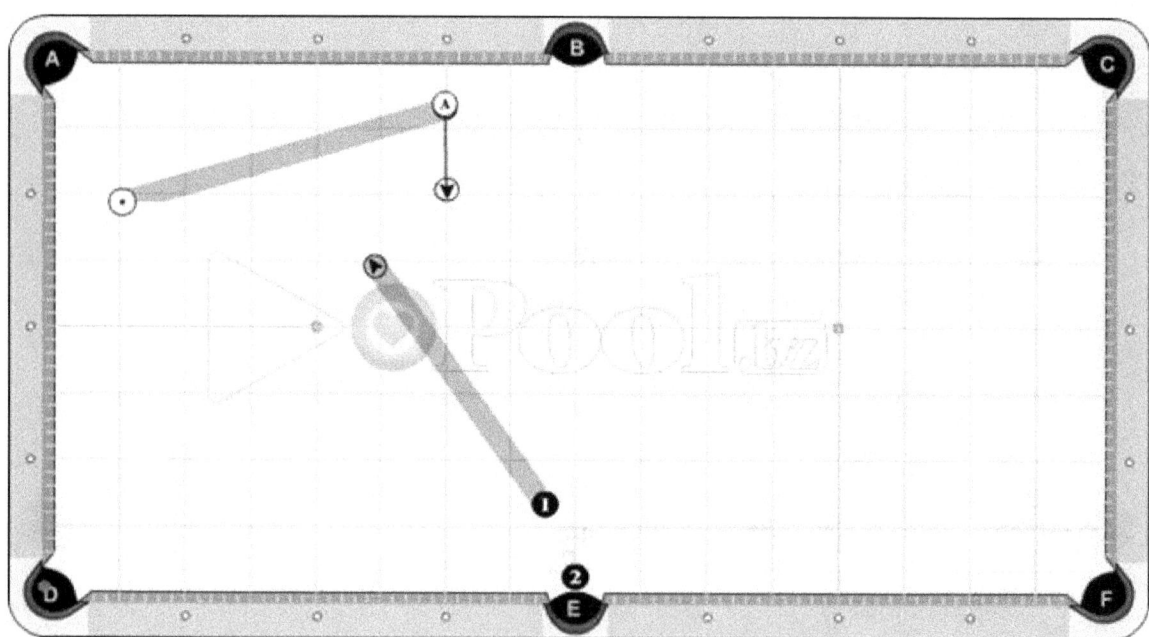

Set 3

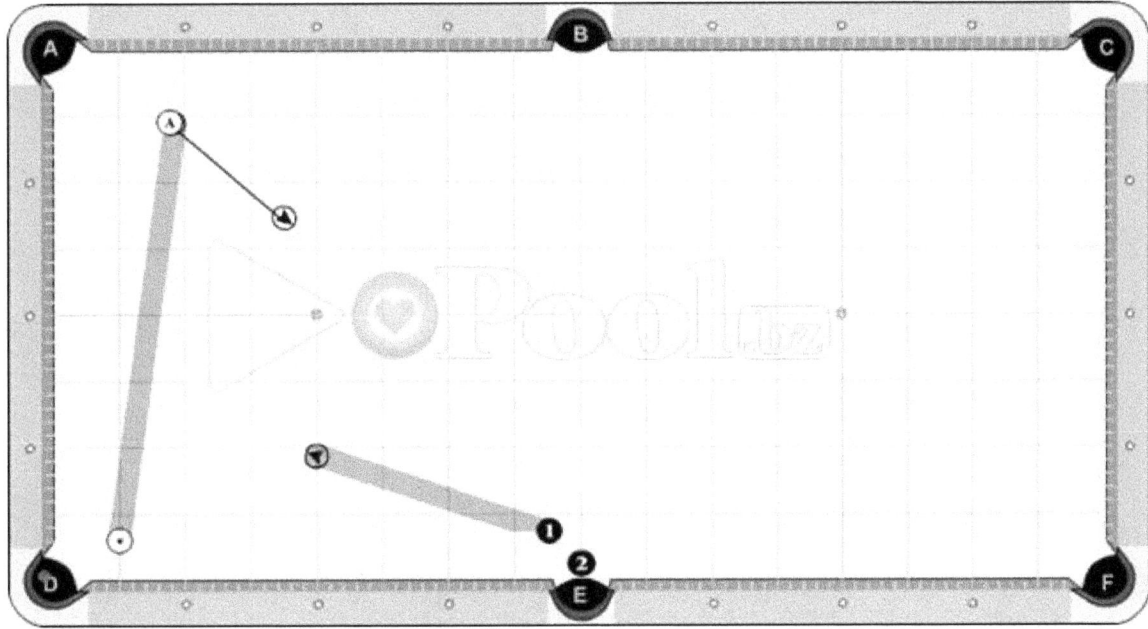

Intermediate Combos

Object: Pocket the second ball. Place CB on grey line and first OB on its grey line.

Set 1

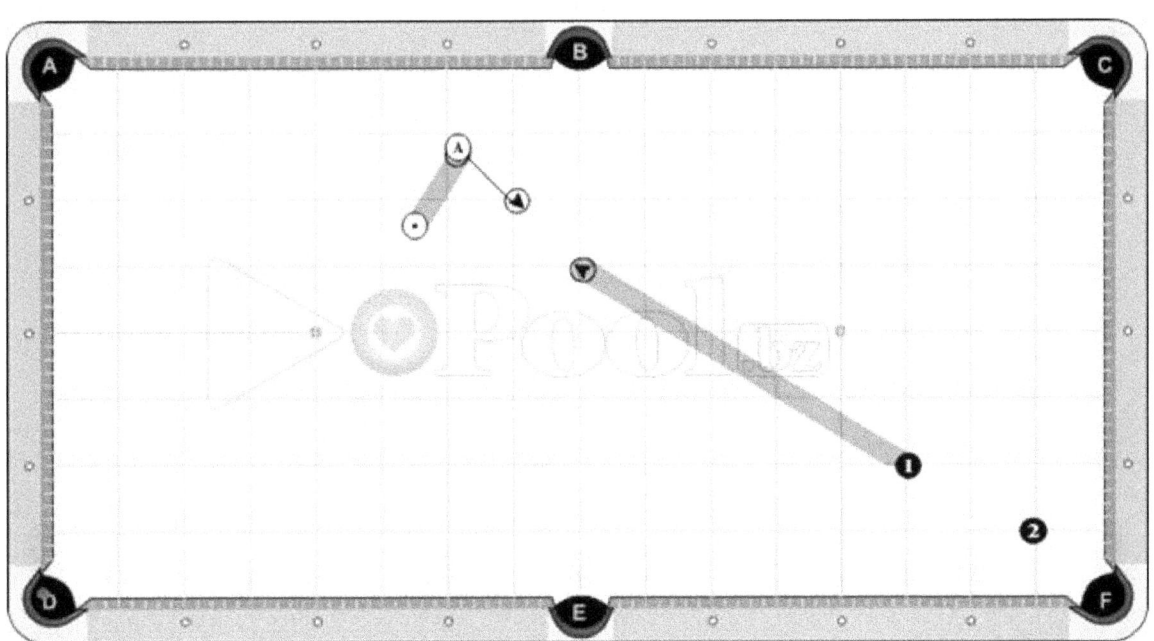

Set 2

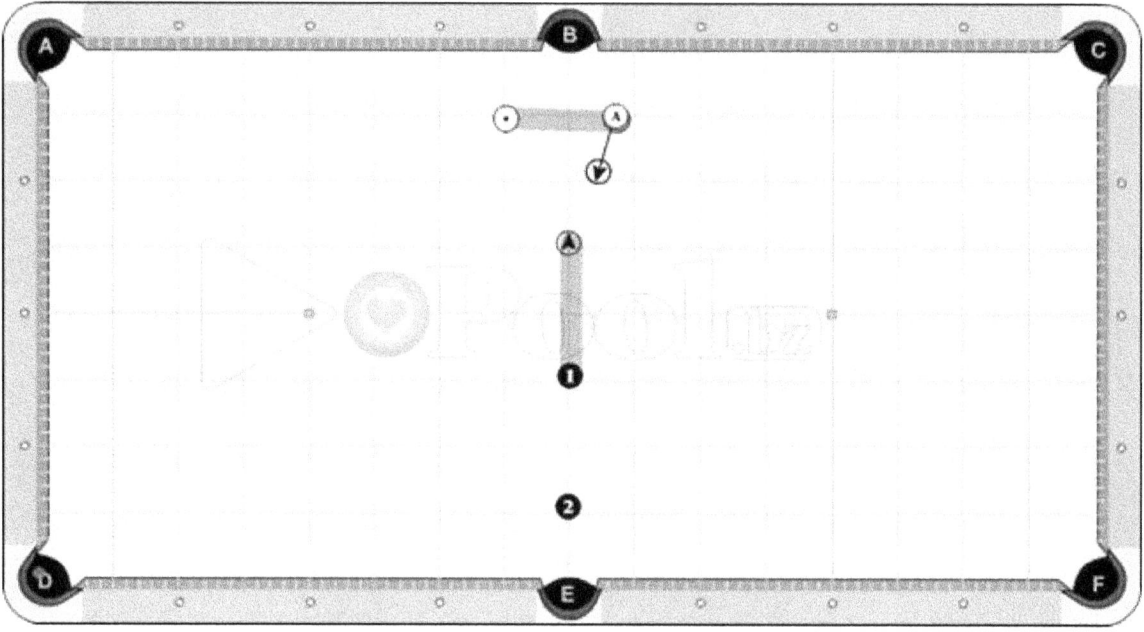

Advanced Combos

Object: Pocket the second ball. Place CB on grey line and first OB on its grey line.

Set 1

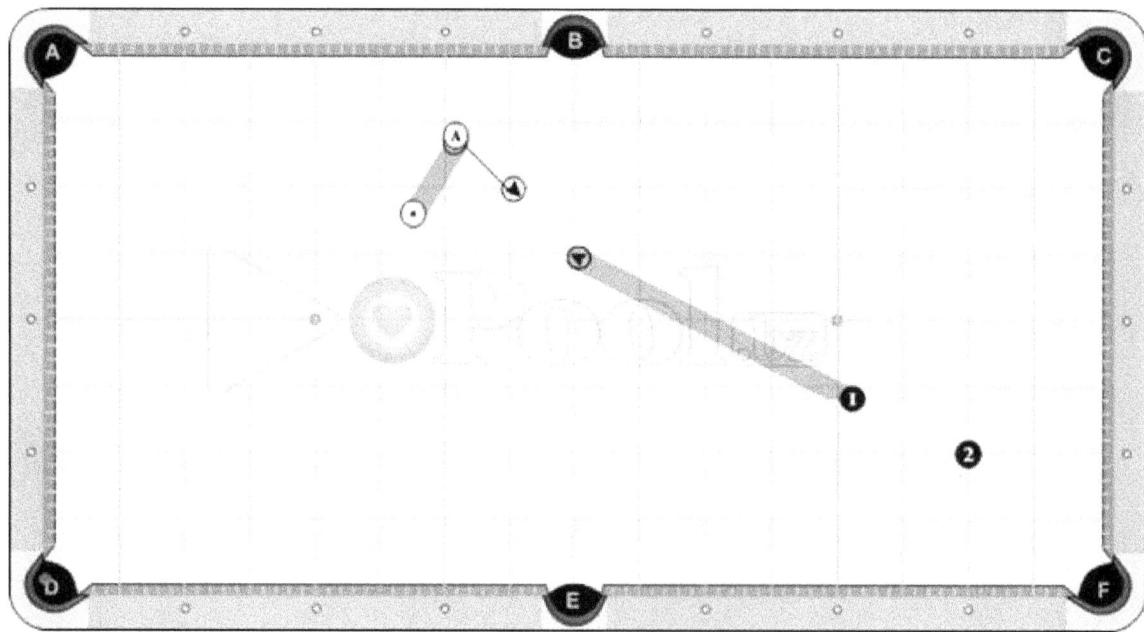

Set 2

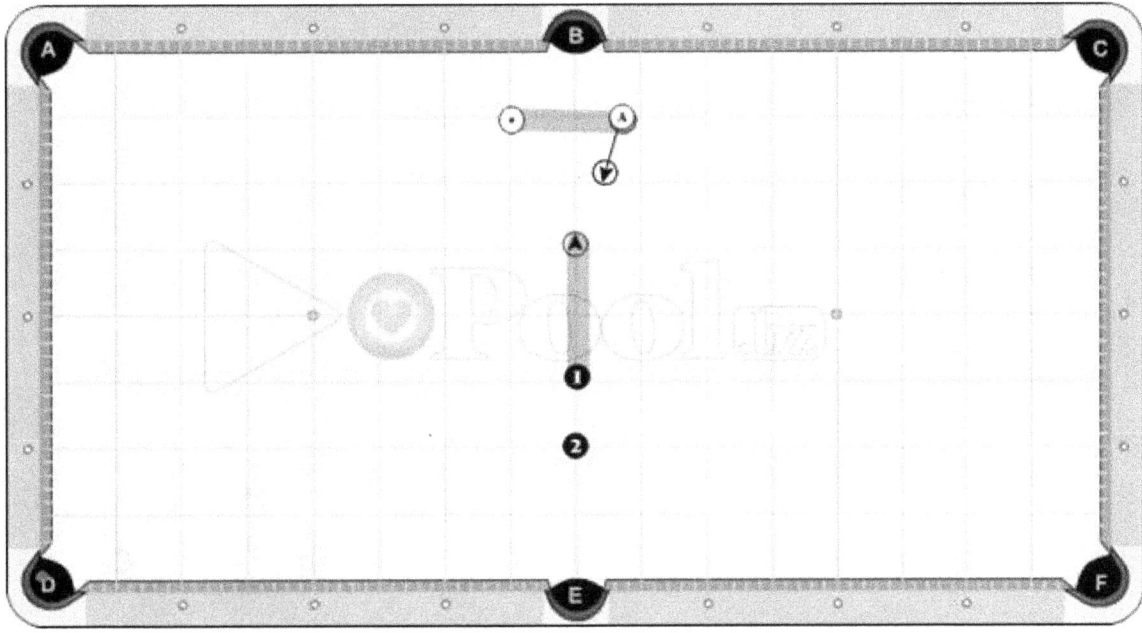

Zig-zag Combos

Object: Pocket the second ball. Place CB on grey line and first OB on its grey line.

Set 1

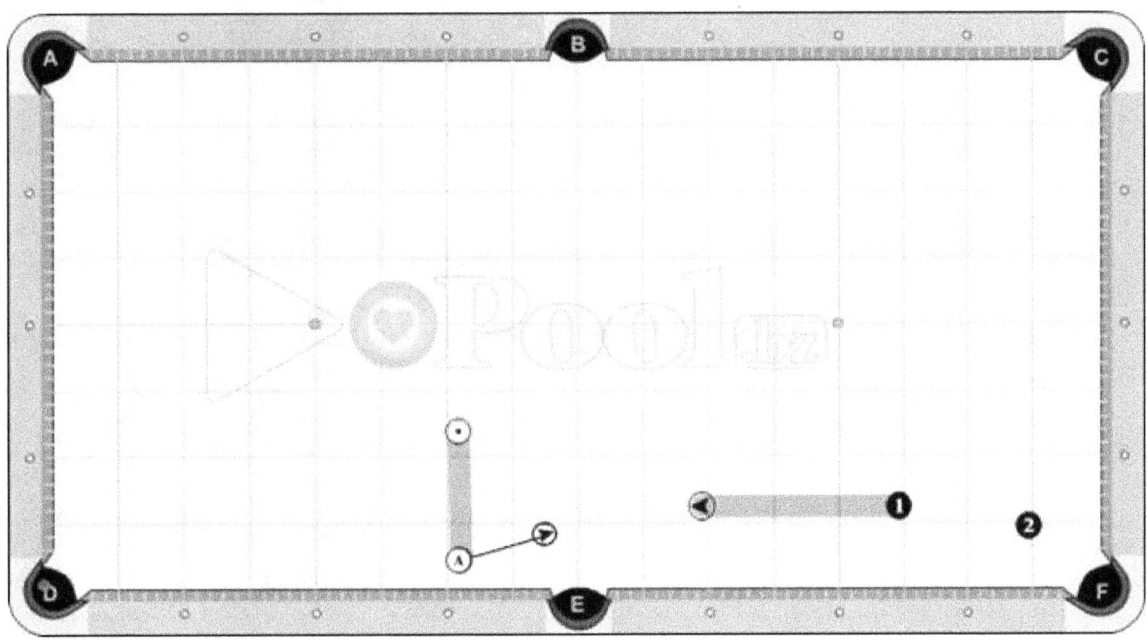

Set 2

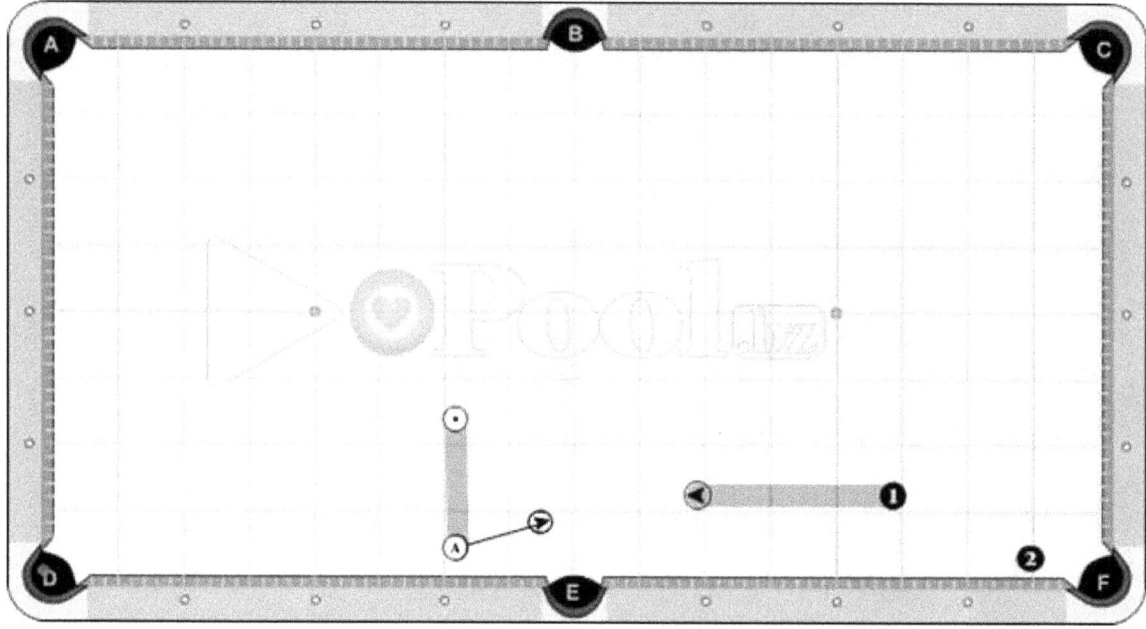

Set 3

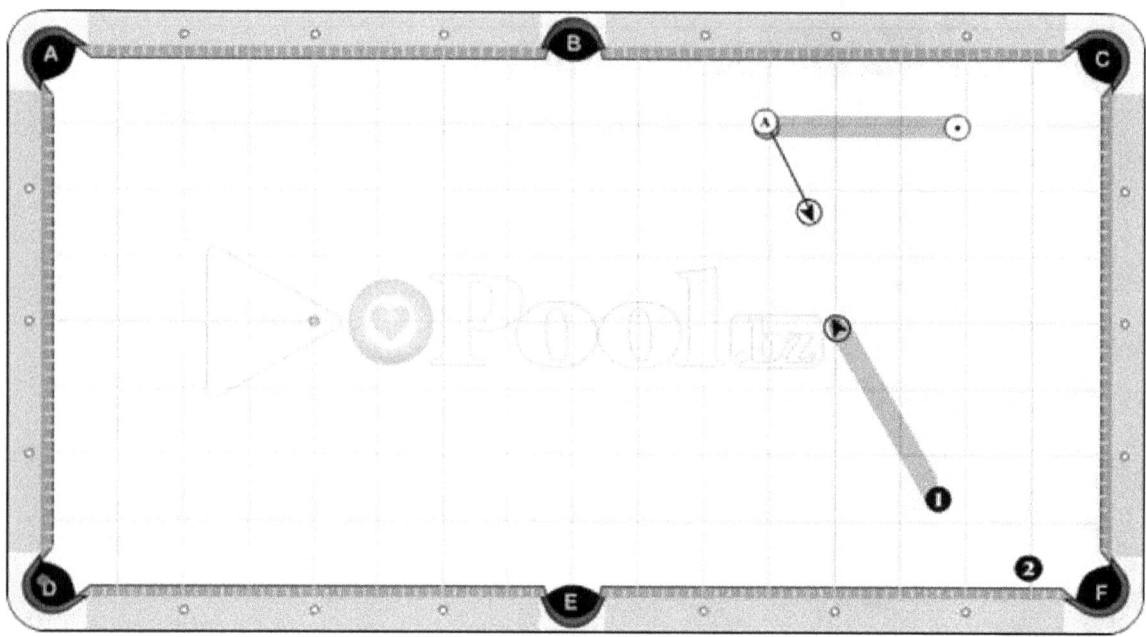

Three Ball Combos

Object: Pocket the third ball OB.

Set 1

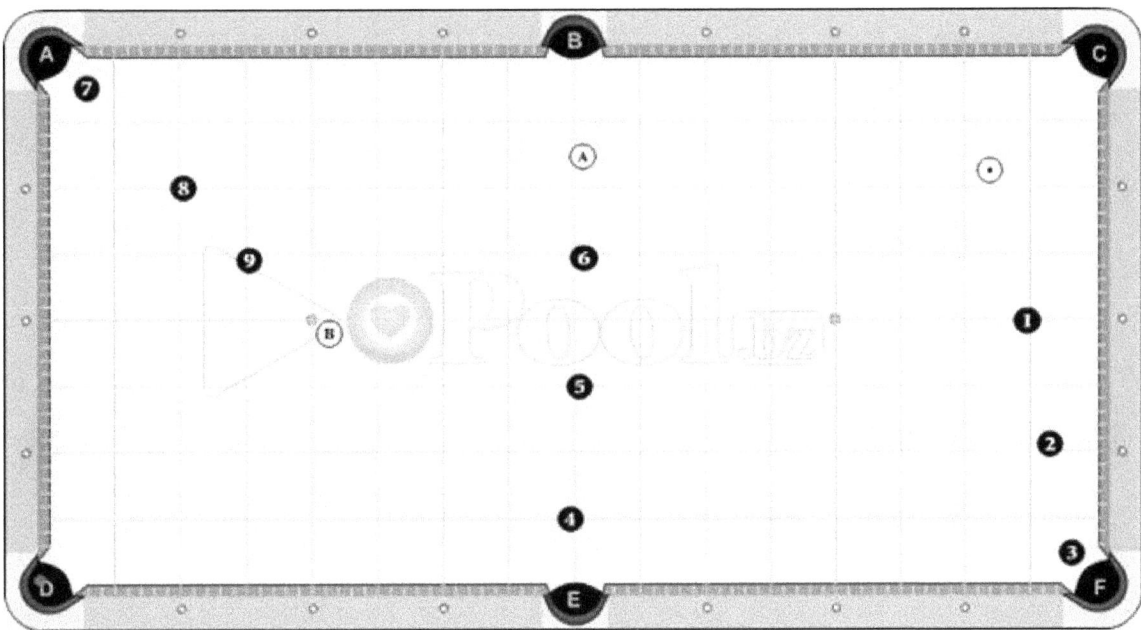

Set 2

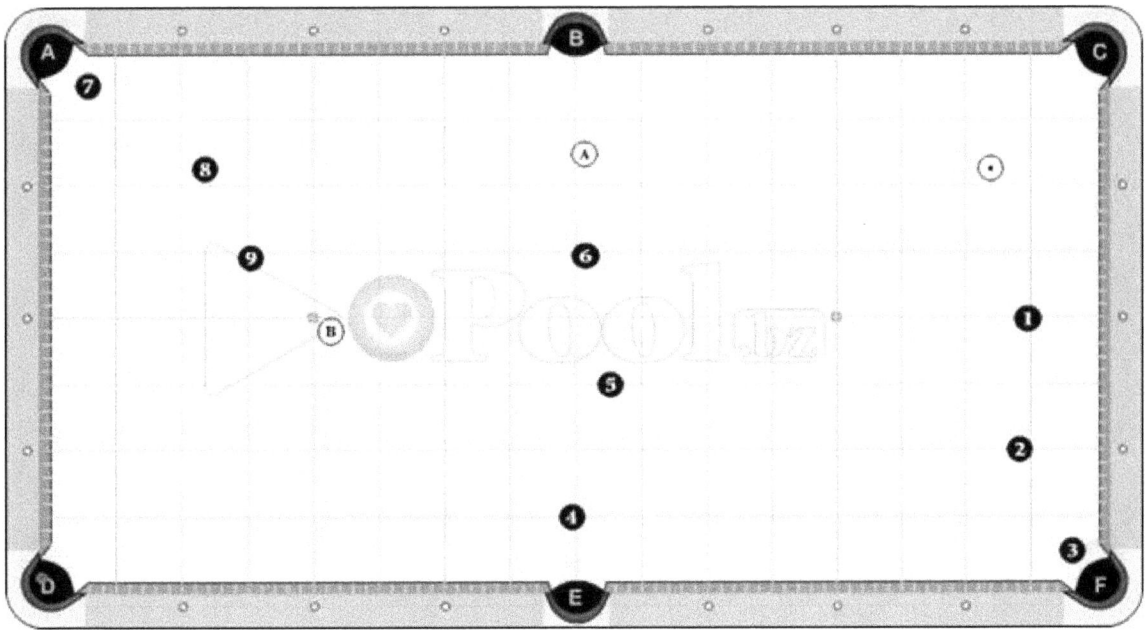

Set 3

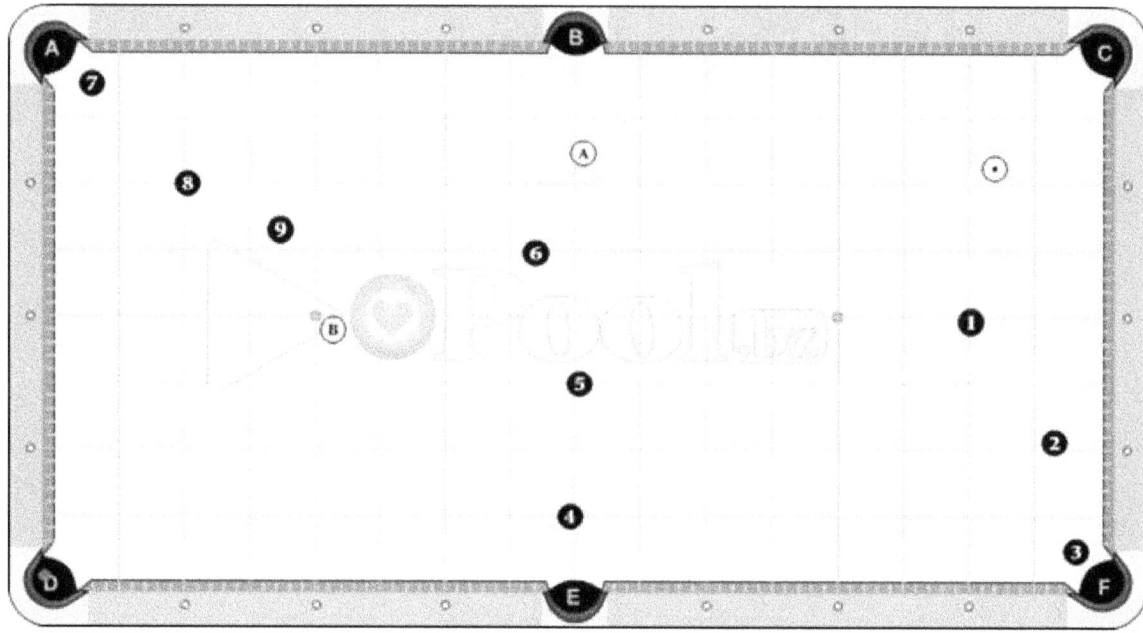

Impossible 4 Ball Combos

Object: Attempt to pocket the 4th OB. Use donuts for positioning. Try these setups to understand the complexities of these shots and why they are not a good idea.

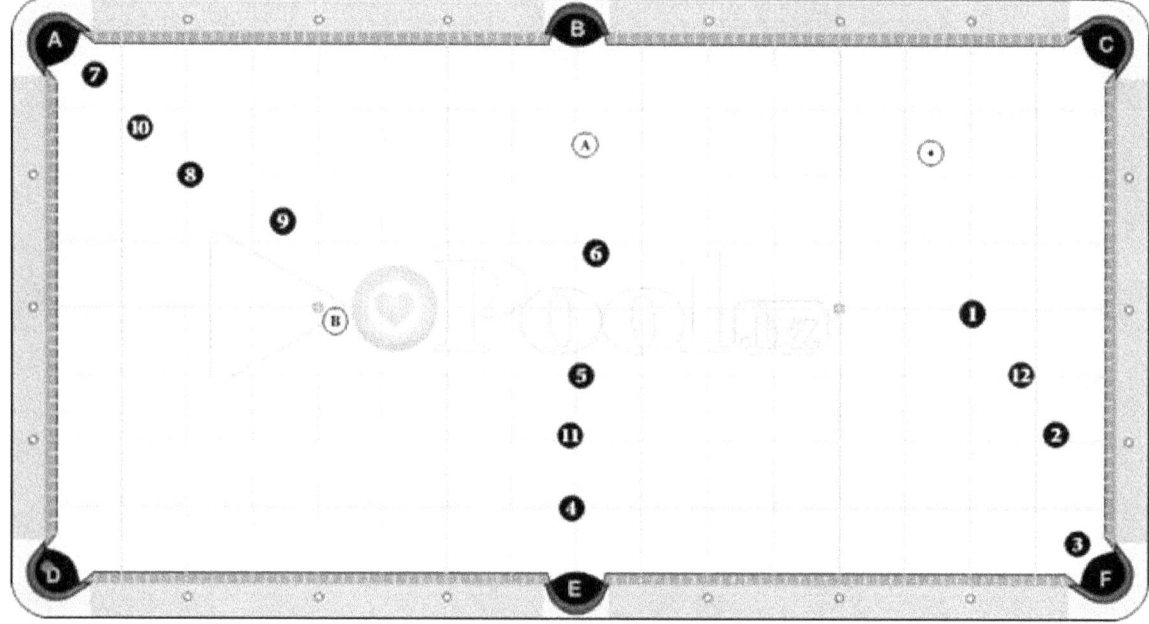

Caroms

These exercises help you become comfortable with using two techniques – tangent line and "Through the Ball". Practice these tangent line caroms. To become

About the Tangent Line

Every time you hit an object ball with a CB, regardless of the speed of the CB and the angle that the CB and object ball contact*, the CB will travel away from the object ball at a right angle. Here is a visual aid. See the line going to the left of the CB/OB contact point? That is the tangent line.

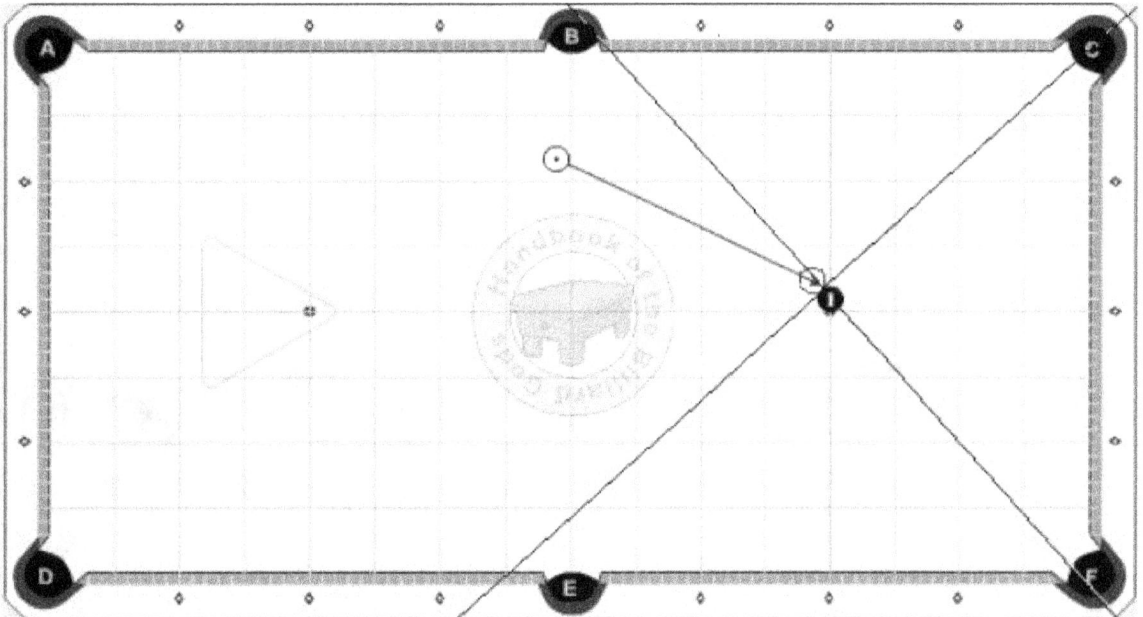

This is as predictable as gravity. You can use this in making successful caroms. Calculate the contact point; shoot the CB into the OB with stun, and you will get predictable results.

Tangent thumb technique

This helps calculate the probable path of the CB after it contacts the OB. This can also help determine whether that path can or should be modified with CB spin.

When the CB travels to the right of the OB, hold your left hand above the OB and form an "L". The index finger points to the pocket, the thumb will point to the CB path.

When the CB travels to the left of the OB, hold your right hand above the OB and form a backwards "L". The index finger points to the pocket, the thumb will point to the CB path.

Tangent Line Caroms

Object: Carom off the first OB and pocket the second OB. Use tangent lines in your calculations.

Set 1

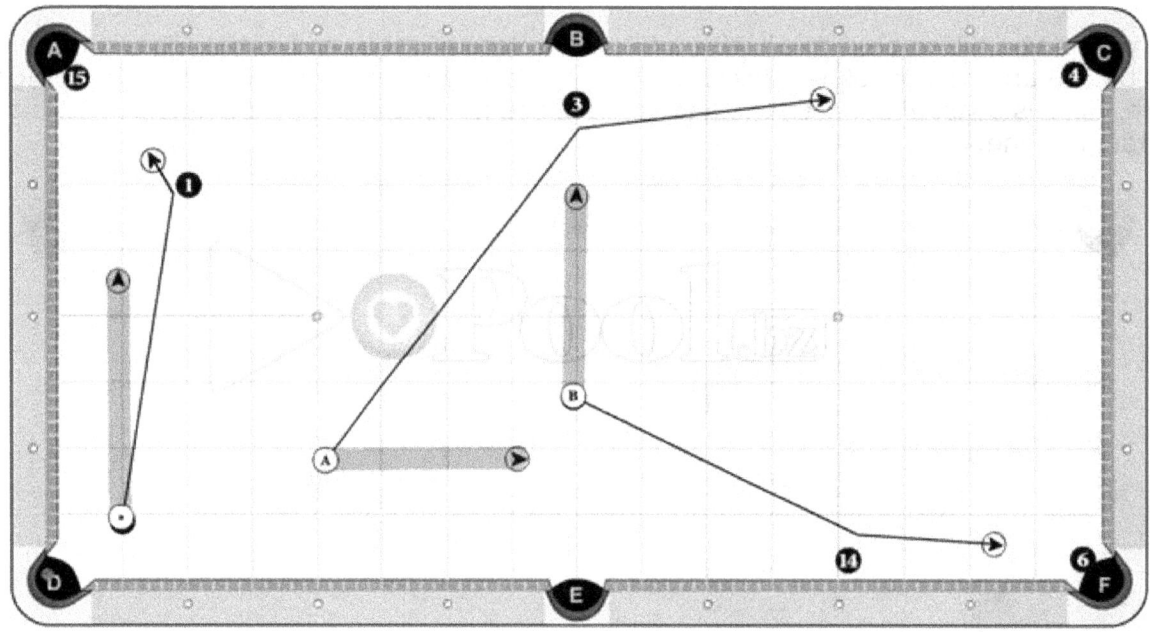

Set 2

Work on each position until you can consistently get successful results.

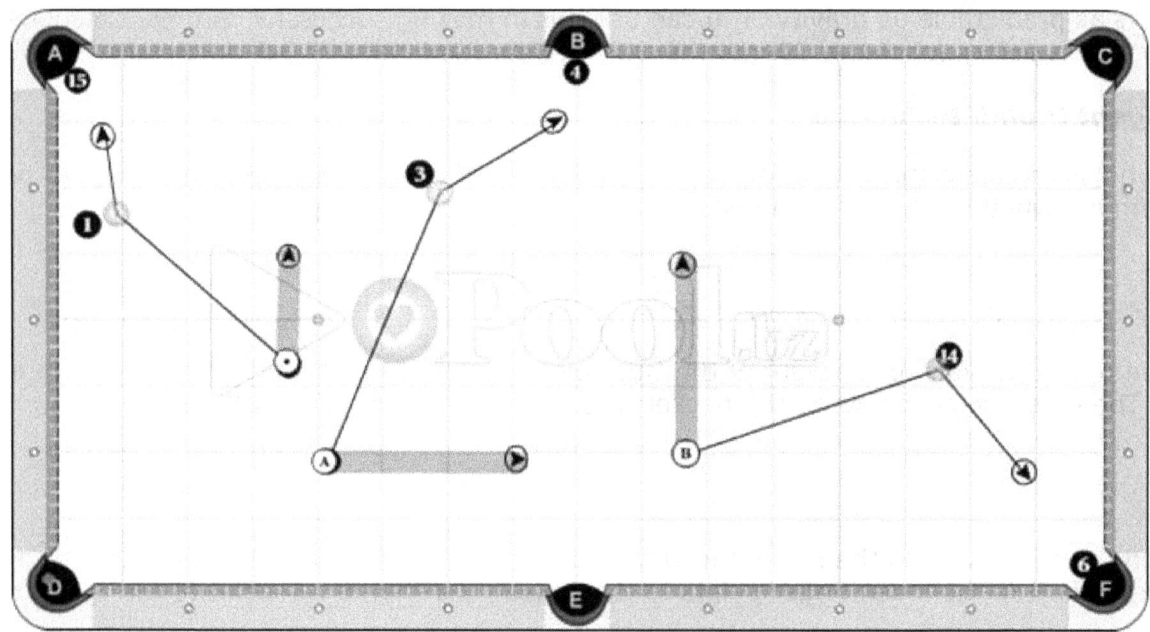

Through the Ball Caroms

Object: Use follow to send the CB through the first OB and pocket the second OB.

Set 1

Tip: Play these with a medium soft stroke and 12:00 follow on the CB.

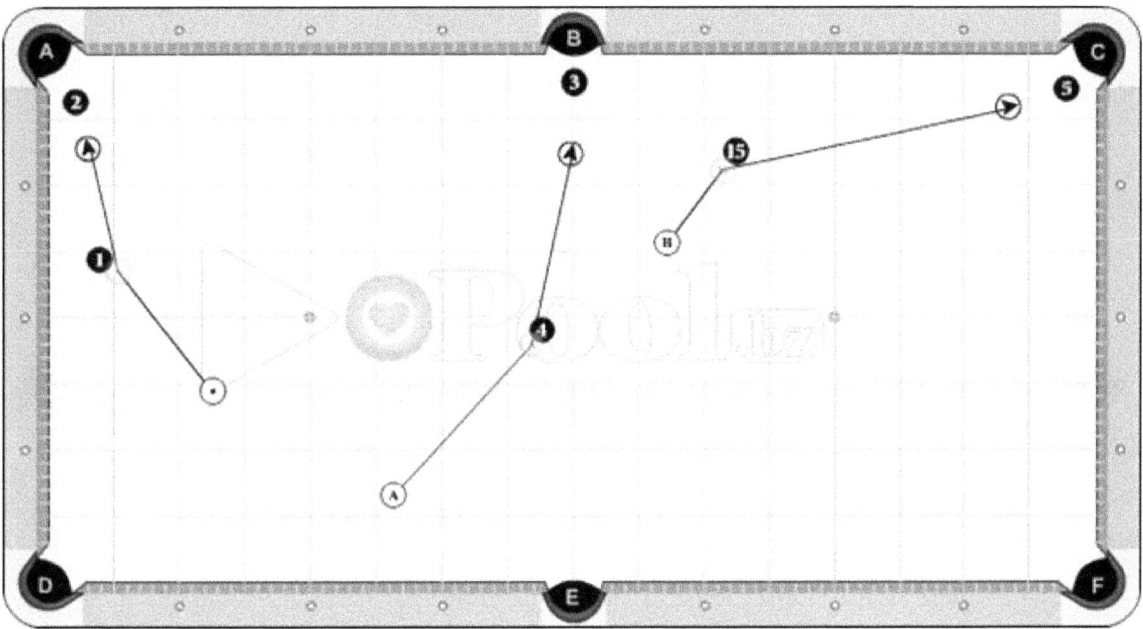

Set 2

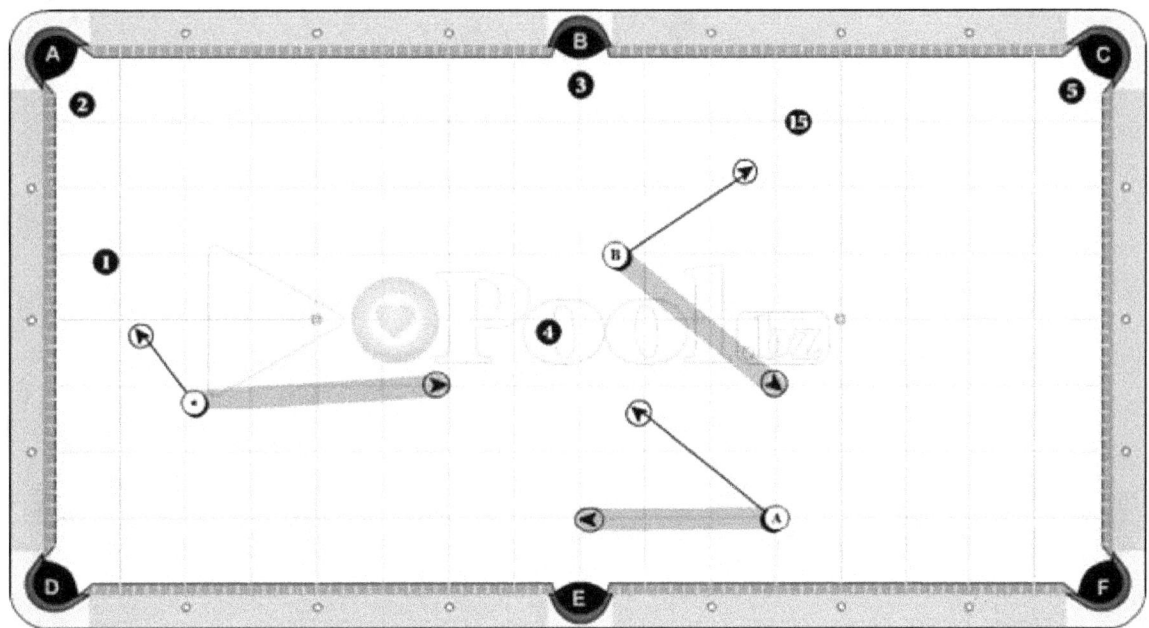

Set 3

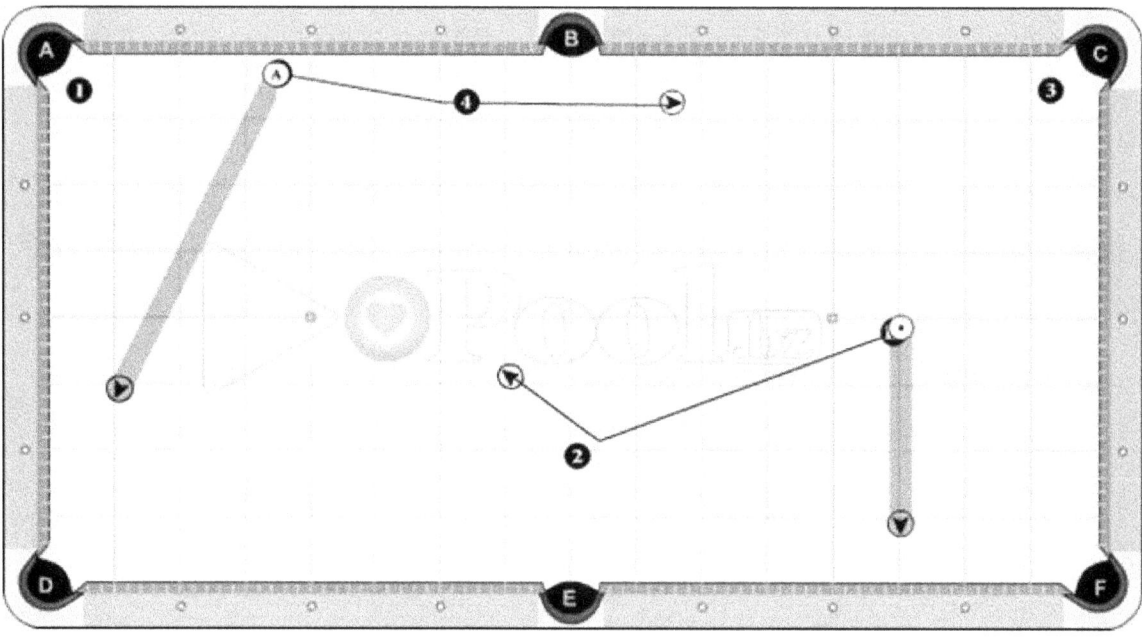

Set 4

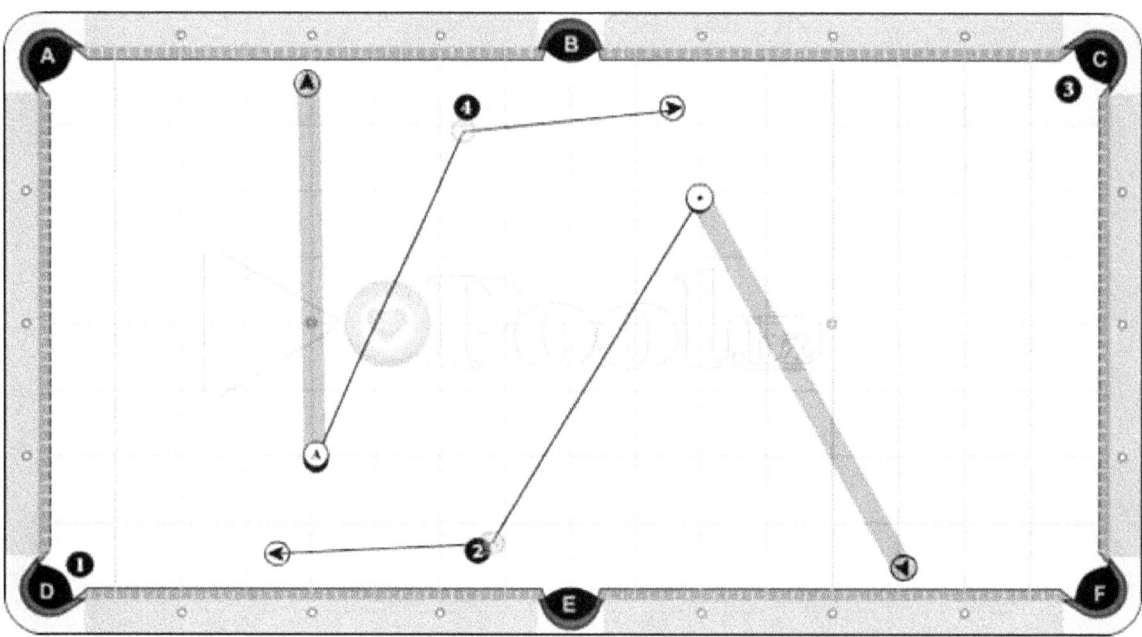

Safeties

Use these safety exercises to recognize good defensive opportunities.

Distance Safeties

Object: Move the CB far away from OB.

Set 1

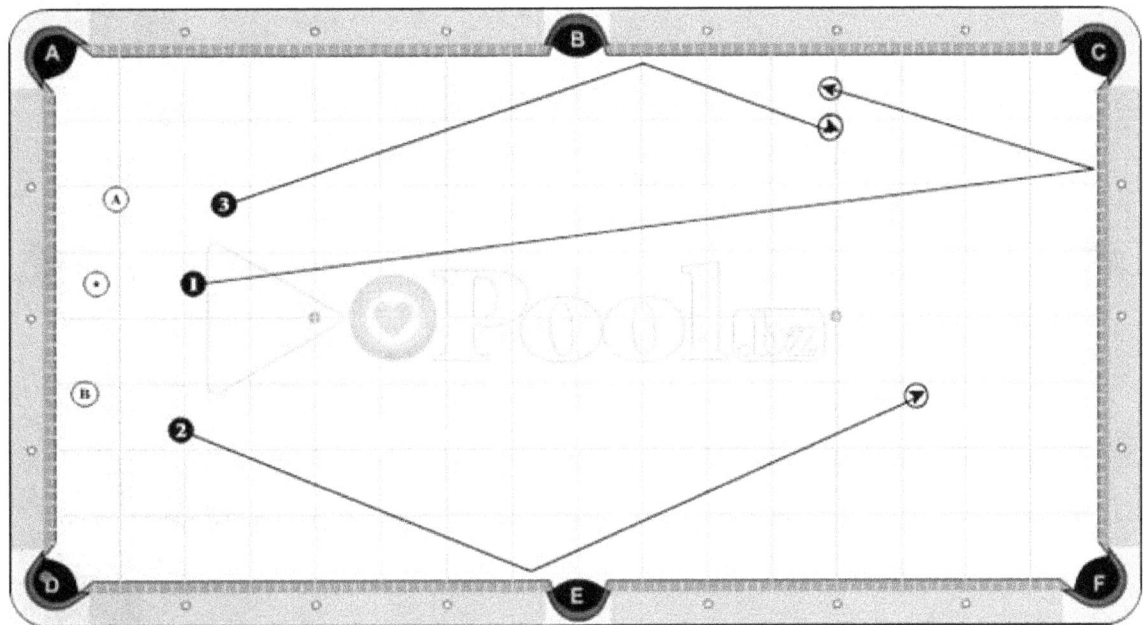

Set 2

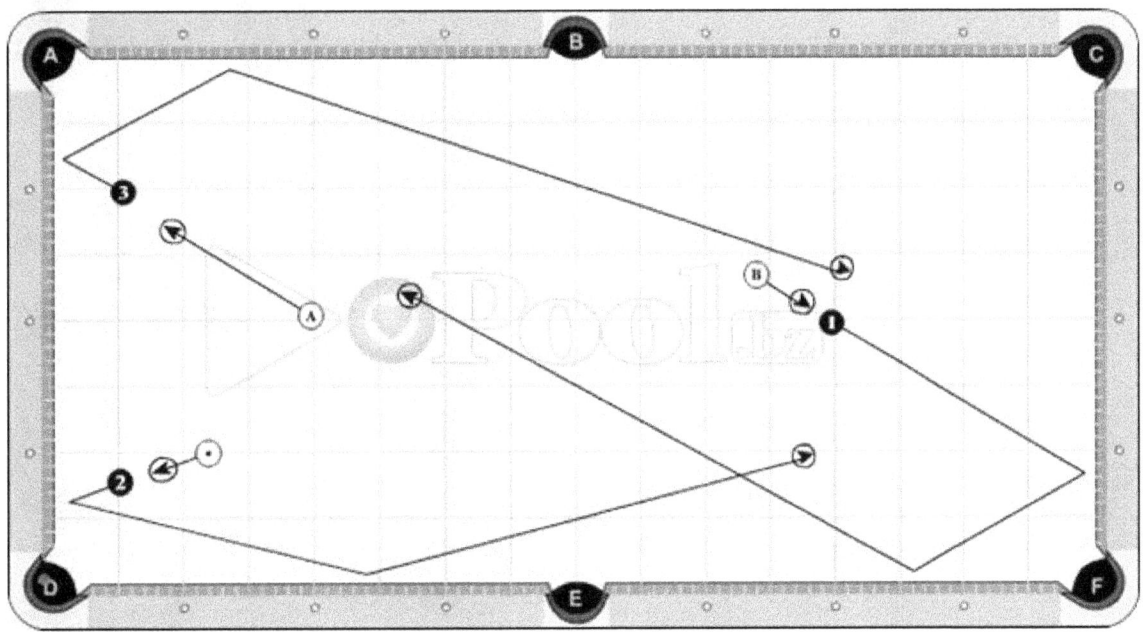

Set 3

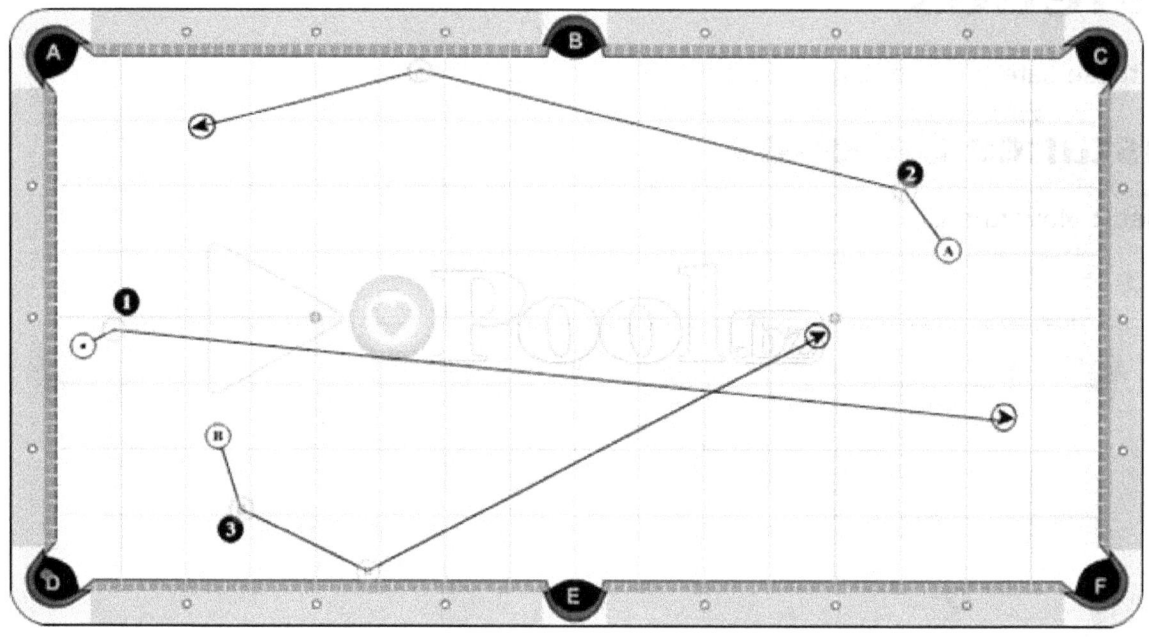

Set

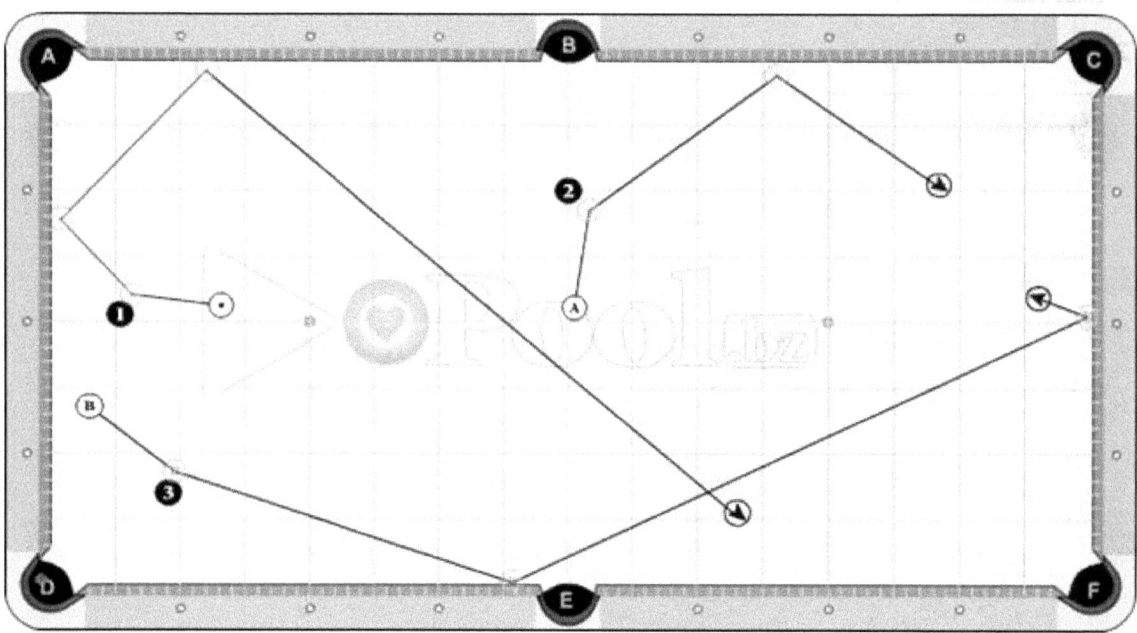

Bad Angle

Object: Contact OB to hit one rail and move OB to leave opponent with no shot.

Set 1

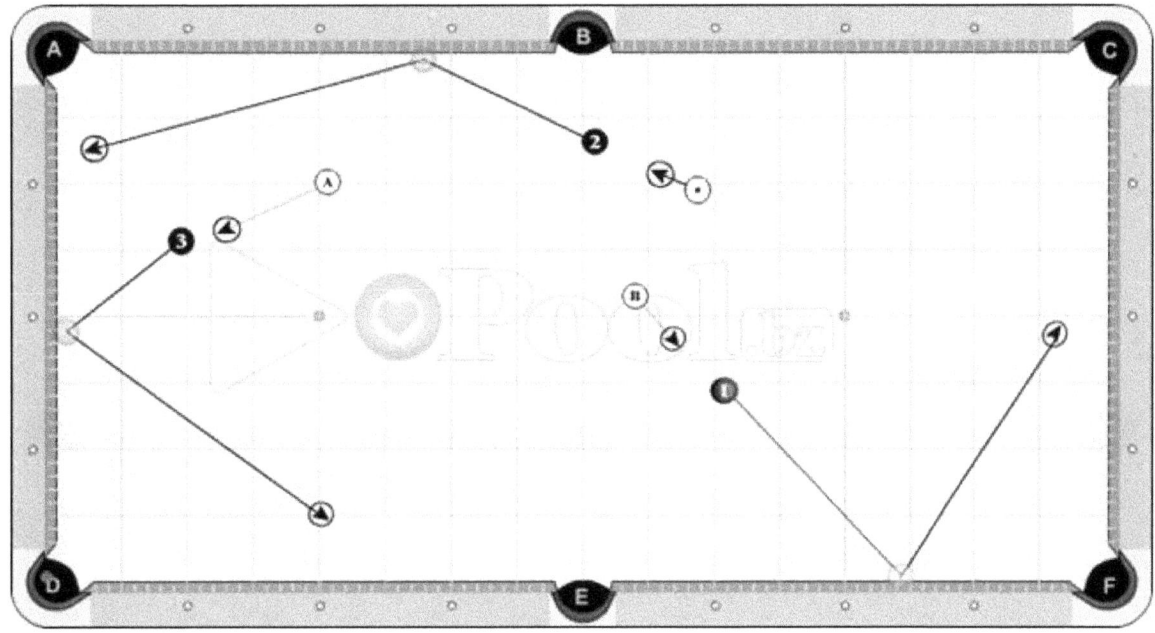

Set 2

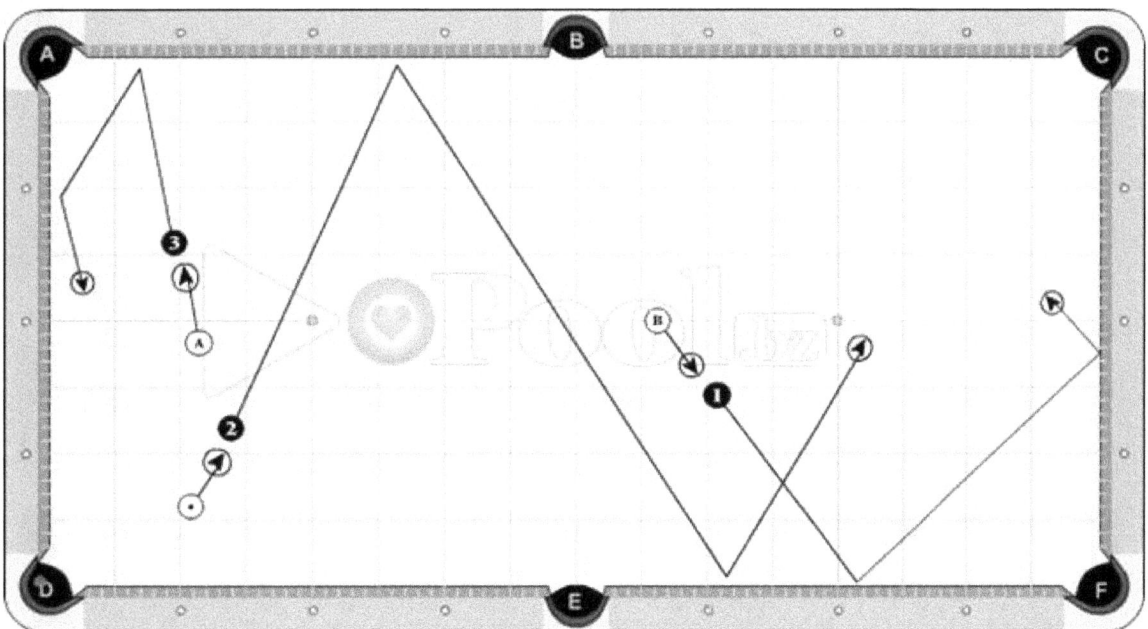

Set 3

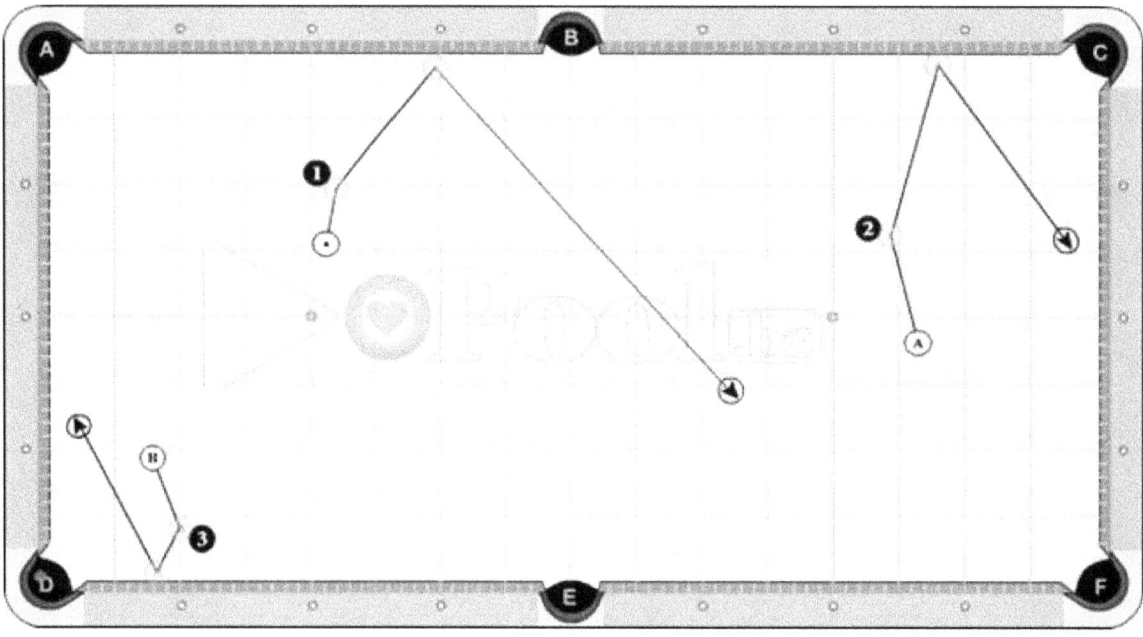

Set 4

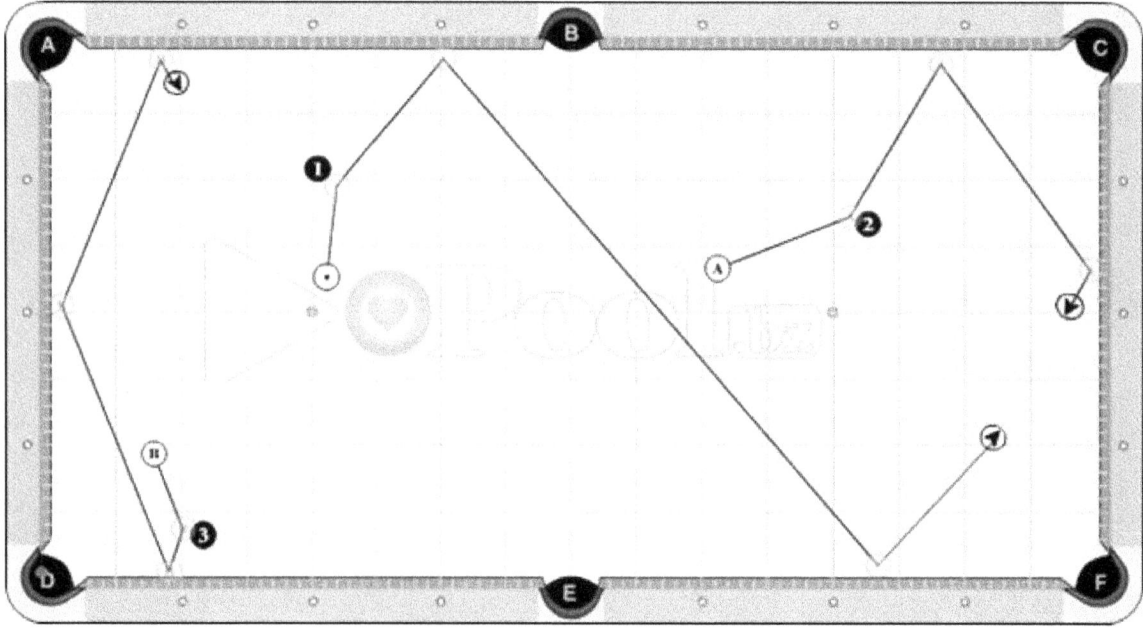

On Cushion

Object: Carom off on OB and leave CB close to cushion..

Set 1

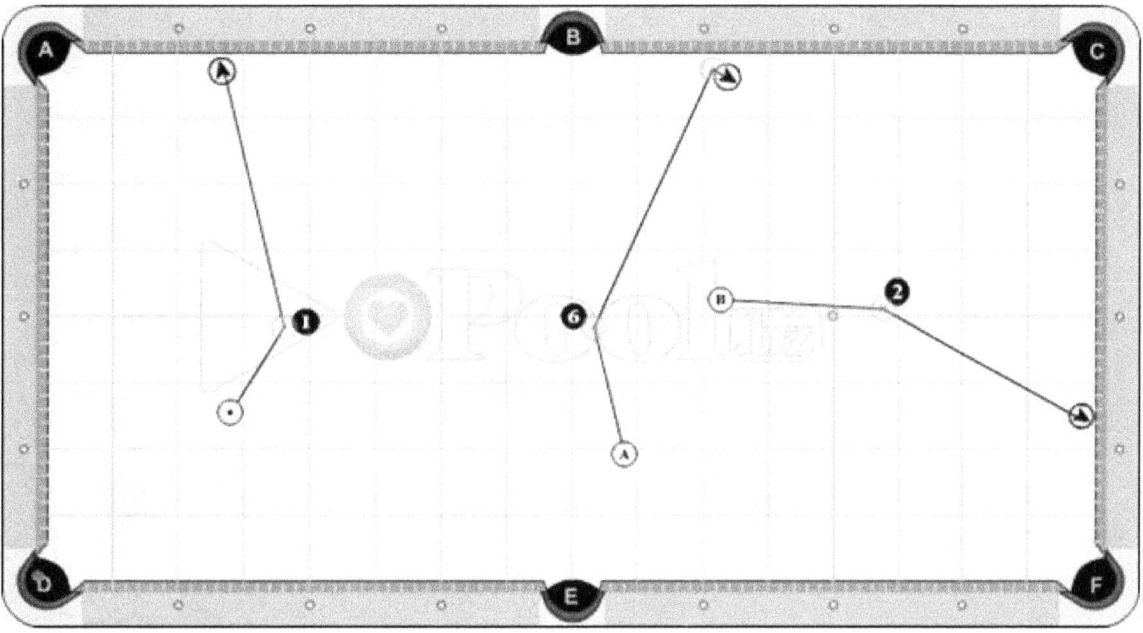

Set 2

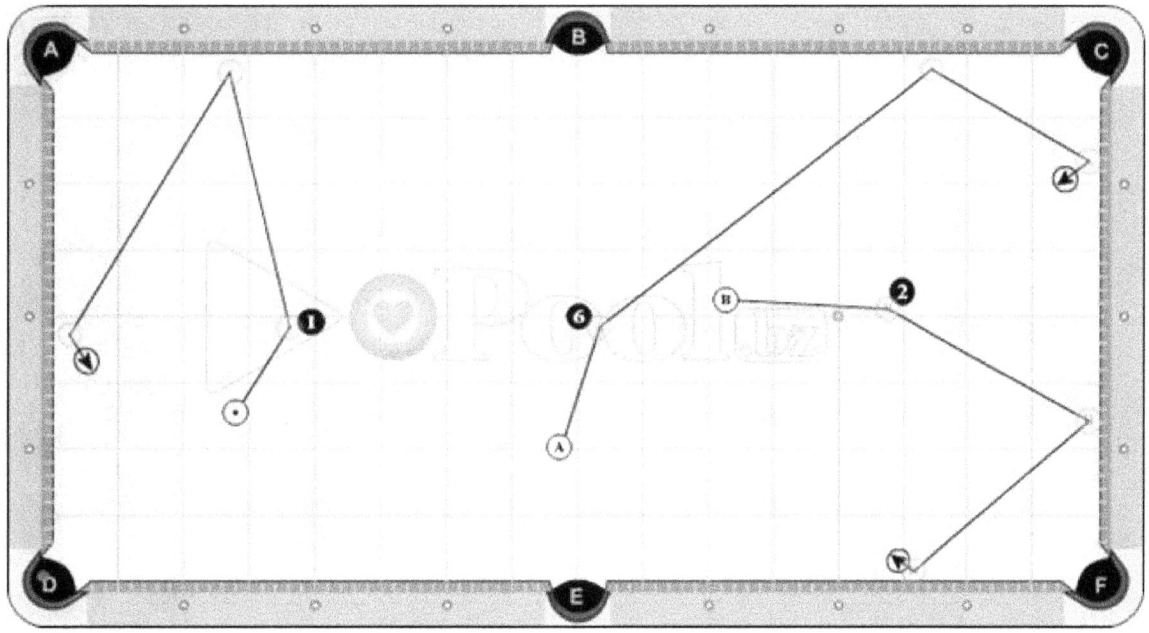

Hidden Ball Safety

Object: Hit OB and hide it from the CB behind the wall of balls.

Set 1 (Stun)

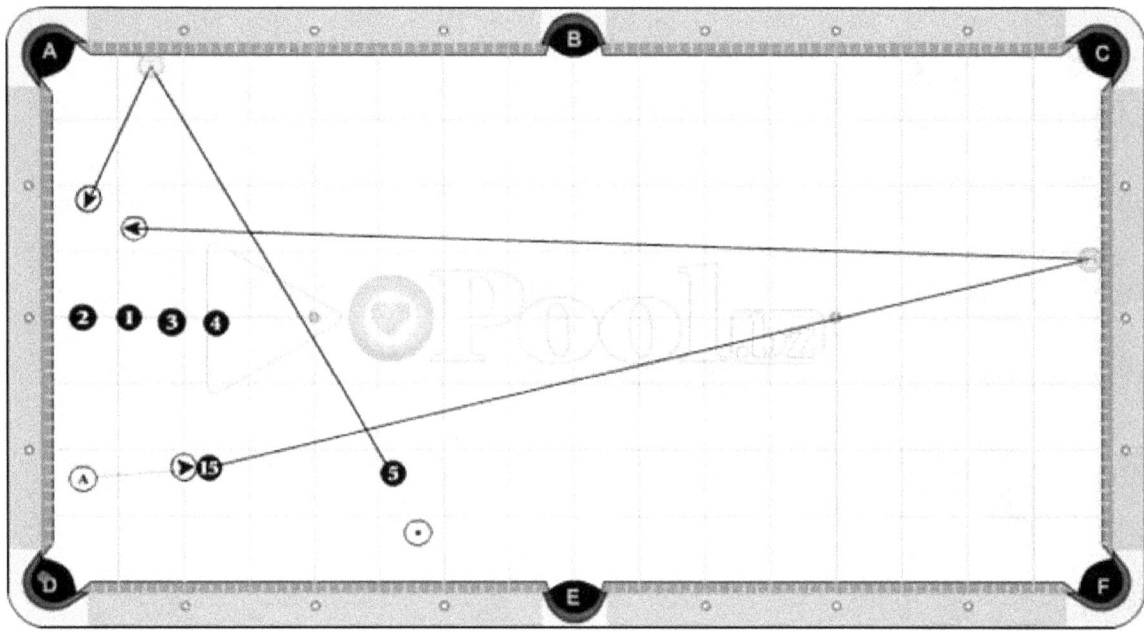

Set 2

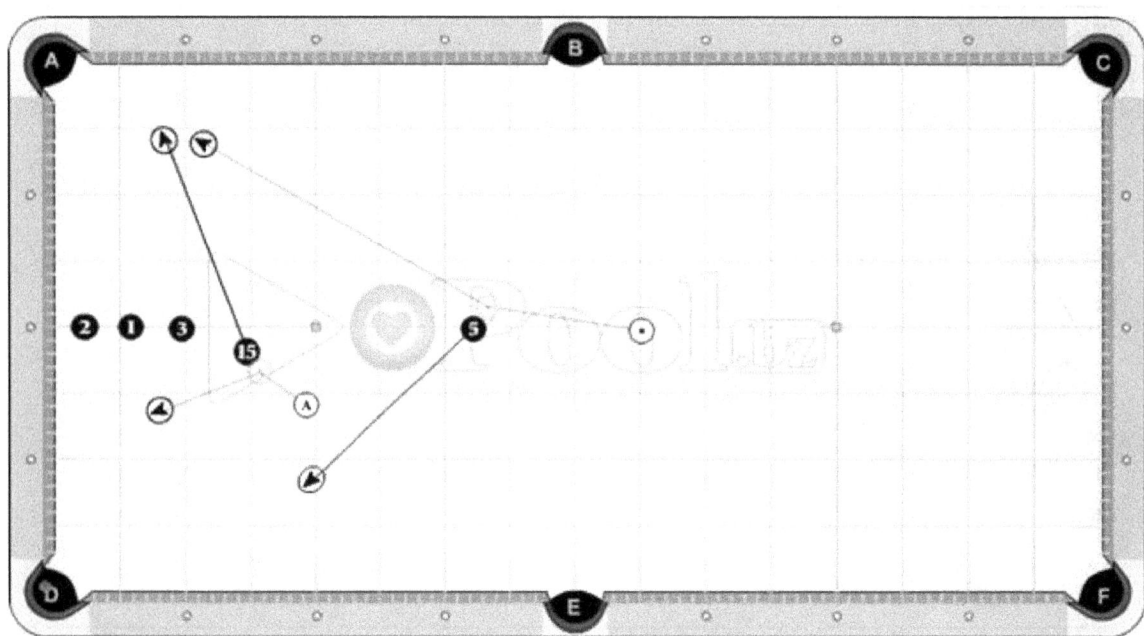

Set 3 (Draw)

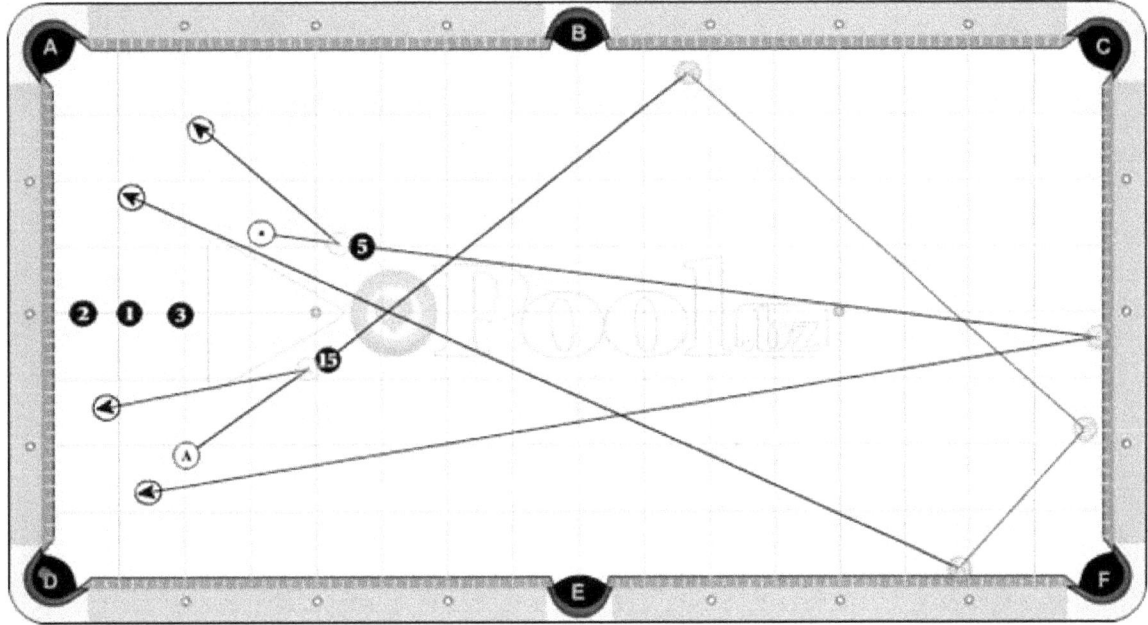

CB Control

Object: Move the cue ball through the OB and lay the CB close to cushion (as shown).

Set 1

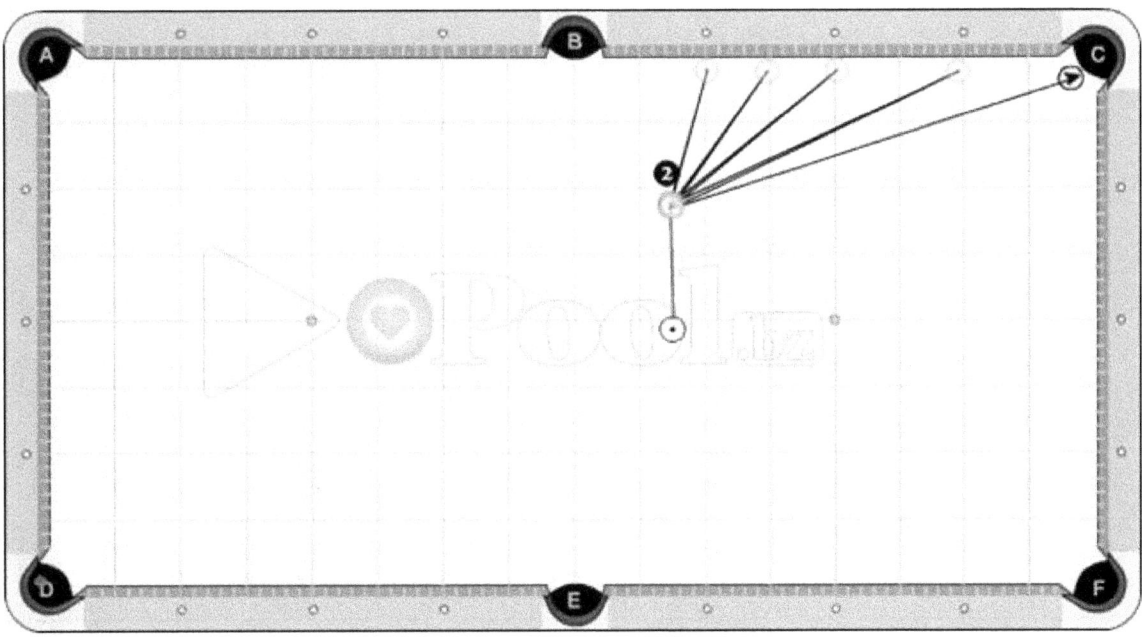

Set 2

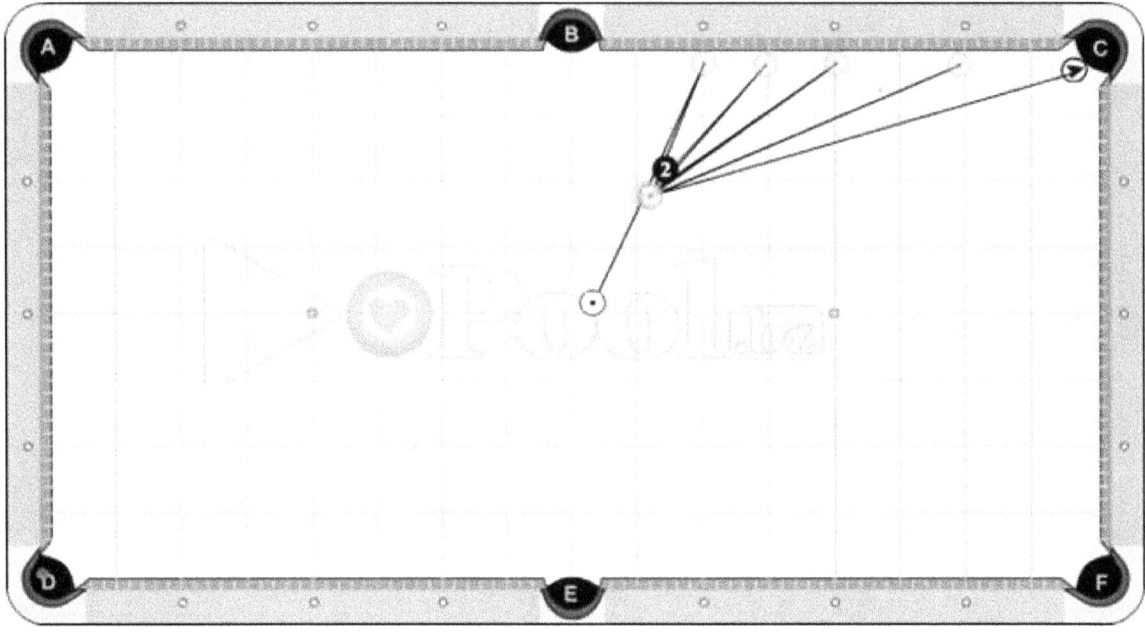

Set 3

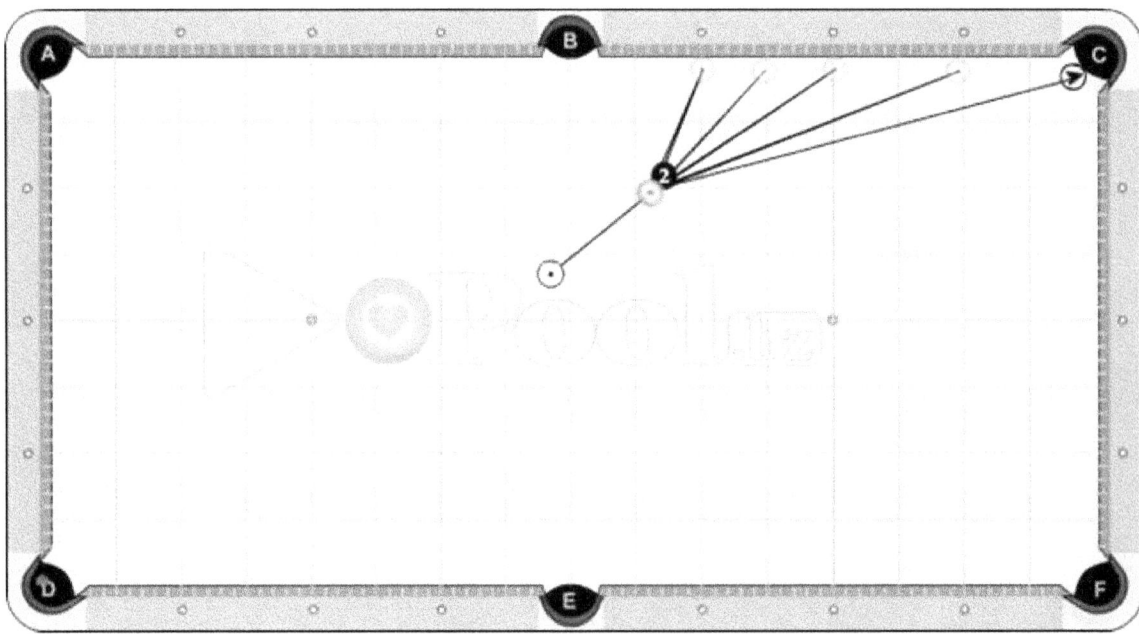

OB Control

Object: Contact OB with CB and move OB near cushion.

Set 1

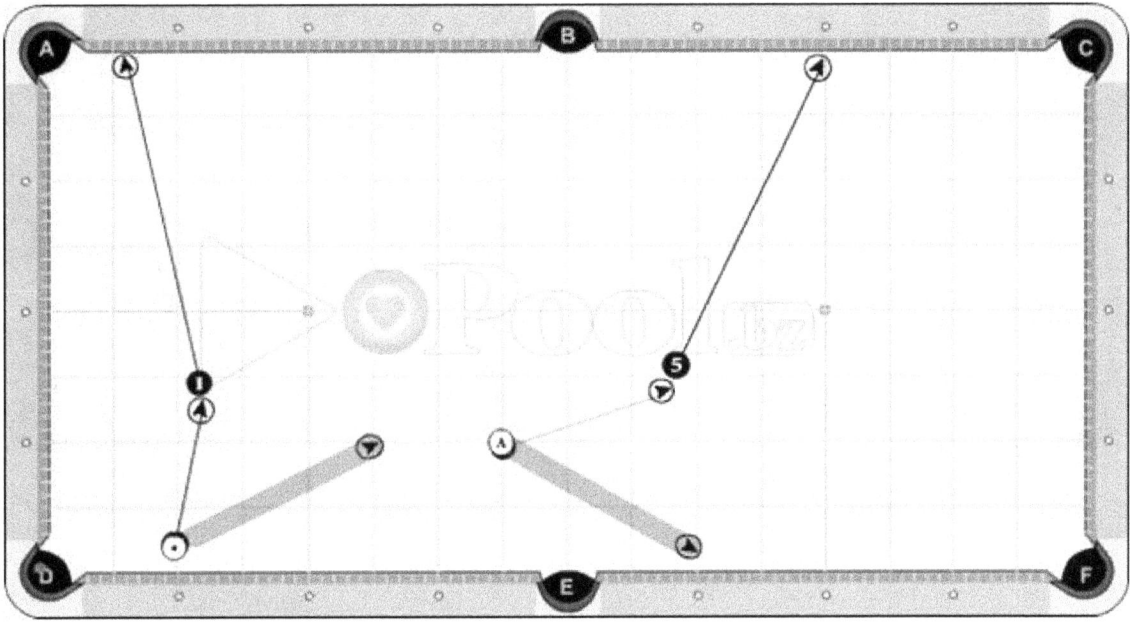

Set 2

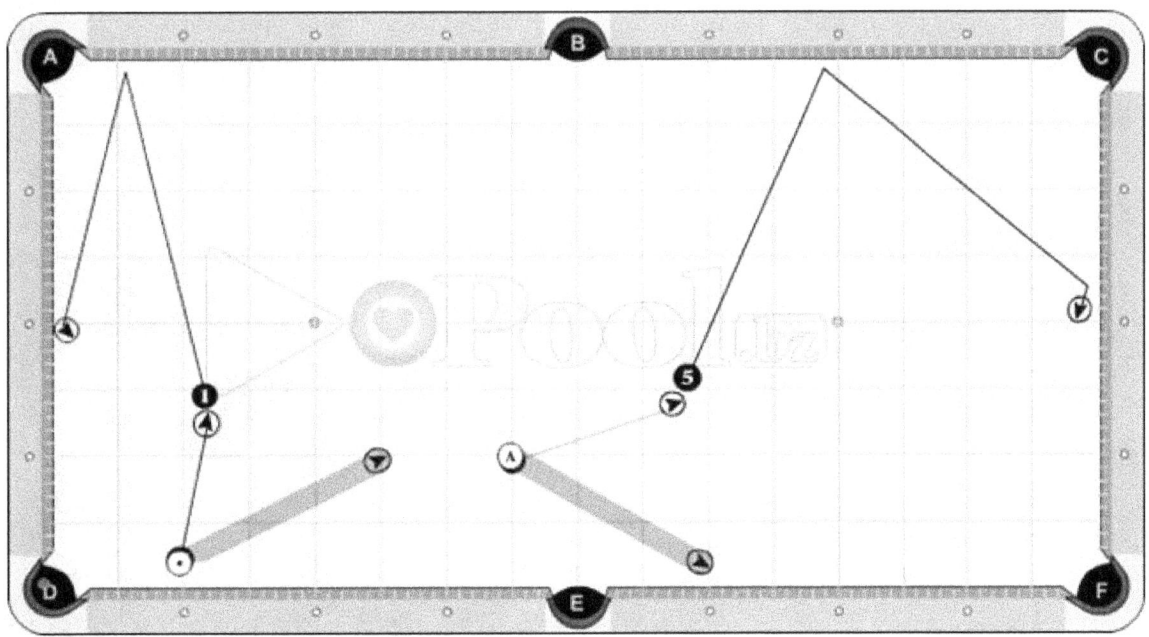

Set 3

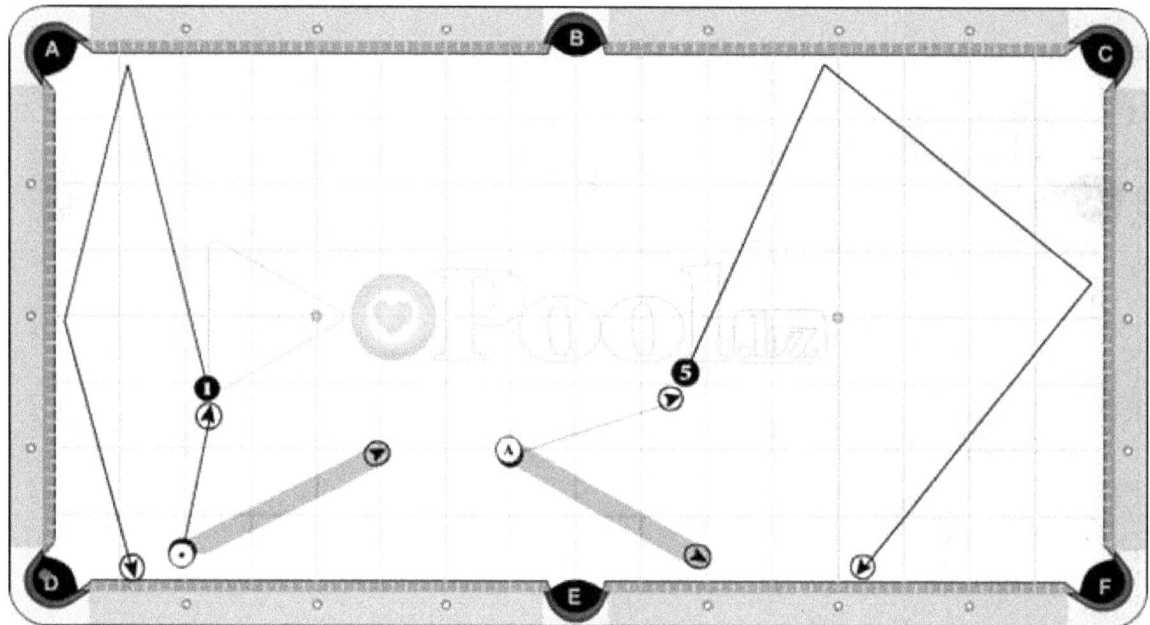

Kicking

Simple Off-Cushion Kicks

Object: CB into cushion and then contact OB into pocket.

Set 1

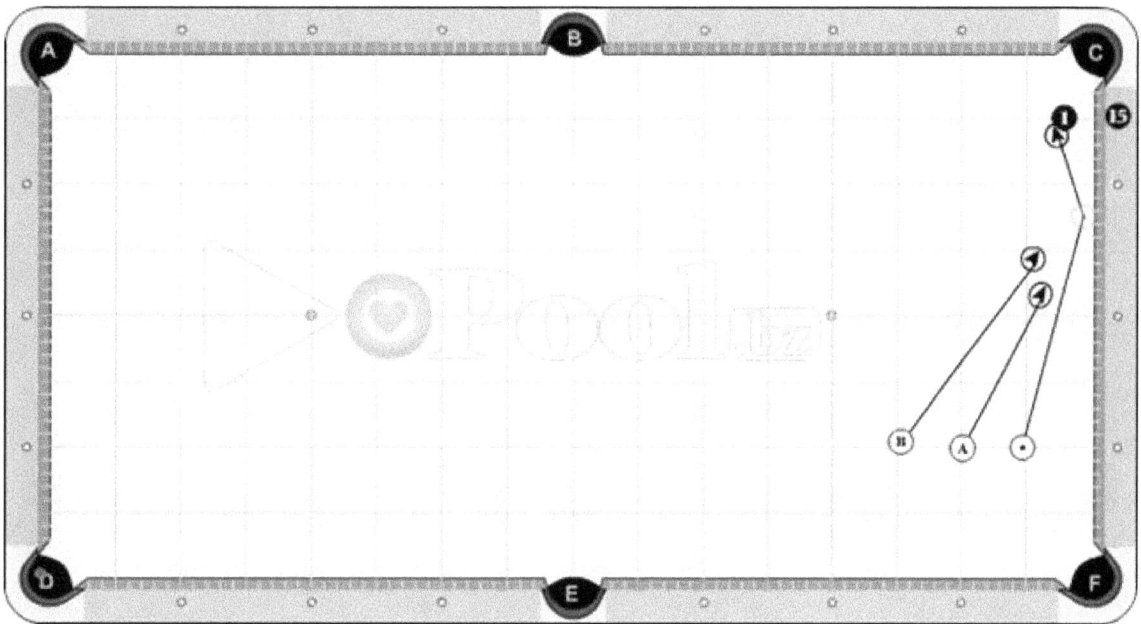

Set 2

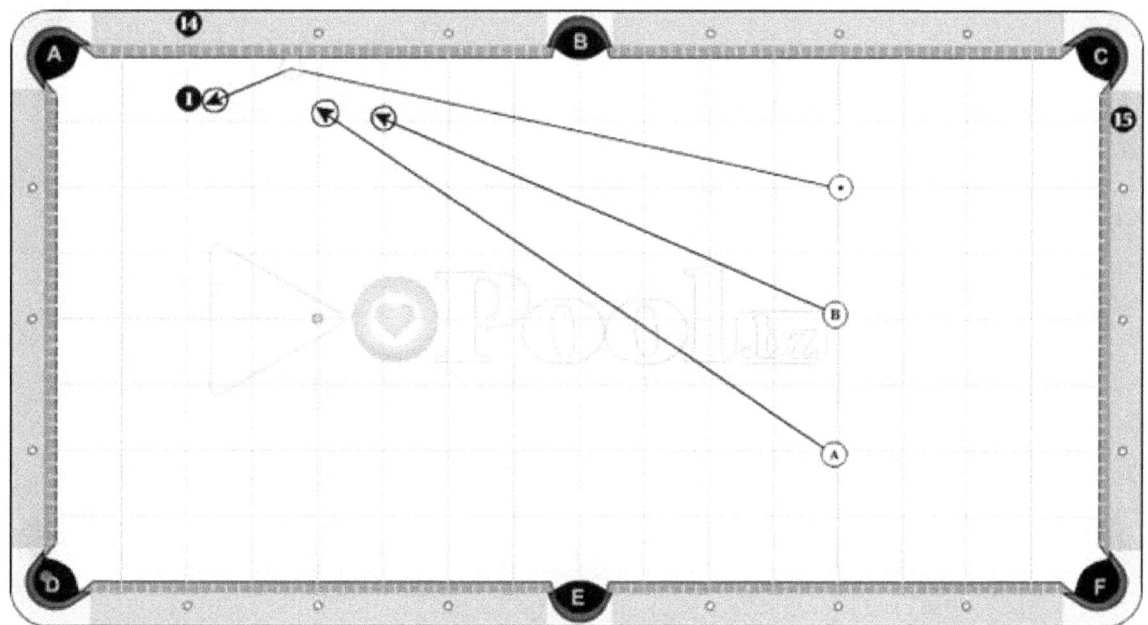

Cross Side Kicks

Object: Shoot CB to cushion and bank into pocket (as shown).

Set 1 (Divide by two technique)

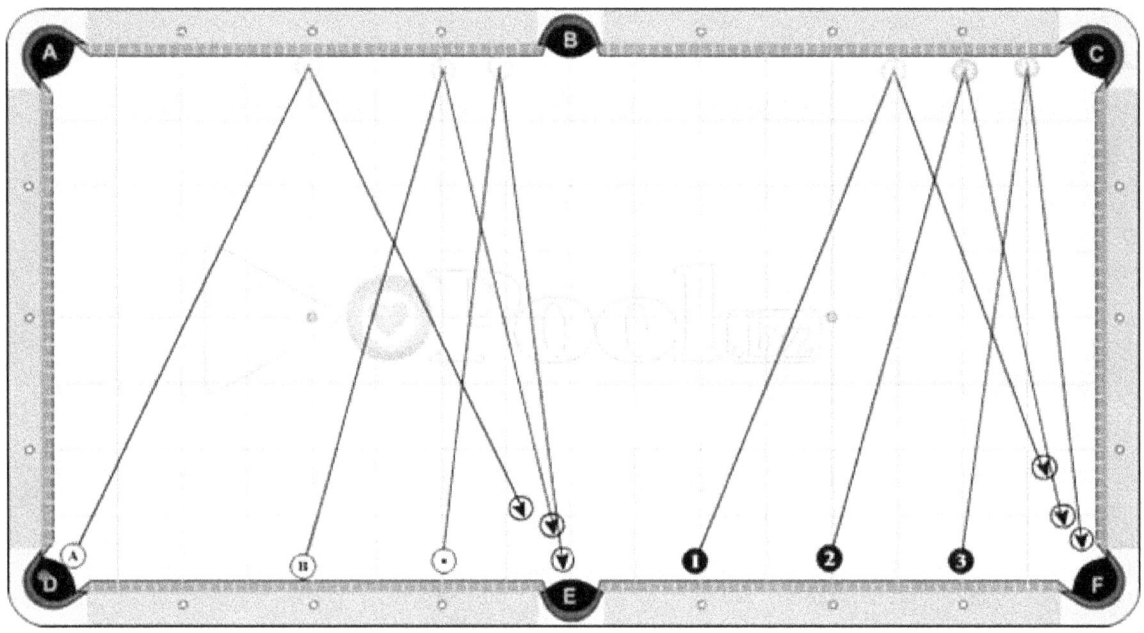

Set 2 (Divide by two technique)

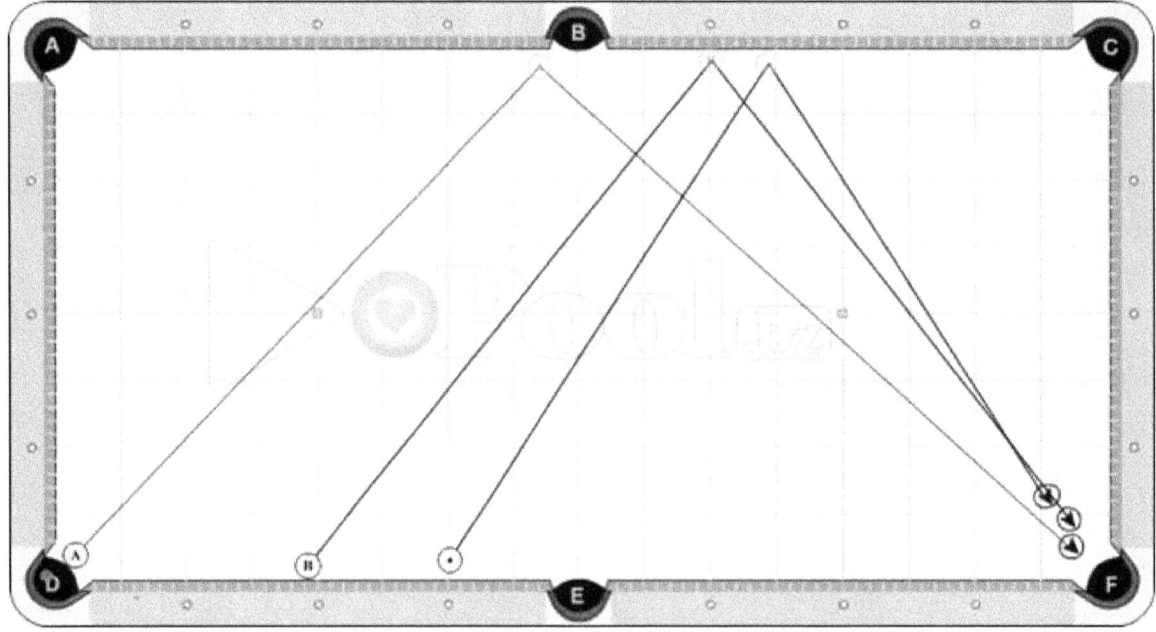

Set 3 (CB 1 D Up)

Divide by two and offset 1/8 on the CB side of the rail contact point. (for Example, if CB and pocket are 2 diamonds apart, divide by 2 = 1 D. CB at 1 D up is offset by 1/8 D (as shown).

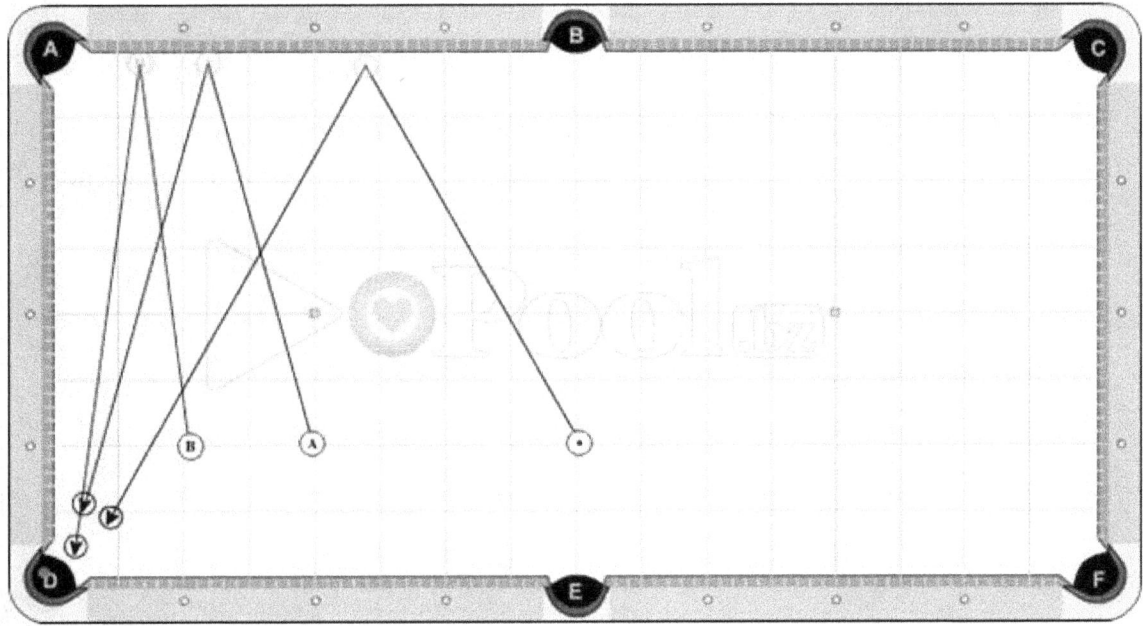

Set 4 (CB 2 D Up)

Divide by two and offset 1/4 on the CB side of the rail contact point. (for Example, if CB and pocket are 2 diamonds apart, divide by 2 = 1 D. CB at 1 D up is offset by 1/4 D (as shown).

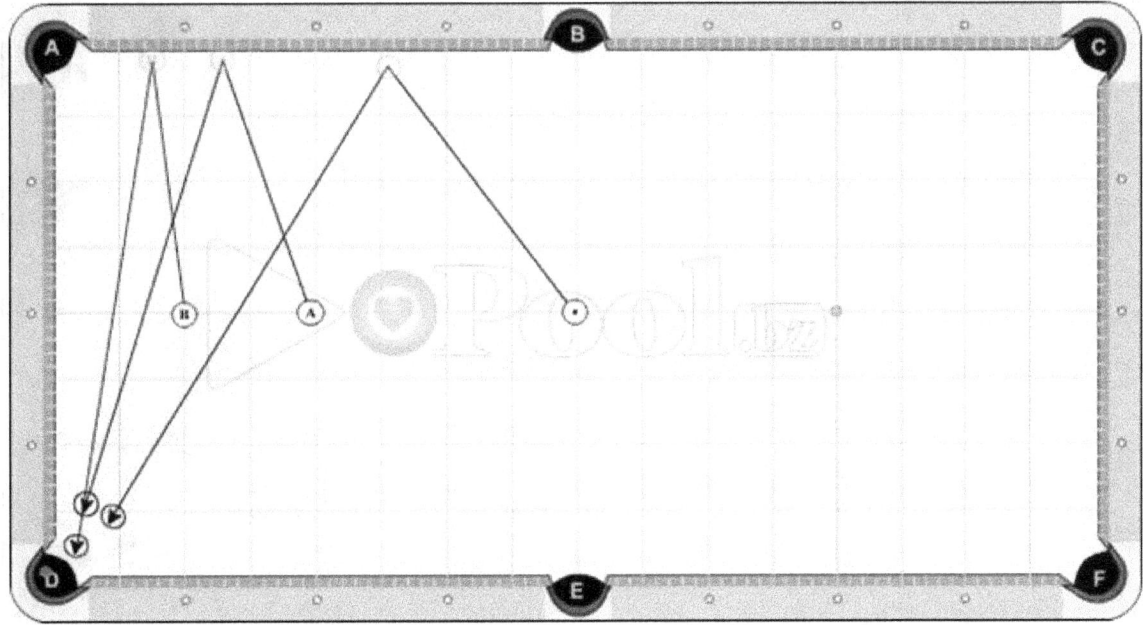

Set 5 (CB 3 D Up)

Divide by two and offset 2/3 on the CB side of the rail contact point. (for Example, if CB and pocket are 2 diamonds apart, divide by 2 = 1 D. CB at 1 D up is offset by 2/3 D (as shown).

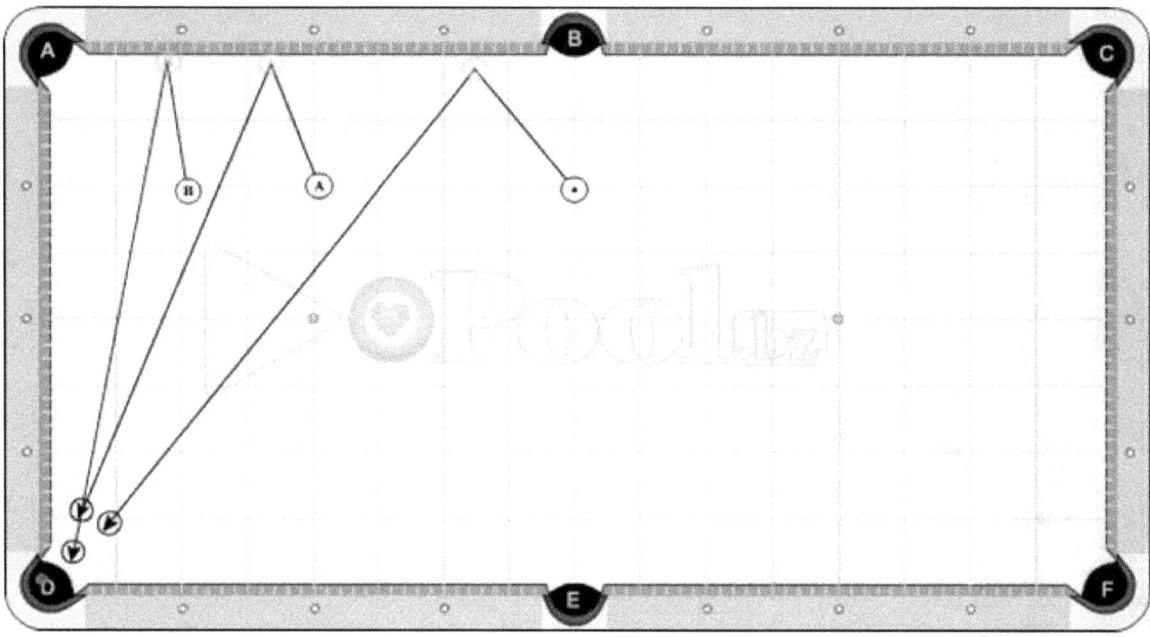

Long Table Kicks

Set 1 (Divide-by-two technique)

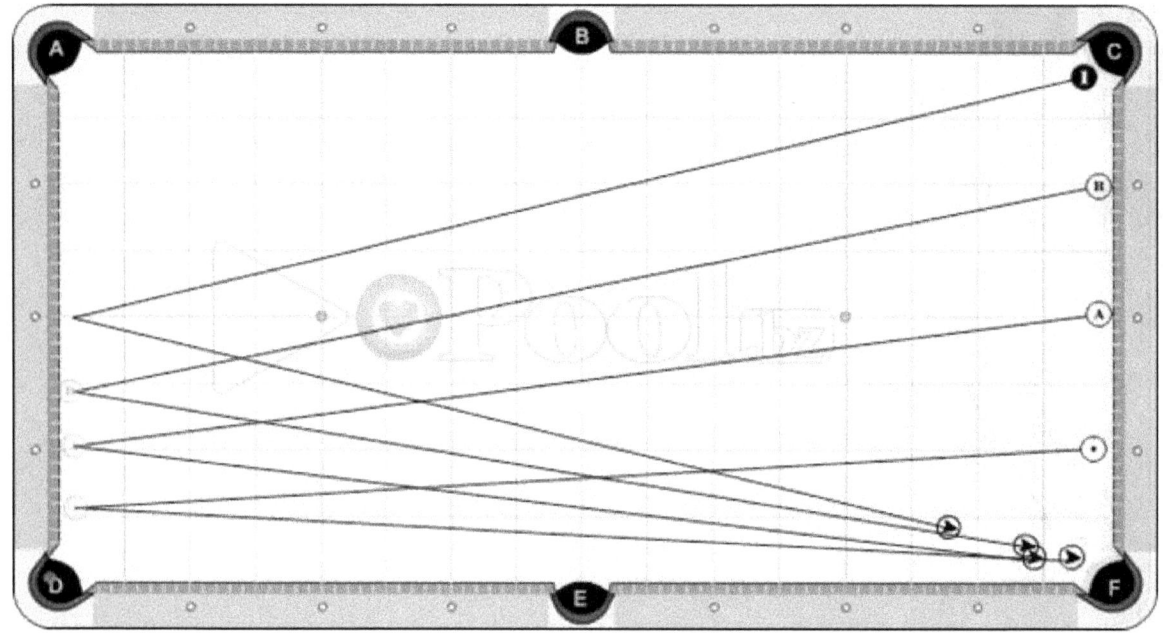

Set 2 (CB 2 D Up)

Divide by two and offset 1/8 on the CB side of the rail contact point. (for Example, if CB and pocket are 2 diamonds apart, divide by 2 = 1 D. CB at 1 D up is offset by 1/8 D (as shown).

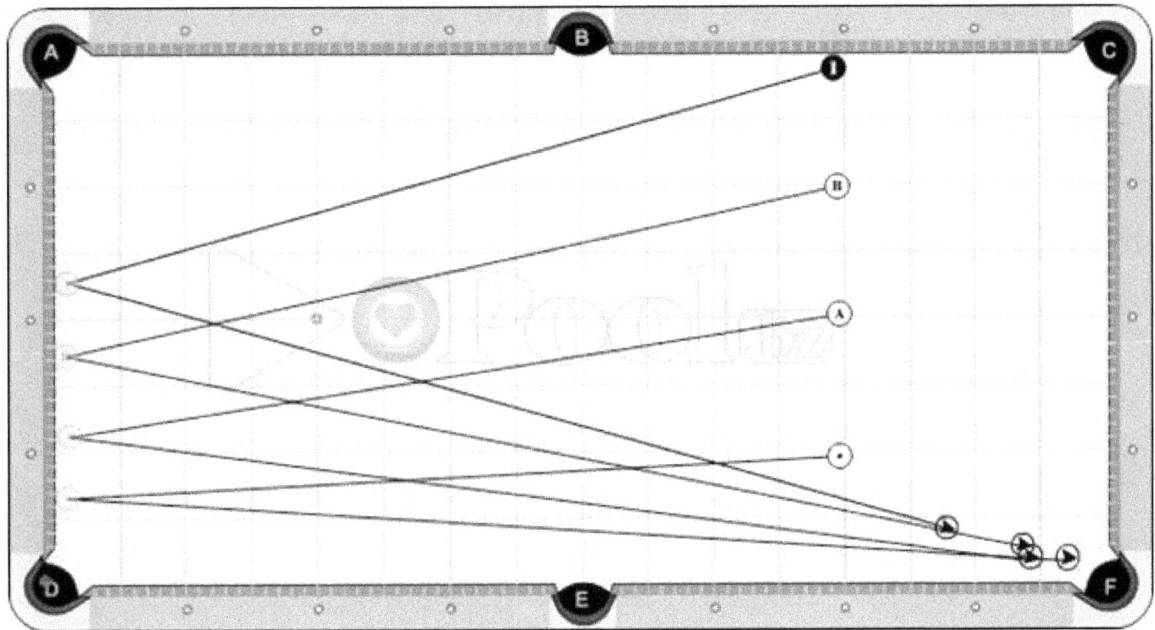

Set 3 (CB 4 D Up)

Divide by two and offset 1/4 on the CB side of the rail contact point. (for Example, if CB and pocket are 2 diamonds apart, divide by 2 = 1 D. CB at 1 D up is offset by 1/4 D (as shown).

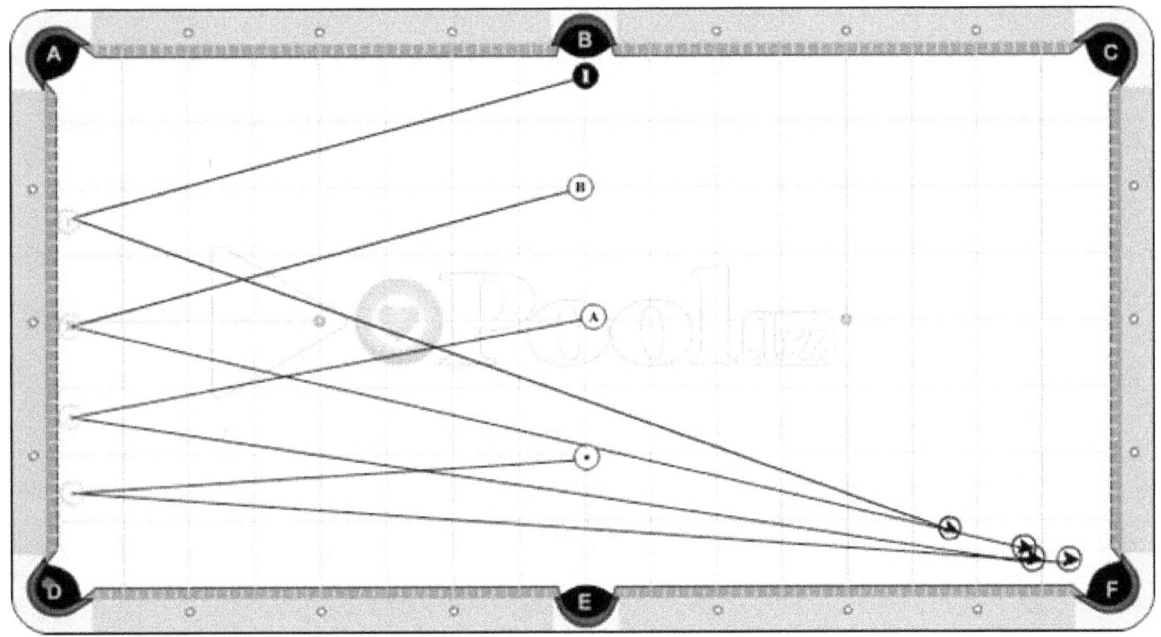

Set 4 (CB 6 D Up)

Divide by two and offset 2/3 on the CB side of the rail contact point. (for Example, if CB and pocket are 2 diamonds apart, divide by 2 = 1 D. CB at 1 D up is offset by 2/3 D (as shown).

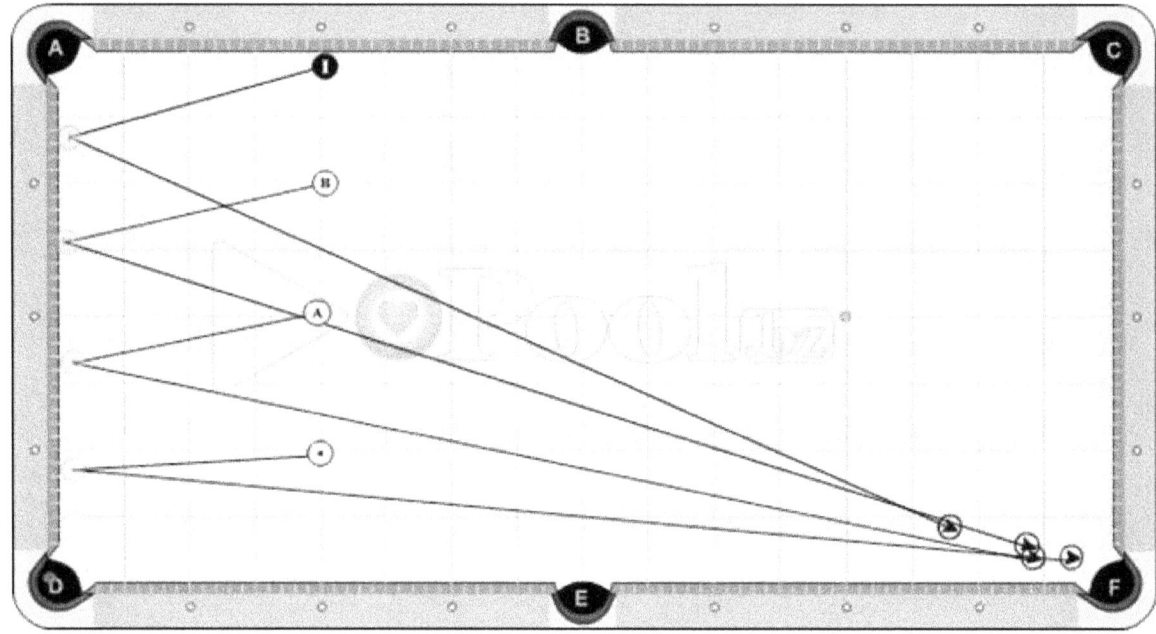

If you want to learn all of the secrets of One-Rail Kicks, there is a 50 minute video "Secrets of One-Rail Kicks" available at the Billiard Gods Store (www.billiardgods.com).

Games to Practice Your Skills

When practicing drills and exercises, sometimes you need a break. Here are some games that help improve your skills.

Bowliards

This game uses the scoring system used in bowling. As a tool to test your improvements over time, it keeps a solitary player's interest. This is similar to *Equal Offense*.

Object

Score a perfect bowling score of 300 points in 10 frames (innings) in solitary play. Scoring uses bowling rules. Each pocketed ball is 1 point.

Opponents

One to four players.

Balls

Set of balls (1-10) plus CB.

Racking

Balls are racked in a four-row triangle.

Breaking

Free break to start inning. Balls pocketed are spotted. If scratch, no penalty. CB goes to the kitchen for the first shot.

Regular play

After break, shoot from kitchen to pocket balls.

Call ball and pocket.

Two innings for each rack. First inning starts after break. On a miss, first inning ends. Second inning starts and ends on a miss.

If all balls pocketed in this frame, scores as a "spare". (10 points for frame plus points in first inning of next frame).

If all balls pocketed in the frame are made on the first inning, scores as a "strike". (10 points for frame plus points from next two innings.)

If a strike or spare in 10th frame, additional innings as necessary.

Balls on the break or jumped balls are immediately spotted.

Fouls (Foul ends inning.)

Bank Pool

Bank Pool is a game where legally pocketed balls must be banked into the pocket using one or more banks.

Opponents

Two sides, individuals or a team of doubles.

Balls

Regular ball set.

Object

Each ball is 1 point. To count, it must be banked 1 or more rails. 8 points to win.

Racking

Regular random rack.

Breaking

Starting player determined by local rules (coin, lag, card draw, etc.)

Legal break is two object balls to the rails with one object ball past the center line. If a ball is pocketed, breaker continues.

If no legal break, incoming player can play the table, or require a new break. No other penalties.

Any pocketed ball, not called, is spotted after shooter's inning.

Regular play

Call ball, rails and pocket. CB contact must be to object ball first. (No rail-first. No double-kiss.)

House rules can permit three or more rail kick to a ball close to a pocket.

Fouls

Penalty is end of inning and one ball spotted. Balls made on foul shot do not count and are re-spotted. Balls can be owed.

- Ball off the table (spotted at end of inning)
- Scratch (shoot from kitchen)
- No legal shot
- Illegal ball touching (optional – moved balls can be replaced with opponent's approval and play continues with no penalty)

On shooting from the kitchen, if all balls inside, ball closest to the head string is spotted.

Variation

9 Ball Bank Pool – one version allows any ball, another version requires banking balls in rotation.

Equal Offense

Based on *14.1 Continuous*.

Object

Score a higher number of total points in a group of opponents with an agreed number of innings. Or, if playing against yourself, beat your previous best score. Generally a game is 10 innings with a 200 point maximum.

Balls

Regular set of balls.

Racking

Standard random rack.

Breaking

Standard break. Any pocketed balls are re-spotted.

Start shooting from the kitchen.

Regular play

After break, first shot is from the kitchen.

Call ball and pocket. See 14.1 rules.

Skill levels

Play at the level of your skills and abilities.

Level 1 - Beginner: After the break, start with ball in hand anywhere. Three misses or fouls to end the inning. After each miss (1st and 2nd), ball in hand anywhere. Advance to the next level when your total score reaches 120.

Level 2 - Intermediate: After the break, start with ball in hand anywhere. Two misses or fouls to end the inning. After the first miss, start with ball in hand anywhere. Advance to the next level if your total score reaches 120.

Level 3 - Advanced: After the break, start with ball in hand from kitchen. One miss or foul ends the inning. Advance to the next level if your total score reaches 120.

Level 4 - Professional: After the break, start with ball in hand in the kitchen. One miss or foul ends the inning. For each inning, the goal is to reach 20 (playing through the rack like 14.1). Reaching 170 would be considered top-level.

Fouls

Penalty is end of turn.

- No legal shot

- Ball off the table

- Scratch

- Illegal ball touching (optional – moved balls can be replaced with opponent's approval and play continues with no penalty)

Chicago (carom-scratch)

Object

Score points by shooting object ball off of CB into pocket. Each ball counts as one point.

Opponents

Two players.

First player determined by local rules (coin, lag, card draw, etc.)

Balls

Regular set of balls.

Racking

Regular random rack. CB is placed on top position (apex ball).

Breaking

Object ball is played from kitchen off of CB. If any object ball is pocketed, play continues.

Regular play

Any object ball is selected and caromed off of the CB into a pocket. If successful, scores one point. Another object ball is shot off the CB, etc.

Incidental object balls pocketed count.

Shooter must make a legal hit off the CB.

Inning ends on a foul or no ball pocketed.

Fouls

Penalties are loss of turn, loss of 1 point, and an object ball re-spotted. (If at zero points, 1 point added to opponent's score.)

- No legal shot

- Ball off the table (re-spotted)

- Illegal ball movement (optional – moved balls can be replaced with opponent's approval and play continues with no penalty)

- Scratch (CB is pocketed) – CB is placed on center spot and incoming player starts

Chase, a game to learn kicking skills

Copyright 2007 Allan P. Sand

This game teaches you how to kick using angles and spins. These rules are for the one player version. The two player game could be played with each person playing a set, or taking turns shot after shot.

Playing

Each shot uses the same CB. Place the CB (can be a solid) on the head spot, a stripe on the foot spot. The player must call and hit a minimum of one rail before a contact with the other ball.

When you have improved with one-rail kicks, move up to two-rail kicks. For very good players, require three-rail kicks. (This can also be a handicap with two player competitions.)

Multi-rail accidents are not counted. You must call the number of rails. If a ball is pocketed, spot it and continue. No penalty.

Scoring

Ten shots equal one frame. Ten frames equal to one game. Points from all 10 frames are added for the final score.

Variations: 5 shots to a frame, 5 frames to a game,

One point is scored when the shooter's designated CB hits the required minimum number of rails and then contacts the object ball.

Fouls

Penalty - 1 point per foul. If score is zero, it goes minus. (For two players, add the penalty point to opponent's score.)

Blank Table Layouts

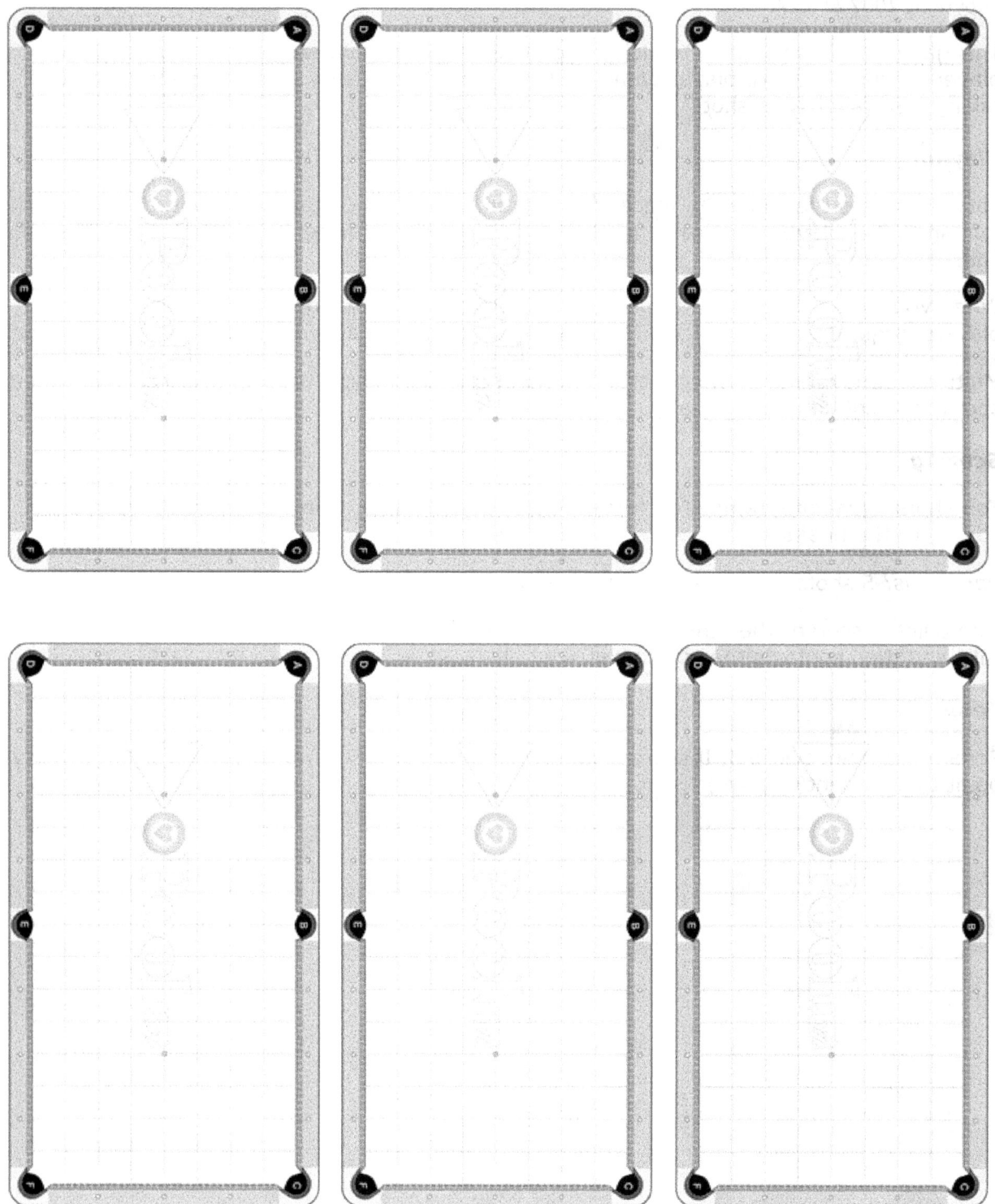